OBJECTS OF WAR

OBJECTS OF WAR

The Material Culture of Conflict and Displacement

EDITED BY LEORA AUSLANDER AND TARA ZAHRA

CORNELL UNIVERSITY PRESS
ITHACA AND LONDON

First published 2018 by Cornell University Press

Printed in the United States of America

Library of Congress Cataloging-in-Publication Data

Names: Auslander, Leora, editor. | Zahra, Tara, editor. | Container of (work): Goff, Alice. Honor of the trophy.
Title: Objects of war : the material culture of conflict and displacement / edited by Leora Auslander and Tara Zahra.
Description: Ithaca : Cornell University Press, 2018. | Includes bibliographical references and index.
Identifiers: LCCN 2017050432 (print) | LCCN 2017051679 (ebook) | ISBN 9781501720093 (epub/mobi) | ISBN 9781501720086 (pdf) | ISBN 9781501720079 | ISBN 9781501720079 (pbk. : alk. paper)
Subjects: LCSH: War and society. | Pillage. | Material culture. | Personal belongings.
Classification: LCC HM554 (ebook) | LCC HM554 .O25 2018 (print) | DDC 303.6/6—dc23
LC record available at https://lccn.loc.gov/2017050432

To all who have found their lives uprooted by violence.

Lad with mother pushing from behind rolls cartload of possessions out of Uerdingen, Germany, moved out by allied military government seeking to prevent loss of life from shelling by Germans on other side of Rhine. Photograph dated March 19, 1945, U.S. National Archives, no. 531255.

Contents

ILLUSTRATIONS

Acknowledgments

This has been a collaborative project from the start, and we are deeply grateful to all of the individuals who have contributed ideas, energy, and support along the way. We are especially indebted to the Neubauer Collegium for Culture and Society at the University of Chicago, which generously funded the two workshops that developed into this volume. We also thank the Chicago Center for Jewish Studies, the Center for the Study of Gender and Sexuality, the Pozen Family Center for Human Rights, the University of Chicago History Department, the Nicholson Center for British Studies, and the France Chicago Center for generous support. We could not have organized our second workshop at the University of Chicago Center in Paris without Sébastien Greppo's invaluable assistance.

Each workshop helped us to advance our thinking about war, mobility, and material culture, and we are indebted to all of the participants for their participation in those events. Susan Gal, Michael Geyer, Daniel Greene, Fiona Rose-Greenland, Emily Osborn, and Holly Shissler provided exceptional feedback to participants in our first conference at the

Neubauer Collegium. We are also grateful to the graduate students in our 2013–14 seminar on migration and material culture at the University of Chicago, for the many conversations that helped advance our thinking.

We also thank our editor, Emily Andrew, for her enthusiasm for and confidence in this project, as well as the anonymous reviewers for their constructive feedback. Our research assistants Natalie Smith and Klara Chomicka assisted us tremendously in the final stages of editing. Finally, we have been grateful for the opportunity to develop this project in the city of Chicago, a city that we hope will continue to embrace displaced people and their things in times of need.

Objects of War

INTRODUCTION

The Things They Carried:
War, Mobility, and Material Culture

Leora Auslander and Tara Zahra

Cell phones, lifejackets, and toys. As over one million refugees flee-ing war in Syria struggled to gain a foothold in Europe in the summer and fall of 2015, newspapers, social media feeds, museums, and galleries were awash with photographs depicting the objects carried by refugees as they made life-threatening journeys across land and sea. Documentary photographer Bryan Sokol's "The Most Important Thing" series shows refugees and items of both sentimental and practical value: a Syrian man with keys to an apartment (which may no longer exist), a little girl with a pair of jeans, a woman and her wheelchair.[1] Other objects are described as precious reminders of home or of missing or dead family members. The website of the nongovernmental organization Mercy Corps depicts a seven-year-old boy with a small toy robot. "Muhamad, 7, and his family have lived in Jordan for two years now," a caption explains. "He's hold-ing a birthday gift from his grandfather. The robot toy reminds him of his grandfather, 'who is now in heaven.'"[2]

Across the centuries, people in flight from war or persecution have carried personal possessions with them, often with great difficulty.[3] They

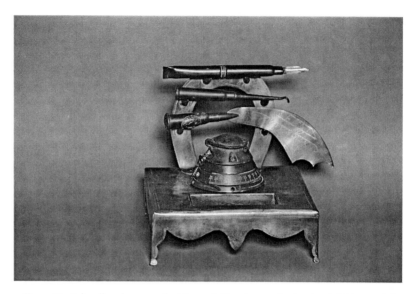

Figure I.1. Inkwell and pens crafted from shell casings and other battlefield material by Gustave Herman, a French soldier mobilized during World War I. He was wounded at Dinan and taken prisoner at Verdun in February, 1916. This inkwell, along with several other pieces of trench art, was found in a cupboard in the family farm in Saint-Nicolas in Pas-de-Calais. Contributed to Wikimedia Commons by Europeana.eu (FRADO62_011). Photo: Marc Serra.

and their descendants have gone to considerable lengths to preserve these objects, despite their everyday-ness, because of the value they accrued as they accompanied displaced people on their travels. Aware of the significance of these things, history museums have sought them out, and many are now on display or languishing in the storerooms of immigration and Holocaust museums around the world. Museum visitors on a quest to understand the lives of migrants of earlier generations turn to glass cases housing the dolls, musical instruments, tools, or dish towels that voyaged with them. In parallel, virtually all Holocaust museums display the suitcases, shoes, and eyeglasses that accompanied victims to the camps. Curators also collect the rings, vases, combs, and other things crafted of found materials by soldiers, prisoners of war, and concentration camp inmates.[4]

These laboriously constructed objects record the resilience and ingenuity of displaced people deprived of the great majority of their possessions.

Through the presentation of the banal things that immigrants, refugees, and prisoners carried with them, these exhibits remind us of how people in desperate circumstances rely on familiar things in their efforts to retain memories and maintain a sense of self. In so doing they transform the ordinary into the extraordinary; a vase crafted from a spent artillery shell does not just hold flowers, a spoon made in a concentration camp is not merely something used to eat, and a pen carried across oceans is as important as a memory prompt as an instrument with which to write.

In most museums, because they are behind glass—visible, but beyond the reach of the other senses—these objects offer empathy only through sight. A few museums are more ambitious and seek to offer visitors a more fully embodied experience. At the Australian National Maritime Museum, for example, visitors can take a short voyage on the *Tu Do* ("Freedom"), the restored fishing boat that brought thirty-one refugees fleeing Vietnam to Sydney in 1977.[5] During that voyage they not only feel the deck moving beneath their feet but also smell Vietnamese food. Visitors to the Lower East Side Tenement Museum in New York crowd into apartments furnished as they would have been in the 1880s. And some Holocaust museums use various strategies, including asking visitors to take their place in a cattle car or to walk on an unnervingly unstable surface, to provide a more vivid sense of deportation than can be evoked by viewing photographs and texts and objects in cases.

Survivors cherish, photographers record, museums preserve and display, and viewers seek out these things because they think that those objects will provide a different kind of knowledge than would a history told in words. The theoretical foundations of that conviction are much debated.[6] Although some scholars refuse the distinctions separating material culture, visual culture, and text, many persuasively argue that images, and especially things, that people have touched create a more immediate sense of connection, a stronger emotional response, to their subjects than do texts. Photographs of victims personalize them in a way that a name on a list does not. Seeing the bra painstakingly assembled by an inmate of a concentration camp effectively conveys the intensity of the quest for dignity, modesty, and sexuality in a context designed to destroy all those qualities.[7] Feeling the Australian sun on one's head while crowded onto the small deck of the *Tu Do* provides the visitor a glimmer of the physical experience of fleeing by sea.

Whether or not one accepts the particular pedagogic capacity of material culture, the fact that refugees, exiles, soldiers, and prisoners went to extraordinary lengths to bring, make, find, and preserve all kinds of things is evidence of their significance *to them*. It is, we argue, because people *need* things that they have made, and make, these efforts to acquire and keep them.[8] Even in times of peace and tranquility, people's need for objects is not limited to the obvious uses: protection from heat and cold, physical comfort, cooking and eating. They need them for many of the activities that are unrelated to physical survival but that define humanness, including writing, making music and art, working, and communicating.[9] People also need things to store memories, to experience pleasure, and to feel in touch with God.[10] As the case of the Syrian refugees with which we opened vividly exemplifies, the meaning of things to individuals is often magnified or transformed entirely in the context of war and displacement. War brings with it the destruction of the stuff of identity, of belonging, and of memory: homes, clothing, and landscapes. Wars also destroy the tools needed for productivity and creativity. Loss of pots and pans brings not only hunger in its wake but also the capacity to nurture. And how could one pray if one's rosary, tefillin, or copy of the Koran were no longer at hand? The rescued remnants take on new meanings when they are all that is left of a formerly much larger array of the stuff of everyday life.

Not only have individuals whose lives have been interrupted and displaced by war invested heavily in things but so, too, have governments and armies. For as long as rulers have raided enemy territories, they have destroyed and stolen the things valued by those they have conquered.[11] When the goal has been domination but not annihilation, only those objects understood to threaten the new form of rule were destroyed as new ones, designed to facilitate governance and compliance, were imposed.[12] Attempts to eradicate entire peoples have resulted in more drastic assaults on the material world, including efforts to wipe out the material culture—and more broadly, the civilization—of those peoples at the same time.[13] Finally, those engaging not in genocide but in revolutionary efforts to completely transform political or religious systems have also had recourse to material destruction, particularly iconoclasm, to make room for a new iconic regime.[14]

Figure I.2. Portraits of the tsars of Russia (including Nicholas II, Alexander II, and Alexander III), which were torn from the walls during the Russian Revolution, 1917. Photo by Three Lions, Wikimedia Commons.

Although both individuals and institutions have assumed that things can be counted on to serve them obediently, many scholars would argue that this is not, in fact, the case. As a consequence of their very materiality, things may counter human will: Statues are accidentally decapitated in transit; wood that has great longevity at home deteriorates quickly in the climate of its site of captivity; and the weight of architectural fragments sinks the ships tasked with carrying them. The thingness of things not only renders them fragile, however, but also makes them impossible to control.[15] The European clothing imposed on a colonized people, intended to shape their minds and bodies to obedience instead, sometimes, inspired revolt. Lead, a source of great beauty when transformed into crystal, poisons those who drink from it. Things, in other words, act in the world; they are not fully subject to human intent. They do not have agency or will but they can be recalcitrant.

This is, then, a book about the displacement of people and things in times of war, in Europe and its former colonies in the nineteenth and twentieth centuries. We have focused on Europe in this broad sense because war

and forced mobility transformed the demography and material culture of
Europe and its colonies so dramatically in the modern era. Europe is therefore rich territory for exploring the use of things in moments of extreme
violence. The diverse experiences examined in this book also begin to illuminate differences and similarities in relationships between humans and
objects across time and space. In each of the distinct cases discussed in
this book, individuals, institutions, and states attempt to use things to
cope, in one way or another, with the violence done to people and their
material environment. And, in virtually all the chapters, the things do
not quite behave, do not do exactly what is asked of them. Including a
wide geographic range within these limits allows us to show that this relation among war, mobility, and things was not limited to the German or
Czech lands, France, or Russia, nor to continental regimes; the chapters
featuring Algeria, the United States, India, and Burma demonstrate the
relevance of this relation well beyond European shores. At the same time,
we can perceive some key differences across time and space, between the
kinds of loot most valued by Civil War soldiers and the men and women
who fought in the Soviet army during World War II or between the ability
of nineteenth and twentieth century states to carry out the mass expropriation and transfer of cultural property. We can also readily distinguish
among the objects produced in an officer's POW camp during the First
World War, a concentration camp during the Second World War, and a
refugee camp in the 1990s.

We have focused on the modern period because although armies and
states have long plundered, and those fleeing war have always attempted
to carry valued objects with them, several developments in the modern
era transformed the relation among people, things, mobility, and violence. The emergence of mass politics intensified pressure on states and
governments to legitimize themselves and build emotional attachments
through things. The development of mechanized warfare and mass armies
enhanced the ability of states to move, transform, or destroy material
objects. The expansion of consumerism profoundly altered the social and
cultural meaning of objects to both individuals and states. Finally, the
birth of the modern museum reconfigured relationships between objects
and individual and collective memory.

Forced mobility and material culture have been inextricably inter-
twined throughout modern history: Each has powerful analytic (and even

causal) significance for the other. We cannot truly understand the dynamics and consequences of war without considering the centrality of material culture to violent conquest, the unmaking and making of empires and nation-states, and the construction of social and cultural identities. Material culture offers, furthermore, a particularly rich and unique form of access to the emotional and social dimensions of war and forced displacement. Crucially, these sources offer insight into the emotional lives and experiences of individuals who did not leave textual records. We also cannot fully comprehend the history of material culture without analyzing the ways in which war and forced migration have reshaped and resignified the things that surround us. Looking at material culture in violent contexts enables and forces reflection about what happens to things when their "normal" life cycles are disrupted. We learn much about the meanings things carry, the identities they generate, how they are physically transformed and repurposed, sometimes in very startling ways.

Because the concern here is to explain how institutions and people have used things and how those things have pushed back, we have left the task of determining what counts as a relevant/meaningful object to our historical actors (rather than defining the boundaries a priori). That has produced a very wide range of goods including but not limited to: sculpture, architectural fragments, fine furniture, paintings, uniforms and other clothing, silverware and porcelain, rifles, medals, watches, bicycles, table linen and hand towels, cookbooks, pianos, doctors' instruments, and school satchels. The source base for this volume is necessarily as rich and varied as the topics addressed. Several authors (Jonker, Dudley, Wallen, Pomerance) examine things themselves, many of which traveled great distances under extreme conditions before landing in the hands of a scholar. Others (Effros, Schechter, Rachamimov, Benninga) focus more on visual and textual sources including drawings, photographs, reports, diaries, memoirs, and written testimony. Still others (Goff, Giustino, Weicksel) draw equally on material, visual, and textual evidence.

As this range of objects and sources indicate, our project requires bringing into dialogue several distinct modes of thinking and bodies of scholarship. Vast interdisciplinary literatures address the dynamics of modern warfare, expropriation, and restitution.[16] And yet how people use things, and how things resist being used, has only rarely entered the purview of military historians or those who specialize in the history of forced mobility.[17] Curators in ethnographic and art museums have been obliged in recent decades to address the violent histories that brought objects into their collections, but those discussions have been little noticed by those who work on war, migration, or material culture.[18] We argue that bringing these fields together sheds unique light on at least four significant and interrelated aspects of war, forced mobility, and material culture: state expropriation/reappropriation; wartime mobilities of people and things; immobilized people and redeployed things; and the afterlives of things. The book seeks to elucidate *both* how states, soldiers, civilians, prisoners, refugees, and museums *have put things to work* and how the things' materiality *has limited the use that those human forces can make of them.*

The first section of the book focuses on how states have attempted to mobilize the things they acquired in war. The success of those efforts was variable: States are not, in fact, unified actors and have not always acted coherently; the citizens of those states have not always been grateful recipients of the pillaged goods; and the things themselves have resisted their redeployment. In the second section we shift our attention from a focus on the state to individuals. Included here are soldiers, colonists, freed people and "contraband," civilians, refugees, prisoners of war, and concentration camp inmates. What binds these diverse categories is that they all found themselves displaced, or in intimate contact with things displaced, by violence, most often by war. Bringing them into a common frame sheds light on the importance people attribute to things in moments when relations among humans are at their most fraught and fragile. The final section addresses the afterlives of things, what happens to them in the calm following the storm. Here we are especially preoccupied with memory-work done by objects, whether in the context of individual and familial histories or in museums.

States of Things: The Making of Modern Nation-States and Empires

The expansion and construction of empires and new nation-states in the nineteenth and twentieth centuries often entailed the violent transformation of the material world as much as political institutions. Millions were displaced or bound to new polities in the aftermath of wars that moved both frontiers over people and people over frontiers. Building on an earlier revolutionary tradition born with the Puritan forces in the English Civil War of the seventeenth century and developed by American and French revolutionaries, material culture became central to the legitimation of new states and to the imagination and consolidation of communities within them.[19] For those displaced by war, meanwhile, objects served as bridges between old and new homes and communities as well as transmitters of memory.

Overseas empires systematically attempted to use material culture to maintain national identities abroad, to "pacify" and govern colonized populations, and to sustain and embody their "civilizing" projects. In French North America, for example, clothing shaped the way that French rulers understood racial categories. An ongoing perception that one could *become* French by adopting French modes of dress challenged the simultaneous transition from a fluid to a more rigid and immutable conception of race.[20] Imperial regimes also sought to influence the form of cities, mosques, and synagogues as well as alter religiously marked dress. The most famous of these conflicts, ongoing into the present day, pivots on the issue of women's dress. In parallel, Belgian, French, German, and British authorities were committed to providing "proper" domestic space and European clothing modified for warmer climates in their empires. These imperial powers also aimed to regulate and control which indigenous populations would be allowed access to which elements of European domesticity and clothing. In all of these examples, material culture was essential to the construction and maintenance of particular norms of gender, sexuality, class, and race in the context of imperial hierarchies.[21]

Material culture was also central to the cultivation of imperial loyalties in Europe's multinational empires. Here, the goal was not to create a homogeneous national culture but to unite a linguistically, religiously, and nationally diverse population across vast stretches of land. The writer Joseph Roth recalled, for example, how the multilingual Habsburg Empire was united in part by a common and recognizable material culture: "Everywhere the gendarmes wore the same cap with a feather or the same mud-colored helmet with a golden knob and the gleaming double eagle of the Habsburgs; everywhere the doors of the Imperial tobacco monopoly's shops were painted with black and yellow diagonal stripes. . . . Everywhere were to be found the same coffee-houses, with their smoky vaulted ceilings and their dark alcoves."[22]

Those strategies were reprised by the Soviet and East German regimes, which set statues of communist leaders on the pedestals where kings and nobles had stood and razed royal palaces to make room for palaces of the people. Habsburg successor states and post-Socialist states in Eastern and Central Europe demolished statues, renamed streets, and remade domestic interiors in the process of creating post-Habsburg and post-Socialist regimes. Some went so far as to rebuild some of those destroyed sites of monarchical rule.

The politicization of material culture likewise took on new life in anticolonial movements and in the construction of postcolonial or post-imperial states and nation-states. From George Washington's homespun, to Gandhi's Swadeshi movement through Mobutu's Abacost, the eradication of imperial everyday materiality and its replacement by "authentic" forms was viewed as essential to the political viability of the new nations.[23]

All of these modern states strove to encourage certain patterns of consumption, certain uses of everyday material culture, in order to facilitate governance. They also, however, saw the potential in the fine arts and antiquities, potential that was fundamentally altered by the advent of the modern public art museum in the late eighteenth century.[24] In premodern times, victorious Vikings and crusaders returned home with trophies and items of religious significance; kings seized neighboring castles; jewels, furs, and works of art traded hands with the rise and fall of states and became emblems of political and military power. In the modern period, objects stolen or appropriated through warfare assumed new symbolic meanings and purposes. More than mere booty that served to enrich rulers or populations, such loot could now represent a victory over a hated national enemy, sustain particular nationalist historical narratives, consolidate expanding empires, or signify a revolution or regime change.[25]

Technological developments in the eighteenth and nineteenth centuries allowed for the transfer of ever more monumental spoils of war; Egyptian, Greek, and Roman statues, architectural fragments, and obelisks were brought to inscribe imperial power into the cityscape of European capitals. Conquering armies encountered highly valued cultural artifacts—Greek, Roman, Latin American, African, and Asian but also Mayan and Aztec. Resources were devoted to the transportation of what might be

termed the "trophies of war"—sculptures, architectural fragments, musical instruments, and everyday things seized by conquering armies. This
booty became the foundation of the collections of the great museums of
Europe and North America, either appropriated as part of a national,
imperial, or western civilization or exoticized as an ethnographic find.

European museums founded on pillaged goods came to face new
challenges in the late twentieth and early twenty-first centuries. These
museums often still hide or obscure the violence that undergird their collections. Here their goal is not to understand the experience of migration
or violence but rather to celebrate or, alternately, normalize the power of
the state or empire. Even after decades of claims by African, Latin American, or European states and Native American Nations for the return of
the cultural goods taken from their territory, most of those things remain
in the museums of the victors. In those museums they are mobilized in the
service of a different historical narrative than the one they would tell were
they to be repatriated.[26]

Neither the continental nor overseas imperial wars of the nineteenth
or twentieth centuries were intentionally genocidal. Correspondingly,
for example, although there was much theft when Egypt lay under British control, the occupying regime did not destroy the area's monumental
heritage, and the same was true of the Ottoman period in Greek history.
That changed in the twentieth century, with important ramifications for
the meaning of things in wartime. In the ethnic cleansing that became
prevalent in the twentieth century, expropriation facilitated the eradication of entire populations. The case of the Nazi regime is the most familiar example. The gradual theft of the possessions that made Jews part of
the national culture—dwellings and their contents, radios, clothing, the
tools needed to practice their trades and professions—was the first step
of their dehumanization and ultimate annihilation. Even those who were
able to flee were forced to leave behind homes and businesses as well as
furniture, artwork, clothing, and jewelry. Those goods stolen from Jews
and occupied territories were stacked up in warehouses and distributed
to bombed-out Germans, serving as both a reward for political complicity and a mark of belonging in the racially defined national community.[27]
This expropriation and annihilation inevitably left ghosts behind. Historians have recently analyzed the cultural, political, and social significance
of former Jewish spaces in Eastern Europe after the Holocaust. They have

focused specifically on material culture, such as former Jewish cemeteries and synagogues, to better understand the "presence of the absence" of Jews in postwar Eastern Europe.[28]

Jews were far from the only victims; Nazi leaders and ideologues justified their conquest and resettlement of Eastern Europe with narratives that linked Slavic racial inferiority and cultural backwardness to the neglect of material (often domestic) spaces and land.[29] The objects left behind were plundered by neighbors, redistributed by government authorities, or reinterpreted as a form of national patrimony.

In the postwar period this process was, in some sense, reversed. As twelve million Germans fled or were expelled from Eastern Europe, their belongings, homes, businesses, and villages were expropriated, evacuated, and resettled. The city of Breslau/Wrocław was transformed from a "German" to a "Polish" space after World War II, for example. This entailed cleansing the city not only of its German inhabitants but also of their material traces: renaming neighborhoods, landmarks, and streets; demolishing "German" statues; and removing gravestones with German names. Scholars have examined the role of material culture (like religious icons and ruins) in the construction of the Iron Curtain between West Germany and Czechoslovakia after World War II and in the formation of expellee communities in postwar West Germany.[30] In the postwar world, material culture, including homes, furniture, cultural artifacts, and the built environment, was central to the politics of retribution, reconstruction, and restitution.

People and Things in Wartime: Soldiers, Civilians, and Prisoners

Mass conscription and mechanized warfare changed the very nature of war and the place of both people and things in it. The second section of the volume moves from state to individual relationships to things. It is impossible to separate the individual use of things from the goals and ideologies of the states that set armies in motion or expelled unwanted minorities. And yet, states were not able to fully control how individuals used and appropriated objects, nor did objects always conform to the uses intended for them. Warfare, displacement, and incarceration meanwhile transformed the meaning and materiality of things as much as the lives and bodies of human beings.

Modern war set huge numbers of *people in motion*. Mass conscription and volunteerism took millions of men, young and old, from their homes and communities. Soldiers were deployed and redeployed, often at great distance from their domiciles. Civilians were impressed into forced labor. Millions more noncombatants were transformed into refugees as they fled the arrival of armies or bombardments. The mass uprooting of soldiers and civilians in the context of war also set things on new trajectories. Individual soldiers stole from the homes abandoned by fleeing civilians and from the corpses of both comrades and enemies on the battlefield. Noncombatants anticipating the arrival of soldiers buried some of their prized possessions, hid small items on their persons, and gave other objects to friends and relations. Refugees, civilian internees, and prisoners took what they could with them, generally that which they most prized for sentimental or pragmatic reasons, and hid or abandoned what they could not transport. The material qualities of objects, as well as the subjective value attributed to them, often determined their fate—their size and durability as well as the ease with which they could be transported, hidden, or resold.

Soldiers did not limit themselves to stealing from occupied or abandoned houses but also from corpses on the battlefield. The boundary between subjects and objects blurred in the context of war and forced migration. Things, such as weapons and medals, prized possessions, or prosthetics, could become vital extensions of bodies. Bodies—deployed, looted, desecrated, transported in cattle cars, or massacred—meanwhile came to be seen by some people and states as "things." Prisoners in Nazi concentration camps were often referred to as "Stücke," the German word for "things" or "pieces." Through these fine-grained studies we gain access to the many meanings attributed to things in time of war, the tactics used by civilians to try to protect the objects they held dear and soldiers to acquire them, and the ways in which the material qualities of objects transformed and shaped their trajectories.

In the twentieth century, the experience of warfare and forced migration was not simply one of *unprecedented mobility*, however, but also enforced *immobility*. "Enemy aliens" were interned; refugees and prisoners of war were held in camps; and, in some cases, individuals were incarcerated solely based on their race, religion, social class, disability, political position, or sexuality. This was in part the consequence of new restrictions on migration introduced during and after the First World War, which meant that individuals fleeing war or state persecution often had no place to turn. While states had long worked to control the movement of populations, their ability to guard frontiers, track identities, and to move and incarcerate people expanded greatly in the modern era. Refugee camps and internment camps emerged as a solution to contain and control the movement of displaced people, soldiers, and unwanted minorities—movement often deemed threatening to state sovereignty and security.

Studying material culture offers a unique perspective on how refugees, POWs, and prisoners have coped with moments of migratory purgatory, often making temporary homes in camps, trenches, ports, or border communities. This work builds on that of recent historians of migration on periods of transit or transition, on the moments of stasis.[31] After the Second World War, for example, efforts by displaced persons in Europe to make temporary homes often reflected and reinforced prevailing norms of gender and sexuality. Jewish survivors worked to foster domesticity in United Nations refugee camps in Germany after World War II; baby carriages in particular became symbols of the regeneration of life in the aftermath of war and genocide. Memoirs and contemporary reports from United Nations social workers after World War II meanwhile emphasized that female refugees often appreciated the opportunity to own small possessions, visit a beauty salon, or make new clothing, which became symbolic of their restoration to good health and a return to a gendered forms of "normalcy."[32]

Afterlives: From Things to Memories

We began this introduction with the contents of refugees' luggage. Analyzing what forced migrants take with them when they leave home reveals a great deal about the context in which they fled, their expectations and hopes for the future, and their subjective, emotional relationship to their old and new homes. As migrants flee their lives in one place and make new ones in another, they take some of the things that make a space home with them and abandon others. Those things vary in scale from the very tiny (a bead or a button) to the huge (a piano, a library, or a lathe). They vary as much in kind; some are utensils needed to prepare food, some tools of a trade, some ritual objects, some bearers of memory.

Memory, migration, and material culture are also linked as particular objects serve as repositories of individual, familial, and collective memories of dislocation. Such material attachments have been key to explaining why people seek to stay where they are or return to a dangerous or almost impossibly difficult home.[33] In the winter of 1939, for example, only weeks before the Third Reich occupied what remained of Czechoslovakia, Anka Roth worried about how to get her furniture out of Prague. Neither Anka nor her furniture ever escaped. But Anka's daughter, Milena, age seven, did reach safety in the United Kingdom on a Kindertransport. Years later, she reflected on her mother's preoccupation with furniture in a moment of extreme peril. "When I first read all her anxious queries about furniture, my mind boggled. Here is a family desperately seeking to flee for survival, but still the dimensions of her furniture preoccupy her to the extent of detailing it in the letters to her rescuer." Milena links her mother's anxiety about her material possessions to the painful decline in social status experienced by Jews in Nazi-occupied Europe, as they lost their homes, their jobs and businesses, their property, and often their friends:

> The furnishings were in fact status symbols in a very deep and necessary way. In that time of extreme peril, when even if my mother survived, she would have become a maid and lost all evidence of her former home and culture, the significance of these symbols became even more important. Similarly, their survival has been of greater importance to me than would otherwise have been normal in my own life. I use this furniture every day and feel a satisfying sense of connection with her.[34]

By contrast, some victims of the Holocaust who could not recover their family's possessions acutely felt the loss of material connections to their loved ones. Franziska/Frances Nunally, a Viennese Jew who escaped to the United Kingdom at the age of sixteen, lost all of her family members in the Holocaust. Sixty years later, when she donated the last letters she had received from her parents and brother to an archive in Austria, she measured their importance in relation to absent things:

> My parents, brother, grandmother, aunts, uncles, etc. all died in the Holocaust. *Nothing* remains from them. No old furniture, works of art, a gold watch, a ring—all the things that are passed from generation to generation in families. There are not even graves for these people. The *only proof* that they were once on this earth lies in their *letters*.[35]

Forced migrants, survivors of deportation and incarceration, veterans and their heirs all have struggled to hold onto or to reclaim the personal possessions that can serve as bridges to the past.[36] Some discovered, when they were successful in their claims, that the outcome was not as expected, that the things refused to serve the role attributed to them. Some blamed their unhappiness with their rescue on their choice of things. Sami Dassa, who survived World War II wrote, for example, "In '42 . . . I was able to get two or three things out of the house but they were banal and useless things," while another survivor wrote of his paralysis in face of the need to select a few objects for rescue.[37] Others found that the recovered items or even entire homes haunted rather than comforted them. Charlotte Delbo recounted how coming back to the home in which her sister, who had died in Auschwitz, had been born was unbearable. "All was still in its place in the house. Dédée's [her dead sister's] things here and there, her room; all was as it had been before . . . all became menacing. I didn't know how to avoid contact with all those objects that encircled, assailed, hit me. How to flee, how to dissolve myself, to no longer be held by the past, bumping into walls, things, memories?"[38] Despite the things' recalcitrance, most people displaced by war either as civilians or soldiers found things to be important memory prompts, a position that sometimes put them in conflict with the museums dedicated to preserving and transmitting that memory.

The conflict between the family of Pierre Lévi-Leleu and the Auschwitz Museum makes the stakes clear. Pierre Lévi (who went by the name Leleu during the war) was forty-four years old at the time of his arrest, deportation, and death. He left a wife and two young sons who survived the war in France. His suitcase, bearing a label in his wife's hand, was recuperated by the Auschwitz-Birkenau Memorial and Museum. In 2005 that suitcase was very reluctantly loaned to the Foundation for the Remembrance of the Shoah in Paris, where it was identified by Pierre Lévi's son, Michel Lévi-Leleu, and granddaughter, Claire. Michel Lévi-Leleu was profoundly moved and shaken by this unexpected encounter with the valise he had last seen more than half a century earlier as it accompanied his father on a trip that would end in Auschwitz, and so he sought to claim the valise. The museum refused to leave the valise in Paris on the grounds that it had an obligation to keep such objects in Poland, on the site of the camp, in order to bear witness to what had happened there.[39] This struggle was a poignant and unresolvable one; both sides, arguably, were right. Those to whom violence was directly done have a right to the things that serve to connect them to the people and places of their pasts, but society also has a need and a right to the things that serve to educate and remind.

Conclusions

Taken collectively, these chapters illuminate critical facets of the forced mobility of people and of things in the last two centuries. They expose several common threads, including the power of objects to legitimate states, to construct and transform individual and collective identities, and to mediate distances of time and space. This is, however, a very partial story. A necessary conclusion of this volume is that every experience of forced mobility is somewhat unique. The relationship between people and objects in flight has varied as much as those experiences.

Paying attention to these objects nonetheless has the potential to illuminate some of the least-understood aspects of war and forced mobility. There is a great deal of excellent research on the political history of forced migration, but we know far less about the semiotics of violence and the cultural and emotional consequences of mobility. Contemporary analysts often analyze forced migration in terms of domestic and international politics or economics. And yet as refugees struggle to breach Europe's frontiers, populist movements often frame opposition to migration in cultural terms, casting migrants as a threat to local material culture.[40] To return to the introduction to this essay, when we want to convey or understand the individual, human dimensions of the experience of war and forced migration, we often turn to objects. This is not coincidental. As we grapple with what it means to be a human during wartime, we need more than words and images. We need to study the objects that move and the objects that are left behind. These objects have powerful stories to tell. People and things moving together, and moving apart, have shaped the experience of war in the modern world.

Notes

1. Cydney Adams, Brinda Adhikari, and Mary Kate Boylan, "'The Most Important Thing' Refugees Carry," September 28, 2015, www.cbsnews.com/news/brian-sokol-documents-refuges-by-the-most-important-thing-they-carry-in-nyc-exhibit (accessed February 4, 2016); Brian Sokol, "The Most Important Thing," http://briansokol.com/syrian-refugees (accessed February 4, 2016).

2. "We Asked Refugees: What Did You Bring with You?" June 15, 2015, www.mercy corps.org/photoessays/jordan-syria/what-do-refugees-need-after-leaving-everything-behind (accessed February 4, 2016). For other examples, see "Current Special Exhibitions," Illinois Holocaust Museum and Education Center, www.ilholocaustmuseum.org/pages/exhibitions/special-exhibitions/ (accessed February 4, 2016); Aimee Levitt, "'What We Carried' Tells the Stories of Iraqi Refugees through Objects," *Chicago Reader*, January 27, 2016, www.chicago reader.com/Bleader/archives/2016/01/27/what-we-carried-tells-the-stories-of-iraqi-refugees-through-objects (accessed February 4, 2016).

3. Maruska Svasek, ed., *Moving Subjects, Moving Objects: Transnationalism, Cultural Production, and Emotions* (New York: Berghahn Books, 2012).

4. Nicholas J. Saunders, *Trench Art: Materialities and Memories of War* (Oxford: Berg, 2003); Gillian Carr and H. C. Mytum, eds., *Cultural Heritage and Prisoners of War: Creativity behind Barbed Wire* (New York: Routledge, 2012); Jane E. Dusselier, *Artifacts of Loss: Crafting Survival in Japanese American Concentration Camps* (New Brunswick, N.J.: Rutgers University Press, 2008).

5. Kim Tao, "A Refugee Boat Called Freedom at the Australian National Maritime Museum," presentation, "People and Things on the Move" conference at the Neubauer Collegium, Chicago, Illinois, May 13–15, 2015. See also "Tu Do: A Boat Called Freedom," Australian National Maritime Museum, www.anmm.gov.au/whats-on/vessels/tu-do (accessed August 29, 2017).

6. Susan M. Pearce, *Museums, Objects, and Collections* (Washington, D.C.: Smithsonian Institution Press, 1992); Elizabeth Edwards, Chris Gosden, and Ruth B. Phillips, eds., *Sensible Objects: Colonialism, Museums, and Material Culture* (Oxford: Berg, 2006); Sandra H. Dudley, ed., *Museum Objects: Experiencing the Properties of Things* (Milton Park, U.K.: Routledge, 2012); Sandra H. Dudley, *Museum Materialities: Objects, Engagements, Interpretations* (London: Routledge, 2010).

7. See, for example, the bra made by Hannah Messinger in the Illinois Holocaust Museum collection. With thanks to Maddie Boyd for the reference.

8. Leora Auslander, "Beyond Words," *American Historical Review* 110, no. 4 (2005): 1015–1045; Bill Brown, *Other Things* (Chicago: University of Chicago Press, 2015); Bill Brown, ed., *Things* (Chicago: University of Chicago Press, 2004); Ian Hodder, *Entangled: An Archaeology of the Relation between Humans and Things* (Chichester, U.K.: Wiley-Blackwell, 2012); Daniel Miller, *Material Culture and Mass Consumption* (Oxford: Basil and Blackwell, 1987).

9. Ian Hodder, ed., *The Meaning of Things: Material Culture and Symbolic Expression* (London: Unwin Hyman, 1989).

10. Serge Tisseron, *Comment l'esprit vient aux objets* (Paris: Aubier, 1999); David Morgan, ed., *Religion and Material Culture: The Matter of Belief* (London: Routledge, 2010); Sally M. Promey, ed., *Sensational Religion: Sensory Cultures in Material Practice* (New Haven: Yale University Press, 2014).

11. Jonathan Roth, *The Logistics of the Roman Army at War: 264 B.C.–A.D. 235* (Leiden, the Netherlands: Brill, 1999); Anders Winroth, *The Conversion of Scandinavia: Vikings, Merchants, and Missionaries in the Remaking of Northern Europe* (New Haven: Yale University Press, 2012).

12. Gwendolyn Wright, *The Politics of Design in French Colonial Urbanism* (Chicago: University of Chicago Press, 1991); Peter Scriver and Vikramaditya Prakash, eds., *Colonial Modernities: Building, Dwelling, and Architecture in British India and Ceylon* (London: Routledge, 2007).

13. See, for example, Michael Meng, *Shattered Spaces: Encountering Jewish Ruins in Postwar Germany and Poland* (Cambridge: Harvard University Press, 2011); Omer Bartov, *Erased: Vanishing Traces of Jewish Galicia in Present-Day Ukraine* (Princeton: Princeton University Press, 2007).

14. Richard S. Clay, *Iconoclasm in Revolutionary Paris* (Oxford: Voltaire Foundation, 2012); Richard Stites, *Revolutionary Dreams, Utopian Visions, and Experimental Life in the Russian Revolution* (New York: Oxford University Press, 1989); Stacy Boldrick, Leslie Brubaker, and Richard Clay, eds., *Striking Images: Iconoclasms Past and Present* (Abingdon, U.K.: Routledge, 2013).

15. Judy Attfield, *Wild Things: The Culture of Everyday Life* (Oxford: Berg, 2000); Carl Knappett and Lambros Malafouris, eds., *Material Agency: Towards a Non-Anthropocentric Approach* (Berlin: Spring, 2008); Jane Bennett, *Vibrant Matter: A Political Ecology of Things* (Durham: Duke University Press, 2010); Bruno Latour, *Reassembling the Social: An Introduction to Actor-Network-Theory* (Oxford: Oxford University Press, 2005).

16. See, for example, Martin Dean, *Robbing the Jews: The Confiscation of Jewish Property in the Holocaust, 1933–1945* (Cambridge: Cambridge University Press, 2008); Götz Aly, *Hitler's Beneficiaries: Plunder, Race War, and the Nazi Welfare State* (New York: Metropolitan, 2007); Sarah Farmer, *Martyred Village: Commemorating the 1944 Massacre at Oradour-sur-Glane* (Berkeley: University of California Press, 1999); Jan Gross, *Golden Harvest: Events at the Periphery of the Holocaust* (Oxford: Oxford University Press, 2012); Mike McGovern, *Making War in Côte d'Ivoire* (Chicago: University of Chicago Press, 2011); Anahit Astoyan, *The Pillage of the Century: Expropriation of Armenians in the Ottoman Empire* (Yerevan, Armenia: Nairi, 2015); Lawrence Rothfield, *The Rape of Mesopotamia: Behind the Looting of the Iraq Museum* (Chicago: University of Chicago Press, 2009).

17. See, however, Paul Cornish and Nicholas J. Saunders, eds., *Bodies in Conflict: Corporeality, Materiality, and Transformation* (Milton Park, U.K.: Routledge, 2014); Nicholas J. Saunders and Paul Cornish, *Contested Objects: Material Memories of the Great War* (London and New York: Routledge, 2009); Nicholas J. Saunders, ed., *Matters of Conflict: Material Culture, Memory, and the First World War* (London and New York: Routledge, 2004).

18. Edwards, Gosden, and Phillips, eds., *Sensible Objects*; John Henry Merryman, ed., *Imperialism, Art, and Restitutions* (New York: Cambridge University Press, 2006); James Cuno, ed., *Whose Culture? The Promise of Museums and the Debate over Antiquities* (Princeton: Princeton University Press, 2012).

19. Leora Auslander, *Cultural Revolutions: Everyday Life and Politics in Britain, North America, and France* (Berkeley: University of California Press, 2009).

20. Sophie White, *Wild Frenchmen and Frenchified Indians* (Philadelphia: University of Pennsylvania Press, 2012).

21. On the British empire, see Mark Staniforth, *Material Culture and Consumer Society: Dependent Colonies in Colonial Australia* (New York: Kluwer Academic/Plenum Publishers, 2003); Zeynep Çelik, *Urban Forms and Colonial Confrontations: Algiers under French Rule* (Berkeley: University of California Press, 1997); Robin D. Jones, *Interiors of Empire: Objects, Space, and Identity within the Indian Subcontinent, c. 1800–1947* (Manchester: Manchester University Press, 2007); Chitralekha Zutshi, "'Designed for Eternity': Kashmiri Shawls, Empire, and Cultures of Production and Consumption in Mid-Victorian Britain," *Journal of British Studies* 48, no. 2, Special Issue on Material Culture (2009): 420–440; Naomi Davidson, *Only Muslim: Embodying Islam in Twentieth Century France* (Ithaca: Cornell University Press, 2012).

22. Joseph Roth, "The Bust of the Emperor," in *Hotel Savoy* (New York: Penguin, 2003), 157–158. On the shared material culture of the Habsburg Empire, see Pieter Judson, *Our Empire* (Cambridge: Harvard University Press, forthcoming) and Daniel L. Unowsky, *The Pomp and Politics of Patriotism: Imperial Celebrations in Habsburg Austria, 1848–1916* (West Lafayette, Ind.: Purdue University Press, 2005).

23. Kariann Akemi Yokota, *Unbecoming British: How Revolutionary America Became a Postcolonial Nation* (Oxford: Oxford University Press, 2010); Peter Gonsalves, *Clothing for Liberation: A Communication Analysis of Gandhi's Swadeshi Revolution* (Los Angeles: SAGE, 2010); Lisa Trivedi, *Clothing Gandhi's Nation: Homespun and Modern India* (Bloomington: Indiana University Press, 2007); Michela Wrong, *In the Footsteps of Mr. Kurtz: Living on the Brink of Disaster in Mobutu's Congo* (New York: HarperCollins, 2001); Yolanda Covington-Ward, *Gesture and Power: Religion, Nationalism, and Everyday Performance in Congo* (Durham: Duke University Press, 2016).

24. Tony Bennett, *The Birth of the Museum: History, Theory, Politics* (London: Routledge, 1995); Andrea Meyer and Bénédicte Savoy, eds., *The Museum Is Open: Towards a Transnational History of Museums, 1750–1940* (Berlin: De Gruyter, 2014).

25. Charlotte Trumpler, ed., *Das Grosse Spiel: Archäologie und Politik zur Zeit des Kolonialismus (1860–1940)* (Cologne, Germany: DuMont, 2008).

26. Sally Price, *Paris Primitive: Jacques Chirac's Museum on the Quai Branly* (Chicago: University of Chicago Press, 2007); Kate Fitz Gibbon, ed., *Who Owns the Past? Cultural Policy, Cultural Property, and the Law* (New Brunswick, N.J.: Rutgers University Press, 2005).

27. Aly, *Hitler's Beneficiaries.*

28. Meng, *Shattered Spaces*; Bartov, *Erased.*

29. David Blackbourn, *The Conquest of Nature: Water, Landscape, and the Making of Modern Germany* (New York: W. W. Norton, 2007), 259–303; Nancy Reagin, *Sweeping the German Nation: Domesticity and National Identity in Germany, 1870–1945* (Cambridge: Cambridge University Press, 2006); Elizabeth Harvey, *Women in the Nazi East: Agents and Witnesses of Germanization* (New Haven: Yale University Press, 2003).

30. Gregor Thum, *Uprooted: How Breslau became Wrocław in the Century of Expulsions* (Princeton: Princeton University Press, 2011); Yuliya Komska, *The Icon Curtain: The Cold War's Quiet Border* (Chicago: University of Chicago Press, 2015).

 31. Kathy Burrell, "Materialising the Border: Spaces of Mobility and Material Culture in Migration from Post-Socialist Poland," *Mobilities* 3, no. 3 (2008): 353–373; Orvar Löfgren, "Motion and Emotion: Learning to be a Railway Traveler," *Mobilities* 3, no. 3 (2008): 331–351.

32. Atina Grossmann, *Jews, Germans, and Allies: Close Encounters in Occupied Germany* (Princeton: Princeton University Press, 2007), 184–236; Tara Zahra, *The Lost Children:*

Reconstructing Europe's Families after World War II (Cambridge: Harvard University Press, 2011), 88–117.

33. On migration, material culture, and memory, see Silvia Spitta, *Misplaced Objects: Migrating Collections and Recollections in Europe and the Americas* (Austin: University of Texas Press, 2009); Kathy Burrell and Panikos Panayi, eds., *Histories and Memories: Migrants and Their History in Britain* (New York: St. Martin's Press, 2006). On loss, see Mikkel Bille, Frida Hastrup, and Tim Flohr Sørensen, eds., *An Anthropology of Absence: Materializations of Transcendence and Loss* (New York and London: Springer, 2010). On displaced persons and personal possessions, see Zahra, *Lost Children*.

34. Milena Roth, *Lifesaving Letters: A Child's Flight from the Holocaust* (Seattle: University of Washington Press, 2004), 83–85.

35. Franziska Nunnally to Sammlung Frauennachlässe, February 21, 2000, NL 36 Frances Nunnally (Franziska Huppert), Sammlung Frauennachlässe, University of Vienna. Emphasis in the original.

36. Leora Auslander, "Coming Home? Jews in Postwar Paris," *Journal of Contemporary History* 40 (2005): 237–259. Sandra Dudley, *Materialising Exile: Material Culture and Embodied Experience among Karenni Refugees in Thailand* (New York: Berghahn Books, 2010).

37. Sami Dassa, *Vivre, aimer avec Auschwitz au coeur* (Paris: L'Harmattan, 2002), 176–177, 192.

38. Charlotte Delbo, *Auschwitz et après*, vol. 3: *Mesure de nos jours* (Paris: Editions de Minuit, 1971), 39–40.

39. Leora Auslander, "Archiving a Life: Post-Shoah Paradoxes of Memory Legacies," in *Unsettling Histories*, ed. Alf Lüdtke and Sebastien Jobs (Frankfurt: Campus Verlag, 2010), 127–146.

40. For more on the senses and antimigrant activism in contemporary Europe, see Leora Auslander, "Negotiating Embodied Difference: Veils, Minarets, Kippas, and Sukkot in Contemporary Europe," *Archiv für Sozialgeschichte* 51 (2011): 401–418.

Part I

States of Things

The Making of Modern Nation-States and Empires

Leora Auslander and Tara Zahra

The essays in this section of the book all focus on the forced mobility of things in the context of war, on the use of stolen objects and antiquities by warring states. The plundering of publicly held artworks and cultural goods more generally as well as the expropriation of individual property have been a central strategy of warfare. These acquisitions have enriched the collections of state museums and royal palaces. This is therefore not only a story of state expropriation and restitution in the immediate context of war. These essays also demonstrate that the importance of things to individual and group identification continues well after the war "ends." In the aftermath of war or ethnic cleansing, restitution cases have turned battles over objects into fierce sites of political contestation, memorialization, and individual and collective struggles for justice and recognition. Throughout the modern era, states have also engaged in heated diplomatic conflicts over the theft and return of stolen objects and cultural patrimony that often last for decades or centuries.

The statues, paintings, furniture, china, tapestries, and architectural fragments themselves have often resisted such theft and redeployment. The fragile materiality of artwork—its propensity to shatter or break in transit—has confounded the political projects assigned to them by humans. They break or tear in transit or capsize the ships used for their transport. Even when they reach their new homes intact, or in a state that allows for repair or restoration, they often don't quite settle in but continue to bear the traces of their earlier lives.

In chapter 1 of this section, "The Honor of the Trophy," Alice Goff explicates how and why during the Napoleonic wars, French armies expropriated artwork from across Europe to be displayed at the new Louvre Museum in Paris in the name of Enlightenment universalism. Focusing on a single work, the bronze statue known as *Adorans* that had been discovered in 1503 in Rhodes and brought to Venice, whence it circulated through noble and royal private collections until it was captured by the French and put on public display in the Louvre. Prussian administrators subsequently repatriated the statue (along with other objects) to serve their own idealistic vision of art's transcendent spirit. The bronze statue was damaged a number of times along this trajectory, so damaged that even fundamental questions such as whether the boy's arms were extended heavenward in supplication or in some other posture became the subject of intense debate. Goff ultimately argues for the importance of the object's materiality and also for the crucial role of its human captors and interpreters. Restorers could not quite eliminate the telltale scars on the statue's body, but the statue did not get to decide if it was praying or not, or how or where it would be displayed, or to what purpose.

Shifting from the context of continental to overseas empire, Bonnie Effros explores how the French discovery of Roman ruins in Algeria was used to legitimate its annexation of the territory. Intellectuals and politicians argued that the Ottoman Empire was illegitimate; France was the true heir of the shared Latinate civilization created by the Roman Empire. The new French Empire would simply reunite the Mediterranean world. Bureaucrats argued further that that Roman heritage had been neglected and abandoned; the French had an obligation to Western civilization to preserve and restore its remains. These efforts were, however, thwarted by both human and material actors. Parisian museum administrators thought that the North African finds were of low quality and not of much interest. French colonists argued, by contrast, that the Roman artifacts should stay in Algeria, to help build a French imperial identity. And the things themselves resisted; they broke when soldiers tried to extract them and their weight sank the ships used to transport them. Alice Goff and Bonnie Effros both suggest, then, that nineteenth-century campaigns to steal, export, and re-signify art and antiquities sometimes fell short of their ambitions.

In the final essay in this part of the volume we move from the nineteenth century to the twentieth and from bronze statues and stone fragments to domestic furnishings, albeit luxurious ones. Cathleen Giustino analyzes how four successive regimes in Czechoslovakia made use of stolen things to reinforce their power between 1938 and 1958. Each regime used this property to legitimate their rule, reward loyalty, and construct new historical and national narratives. Chateaux that had been the residences of Czech nobles were appropriated first for Nazi use, then reclaimed immediately after World War II and transformed from enemy property into a form of national patrimony that symbolized the cleansing of Germans from "Czech" space. They acquired yet another life under the socialist regime, becoming retreats for writers whose work was sanctioned by the state. Each of these redeployments of the buildings required reallocation of their contents and a reconceptualization of whether those household furnishings' purpose in life was to be used in the present or preserved for the future.

In all three of these chapters the powerful investment of the modern state, whether imperial, monarchical, republican, or socialist, in the wartime seizure not only of territory but also of movable property becomes clear. Those appropriated goods were then redeployed to serve the states' political and material interests. French, Prussian, German, and Czech regimes discovered, however, that they had less power over these mere things than they thought they had. The things themselves did not always behave—they broke, wore out, or bore scars that raised questions—and people did not always react to them as they were intended to react. The traces of violence had their costs.

THE HONOR OF THE TROPHY

A Prussian Bronze in the Napoleonic Era

Alice Goff

Protect me from the surging horde
That pulls us against our will toward the maelstrom
No, lead me to the quiet corner of heaven
Where new joy blossoms for the poet alone. . . .
—Goethe, *Faust*, 1808

In November 1806, the members of the Academy of Sciences in Berlin gathered to draft a desperate plea. France had defeated Prussia a month earlier at the battles of Jena and Auerstadt, and Napoleon and his army were now occupying the city. In a by then well-established feature of French military policy in the Revolutionary and Napoleonic Wars, the occupiers sought out objects of cultural value from the vanquished state to transport back to France. The director of the Musée Napoleon, Dominique-Vivant Denon, led the endeavor, selecting works of art, coins, books, maps, and curiosities from the royal palaces and galleries in Berlin and Potsdam to enrich his museum's collections in Paris. As the objects were readied for transport, the distraught members of the Academy in the Prussian capital decided to intervene with the French emperor himself.[1] In the resulting petition, the members invoked one of the threatened objects to represent their plight. The most prized antiquity in the Prussian collections, an ancient bronze boy just over

Figure 1.1. Bronze statue of a young man (*Adorans*), late 4th century BCE.
Antikensammlung, Staatliche Museen Berlin, Sk. 2. Erich Lessing,
Art Resource, New York.

four feet tall with head raised and arms stretched upward, implored the mercy of its captors.

> The only monument of the collection that could merit the honor of being taken away as a trophy is the . . . image of an *Adorans*. He raises his eyes and his hands as if to implore the great and generous spirit of the victor. This beautiful bronze represents so well the state of the supplicant, and portrays so well our situation, to which we cannot add anything to express more strongly and more deeply our prayers and our hopes.[2]

It was a strange formulation. The artwork, with its arms outstretched, pleading to the French captors to spare it, was at the same time a worthy trophy. Stranger still, the Academy seemed to concede that the very gesture that made the boy such a fitting representative of their supplication also assured its own capture. The allegory of the praying statue had overshot its target. By embodying so perfectly the plight of the conquered, the statue was the perfect emblem of the conqueror. By interceding on its own behalf, the *Adorans* condemned itself.[3]

This figurative sacrifice was too evocative for the classicist Aloys Hirt, a drafter of the appeal. To concede that "the only monument . . . that could merit the honor of being taken away as a trophy" might give the impression that the sculpture was a fair prize, Hirt cautioned.[4] While the bronze boy might be a fitting trophy, what that status should entail need not be so blatantly explicated. He thus proposed excising the mention of the act—"the honor of being taken away"—and replacing it with the more abstract "the honor of a trophy." "I believe it is better to wrap these matters in a kind of chiaroscuro," Hirt wrote to his colleagues. "Besides, if the conqueror were to leave this ancient trophy in our hands, would this not be just as fitting a memorial to his victory and his greatness?" The director of philology at the Academy agreed, amending only the grammaticality of the construction into idiomatic French.[5]

For all their quibbling about language, the Academy members remained silent on the boldest aspect of their invocation of the Adorans, which is that they should call this object an Adorans at all. The statue, perhaps the most famous work in the Prussian collections, was widely known at the turn of the nineteenth century not as *Adorans*, but as *Antinous*, the favorite youth and lover of the Roman emperor Hadrian. By calling it an

Adorans, an unnamed individual in an act of worship, the Academy was claiming an entirely new identity for the ancient bronze. In their last-ditch effort to save their collections from the French occupiers, why should they not only invoke but literally invent an artwork whose prayers would go unanswered? More than unanswered, an artwork whose prayers secured the very thing these strove to prevent? Of all the rhetorical tools, of all the metaphorical figures at the disposal of the most learned men of the Prussian capital, why this deeply flawed and, as Hirt himself recognized, deeply risky one?

This question, which will concern the following pages, is larger than it seems. Through the figure of the bronze statue made to pray, the Academy's petition contained an argument about the power of art in a moment of political instability, material uncertainty, and upheaval. The devastating losses to the French in October 1806 and the subsequent two-year occupation created a crisis within the Prussian state, exposing the ineptitude of its military, the fragility of its economy, and the vulnerabilities of its government, which was fractured by local traditions and privileges.[6] Drawing on the aesthetic theory of the eighteenth century, the learned bureaucrats addressing these problems in the aftermath of Prussian defeat saw the arts as a means of both social reform and spiritual uplift.[7] The creation of the *Adorans* as such conveyed not only the position of the Academy members but also a new vision for Prussia defined by its commitment to the sovereignty of culture within the political order.

This commitment was a theoretical proposition, but it was also a material one. And the material world of the arts in Prussia in 1806 was in disarray. As news of the impending French occupation arrived in Berlin, administrators of the royal collections struggled to spirit their objects away, anticipating the despoliations of artworks that had accompanied French military campaigns since the invasion of the Low Countries and the Rhineland in 1794.[8] Their efforts were mostly for naught. Over the winter and spring, Denon and his associates made substantial incursions into collections in Kassel, Braunschweig, Schwerin, Berlin, and Potsdam, sending convoys of artworks across the northern German countryside and into the galleries and storerooms of Europe's new cultural capital. The *Adorans*, despite its desperate prayer, was by December on its way to Paris.

The following article argues that the *Adorans*' prayer and the *Adorans*' despoliation were closely connected. As many of the following chapters reveal, the displacement of objects in times of violent conflict throws both their symbolic power and their material vulnerability into stark relief. This is particularly true of objects of culture, which as sources of political legitimacy are both afforded special protections and made special targets in the devastation of modern warfare. The elevation of cultural objects to the status of national patrimony is a project underwritten by violent takeovers and dispossessions, as Bonnie Effros's and Cathleen Giustino's contributions to this volume make clear. I join these authors in arguing that the terms of this relationship must be illuminated if we are to understand the place of art in the exercise of state power.

This duplicity between the symbolic strength and material vulnerability of objects provokes important questions for the historian of the material cultures of warfare and violent displacement. If the objects embroiled in these conflicts also provide a platform for imagining a world beyond prevailing realities, does the material cultural record provide a way into the depths of catastrophe or a way out of it? How can both perspectives be managed at once in historical thinking and writing? The contributions to this volume navigate these questions in different ways, invoking objects' agency or indifference to illuminate their significance as sources for understanding disastrous times. An object that is displaced, Sandra Dudley notes in the final chapter, entails the possibility of rupture and continuity, loss and presence, mobility and immobility. For Dudley, the simultaneity of these meanings can best be understood by taking the object's point of view, a view that may contain multitudes (see Sandra Dudley's contribution to this volume). This chapter follows a somewhat different path. The *Adorans* is a statue enchanted through its displacement. My focus, however, is on the question of how and why it came to be thought of in this way and what its spiritual charge meant for its participation in the military and political conflicts of the early nineteenth century. And while the vitality and the vulnerability of the *Adorans* are importantly linked, they are not in this case complementary forces. In the story of the *Adorans* we see how the very hope that a work of art might metaphorically come alive to point the way beyond the maelstrom, in the words of Goethe's poet, may condemn the body of the work to which this hope so faithfully clings.

The Journey to Prayer

By the time it was called upon to pray for the rescue of the Prussian collections, the *Adorans* had a tumultuous journey behind it. The bronze
statue was discovered in 1503 on Rhodes and brought to Venice, where
it became well known among leading collectors and dealers of the Italian Renaissance.[9] Over the next seventy years it traveled through the
collections of the northern Italian nobility, during which time it was
copied, restored, coveted, and praised in the accounts of its beholders.
In 1631, the Gonzaga family of Mantua, facing financial crisis, sold the
statue through a dealer to Charles I of England, and it began a twenty-
year term in Whitehall. After the king's execution the work was given as
payment for an outstanding debt to an upholsterer, who quickly sold it
in 1651 to the superintendent of finances for Louis XIV, Nicholas Fou-
quet, who installed it at Vaux-le-Vicomte, southwest of Paris. In 1717
the statue became a resident of Vienna, first in the lavish collections of
Prince Eugen of Savoy in the Lower Belvedere and from 1736 in the palace of Prince Joseph Wenzel of Liechtenstein. In 1747 the aesthetically
inclined Prussian king Friedrich II purchased the statue and installed it
in a lattice cupola outside his library window at his Potsdam palace,
Sanssouci.[10]

From its arrival in Potsdam, carefully supervised by the king himself,
the bronze held a privileged position within the royal collections. The circumstances of its purchase, motivated in part by Prussia's influence over
the House of Liechtenstein after the First and Second Silesian Wars, might
have immediately connected the work to a narrative of Prussian supremacy and prestige.[11] That the work even came from Liechtenstein, however,
seems to have been kept out of the public record.[12] The statue appears
infrequently in published descriptions of Sanssouci and Friedrich's collections, a remarkable silence for such a rare and complete ancient bronze.
Even the renowned historian of classical art, Johann Joachim Winckelmann, who saw the work during numerous visits to Potsdam and knew it
to be one of only three Greek bronzes in the entire Holy Roman Empire,
afforded it only passing reference in his *History of Ancient Art*: "a naked
figure with raised hands looking into the distance."[13]

Instead, the statue's distinction came from its special relationship to
Friedrich II himself. The work had been called many things during its

journeys through the courts of Europe—"*Apollo giovani in bronzo*,"[14] "a brass figure less than ye life,"[15] "*un adolescent tendant les bras*"[16]—but by 1747 it was popularly known as an *Antinous*. The artwork's designation as such gave the art historically inclined a clear indication of its significance to the Prussian king. Antinous, the boy lover of Hadrian, had, according to ancient sources, jumped into the Nile and drowned, sacrificing himself to the gods for his beloved emperor.[17] Upon his death, Hadrian built a cult around the figure of the boy, elevating him to the status of a god, dedicating a city to him and commissioning temples filled with his likeness in sculptures and reliefs. Images of Antinous were legible to eighteenth-century viewers as expressions of homoerotic love in collections of art across Europe, perhaps especially in the court of Friedrich II, where rumors of the king's desire for men circulated openly.[18] The Prussian *Antinous*, stepping forward with arms outstretched in the moment of his sacrificial leap, gestured toward the life of the monarch at the most intimate register, and in an especially direct way. This ancient work was, after all, not simply a representation of Antinous but itself a material artifact of Hadrian's devotion to him, its existence a result of the mourning emperor's enthusiastic commission of his lost lover's image across the empire following his death.[19] The body of the bronze stood quite literally for a love between subject and sovereign.[20]

After Friedrich II's death in 1786, his successor, Friedrich Wilhelm II, ordered that the *Antinous* be brought indoors in order to protect it from the weather. The move signaled a shift in the sculpture's representative function. Taken out of its cupola in Sanssouci and installed in a room for the reception of military guests in the city palace in Berlin, the bronze retained its identification as Antinous. But here, surrounded by decorative swords and statues of Victoria, the youth no longer embodied the king's lives and loves but modeled instead the sacrifice of the soldier for his ruler on the battlefield.[21] It was from this position in the military reception hall that on November 5, 1806, the bronze was taken down from its pedestal, packed up, and shipped off to Paris along with the rest of the spoils: hundreds of additional works of ancient and modern sculpture, paintings, and many thousands of ancient and modern coins, medals, and gemstones.[22]

It was at this moment that, in the hands of the Academy, the sculpture became an *Adorans*, thereby abandoning its identity as Antinous and the particular association with the Prussian monarchy this identity had signaled. This may appear surprising: Given its gesture of patriotic sacrifice on one hand and its connection to Friedrich II on the other, Antinous might have fit perfectly into the Academy's petition as an ambassador of Prussian interests and a symbol of a recent past of Franco-Prussian sympathies. There was more at stake in this plea, however, than finding a persuasive rhetorical device. In inventing the *Adorans*, the Academy made an argument for what art should mean to a state in a crisis of legitimacy and a political order in chaotic disarray. As Antinous, whether caught in an act of homoerotic love or of patriotic loyalty, the material presence of the sculpture was the source of its meaning. Its connection to the Prussian state derived from the fact of its body, from a lineage of ownership that began with Hadrian and ended in Berlin. The *Adorans* did the opposite: In its inclination toward the heavens it left its body behind, a worthy trophy open to the French army's acquisitive grasp. But as an *Adorans*, the looting of the sculpture didn't matter. Through the *Adorans* the Academy claimed that the work of art would enable Prussia's legitimacy beyond the desperate material realities of occupation and defeat.

Prayer 1

In 1806, the bronze statue stood at the precipice of a cultural world in danger of grave violation. The arrival of Napoleon and Denon in Berlin on October 24, 1806, along with the French troops and cadres of officers that would occupy the city for the next two years, evoked a cultural kinship between the German and the French that had thrived particularly in the Frederician period. Indeed, the members of the Academy invoked this spirit in their appeal to the French emperor: "Up until now there has existed a useful rivalry of scientific and artistic progress between the learned men of Italy, France, and Germany," the drafters asserted. "Now it is the task of the hero, whose genius has produced such marvels before the astounded eyes of Europe, to encourage more and more this happy exchange between these countries."[23] Even Denon, known as "the eye of Napoleon," stood for a cosmopolitan European community of arts and letters that remained active at the time.[24] An internationally well-regarded artist and scholar by 1806, he had spent his youth in the salon culture of Venice and attracted the attention of German intellectuals with his account of his travels with Napoleon in Egypt, which was translated into German in 1803, just as he became director of the Musée.[25] Denon thus entered German cities in 1806 as the figurehead of this institution's awe-inspiring breadth, its unprecedented openness, and its energetic support of scholarship in the arts and sciences. Such was Denon's stature, not to mention his oft-cited charming demeanor, that he was received as a friendly colleague by many German artists and writers, including Johann Gott-fried Schadow and Johann Wolfgang Goethe, the latter of whom risked showing him his coin collection.[26] He was even welcomed measuredly by the very supervisors of the collections whose loads he was lightening. "He was a . . . truly good-natured man," the administrator of the gallery of paintings at Sanssouci, Johann Gottlieb Puhlmann, recalled in a report to Friedrich Wilhelm III. "Instead of inspecting paintings, he walked up and down the gallery with me and spoke much of Rome."[27] The family of the director of the Royal Cabinet of Arts, Jean Henry, went so far as to invite him to breakfast.[28]

Denon's incursions into the royal art collections constituted in this con-text a particularly poignant transgression. That an occupying army would claim trophies as spoils of war was no particular surprise. Although cul-tural property had emerged as a protectable legal category in times of military conflict and occupation in the early modern period, there were no formal prohibitions against its seizure.[29] The *Kunstraub* ("art robbery"), however, perpetrated in the name of universal learning by participants in a European community of intellectual exchange, exposed the fragility of the cosmopolitanism on which such a community was built. If the Musée Napoleon were to have a motto, the Dresden art historian Karl August Böttiger posited, it might read: "These old artworks belong indeed to the entirety of educated and education-seeking humanity; however the people who are called to be the keepers and protectors of these treasures are only those whose arm can use the sword to defend their ownership."[30] Juxtaposing two registers of possession—"belonging" for humanity and "ownership" for the sword bearers—Böttiger exposed a challenging para-dox of the Musée: that the treasures of humanity ought to be regulated by the force of arms and that by extension the property of all must, in its material form at least, rest in the hands of the few.

The members of the Academy of Sciences were looking for answers to these problems. So too were Prussian bureaucrats, who saw cultural education to be a source of social reform.[31] How to foster a community of scholarship that transcended the particularities of individual objects and individual places while advocating for the preservation of particular objects in particular places? How, further, to maintain a grasp on these works of art in the face of their material loss? A growing literature that emphasized the spiritual nature of aesthetic experience provided useful language for articulating the place of art in Prussia in the face of the devastation of the royal collections at home and the brilliance of the national museum in Paris abroad.[32] For Karl Freiherr vom Stein zum Altenstein, who would become Prussia's first minister of culture in 1817, art's capacity to elevate the state and its subjects toward a realm of moral goodness and truth was a means of distinguishing Prussian cultural politics from the French. France valued the arts only in as much as they were useful to the exercise of power, Altenstein asserted in an 1807 memorandum written in Riga, to which he had fled along with other Prussian ministers following the occupation of Berlin.[33] Prussia must come to understand that the state must make itself subservient to the arts rather than make the arts subservient to the state, he argued: "All that is touched by [the arts] will approach this higher status. With their complete power they will capture all that nears them with omnipotence."[34] While the conqueror might make Prussian artworks their trophies, Prussia would make art the conqueror, omnipotent and capable of reforming the state according to higher ideals. If the state were going to seize the ideal power of the arts, the arts would do the seizing.

Here Altenstein gestured toward the most influential theorist of the value of art in public life at the turn of the nineteenth century, Friedrich Schiller. Schiller's *Aesthetic Letters on the Education of Man*, written in the shadow of the Terror, had provided the theoretical framework through which art might bring the ideals of the Enlightenment into social and political life while avoiding the perversions of revolutionary violence: "Humanity has lost its dignity, but Art has rescued and preserved it in significant stones [*bedeutende Steinen*]," Schiller wrote.[35] Six years later, in the wake of Napoleon's Italian campaigns, Schiller went a step further in a poem written about the antiquities displaced from Rome to Paris:

> They to him are silent ever,
> Into life's fresh circle never

From their pedestals come down.
The muses are alone possessed,
By he who holds them in warm breast;
To the Vandal they are stone![36]

Schiller and Altenstein, poet and statesman, offer a brilliant solution to the dilemma of the *Kunstraub*: stone, or the material object turned profane, was the purview of the vandal. Virtuous and true engagement with art, both suggested, was now predicated on a physical impossibility: the statue that could transcend its earthly parameters and step off its pedestal "into life's fresh circle" was, after all, no statue at all.[37]

The *Adorans* was an answer to the dilemma of its displacement in this vein. The sculpture's prayer signaled a new place for art in the Prussian state that no longer relied on the material presence of objects for their ultimate meaning. The act of worship became in this invocation a betrayal of the sculpture's body and the body an embarrassment to the transcendent impulse of its gesture. As the *Adorans* strove toward the heavens, it served as the perfect disembodiment: an intellectual community of spirit over matter. That in its gesture toward transcendence it foiled its own material salvation made it all the more fitting an ambassador of the Academy's difficult position.

Prayer 2

The body of the bronze, however, would not be so easily dispensed with. The members of the Academy were, after all, neither poets nor visionary statesmen but rather art-historical scholars of a more ruthlessly antiquarian bent: The *Adorans* was not only a symbolic figure but also an artifact whose interpretation should be grounded in concrete evidence.[38] And in 1806 the evidence for the identification as *Adorans* was not great. The idea for its re-designation seems to have come from an 1803 article by the classicist Jakob Andreas Konrad Levezow that had called its interpretation as Antinous into question.[39] Levezow contended that its head and facial expression had nothing in common with other extant portrayals of the youth and that the position of its body made impossible the claim that it was about to jump into a river. The notion of the sculpture's subject in an act of worship emerged from an effort to suggest one, and perhaps any, alternative. Levezow wrote of then-*Antinous*: "One might sooner arrive at the hypothesis that the gaze of this youth towards the heavens, along with its arms and hands stretched in this same direction, portray an Adorant, appealing to the Gods."[40]

And yet, Levezow seems to have offered this as an only marginally more plausible reading. The dispersal of the royal collections across various locations in Berlin, Potsdam, and Charlottenburg, where they could neither be compared nor regarded as a whole, impeded their true study and appreciation, he complained. In the case of the bronze boy, isolated in the city palace and perched in a "quite disadvantageous and very high position," there was no possibility of proper critical examination. More unsettling to the ascription of the *Adorans*, however, was a new and damning finding. Even in compromised conditions, Levezow had managed to get close enough to the work to identify breaks in the bronze near the shoulders. Comparing these to copies of the work, he concluded: "One can say with near certainty, that both arms of the statue, as they appear now, are of modern origin."[41] Nor was there, according to Levezow, any assurance that the original arms had assumed this elevated position. Indeed, he sensed that the boy's expression was rather set off-kilter by its gesture. The uncertainties surrounding the arms required a reading of the statue based on its body alone. Levezow settled on Ganymedes, cupbearer to the gods and favorite of Jupiter: "Most likely with a different position of the arms, he once held a cup of nectar in an elevated hand . . . and in the other [hand] the vessel from which he filled it."[42] An engraving of the statue accompanying his article shows the work on a square base, facing forward toward the viewer, and sporting the confident title *Ganymedes*.

By 1806 the *Adorans* was thus on shaky art historical ground. The members of the Academy would have recognized this. Levezow was an active participant in Berlin's scholarly and antiquarian networks, and his 1803 article was certainly well known. Further, Aloys Hirt, the petitioner who took exception to the explicit mention of the bronze being "taken away" (but none to the work's designation) was one of the most rigorously physical interpreters of objects in the classical field at the time, lampooned by his romantically inclined contemporaries for his "surgical" methods.[43] It seems that in the desperation of the moment of invasion, the allure of the metaphor won out over scholarly precision, at least temporarily.

The *Adorans* made its public debut in the Salle de Diane of the Musée Napoleon in October 1807 as part of an exhibition commemorating the French victories at Jena and Auerstadt. In the catalogue for the exhibit, it acquired a new line on its roster of identities, "*Jeune athlète*," and a new explanation. "It appears to give thanks to the Gods," proclaimed the catalogue, and given the tenor of the exhibition, one may presume that the athlete's gratitude is for his victory.[44] There is an inflection of the Academy's *Adorans* in this description, translated into a triumphant rather than beseeching mode, and while it is uncertain that they would have heard of the petition, the catalogue's compilers were familiar with the 1803 article, especially in light of their adamant defense of the authenticity of the statue's posture: "The expression of his head matches perfectly with his attitude, and his gesture is certain," the description asserted.[45]

Once the *Adorans* was installed in the Musée Napoleon, visible for the first time to a broad viewing public, the prayer theory could acquire proper scholarly credence, and Konrad Levezow got to work right away. Levezow, who had complained of the work's poor exhibition in Berlin, found that its new installation in better light and on a lower pedestal afforded more precise observations of its physical particularities. His investigations yielded the first definitive treatise on the bronze, published in 1808: *De iuvenis adorantis signo ex aere antiquo*.[46]

Levezow began his text with a lamentation of the statue's seizure in Berlin. However, the research made possible by its displacement to Paris soon eclipsed the injustice of the act, as he contrasted the results of his thorough investigation in the Salle de Diane with his previous assumptions in Berlin:

> At first it had seemed to me that from far off . . . each arm had been newly joined to the shoulders, and I suspected from several clues [the arms] to have been remade by a more recent hand. . . . However, upon a repeated examination, and one undertaken from very close up, so that all things could be observed most clearly, I found that in the original excavation of the work not only had both arms been broken off at the shoulder, but also that the left one had been broken in addition in another place, namely near the forearm.[47]

At this point in his treatise, the discovery of another fracture on the left arm, in addition to confirmation of the two breaks in the shoulders, would seem to be bad news for the *Adorans* as such. More fissures lent credence to his "near certain" thesis of 1803 that the arms were indeed of modern origin. Levezow's conclusion based on this new evidence, however, went in an unexpected direction: "but then, when [the left arm] was lifted from the shadows, in which it lay buried . . . it was cemented and fit back perfectly onto the ancient shoulder; . . . And likewise, I could observe that the right arm had also been returned to the shoulder; and that another [modern] hand had taken pains at forming and polishing its whole surface, and that . . . the ancient arm . . . was similarly formed and joined to the body, and thus that the boy had also been raising this arm in the same gesture."[48]

Levezow came away from his investigations with the conclusion that the breaks in the arms confirmed rather than disputed the authenticity of their contemporary position. The left arm was original after all, having been broken during excavation but then reattached. The right arm was modern but had been joined to the body in exactly the same way as the ancient and now-lost right arm. To test his theory, Levezow recruited a sixteen-year-old boy similar in stature to the bronze to stand by the statue in the Musée so that he could compare the bronze musculature to that of a living specimen.[49] With his observations complete, "there can be no more doubt about the authentic form and gesture of the arms of the statue," he asserted.[50] Levezow could now take up an understanding of the statue's meaning entirely dependent on its gesture.

Levezow's treatise, backed up with pages of references from classical literature and published, somewhat anomalously for the day, in Latin, makes his treatment of the *Adorans* appear to be the height of empirical inquiry, conclusions won through the hard and rigorous practice of close material investigation that reaps a divine reward. It is irresistible to imagine Levezow in the Salle de Diane of the Musée Napoleon vigorously scrutinizing the limbs of the bronze next to his live model. From the effort of squinting at the fissures in the work's pocked surface and the extensive physiognomic analysis a divine connection was elicited, a prayer. This was exactly the kind of art historical inquiry that Levezow had envisioned when he wrote of the benefits of a publicly accessible and centralized museum of art for Prussia in his 1803 article and for which he had repeatedly advocated in the introductions to his published studies. "In perhaps no other kind of science is it as necessary . . . to arm oneself against the

appeal of overly hasty, if seemingly obvious judgments through cold delib-
erateness and through tireless patience in the examination [of objects] as
in the study of antiquities," he wrote in an 1801 treatise on ancient stone
carvings.[51] This was the type of engagement that the Musée Napoleon was
equipped to foster.[52]

It is thus somewhat peculiar that in his inspection, "one undertaken
from very close up," Levezow, who had also had the opportunity to examine the *Adorans* before it had left Berlin, would have missed the significant
changes to the work after its arrival in Paris.[53] Because of the thin walls
of its bronze body, the statue was in a delicate condition from the start,
and it had incurred serious damage on the voyage from Berlin to Paris.
When it arrived, its head had cracked at the neck, its feet had broken
into pieces, and its arms had nearly detached from the body. A massive
restoration project ensued, led by the sculptor and metalworker Charles
Stanislas Canlers, who fashioned internal struts and sockets in order to
reattach and stabilize the broken appendages.[54] Canlers repaired the arms
by fitting them with internal iron rods embedded in a plaster filling that
bolted onto a plate in the statue's chest. The details of how he repaired the
seams in the bronze after reattaching the arms remain unclear, but given
the severity of the intervention, it is surprising that Levezow overlooked
its evidence on the surface of the statue itself, and that he had not heard
of the repairs through his scholarly networks.[55]

Perhaps, however, Levezow's omission can be attributed to his recognition that establishing the physical certainty of the statue's arms only
got him so far. He had explicated the mechanics of the statue's gesture
in exquisite detail, and yet to call this gesture an act of prayer required a
step further. He turned thus in the last words of his reading of the work
to the importance of the feeling and idea of the gesture, rather than its
anatomy:

> If [the viewer] properly considers the expression of the mouth and especially
> of the eyes as suffering (πάθημα), he will necessarily understand that this is di-
> rected towards the sky, the image of someone praying and making an urgent de-
> mand. And if you perceive, and join together in your mind, the appearance of
> the face and expression gazing [upwards], together with the arrangement of the
> arms and the form of the whole body standing . . . it cannot be otherwise than
> that willingly . . . you will form for yourself the idea of a certain youth wor-
> shipping, that is, pouring forth prayers and reverently worshipping the gods.[56]

Here Levezow transposed the imperative of the Academy's first invocation of the *Adorans* into his art-historical treatise. The statue was praying,
but so too must its viewer. In a move away from the difficult decoding of
cracks and surfaces, Levezow asked his readers to follow the statue's gaze
into the skies and to allow the idea of the prayer to derive from an act of
imagination. In the end, the ascription of the statue as an *Adorans* was a
leap of faith.

The leap of faith has stuck. While there is some variation of opinion
among classicists and archaeologists, the statue continues to be known
by its "praying" gesture, as the *"Betende Knabe"* (The Praying Boy) in
scholarly literature and in the official catalogues of the Altes Museum in
Berlin, where it is currently on display. At the same time, Levezow's rejection of the modern origins of the statue's arms has been overturned. Both
arms are now thought to have been added during its French tenure in the
seventeenth century. There is no consensus, however, on whether or not
they occupy the position of the original gesture.[57]

The invention of the *Adorans* responded to the crisis of the Prussian
state and the displacements of cultural property in the wake of the Napoleonic Wars. First as allegorical fantasy and then as art historical certainty,
both of the *Adorans'* prayers elided the work's material frame. This was
no casualty of language or accident of method: It was exactly the point.
By converting the *Antinous* into the *Adorans*, Levezow and the Academy members were fashioning a new power for a work of art that relied
on spiritual affinity rather than material ownership. The *Adorans* was
designed, in other words, to account for the absence of the work from
Prussian territory and to make it meaningful, despite its displacement, to
Prussian cultural identity.

Coda: The *Adorans* Acquires a Temple

The work's return to Prussia in 1815, however, did not end its identity
as an *Adorans* but rather shifted its prayer into a new key. After the fall
of the Napoleonic regime, Prussia successfully reclaimed vast quantities
of artworks seized in the intervening decades, and the prized bronze was
installed once again in the military reception room of the city palace in
Berlin where it had stood in 1806. This would not be a restoration of an

old regime of cultural politics, however, Prussian bureaucrats made clear. The achievement of the Musée Napoleon and the trauma of the looting had given impetus to longstanding proposals to create a museum of art in the Prussian capital, and the works that were returned from Paris quickly became part of the plans. The museum would centralize the dispersed royal art collections and provide an opportunity to transform Altenstein's 1807 vision for a state oriented toward ideal truths through art into concrete practice. In 1823, Karl Friedrich Schinkel's proposal won the endorsement of Friedrich Wilhelm III, and the project began in earnest.

Schinkel's museum design drew heavily on the theories of aesthetic engagement found in the work of his romantic and idealist contemporaries.[58] In line with Altenstein's formulations, this was to be a sanctuary devoted to the spiritual sovereignty of the arts and the moral elevation of the populace through them. The central architectural element of the museum was a cathedral-like rotunda, which was to be bordered by ancient sculptures. In the middle of a building filled with galleries presenting the geographical and chronological development of the western art tradition, the rotunda was an emblem of the unassailable and timeless supremacy of the ideal of beauty achieved by ancient art.[59] In the passage from the rotunda into the galleries—that is, between the place of the ideal and the place of the historical—stood the *Adorans*, described by Christian Friedrich Tieck in the catalogue at the museum's opening in 1830 as "*Anbetender Knabe*" (worshipping boy).[60]

The *Adorans* seemed the perfect symbol for Schinkel's temple of art. But unlike its previous iterations in the Academy's petition and in Levezow's treatise, in the Berlin museum the *Adorans* was neither a construction of language nor an artifact of scholarly interpretation but a material object standing in front of a viewer who could only wonder what to make of it. The catalogue did not help much. Unlike Levezow's exhaustive treatise or Visconti's description in the catalogue of the Musée, each of which spoke of the gods and the gestures associated with ancient prayer, Tieck did not indicate to whom or for what the boy might be praying. And yet the absence of this information suggests that for its new status as Prussian museum object, more important than the destination of its prayer was that it was praying at all. Positioned between the sacred space of the rotunda and the art-historical space of the galleries, the *Adorans* modeled the type of viewership the institution hoped to promote: an attitude toward art that looked up and out into a world of ideal beauty and moral truth rather than down into one of profane materiality. Or in the words of the romantic writers Wilhelm Heinrich Wackenroder and Ludwig Tieck: "I compare the enjoyment of the finest works of art to a prayer. . . . He who is beloved by the heavens . . . lays bare his noble soul; then he kneels, and turns his open breast in silent rapture towards heaven's brilliance and nourishes himself with ethereal light; then he stands up . . . full and light of heart, and puts his hand on a great and good work of art. This is the true meaning of prayer."[61] In this context, the *Adorans'* prayer for the first time figured as a physical proposition rather than a theoretical one. It gave body to the ideal museum experience. Immediately visible to visitors upon entering the building, the *Adorans* raised its arms toward the domed ceiling in prayer perhaps to the museum itself, entreating its viewers to adopt its reverential gaze as they proceeded through Schinkel's temple of art.

And yet museums, despite their loftiest motives, are places where the profane is difficult to banish. The *Adorans* was a material object that needed to be managed rather than merely revered. Indeed, the visitor devout enough to follow Wackenroder and Tieck's instructions for proper viewership to reach out to touch the *Adorans* would have been met not only with a stern reprimand from the attending gallery servant but also with a surprise feature of the work in its new installation. Upon positioning it in the primary sight line of people entering the building through the rotunda, museum planners had discovered that the bronze was terribly backlit from the windows in the gallery behind it.[62] As a solution to the problem, Wilhelm von Humboldt proposed that it be mounted on a swiveling base "so that the most beautiful of our statues . . . can be seen from the front and from the sides in good lighting."[63] In the museum, prayer was a matter of engineering.

The *Adorans* had acquired a temple to frame its tenuously constructed gesture. But in this temple it stood for more than a vault into an ideal aesthetic world. It stood also for the institutional and infrastructural challenges that this vault would require to support it. The *Adorans* brought the difficult confrontation between its body and its prayer, born of the crisis of the Napoleonic *Kunstraub*, into the Prussian museum.

At the beginning of the nineteenth century, the Napoleonic Wars in Europe occupy an ambiguous position in the history of modern warfare. As the site of new forms of violence and military strategy that conscripted all aspects of society into the throes of conflict, these wars were also underwritten by a belief, common to the European powers, in the sovereignty of culture and the sanctity of the arts in the midst of grave political upheaval. Without the *Adorans*, it might be possible to see in this juncture a confrontation between new and old regimes: an early modern commitment to the essential cosmopolitanism of cultural inquiry out of joint with a consolidated nationalist militarism that would define European conflict into the twentieth century. The history of the *Adorans* makes evident, however, that this faith in the transcendent capacities of art was not at odds with the brutal realities of the Napoleonic conflicts but was in fact dependent on them. It was the very despoliation of the art object that produced the statue's spiritualized meaning, a meaning that effaced the violence in which the material world of art was entangled. In the body of the *Adorans* this act of effacement slides back into view, revealing an unresolved duplicity between spiritual sovereignty and material destruction with which the museum, despite its devotion to the bloodless transformation of society, must ultimately contend.

Notes

I am grateful to the members of Der Kreis at UC Berkeley, the Michigan Society of Fellows, and in particular Amanda Armstrong-Price, Leora Auslander, Jennifer Nelson, Helmut Puff, Anicia Timberlake, Tara Zahra, and the contributors to this volume for their very helpful comments on this piece.

1. The Academy of Science was joined in a similar effort by their colleagues in the Prussian Academy of Arts, who submitted a petition days before their own. Bénédicte Savoy, *Kunstraub: Napoleons Konfizierungen in Deutschland und ihre europäische Folgen* (Vienna: Böhlau, 2009), 231.

2. Akademie der Wissenschaften to Napoleon, November 22, 1806, Historische Abteilung, PAW I–XV: 8a, fol. 1v, Archiv der Berlin-Brandenburgischen Akademie der Wissenschaften, Berlin.

3. This chapter will generally refer to the bronze sculpture in question as "the *Adorans*," preserving the form in the Academy's petition. Later works in German, English, and French refer to the work as "*Adorant*." It is now commonly known as the "*Betende Knabe*" (Praying Boy).

4. Aloys Hirt to Frédéric de Castillon, November 23, 1806, Historische Abteilung, PAW I–XV: 8a, fol. 3r, Archiv der Berlin-Brandenburgischen Akademie der Wissenschaften, Berlin.

5. Frédéric de Castillon to Aloys Hirt, November 24, 1806, Historische Abteilung, PAW I–XV: 8a, fol. 3v, Archiv der Berlin-Brandenburgischen Akademie der Wissenschaften, Berlin. Bénédicte Savoy reads this pedantic exchange as evidence of Castillon's reluctance to explicitly resist the French incursions. See Savoy, "'Die Ehre einer Trophäe': Aloys Hirt und der

französische Kunstraub," in *Aloys Hirt: Archäologe, Historiker, Kunstkenner*, ed. Claudia Sedlarz (Hannover-Laatzen, Germany: Wehrhahn Verlag, 2004), 143.

6. The significance of the losses of 1806 for the Prussian state has been treated by a large body of scholarship: on its impact on civilian life, see Karen Hagemann, *Revisiting Prussia's Wars against Napoleon: History, Culture, and Memory* (Cambridge: Cambridge University Press, 2015); on its consequences for military thinking, see Peter Paret, *The Cognitive Challenge of War: Prussia 1806* (Princeton: Princeton University Press, 2009); on its importance for the Prussian reform movement, see Matthew Levinger, *Enlightened Nationalism: The Transformation of Prussian Political Culture, 1806–1848* (Oxford: Oxford University Press, 2000).

7. James Sheehan, *Museums in the German Art World: From the End of the Old Regime to the Rise of Modernism* (Oxford: Oxford University Press, 2000), 56–58.

8. This "*Kunstraub*" (art robbery) had attracted the particular outrage of German audiences during the Italian campaigns as Napoleon's army removed the most celebrated works of painting and sculpture in the European tradition to the burgeoning collections of the museum in the Louvre, as of 1803 known as the Musée Napoleon. On the significance of the French looting for the development of this institution, see Andrew McClellan, *Inventing the Louvre: Art, Politics, and the Origins of the Modern Museum in Eighteenth-Century Paris* (Cambridge: Cambridge University Press, 1994). For a comprehensive treatment of German reactions to the French looting, see Savoy, *Kunstraub*.

9. For the work's tenure in Italy, see Marilyn Perry, "A Greek Bronze in Renaissance Venice," *The Burlington Magazine* 117, no. 865 (1975): 204–211, www.jstor.org/stable/877977; Nele Hackländer, "Der Betende Knabe: Eine Antike auf Wanderschaft," in *Der Betende Knabe, Original und Experiment*, ed. Gerhard Zimmer and Nele Hackländer (Frankfurt am Main: Peter Lang, 1997), 25–28.

10. Hackländer, "Der Betende Knabe," 29.

11. Thomas Fischbacher, *Des Königs Knabe: Friedrich der Grosse und Antinous* (Weimar, Germany: Verlag und Datenbank für Geisteswissenschaften, 2011), 47–63.

12. The official catalogue of the Prussian collections, published in 1774, leaves out any mention of Liechtenstein, citing the previous owner as Prince Eugen of Savoy. Fischbacher, *Des Königs Knabe*, 100. Matthias Oesterreich, *Description et explication des Groupes, Statues . . . qui forment la Collection de S.M. le Roi de Prusse* (Berlin: George Jacques Decker, 1774), 14–15.

13. Johann Joachim Winckelmann, *Geschichte der Kunst des Alterthums*, vol. 1 (Vienna: Akademischer Verlag, 1776), 546. Perhaps, Thomas Fischbacher argues, Winckelmann hesitated to draw attention to the discrepancy between his identification of the statue as Greek and the prevailing interpretation of the work, confirmed in the official royal catalogue, as Roman. Fischbacher, *Des Königs Knabe*, 99.

14. From a description within the Bevilacqua estate papers, 1594, quoted in Hackländer, "Der Betende Knabe," 27.

15. Inventory of Charles I, 1649, quoted in Hackländer, "Der Betende Knabe," 28.

16. Inventory of Foucquet, 1665, quoted in Hackländer, "Der Betende Knabe," 29.

17. See for example the account in Dio Cassius, *Roman History*, book 69, trans. Earnest Cary, *Loeb Classical Library* vol. 176 (Cambridge: Harvard University Press, 1925), 444–447. For an overview of the textual evidence for Antinous' life and death, see Caroline Vout, *Power and Eroticism in Imperial Rome* (Cambridge: Cambridge University Press, 2007), 54–61.

18. Whitney Davis, *Queer Beauty: Sexuality and Aesthetics from Winckelmann to Freud and Beyond* (New York: Columbia University Press, 2010), 24–29.

19. Caroline Vout lays out this argument for a correspondence between the history of Antinous and the image of Antinous. See Vout, *Power and Eroticism,* 52–135.

20. It continues to serve in this way, a tantalizing if enigmatic source of insight into a monarch who was, as Christopher Clark writes, "loquacious . . . but rarely self-revealing." Clark, *Iron Kingdom: The Rise and Downfall of Prussia, 1600–1947* (London: Penguin, 2007), 183.

21. Fischbacher, *Des Königs Knabe,* 129–130.

22. Totals of objects taken out of the collections of the city palace are in Dominique-Vivant Denon, "Inventaire des objets d'Art et de curiosité énléves du Palais du Roi de Prusse à Berlin par ordre de S.M. l'Empereur pour être transportés à Paris," April 5, 1807, Historische Abteilung, PAW I–XV: 9, fol. 69–74, Archiv der Berlin-Brandenburgischen Akademie der Wissenschaften, Berlin. Götz Eckardt calculates the loss of 38 statues, 79 busts, 10 reliefs, and 116 paintings from the royal palaces, which excludes the contents of the royal Kunstkammer: Götz Eckardt, "Der napoleonische Kunstraub in den königlichen Schlössern von Berlin und Potsdam," in *Studien zur Berliner Kunstgeschichte,* ed. Karl-Heinz Klingenburg (Leipzig: VEB E.A. Seemann Verlag, 1986), 126.

23. Akademie der Wissenschaften to Napoleon, November 22, 1806, Historische Abteilung, PAW I–XV: 8a, fol. 1r, Archiv der Berlin-Brandenburgischen Akademie der Wissenschaften, Berlin.

24. Savoy, *Kunstraub,* 120.

25. Dominique-Vivant Denon, *Voyage dans la Basse et la Haute Égypte* (Paris: P. Didot L'Aine, 1802); Dominique-Vivant Denon, *Reisen durch Ober- und Unter-Ägypten während Bonapartes Feldzügen,* trans. Dietrich Tiedemann (Hamburg and Berlin: Anton Doll, 1803).

26. Savoy, *Kunstraub,* 124. Johann Gottfried Schadow writes of a visit from Denon, who assisted him in sketching from memory a portrait of Copernicus. Johann Gottfried Schadow, *Kunst-Werken und Kunst-Ansichten* (Berlin: Verlag der Deckerschen Geheimen Ober-Hofbuchdruckerei, 1849), 88.

27. Johann Gottfried Puhlmann to Friedrich Wilhelm III, March 10, 1810, I.HA Rep. 89: Geheimes Zivilkabinett, jüngere Periode, no. 20418, Geheimes Staatsarchiv Preußischer Kulturbesitz, Berlin.

28. Minette Henry, diary entry from November 2, 1806, transcribed by Emil Dubois-Reymond, "Aus dem Tagebuche von Minette Henry," Runge-Dubois-Reymond Papers, no. 178, Heft 3, Staatsbibliothek Berlin.

29. On the protection of cultural property in this period, see Margaret M. Miles, *Art as Plunder: The Ancient Origins of the Debate about Cultural Property* (Cambridge: Cambridge University Press, 2008), 297–348.

30. Karl August Böttiger, *Über Museen und Antikensammlungen: eine archäologische Vorlesung* (Leipzig: Dyk'schen Buchhandlung, 1808), iii.

31. Suzanne Marchand, *Down from Olympus: Archaeology and Philhellenism in Germany, 1750–1970* (Princeton: Princeton University Press, 1996), 25–28.

32. The genre of the gallery dialogue, argues Theodore Ziolkowski, became a central locus for this construction of a romantic concept of cultural politics with an eye toward developments in France. Theodore Ziolkowski, *German Romanticism and Its Institutions* (Princeton: Princeton University Press, 1990), 355–372.

33. Karl Sigmund Franz Freiherr vom Stein zum Altenstein, "Denkschrift über die Leitung des Preußischen Staates (an Hardenberg)," in *Die Reorganisation des Preussischen Staates unter Stein und Hardenberg; veranlasst und unterstützt durch die preussische Archivverwaltung in Verbindung mit der Notgemeinschaft der deutschen Wissenschaft,* ed. Georg Winter and Rudolf Vaupel, vol. 1 (Leipzig: Hirzel, 1931), 454.

34. Altenstein, "Denkschrift," 454.

35. Friedrich Schiller, "Über die ästhetische Erziehung des Menschen in einer Reihe von Briefen," in *Schillers Werke: Nationalausgabe*, ed. Lieselotte Blumenthal and Benno von Wiese, vol. 20. bk. 1, *Philosophische Schriften* (Weimar, Germany: Hermann Böhlaus Nachfolger Verlag, 1962), 334. Translation from Friedrich Schiller, *On the Aesthetic Education of Man in a Series of Letters*, trans. Reginald Snell (London: Routledge, 1954), 52.

36. Friedrich Schiller, "Die Antiken zu Paris," in *Schillers Werke: Nationalausgabe*, ed. Norbert Oellers, vol. 2, book 1, *Gedichte in der Reihenfolge ihres Erscheinens 1799–1805* (Weimar, Germany: H. Böhlaus Nachfolger Verlag, 1983), 408; translation from Friedrich Schiller, "The Antiquities in Paris," in *The Poems of Schiller*, trans. Edgar Alfred Bowring (London: John W. Parker and Son, 1851), 242.

37. Gerhard Kaiser, "Ideen oder Körper: zu Schillers und Goethes Rezeptionsweise antiker Plastik," in *Antiquitates Renatae: deutsche und französische Beiträge zur Wirkung der Antike in der europäischen Literatur: Festschrift für Renate Böschenstein zum 65. Geburtstag*, ed. Verena Ehrich-Haefeli, Hans-Jürgen Schrader, and Martin Stern (Würzburg, Germany: Königshausen & Neumann, 1998), 168.

38. Indeed, the mandate for evidence-centered scholarship, whether textual or material, was, as Suzanne Marchand argues, importantly linked to the political value of classical studies in a particularly nineteenth-century project Marchand terms *neohumanism*. See *Down from Olympus*, 37–38.

39. Konrad Levezow, "Die Kunstschätze des Königl. Preußischen Hauses," *Die Freimüthige oder Berlinische Zeitung für gebildete unbefangene Leser* 17 (January 31, 1803): 67–68.

40. Levezow, "Die Kunstschätze," 67.

41. Levezow, "Die Kunstschätze," 67.

42. Levezow, "Die Kunstschätze," 67–68.

43. August Wilhelm Schlegel in Inka Mülder-Bach, "Sichtbarkeit und Lesbarkeit: Goethes Aufsatz Über Laokoon," in *Das Laokoon-Paradigma. Zeichenregime im 18. Jahrhundert*, ed. Inge Baxmann et al. (Berlin: Akademie Verlag, 2000), 466.

44. *Statues, bustes, bas-reliefs, bronzes, et autres antiquites . . . dont l'exposition a eu lieu le 14 octobre 1807, premier anniversaire de la Bataille d'Iéna* (Paris: Dubray, 1807), 7. Because the compilers of the 1807 catalogue wrote it before all the works of art could be unpacked, it is unclear whether the ascription of "*jeune athlete*" relied on actual examination of the statue. Francis Haskell, *The Ephemeral Museum: Art Exhibitions and Their Significance* (New Haven: Yale University Press, 2000), 171n34.

45. *Statues, bustes*, 7.

46. Konrad Levezow, *De Iuvenis Adorantis Signo Ex Aere Antiquo* (Berlin: August Friedrich Kuhn, 1808). I am grateful to Dr. Susannah Brower for her assistance with the Latin. The treatise was reviewed in the *Göttingische Gelehrte Anzeige* 203 (1807): 2023.

47. Levezow, *De Iuvenis*, 6–7.

48. Levezow, *De Iuvenis*, 7.

49. Levezow, *De Iuvenis*, 7.

50. His description was corroborated and expanded upon a year later by the director of antiquities at the Musée Napoleon, Ennio Quirino Visconti. Hackländer, "Der Betende Knabe," 33. Visconti's essay is reprinted in Ennio Quirino Visconti, *Opere varie*, vol. 4 (Milan: Presso Antonio Fortunato Stella e Figli, 1831), 159–162.

51. Karl Levezow, *Über den Raub des Palladiums auf den geschnittenen Steinen des Alterthums* (Braunschweig, Germany: Friedrich Vieweg, 1801), vi–vii.

52. On the scholarship generated by German collections in the Musée Napoleon, see Savoy, *Kunstraub*, 339–379.

53. Levezow, *De Iuvenis*, 6.

54. Savoy, *Kunstraub*, 330–332; Uwe Rohnstock, "Die neue Aufstellung und die Altrestaurierungen," in *Der Betende Knabe, Original und Experiment,* ed. Gerhard Zimmer and Nele Hackländer (Frankfurt am Main: Peter Lang, 1997), 113–116.

55. There is some disagreement between historical and conservation scholars on which elements of the *Adorans*' many restorations in the centuries after its excavation can be attributed to Canlers. Based on Canlers's own unpublished report on the project, Savoy asserts that the intervention with iron rods and plaster filling derives from this 1806–7 work. See Savoy, *Kunstraub*, 330–331. This is in contrast with the findings of the conservator Uwe Rohnstock during the last major conservation of the *Adorans* in 1997, that these elements date from the mid-nineteenth century: Uwe Rohnstock, "Die Odyssee des 'Betenden Knaben': Altrestaurierungen bei einer antiken Großbronze auf Wanderschaft," *Restauro* 3 (1998): 175–176.

56. Levezow, *De Iuvenis*, 8.

57. Archaeologists assert that the ancient Greeks frequently offered up sculpted replicas of limbs and body parts to the gods, including eyes, ears, genitalia, legs, arms, and internal organs, though there is some uncertainty whether these represented complete offerings or fragments. See Heike Tahödl, "Zu Antiken Gliederweihungen," in *Die Götter Beschenken: Antike Weihegaben aus der Antikensammlung der Staatlichen Museen zu Berlin,* ed. Moritz Kiderlen and Volker Michael Strocka (Munich: Biering & Brinkmann, 2005), 27–29. Perhaps if the *Adorans* can be said to be praying, it may be doing so in offering up its original arms to the gods.

58. On the romantic idealism of Schinkel's design, see Elsa van Wezel, "Die Konzeptionen des Alten und Neuen Museums zu Berlin und das sich wandelnde historische Bewusstsein," *Jahrbuch der Berliner Museen* 43 (2001); James Sheehan, *Museums in the German Art World from the End of the Old Regime to the Rise of Modernism* (New York: Oxford University Press, 2000); Ziolkowski, *German Romanticism and Its Institutions*.

59. Beat Wyss, *Trauer der Vollendung: Von der Ästhetik des deutschen Idealismus zur Kulturkritik an der Moderne* (Munich: Matthes & Seitz Verlag, 1985), 143.

60. Christian Friedrich Tieck, *Verzeichniss der antiken Bildhauerwerke des Königlichen Museums zu Berlin* (Berlin: Königliche Akademie der Wissenschaften, 1831), 7.

61. Wilhelm Heinrich Wackenroder and Ludwig Tieck, *Herzensergießungen eines Kunstliebenden Klosterbruders* (Berlin: Johann Friedrich Unger, 1797), 159. Ludwig Tieck was the brother of the author of the museum's antiquities catalogue, Christian Friedrich Tieck.

62. Christoph Martin Vogtherr, "Das Königliche Museum zu Berlin: Planungen und Konzeption des ersten Berliner Kunstmuseums," *Jahrbuch der Berliner Museen* 39 (1997): 164.

63. Wilhelm von Humboldt to Christian Friedrich Tieck, August 10, 1830, Autographensammlung 0643.001, Zentralarchiv, Staatliche Museen zu Berlin. Uwe Peltz, "Mounting and Patina: Nineteenth Century Solutions in the Restoration of Large Bronzes in Berlin's Antikensammlung," in *The Restoration of Ancient Bronzes: Naples and Beyond,* ed. Erik Risser and David Saunders (Los Angeles: J. Paul Getty Museum, 2013), 98–100.

2

Colliding Empires

French Display of Roman Antiquities Expropriated from Postconquest Algeria, 1830–1870

Bonnie Effros

> In every epoch, the establishment of colonies has been the most useful and fruitful work of humanity; this expansive force against the barbarian world has been destined by its incessant action to enlarge the domain of civilization and prepare the way for Roman unity. For nations foreign to the great city-state, it became the upper limit of the political and social progress that they could attain.
>
> Let us therefore do research on the remains of Roman domination, not in order to propose a servile imitation of it that would reject the bold allures of our own century and the adventurous spirit of our nation, but rather to inspire us with the wisdom of the ancients, and leave, if we can, to our descendants, some examples of our own wisdom.
>
> —Azéma de Montgravier, May 1846

The French Invasion and Conquest of Algiers

In June 1827, two months after Hussein Dey of Algiers' insult of the French consul, Pierre Deval, an event known in French sources as the "le coup d'éventail du Dey d'Alger" (fly whisk affair), the French king ordered a naval blockade of the city of Algiers. This response was an aggressive rebuff to repeated demands that the French pay eight million francs still owed to two Jewish merchant families in the Ottoman Regency of al-Jazā'er for the supply of wheat to the French army between 1793 and 1798.[1] Yet after the trade embargo created an economic crisis in the south of France, King Charles X sought a way to save face. With the pretext of combating piracy and white slavery on the Barbary coast, the Bourbon monarch chose a military assault to restore the honor of the French army and to shore up his failing regime. Although the July 1830 campaign in Algiers proved successful, Charles X abdicated within weeks of the French army's landing at Sidi Ferruch.[2]

Charles' cousin Louis-Philippe, whose eighteen-year reign was otherwise characterized by a largely pacifist foreign policy, inherited the poorly strategized invasion by the Armée d'Afrique, which had created a power vacuum through the exile of the Regency's semiautonomous Ottoman administrators. Although initially ambivalent toward this undertaking, the new king oversaw the dramatic expansion of the Armée d'Afrique from thirty-seven thousand men to almost three times its original size in little more than a decade.[3] Indeed, the July Monarchy tacitly supported the army's transformation of the poorly defined military venture into a costly, if not always well organized, imperial campaign. By the late 1830s, France had invested deeply in the North African colony it christened Algeria.[4] Among the military officers who participated in the venture, especially those who were graduates of the École polytechnique, were many dedicated disciples of Saint-Simonian thinking. Building on the ideas of social reformers like Barthélemy Prosper Enfantin, they aspired to use their scientific and humanistic expertise to bring scientific and technological advances to the new colony.[5] In their eyes, the French invasion of the nominally Ottoman-ruled territory of al-Jazā'er offered the opportunity to reinvigorate the material and moral circumstances of both metropolitan France and the colonial territory.[6]

However, the idealism of French officers was all too often at odds with the brutal realities of their military campaign. Although the initial surrender agreement of July 5, 1830, included General Louis-Auguste-Victor Bourmont's assurances that the French would respect the Islamic religion and the property rights of the existing inhabitants, the invading forces soon violated those agreements and resorted to deadly measures against the civilian population.[7] From the earliest days of the "pacification" and

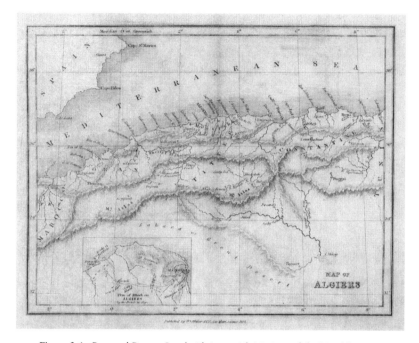

Figure 2.1. Perceval Barton Lord, *Algiers, with Notices of the Neighbouring States of Barbary*, vol. 1. (London: Whittaker and Co., 1835).

settlement of the territory of Algiers, the Armée d'Afrique appropriated homes, agricultural land, and mosques from the Arab and Kabyle (Berber) population and massacred tribes that resisted French domination.[8]

In fall 1837, the French expanded their footprint in the region with the conquest of the neighboring Regency of Constantine. Between 1840 and 1850, the number of civilian settlers grew from roughly twenty-seven thousand to one hundred and twenty-five thousand Europeans.[9] Few colonists, of whom roughly half were French,[10] questioned the oppressive military regime that deprived the Indigenous residents of shelter, food, fertile lands, their former livelihoods, and too often, their lives. The conquest granted individuals of European extraction, even those who were not French citizens, stark privilege over Arab, Kabyle, and Jewish inhabitants, who suffered greatly under the yoke of French domination.[11]

Even if the proportion of those who died directly at the hands of the French army was small relative to the hundreds of thousands of Arab and Kabyle residents of Algeria who were displaced, administrative policies put into place over the course of the first forty years of French colonial rule contributed to the deaths of many. The loss of homes and villages subjected residents to extreme weather conditions; the loss of fertile lands and herds caused severe malnourishment. Both factors magnified the effects of drought (1868–70), swarms of locusts, and unusually severe winter weather from 1867 to 1869. In 1866 and 1867, the crisis caused by these environmental and man-made conditions in Algeria magnified the effects of epidemics of cholera, typhus, and the bubonic plague that disproportionately ravaged vulnerable Indigenous communities.[12] The consequence was demographic collapse: The historian Djilali Sari estimates that the resulting humanitarian disaster caused the death of roughly one-third to one-half of the non-European population of Algeria, between eight hundred twenty thousand and a million individuals.[13]

Simultaneous with the normalization of violence against native Algerian civilians and the systematic confiscation of both privately held and communal property, French church authorities sought to build on the ancient Christian heritage of North Africa and revive what had been a vibrant community until the late seventh-century conquest of Islam. The first step in this direction occurred in August 1838, when French administrators gave Pope Gregory XVI permission to make the long-delayed appointment of a bishop in Julia Caesarea (modern Cherchel) and Hippo Regius (modern Annaba, which was called Bône by the French).[14] Just four years after taking up his duties in the colonial capital of Algiers, Bishop Antoine-Adolphe Dupuch, formerly a priest in Bordeaux, successfully petitioned the archbishop of Pavia, Aloysius Tosi, for a bone of Saint Augustine. After erecting a monument in the fifth-century bishop of Hippo's episcopal seat at Bône in 1842, Dupuch celebrated the installation of the powerful relic of the right forearm of the holy Church Father.[15] This translation of a bone from the arm with which Augustine presumably wrote his famous treatises, sermons, and letters was considered an unwelcome development by French military officials, who discouraged Catholic proselytism in the French colony in order to avoid further unrest among the Kabyle and Arab populations.[16] However, the symbolic transfer of a relic of Augustine attracted a steady stream of French pilgrims to the region.[17] And during the humanitarian nadir of 1867, more concerted missionary activities among Kabyles and Arabs were organized under the authority of the newly appointed Archbishop Charles Lavigerie.[18]

During the early decades of the French conquest, however, most military officers and scholars were far more interested in the ancient Roman imperial monuments they encountered in Algeria than in the ancient church of North Africa. Although the ruins of Roman cities, military camps, and infrastructure like roads, aqueducts, and cisterns were not foreseen as a reason for French involvement in the region (in contrast to Napoleon I's anticipation of ancient monuments on the occasion of his expedition to Egypt thirty years earlier), they rapidly became an integral part of the French efforts to establish control of the new North African colony. From a practical military standpoint, the cut stone found at Roman sites was invaluable for building fortifications, paving roads, and constructing army barracks.[19] From an ideological perspective, moreover, these monuments had considerable agency: They reminded French officers and soldiers of the historical legacy of foreign invaders who had controlled the region. Thus, when Claude-Antoine Rozet, a graduate of the École polytechnique and a captain in the royal corps of the army's general staff, recounted the vast number of antiquities visible on the ground at Cap Matifou in 1832, he remarked on "those [monuments] that recalled the passage of the ancient masters of the world."[20] For Rozet, these ancient remains held valuable lessons for the French, who identified with the Romans and could follow their army's precedent of colonizing and bringing "civilization" to the barbarous inhabitants.[21]

Twenty years later, in an essay published in the *Revue archéologique*, the leading French archaeological journal of the day, the epigraphical specialist Léon Renier tried to convey to a metropolitan audience of antiquaries and archaeologists the deep attraction and powerful agency of the ancient Roman patrimony among French officers and colonists. Writing from the ancient Roman military camps of Lambaesis (1850–51) in the Aurès Mountains, where he conducted several months of research, he alleged in an apocryphal passage that

> Roman monuments, especially the inscriptions, are in the eyes of the Arabs our most legitimate title to the possession of Algeria. During my stay in Zana, the sheik of the country and a venerated marabout Si Mohammed Bokarana, came one day and found me amongst the ruins. I copied an inscription: "You understand this writing?" he asked. I answered, "Not only

do I understand, but I can write it; look: these are our letters, this is our language." He responded by addressing the Arabs who accompanied him, "It is true; the *Roumis* are the sons of the *Roumâns*; when they took this land, they were simply taking back the property of their fathers."[22]

Renier thus made the case that ancient inscriptions found in Algeria were irrefutable evidence of the French responsibility to follow the lead of the ancient Romans. They were, after all, the conquerors not only of North Africa but also of the ancient Gauls.[23] By this logic, whereas the Romans had led the Gauls, ancestors of the French, to a more glorious existence,[24] the French, now the self-proclaimed heirs of the ancient Romans, were in a position to assert their right to wear the victor's mantle. Roman stone inscriptions and monuments, largely pagan military ones, helped bridge the temporal distance that separated the French from their ancient predecessors.

This teleological narrative justifying French conquest pointedly excluded the Arab and Kabyle populations from sharing in Roman heritage. Instead, for at least a century prior to the conquest, European scholars like Jean-André Peyssonnel, Thomas Shaw, and James Bruce, describing the Berber tribes as descended from the Vandals, cast them as the alleged enemies of Roman civilization.[25] In the early decades of the conquest, French propaganda of this nature was aimed almost exclusively at stakeholders in the metropole as well as at French military officers and civilian settlers in Algeria. Given the extreme violence of the military undertaking and the near-total erasure of contemporary Indigenous voices, surviving evidence suggests that little or no effort was made to direct the historical justification of French presence in the Algerian territory toward the Arab and Kabyle inhabitants.[26] The physical and hermeneutical appropriation of Roman antiquities allowed French authors to glorify their conquest of the territory of Algeria to audiences at home and downplay the unsavory aspects of the French extralegal and brutal campaign in North Africa as the inexorable result of historical destiny.[27] Even if it had been directed toward the Indigenous residents of Algeria, this warped French version of contemporary events contributed only indirectly toward the the conquest and "pacification" of the region. No survivor of the French offensive, knowing firsthand the realities of French military rule, would have believed such a skewed narrative of bringing "civilization" to the region.

Claiming the Legacy of Ancient Rome

Suzanne Marchand has recently outlined some of the parameters of what she calls the "dialectics of the antiquities rush," namely the set of global cultural dynamics by which the unregulated and competitive "collecting" of classical monuments and artifacts was undertaken by European powers starting in the early nineteenth century. Inspired by the Napoleonic Army's invasion and pillage of Egypt and Rome, French military forces appropriated monuments and antiquities with the purpose of enriching the metropole, a practice normalized over the following decades through repetition and legitimized by the success of these ventures.[28] The classical focus and scope of such raiding enterprises was distinct from the kind of collecting that characterized European exploration and colonialism in previous centuries, which brought a blend of curiosities, natural wonders, and valuables back to the British Isles and the Continent.[29] It also differed from the infinitely more courteous manner in which western Europeans appropriated artifacts from one another in theaters of war, as Alice Goff and Cathleen Giustino have also demonstrated in this volume. The combination of military and scientific missions allowed Europeans to hone so-called archaeological enterprises as instruments of imperial domination.[30] Egyptian antiquities, once transported from North Africa, were displayed triumphally and occupied places of prominence in imperial museums dedicated to this purpose in Paris, London, Berlin, and other European capitals.[31]

In Egypt, Algeria, and other colonial venues, antiquarianism (succeeded by archaeological practice in the second half of the nineteenth century), maps, and museums made it possible for the French state to reorder not just the contemporary social hierarchy but also the history of past events in the new colony.[32] As Lynn Meskell notes, "Archaeology is not free from hegemonic flows, rather it has been indelibly entwined with their politics."[33] From this perspective, we can see that within a decade, French authorities began to view the Algerian colony as an extension of the metropole and in discrete cases sought to incorporate Roman antiquities not only in a narrative of Algerian history but also in a new history of France that included Algeria. This narrative, illuminated by impressive stone artifacts, emphasized French historical claims to the rule of conquered subjects and settlement of its citizens in this territory.[34]

Efforts to procure Roman antiquities in Algeria for French collections in urban centers within the colony as well as in the metropolitan capital, at the same time that Arab and Kabyle villages were being destroyed, offer vivid examples of French confidence in a historical connection to the Roman past of the French colony.[35] The French officers and civilian scholars idealized and reimagined ancient Roman fragments found on Algerian soil as part of a living classical culture to which they were the exclusive heirs.[36]

An integral part of archaeological exploration as a knowledge-generating process was the study, collection, and redistribution of Algerian antiquities.[37] In the first forty years of the French occupation, the vast majority of sites that attracted French interest were, for both practical and ideological reasons, of imperial Rome (as opposed to ancient Punic remains, which were not widely accessible, or more recent Byzantine and Islamic monuments, which were seen as inferior).[38] As early as the mid-1830s but more commonly from the 1850s onward, French officers and civilian antiquaries founded museums in the new colony and filled them predominantly with imperial Roman artifacts rescued, when possible, from the destructive reach of the Armée d'Afrique. Gathered in open-air museums and confiscated buildings in the cities of Algiers, Constantine, Philippeville (modern Skikda, ancient Russicada), and Cherchel, pagan Roman statues, inscriptions, architectural remains, and smaller objects like coins and medals became part of makeshift displays directed largely at the edification of European residents.

However, there is no evidence that the Indigenous population of Algeria was ever the envisioned audience of such museological edification. Rather than serving as part of what became during the Third Republic the official doctrine of the *mission civilisatrice*, colonial museums in Algeria were intended to aid in the acculturation of recent European transplants to the French colony.[39] In the midst of a violent military undertaking, ancient Roman artifacts became part of a new system of value for the colony. Wrenched from the ruins of ancient Roman temples, fortresses, military camps, cemeteries, and baths, fragmented remains of mosaics, statues, mile markers, inscriptions, and coins became potent icons of the colonial enterprise. The French pillaged Roman antiquities in the belief that they valorized the historical claims underlying French rule in Algeria.[40]

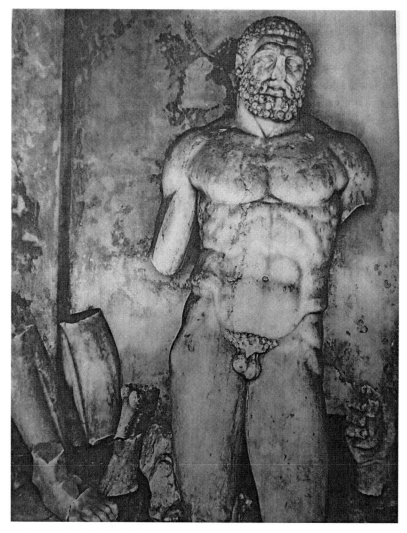

Figure 2.2. Displayed at the Musée de Cherchel, this statue of Hercules revealed
something of the circumstances in which it had been procured. Paul Gauckler,
Musée de Cherchel (Paris: Ernest Leroux, Éditeur, 1895).

As they had done previously in Rome, Egypt, and the Peloponnese,
the French also exported some of these artifacts to metropolitan France,
where they were put on display in Paris in prominent collections held at
the Louvre and the Bibliothèque royale. There, instead of highlighting the
exoticism of new possessions as was done with artifacts procured from

many other colonial contexts, curators repackaged modest collections of Roman fragments to glorify France's controversial military undertaking.[41] For instance, one of the earliest, if not the earliest, documented exports of antiquities from the Algerian territory to France was a stone epitaph in Latin dedicated to a Christian woman named Aprilia Fidelis (d. August 29, 557 CE). French soldiers removed the marker from the city of Bône and transported it first to Algiers and then to the Cabinet des médailles in the Bibliothèque royale in Paris.[42] In contrast to the pride that some European settlers in colonial Algeria took in such collections, however, the display of such modest and often damaged remains were not as successful among French metropolitan audiences as they had been in the colony. The epitaph of Aprilia Fidelis was largely forgotten and went unlisted in catalogues of the metropolitan capital's premier library.[43]

As will be discussed in the pages that follow, the reasons for the muted reception of Roman antiquities are complex. In part it had to do with the poor relationship between civilian and military authorities in war-torn Algeria, which hampered the movement to France of the ponderous stone monuments erected by the ancient Romans in North Africa. Consequently, many fragile sculptural remains, mosaics, and inscriptions were damaged during military operations and the inexpert, hasty, and poorly funded efforts to extract them from their original settings. Moreover, would-be "rescuers" of antiquities underestimated the expense and technical challenges of overland transport of heavy stone remains to coastal ports, and only some were able to overcome the reluctance of the minister of war to grant cargo space to these bulky artifacts. Even more critical was the quality of the remains in question: The often forlorn-looking plunder did not translate effectively to Parisian audiences. This manifestation of the "antiquities rush" in colonial Algeria thus suggests that the values that French military officers and settlers understood to be embedded in Roman artifacts did not translate readily to the metropole once the pieces had been removed from war-torn Algeria in the mid-nineteenth century.

Transporting Ancient Trophies to the Metropolitan Capital

If we look in greater detail at the French military undertaking in Algiers, we may see that the French officers and scholars who identified the ideological and practical potential of Roman antiquity faced an uphill battle in convincing military officials of the merits of ancient Roman antiquities in furthering French strategic objectives in the region. An early attempt to establish collaboration between the French army and academics was initiated by the Maréchal Jean-de-Dieu Soult, who wrote in 1833 to the perpetual secretary of the Académie des inscriptions et belles-lettres that

> the occupation of the Regency of Algiers by French troops . . . does not have to remain without benefit for science, and from its side, science can compete in this work of civilization that is beginning in Africa with the protection of our armies . . . the advantages of this mutual relationship could provide a good geography of the ancient civilization of Mauretania and a history of Roman colonization in this region, the institutions that they founded, and the relations that existed between themselves and the indigenous peoples.[44]

Although the Académie expressed interest in fulfilling such a mission, which paralleled activities it had carried out most famously in Napoleon's invasion of Egypt and in the Peloponnese in the 1820s, it nonetheless found its civilian members excluded from the territory of Algeria by the minister of war until 1839.[45] Scholarly research on these topics in the first decade of the conquest was thus conducted indirectly. It depended on the willingness of the minister of war to work with the governor-general of Algeria to gather basic information about ancient monuments and inscriptions, a level of cooperation that was often not forthcoming.[46]

The minister of war's reluctance to allow civilian scholars to travel to Algeria stemmed from the violence of the imperial undertaking and, to a lesser extent, from the negative impact that French military activities were having on ancient monuments. Although officers in the invading Armée d'Afrique found it practical to refer to the accomplishments of ancient Rome to claim the Algerian territories as the possession of metropolitan France, in the course of military operations the armed forces destroyed numerous ancient sites.[47] They used the cut stone thereby freed up as materiel for the construction of fortifications, barracks, roads, and, in time, housing for the growing European civilian population.[48] No doubt, the rapid disappearance of centuries-old ruins caused trepidation for at least some officers and moved them to record their distress at the loss of so many of the Roman monuments they encountered.[49] This interest—as suggested by both the letters and the independent publications of contemporary military men and the official military record of the war—indicates how important these individuals believed it was to record the physical remains of Roman antiquity before they vanished. Latin inscriptions, above all, shaped the way in which French officers envisioned their contribution to the spread of Roman civilization, an inheritance they believed to have been unbroken by the interlude of the Arab conquest of Roman North Africa in the seventh century.[50]

Beyond the difficulty of deterring the destruction of Roman sites to any significant degree during the early decades of colonial occupation, there were structural impediments that complicated their documentation, study, and preservation. The field of classical archaeology was still relatively new in the late 1820s and early 1830s despite some well-known precedents such as the famous excavations of Pompeii and the publications of leading French antiquaries like Aubin-Louis Millin.[51] It thus would be anachronistic to have expected French military or civilian officials to be anything but ambivalent toward antiquarian research, which was seen by many as a distraction from the war effort. Consequently, authorities relegated such concerns to a much lower priority than military endeavors, as reflected in the consistent shortfalls in funding for research and conservation.[52] However, in response to complaints by members of the Académie des inscriptions et belles-lettres about the grievous destruction of ancient sites, Governor-General Thomas-Robert Bugeaud appointed Charles Texier to be inspector general of civil structures in Algeria in 1845. The position left the woefully underfunded and outmanned Texier to fight, usually unsuccessfully, in defense of the Roman monuments threatened by the military.[53] Neither the creation of this position, which had a brief existence, nor its replacement in the mid-1850s by the Office of the Inspector General of Historical Monuments and Archaeological Museums of Algeria, had a significant effect on conservation efforts in the French colony.[54]

Despite the challenges of an ongoing war, many French officers were not immune to the attractions of ancient Rome, a period that had played such an important role in their formal training at military academies like the École polytechnique and the École spéciale militaire de Saint-Cyr.[55] Ferdinand-Philippe, the duc d'Orléans and the oldest son of Louis-Philippe then serving in the Armée d'Afrique, was among those interested in the symbolic potential of the monuments of imperial Rome.[56] In 1839, following the precedent of the Napoleonic Army's plunder of ancient monuments in Italy and Egypt, he visited Djémila (ancient Cuiculum) and observed of the pristine archaeological ruins:

> This place has remained a sort of unexploited Herculaneum that would offer an inexhaustible mine for science. There is an immense space covered with column shafts of stone or European granite, capitals, sculptures, mosaics, etc., that one can hardly gather. I chose two capitals, two medals that a soldier had just uncovered, and a column of which only the end would come out, so that they could be sent to Paris for me. I indicated the place where I wanted someone to dig to find some more objects and, with the heel of my boot, I discovered a mosaic that had not yet been noticed.[57]

He thereafter tenaciously pushed forward an ambitious plan to move the third-century triumphal arch of Djémila to France. In a period when the violence of the war was already becoming so extreme that information coming out of the Algerian campaign was heavily censored,[58] the Duc d'Orléans planned to mount it in the Tuileries to celebrate the continuing success of the African army.[59] Although efforts to transport the arch to Paris ultimately failed due to the technological challenges of moving a monument of this size and weight overland and the lack of impetus for the project following the premature death of the duc d'Orléans in a carriage accident in 1842, the plan illustrated the potential attraction of antiquities for the metropole.[60] Legally affirmed in the 1840s and defended thereafter by the minister of war, however, this policy made it difficult for successive military governors-general to protect colonial museums by prohibiting the removal of antiquities from Algeria.[61]

In November 1839, two years after the French defeated the bey of Constantine and seized the eastern province of the growing colony of Algeria, members of the Commission d'exploration scientifique d'Algérie finally arrived in the Maghreb to begin their on-site study of a variety of features of the newly conquered territory. Among the group were two individuals whose work was primarily archaeological: Captain Alphonse Delamare, an artillery officer whose responsibility to record ancient monuments resulted mainly from his artistic skill rather than any antiquarian background,[62] and Amable Ravoisié, an architect whose role in the commission was to study ancient monuments.[63]

Figure 2.3. This badly damaged head of Agrippa sculpted in marble was procured by Alphonse Delamare in Philippeville (ancient Russicada) on the coast of Algeria during the colonial makeover of the ancient city in the mid-nineteenth century. The fragment, thought to date to 45–50 CE, arrived at the Louvre in 1848. Louvre LP 3029. Photograph by the author.

Due to ongoing hostilities, however, the scope of the mission was limited to two years for most members (though Delamare would stay longer), and many important sites in the region of Constantine, especially the Aurès Mountains, remained inaccessible to participants because of the danger involved in visiting them.[64] Extant correspondence nonetheless reveals that the ambitions of the expedition went beyond publishing research conducted in the colony.[65] Both Ravoisié and Delamare identified exceptional objects as worthy of transport to and display in Paris. Following the formal conclusion of the expedition, the latter documented the imposing mosaic of the "Triumph of Neptune and Amphitrite" discovered on the hill of Koudiat-Ati near the city of Constantine.[66] Plans for the transport of the piece to the Louvre were rapidly drawn up, taking into account the technological and financial challenges this objective entailed.[67] As we shall see, however, the shipping of this particular mosaic was delayed for several years.

Although the bureaucratic protections that existed for private property in metropolitan France were not an issue in Algeria, military officers and scholars who sought to export antiquities to France were challenged by the logistics of extracting ancient remains and the expense of transporting heavy stone antiquities.[68] Ironically, these efforts often resulted in their harm or destruction. For example, in a letter of December 31, 1843, the minister of war requested that Governor-General Bugeaud send a bust found in Orléansville.[69] In this case, when troops from the subdivision of Orléansville inexpertly attempted to remove the statue from its location, they damaged it badly with a pick-axe. It is unclear whether authorities subsequently bothered to transport the now-fragmented object to France.[70] Similarly, a mosaic found in the city of Aumale in July 1851 was destroyed by a combination of bureaucratic infighting, shortage of funds, a bungled attempt to extract it quickly, and general incompetence.[71] Consequently, recommendations made by Renier in 1850 and 1871 for the removal of inscriptions and stone carving went unheeded for decades because of the cost involved.[72] These constraints meant that the number of items slated for removal from Algeria was necessarily small in comparison to other former parts of the Ottoman Empire, which had antiquities closer to coastal locations or along navigable rivers, as was the case in Greece, Egypt, and Asia Minor.[73] Consequently, the monuments in Algeria that were not selected for transport abroad, if they were lucky enough to survive intact, found their way to colonial museums in Algiers (1835), Cherchel (1844), Constantine (1853), and Philippeville (1859), to name the most prominent.[74]

The Migration of Roman Artifacts to Paris and Their Reception

Despite these many challenges, by June 1845 some Roman monuments had made the arduous journey overland and across the Mediterranean to enter French metropolitan collections in significant quantities for the first time since the conquest. The duc de Dalmatie, then minister of war, wrote to King Louis-Philippe with great excitement that the mosaic found

several years earlier at Koudiat-Ati, as described above, had been successfully removed from its location by Captain Delamare. The officer then
oversaw its transport to Paris along with a host of other artifacts found in
Algeria, including busts, marble and bronze statues, and inscriptions.[75] By
mid-July 1845, the 343 cases of artifacts weighing approximately seventy
thousand kilograms that comprised this shipment on *Le Progrès*, most but
not all from the region of Constantine, reached the port of Le Havre; these
items continued their journey to the Port de la Villette in Paris in early
August and were deposited in the collection of the Palais du Louvre.[76]
These artifacts joined a small number of antiquities from the Maghreb
already in the Louvre, including a group of four mosaics or mosaic fragments from Carthage acquired by M. de Lagau, the French consul in
Tunis, which had arrived at the museum in February 1845.[77]

There is no doubt that these important accessions encouraged Louis-
Philippe to abandon his tepid position on the acquisition of Roman
remains from North Africa and take rapid steps, on the basis of a proposal by the minister of war, to create a "Musée algérien" in the Louvre.
As noted in the circular that went out from the governor-general to all of
the provincial commanders of Algeria and those officers who served in
their command on August 26, 1845, they were to inform authorities in
Algiers of any items suitable to be transported to Paris. Their objective
was to highlight the cultural wealth of the new colony as had been done
a half-century earlier with the spoils of Napoleon I's Egyptian venture.[78]
Later that summer, the shipment overseen by Delamare was joined by a
group of sculptural remains with a provenance of Cherchel (ancient Julia
Caesarea). Collected by the architect Ravoisié, who was also a member of
the commission, this group of artifacts, which had originally gone to the
Palais des Beaux Arts, was now transferred to the Louvre.[79]

The 1850s saw a continuous stream of artifacts arriving at the Louvre
from the Maghreb, including three cases of stone monuments from Oran
weighing close to three thousand kilograms that arrived in 1851,[80] an
epitaph of the tribune of the Imperial Officer's Guard of the Third Augustan Legion taken by Renier from Batna in 1851,[81] and a sarcophagus
found near Cherchel in late 1850 that weighed around 1,800 kilograms.[82]
Another six cases of statues arrived from Tunis in February 1856,[83] along
with a marble bas-relief sent from Carthage in 1856 by the consul-general
of Tunis, Léon Roches,[84] and a gift to the Louvre of a bas-relief from

Cherchel by M. Rattier, an architect in Algiers.[85] Napoleon III's visit to the ancient Roman camps of the Third Augustan Legion at Lambaesis in 1865 likewise brought to the Louvre fragments of a colossal statue thought to be of Jupiter.[86] In addition, sometime before 1889, two pieces of an inscription from Lambaesis, which commemorated lower officers of the Third Augustan Legion who had contributed to the erection of gilded statues in honor of the Roman emperor, were embedded in a wall near the stairwell of the Département des medailles et antiques in the Bibliothèque nationale.[87]

Archaeological societies and the museums founded by the French in Algeria in the 1850s and 1860s, however, began to compete with the Louvre for these remains and protest their removal. The members of learned societies in cities like Algiers, Constantine, and Cherchel, who were without exception of European extraction, complained that they wanted to keep Roman artifacts in the colony for the benefit of future immigrants.[88] Although the export of antiquities from the French colony did not cease in the 1870s and 1880s, it is clear that those that did transpire excited greater controversy and made such appropriations more complex. By 1874, when Antoine Héron de Villefosse transported fifteen crates of antiquities from Lambaesis (modern Tazzoult) via Philippeville (modern Skikda) and Marseille to Paris, many of them items that Renier had identified two decades earlier, archaeological enthusiasts in Algeria expressed considerable consternation that so many artifacts were departing the colony. Some tried unsuccessfully to block the shipments.[89]

There were also unfortunate circumstances that made clear the stakes of exporting antiquities. In 1875, Évariste-Charles Pricot de Sainte-Marie, the leading dragoman in the French consulate in Tunis, attempted to ship 2,088 inscriptions and antiquities from the Maghreb to the Bibliothèque nationale and the Louvre. After a fire on the *Le Magenta* ignited the battleship's gunpowder magazine, both ship and cargo sank near Toulon. Very few of the roughly 1,400 artifacts could be salvaged from the harbor.[90] More successful in its outcome was the shipment of a group of inscriptions thought to come from an imperial slave cemetery in Carthage and excavated in 1880 by Père Alfred Delattre, a member of the Missionaires d'Afrique (also known as the Pères blancs). Yet these artifacts do not appear to have been valued highly by recipients in the Département des médailles et antiques of the Bibliothèque nationale de France: although they were displayed, they were embedded permanently in the wall of a small room on the ground floor facing a guard's station.[91]

Indeed, beyond listing which artifacts entered the collections of the Louvre, extant documents make it difficult to understand the authorities' precise vision for the proposed Musée algérien. Published complaints surfaced in the late 1840s that the exhibition at the Louvre of artifacts from the Algerian colony was severely lacking in ambition and that its tenure was too short.[92] This situation may have been caused by curators' resistance to the quality of the material itself: Adrien de Longpérier remarked that many of the artifacts from Algeria offered to Louvre were not up to the museum's high standards.[93] Even a decade later, the organization of the Musée algérien remained incomplete, despite the addition of additional statues and a colossal bust of Jupiter offered as a gift to France by the bey of Tunis.[94] Ultimately, as a consequence of the reluctant embrace of the Roman antiquities from Algeria, this dedicated section of the Louvre (in contrast to the popular gallery dedicated to Egyptian remains) never became a permanent feature of the metropolitan institution.

French Provincial Interest in Roman Antiquities

By contrast, some antiquarians in the French provinces expressed interest in acquiring antiquities in Algeria, perhaps motivated in part by the fact that provincial institutions had a more difficult time getting access to desirable ancient remains than museums in the metropolitan capital. On October 3, 1831, Alexandre du Mège, cofounder of the Société archéologique du Midi, a former military engineering officer, and a widely known antiquary in Toulouse,[95] posted a letter to the aide-de-camp of General Pierre Berthézène, who was then leading the sixteen-month-old campaign in the former Ottoman Regency. Du Mège, a legitimist and defender of Toulousan culture, indicated that he had learned of the wealth of antiquities available for the taking in Bône.[96] Referring to an earlier exchange with General Jean-Jacques-Germain Pelet-Clozeau, who hailed originally from Toulouse, he requested that French officers stationed in the famous Roman city send a few pieces for display in the newly founded Musée de Toulouse. He also suggested how they go about this endeavor, noting that "a few blows from pick-axes near the remains of an ancient building would produce a beautiful head made of marble and some other very interesting fragments."[97] This petition, disturbing in terms of the violence it normalized against any number of Roman monuments found in Bône, is suggestive of the callousness of the majority of French officers toward the extreme ferocity of the campaigns suffered by the Indigenous population not even a year and a half after the French first set foot in Algiers. It is clear that the colonial war—just as the American Civil War discussed elsewhere in this volume by Sarah Weicksel—blurred the boundaries of ownership and made plunder more acceptable even in the midst of great suffering. Du Mège's letter was motivated no doubt by his interest in acquiring antiquities from the place associated with Saint Augustine of Hippo.[98]

And, indeed, du Mège's request was not too far off the mark. As Berthézène himself later complained, soldiers were too often seen looting the ancient architectural remains of Algiers, including marble stones, window casings, and columns, which were on occasion sold and exported to France.[99] However, despite du Mège's entrepreneurial efforts to acquire ancient fragments from Bône through the agency of fellow military officers, French North Africa does not appear to have yielded any antiquities during the early 1830s for the growing collection of the Toulouse museum. The institution displayed in its inaugural years an impressive assortment of ancient and medieval remains found both regionally (including artifacts from Toulouse, Narbonne, and Martres, among others) and from Italy (mainly from the ancient cities of Pompeii and Luni). Interestingly, the collection also contained an assortment of antiquities from Egypt, items that appear to have been acquired as a result of French military exploits in the region earlier in the century.[100] By 1835, however, none of the artifacts documented in the institution's first catalogue hailed from the Maghreb.

A decade later, however, it seems that another specific petition from a provincial collector in France yielded the desired response. In a letter of February 6, 1844, the minister of war reported that an unnamed officer had transported from Cherchel (ancient Julia Caesarea) a Roman statue thought to have portrayed a likeness of Ptolemy (d. 40 CE), the king of Mauritania. This statue, which was taken from Algeria without official authorization, was held by M. Denis, the deputy of the department of Var. The incident caused the minister considerable consternation, mainly because he deplored the fact that the illegal removal was destined for a private collection rather than a metropolitan institution like the Louvre.[101] The outcome of other roughly contemporary requests is less clear. In 1852, the Musée de Guéret (Creuse), a provincial museum founded in 1832 by the Société des sciences naturelles et archéologiques de la Creuse, sought to acquire Roman antiquities in Algeria. Although the prefect of Creuse asked the minister of war for free transport to France of artifacts, including coins, manuscripts, and archaeological objects, which had been offered to the learned society by Commandant Montaudon of the Zouaves, it is uncertain how the minister responded.[102] Keeping in mind Governor-General Jacques-Louis Randon's backing for the creation of archaeological societies and museums in Algeria, we may surmise that his answer was likely negative.

Thus, we should observe that even in this early phase of the war, du Mège's request for antiquities was exceptional mainly because it came from the provinces rather than the metropolitan capital. As a former officer himself, du Mège clearly recognized that French intervention in Algeria might offer, among other things, an unparalleled opportunity to acquire classical artifacts. This circumstance became especially important for French provincial museums that desired to display more than local finds, museums that typically lacked the financial resources and connections possessed by their counterparts in Paris.[103] The war in Algeria may thus have fueled hopes among local institutions that wished to participate in the acquisition of the classical antiquities in vogue at least since the French Revolution. It is possible that du Mège and others thought that they might profit from events influenced by the precedent of Napoleon I's seizure of antiquities in Rome for the Louvre in the late 1790s, and thus succeed in building up local collections that enhanced provincial identity.[104] There were also earlier nonmilitary precedents in North Africa such as Claude Le Maire, French consul in Tripoli, who exported marble from the famous Roman site of Leptis Magna in the late seventeenth century.[105]

In the end, however, the fruit of wartime looting of ancient monuments from newly conquered Algerian territory, framed as collecting, almost exclusively benefited national institutions like the Louvre and the Bibliothèque nationale. Despite the eagerness of du Mège and his provincial contemporaries to participate in this arena and their greater willingness (compared to Parisian curators) to accept less-than-perfect specimens, they were discouraged from doing so. Moreover, they did not possess the soldiers, financial resources, and vessels necessary to transport ponderous stone antiquities to their institutions. While there is no extant documentation to suggest that restricting antiquities to Parisian museums was an official policy, contemporary circumstances suggest that chances were slim at best that provincial institutions might acquire Roman antiquities from Algeria in the early decades of the colonial endeavor.

Conclusion: Roman Antiquities Abroad

On the whole, the display of Roman antiquities expropriated from Algeria by French officers and scholars seems to have been largely lost on metropolitan audiences of the mid-nineteenth century. The costly initiatives to bring sculptures, mosaics, and inscriptions over land and sea from the military zone often resulted in their damage before they arrived in Paris. Beyond the fragmentary nature of these Roman remains, they were perceived by some art historians as provincial and thus inferior to those acquired from the Italian peninsula and southern France. Consequently, despite some interest from regional French museums to bolster their collections with such prizes, these Roman objects never earned a level of acclaim anywhere close to that of the Egyptian antiquities in the metropolitan capital. As a consequence of the ambivalence of even its own curators toward North African antiquities, efforts to integrate these objects into the galleries of the Louvre between the 1840s and 1870s proved largely unsuccessful.

Beyond the question of aesthetics, it appears that the ancient monuments in question were not an effective medium by which to communicate the ideological message and symbolic significance of the place of Rome in the historic past of France. Once removed from the context of the Algerian colony, these items could not activate a logic that was poorly understood by most Louvre visitors who had never been to North Africa, nor participated in the bloody conflict. Indeed, this vision of the past was in competition with Napoleon III's contemporary excavations of Alésia and ultimately lost out to widespread interest in the Gallic origins of France.[106] By the 1870s, moreover, facing significant resistance from European colonists in the Maghreb, French efforts to appropriate artifacts from Algeria for the metropolitan capital began to dry up. Settlers in Algeria complained that French authorities were stealing objects that rightly belonged in the local museums that they had established to celebrate the ancient heritage of their cities and help acculturate the new European residents of the colony.[107] Facing such odds, supporters of the proposed Musée algérien at the Louvre largely appear to have abandoned their project. And, following the mission of Héron de Villefosse in the mid-1870s, the export of antiquities from Algeria and Tunisia to the Louvre slowed while the existing collection of fragments from Algeria was seamlessly and quietly integrated with other Roman antiquities held by the institution.

Notes

This essay was made possible by the support of the Rothman Endowment at the Center for the Humanities and the Public Sphere at the University of Florida (2009–15), a NEH Summer Stipend (2013), and a George Kennan Membership in the School of Historical Studies at the Institute for Advanced Study, with additional funding provided by the Hetty Goldman Membership Fund (2013–14). Travel to Rome and Paris in spring 2016 was supported by a travel grant from the Center for European Studies at the University of Florida. I am grateful for the generous and encouraging feedback of Leora Auslander, Tara Zahra, and the conference participants, which helped a great deal in refining and sharpening my contribution to this volume.

1. Jamil M. Abun-Nasr, *A History of the Maghrib,* 2nd ed. (Cambridge: Cambridge University Press, 1975), 236–238.

2. Jennifer E. Sessions, *By Sword and Plow: France and the Conquest of Algeria* (Ithaca: Cornell University Press, 2011), 19–22.

3. Sessions, *By Sword and Plow,* 83–94.

4. Cheryl B. Welch, "Colonial Violence and the Rhetoric of Evasion: Tocqueville on Algeria," *Political Theory* 31, no. 2 (2003): 235–264.

5. Patricia M. E. Lorcin, *Imperial Identities: Stereotyping, Prejudice, and Race in Colonial Algeria* (London: I. B. Tauris Publishers, 1995), 99–102.

6. Osama W. Abi-Mershed, *Apostles of Modernity: Saint-Simonians and the Civilizing Mission in Algeria* (Stanford: Stanford University Press, 2010), 27–33.

7. Hamdan Khodja, *Le Miroir: Aperçu historique et statistique sur la Régence d'Alger,* vol. 2 (Paris: Sinbad, 1985), 155.

8. Pierre Nora, *Les français d'Algérie* (Paris: René Julliard, 1961), 87–92; Benjamin Claude Brower, *A Desert Named Peace: The Violence of France's Empire in the Algerian Sahara, 1844–1902* (New York: Columbia University Press, 2009), 15–18.

9. John Ruedy, *Land Policy in Colonial Algeria: The Origins of the Rural Public Domain* (Berkeley: University of California Press, 1967), 30–31.

10. Julia A. Clancy-Smith, *Mediterraneans: North Africa and Europe in an Age of Migration, c. 1800–1900* (Berkeley: University of California Press, 2011).

11. Annie Rey-Goldzeiguer, *Le royaume arabe: La politique algérienne de Napoléon III, 1861–1870* (Algiers: Société national d'édition et de diffusion, 1977), 69–70.

12. Djilali Sari, *Le désastre démographique* (Algiers: Société nationale d'Édition et Diffusion, 1982), 135–165, 217–221.

13. Sari, *Le désastre démographique*, 129–132.

14. Marcel Emerit, "La lutte entre les généraux et les prêtres aux débuts de l'Algérie française," *Revue africaine* 97 (1953): 66–97.

15. Archives de la Société des Missionaires d'Afrique A16 251 (Rome): *Procès-verbal de la visite et inspection de la châsse de cristal, contenant les sacrées dépouilles du corps de Saint-Augustin*, Pavia, April 12, 1842; Antoine-Adolphe Dupuch, *Lettre pastorale de Monseigneur l'évêque d'Alger* (Marseille: Marius Olive, Imprimeur de Monseigeur l'evêque, 1842).

16. Service historique de l'armée de la terre (SHAT) 1 H 86-2: Letter dated October 21, 1842, from the Duc de Dalmatie, minister of war, to the governor-general of Algeria. SHAT 1 M 1317: Capitaine Adjudant-Major Amable Joseph Ardiet, *Mémoire militaire sur la reconnaissance de l'emplacement de l'ancienne ville d'Hippone et ses environs* (1851).

17. M. Poujoulat, *Études africaines: Récits et pensées d'un voyageur* 2 (Paris: Comptoir des Imprimeurs-Unis, 1847), 128.

18. Karima Direche-Slimani, *Chrétiens de Kabylie (1873–1954): Une action missionaire dans l'Algérie colonial* (Saint-Denis, France: Éditions Bouchene, 2004), 9–10, 24–26.

19. Michael Greenhalgh, *The Military and Colonial Destruction of the Roman Landscape of North Africa, 1830–1900* (Leiden, the Netherlands: E. J. Brill, 2014).

20. Claude-Antoine Rozet, *Voyage dans la Régence d'Alger ou Description du pays occupé par l'armée française en Afrique*, vol. 3 (Paris: Arthus Bertrand, Libraire-Éditeur, 1833), 179.

21. Rozet, *Voyage dans la Régence d'Alger*, vol. 3, 412.

22. Léon Renier, "Notes d'un voyage archéologique au pied de l'Aurès," *Revue archéologique* 8, no. 2 (1851–1852): 513.

23. A fuller exposition of this topic is the subject of my forthcoming book, Bonnie Effros, *Incidental Archaeologists: French Officers and the Rediscovery of Roman North Africa* (Ithaca: Cornell University Press).

24. Michael Dietler, "'Our Ancestors the Gauls': Archaeology, Ethnic Nationalism, and the Manipulation of Celtic Identity in Modern Europe," *American Anthropologist* 96, no. 3 (1994): 584–605. On French reluctance to embrace the Frankish past during the course of the nineteenth century, see Bonnie Effros, *Uncovering the Germanic Past: Merovingian Archaeology in France, 1830–1914* (Oxford: Oxford University Press, 2012).

25. Effros, *Incidental Archaeologists*, ch. 3.

26. There is no room within the scope of this brief essay to discuss Indigenous attitudes toward Roman antiquities, a subject I have discussed elsewhere. Bonnie Effros, "Indigenous Voices at the Margins: Nuancing the History of French Colonial Archaeology in Nineteenth-Century Algeria," to appear in Bonnie Effros and Guolong Lai, eds., *Unmasking Ideology in Imperial and Colonial Archaeology: Vocabulary, Symbols, Legacy* (Los Angeles: Cotsen Institute of Archaeology, in press).

27. David Mattingly, "From One Colonialism to Another: Imperialism and the Maghreb," in his *Imperialism, Power, and Identity: Experiencing the Roman Empire* (Princeton: Princeton University Press, 2011), 47–50.

28. Suzanne Marchand, "The Dialectics of the Antiquities Rush," in *Pour une histoire de l'archéologie XVIIIe siècle—1945. Hommage de ses collègues et amis à Ève Gran-Aymerich*, ed. Annick Fenet and Natacha Lubtchansky (Bordeaux: Ausonius, 2015), 191–206.

29. Chris Gosden, *Anthropology and Archaeology: A Changing Relationship* (Oxford: Routledge, 1999), 15–25.

30. Bruce G. Trigger, "Alternative Archaeologies: Nationalist, Colonialist, Imperialist," *Man* 19, no. 3 (1989): 355–370.

31. Donald Malcolm Reid, *Whose Pharoahs? Archaeology, Museums, and Egyptian National Identity from Napoleon to World War I* (Berkeley: University of California Press, 2002).

32. Michael J. Heffernan, "An Imperial Utopia: French Surveys of North Africa in the Early Colonial Period," in *Maps and Africa: Proceedings of a Colloquium at the University of Aberdeen, April 1993,* ed. Jeffrey C. Stone (Aberdeen: Aberdeen University African Studies Group, 1994), 80–107; Benedict Anderson, *Imagined Communities: Reflections on the Origin and Spread of Nationalism* (London: Verso, 2006), 178–185.

33. Lynn Meskell, "Archaeology Matters," in *Archaeology under Fire: Nationalism, Politics, and Heritage in the Eastern Mediterranean and Middle East,* ed. Lynn Meskell (London: Routledge, 1998), 1–12.

34. Frantz Fanon, *The Wretched of the Earth,* trans. Richard Philcox (New York: Grove Press, 2004), 15.

35. Fanny Colonna, "La carte Carbuccia au 1: 100.000e de la subdivision de Batna, ou le violon d'Ingres du 2e régiment de la Légion étrangère (vers 1850)," in *L'invention scientifique de la Méditerranée, Égypte, Morée, Algérie,* ed. Marie-Noëlle Bourguet, Bernard Lepetit, Daniel Nordman, and Maroula Sinarellis (Paris: Éditions de l'École des hautes études en sciences sociales, 1998), 53–70; Patricia M. E. Lorcin, "Rome and France in Africa: Recovering Colonial Algeria's Latin Past," *French Historical Studies* 25, no. 2 (2002): 295–329.

36. Nabila Oulebsir, "From Ruins to Heritage: The Past Perfect and the Idealized Antiquity in North Africa," in *Multiple Antiquities—Multiple Modernities: Ancient Histories in Nineteenth-Century European Cultures,* ed. Gábor Klancizay, Michael Werner, and Ottó Gecser (Frankfurt: Campus Verlag, 2011), 335–364.

37. Nadia Abu El-Haj, *Facts on the Ground: Archaeological Practice and Territorial Self-Fashioning in Israeli Society* (Chicago: University of Chicago Press, 2001), 8–16.

38. Nabila Oulebsir, *Les usages du patrimoine: Monuments, musées et politique coloniale en Algérie (1830–1930)* (Paris: Éditions de la Maison des sciences de l'homme, 2004), 14–19.

39. Bonnie Effros, "Museum-Building in Nineteenth-Century Algeria: Colonial Narratives in French Collections of Classical Antiquities," *Journal of the History of Collections* 28, no. 2 (2016): 243–259.

40. Arjun Appadurai, "Introductions: Commodities and the Politics of Value," in *The Social Life of Things: Commodities in Cultural Perspective,* ed. Arjun Appadurai (Cambridge: Cambridge University Press, 1986), 3–63.

41. Shaun Hides, "The Genealogy of Material Culture and Cultural Identity," in *Cultural Identity and Archaeology: The Construction of European Communities,* ed. Paul Graves-Brown, Siân Jones, and Clive Gamble (London: Routledge, 1996), 25–47.

42. René Cagnat, "Notice sur les inscriptions romaines découvertes jusqu'à ce jour à Bône et aux environs," *Bulletin de l'Académie d'Hippone* 17, no. 45 (1882): 72.

43. M. Chabouillet, *Catalogue général et raisonné des camées et pierres gravées de la Bibliothèque impériale* (Paris: J. Claye, 1858); *Notice sommaire des principaux monuments dans le Département des médailles et antiques de la Bibliothèque nationale* (Paris: Imprimerie nationale, 1889).

44. M. Walckenaer, "Rapports sur les recherches géographiques, historiques, archéologiques, qu'il convient de continuer ou d'entreprendre dans l'Afrique septentrionale," *Mémoires de l'Institut royal de France. Académie des inscriptions et belles-lettres* 12 (1831–38): 98; Paul-Albert Février, *Approches du Maghreb romain: Pouvoirs, différences et conflits* 1 (Aix-en-Provence, France: ÉDISUD, 1989), 30.

45. M. Raoul-Rochette, "Rapport sur les recherches archéologiques à entreprendre dans la province de Constantine et la régence d'Alger," *Mémoires de l'Institut royal de France. Académie des inscriptions et belles-lettres* 12 (1839): 135–181; Bernard Lepetit, "Missions

scientifiques et expéditions militaires: remarques sur leurs modalités d'articulation," in *L'invention scientifique de la Méditerranée: Égypte, Morée, Algérie*, ed. Marie-Noëlle Bourguet, Bernard Lepeit, Daniel Nordman, and Maroula Sinarellis (Paris: Éditions de l'École des hautes études en science sociales, 1998), 97–116.

46. Request of the Ministry of War to the governor-general of Algeria on behalf of the Académie des inscriptions et belles-lettres dated February 24, 1835. SHAT 1 H 30-1.

47. Marcel Bénabou, "L'impérialisme et l'Afrique du Nord: le modèle romain," in *Sciences de l'homme et conquête coloniale: Constitution et usages des sciences humaines en Afrique (XIXe–XXe siècles)*, ed. Daniel Nordman and Jean-Pierre Raison (Paris: Presses de l'École normale supérieure, 1980), 15–22.

48. Greenhalgh, Military and Colonial Destruction.

49. Monique Dondin-Payre, "L'*Exercitus africae* inspiratrice de l'armée française d'Afrique: *Ense et aratro*," *Antiquités africaines* 27 (1991): 141–149.

50. Jacques Frémeaux, "Souvenirs de Rome et présence française au Maghreb: Essai d'investigation," in *Connaissances du Maghreb: Sciences sociales et colonisation*, ed. Jean-Claude Vatin (Paris: Éditions du Centre national de la recherche scientifique, 1984), 29–46.

51. Ève Gran-Aymerich, *Naissance de l'archéologie moderne, 1798–1945* (Paris: CNRS, 1998), 36–62.

52. Monique Dondin-Payre, *La Commission d'exploration scientifique d'Algérie: Une héritière méconnue de la Commission d'Égypte* (Paris: Imprimerie F. Paillart, 1994), 33–36.

53. Charles Texier, "Extrait d'un aperçu statistique des monuments de l'Algérie," *Revue archéologique* 3, no. 2 (1846–47): 724–725.

54. Monique Dondin-Payre, "La mise en place de l'archéologie officielle en Algérie, XIXe–début du XXe," in *Aspects de l'archéologie française au XIXe siècle: Actes du colloque international tenu à La Diana à Montbrison les 14 et 15 octobre 1995*, ed. Pierre Jacquet and Robert Périchon (Montbrison, France: La Diana, 2000), 355–357.

55. William Serman, *Les origines des officiers français, 1848–1870* (Paris: Publications de la Sorbonne, 1979), 20–21, 103–107; Abi-Mershed, *Apostles of Modernity*, 27–37.

56. Sessions, *By Sword and Plow*, 75–85.

57. Ferdinand-Philippe, duc d'Orléans, *Récits de campagne, 1833–1841*, ed. the comte de Paris and the duc de Chartres (Paris: Calmann Lévy, Éditeur, 1890), 216–217.

58. Jennifer E. Sessions, "'Unfortunate Necessities': Violence and Civilization in the Conquest of Algeria," in *France and its Spaces of War: Experience, Memory, Image*, ed. Patricia M. E. Lorcin and Daniel Brewer (New York: Palgrave Macmillan, 2009), 29–44.

59. On efforts to bring the triumphal arch of Djémila to France, see Ferdinand-Philippe, *Récits de campagne, 1833–1841*, 426–427; Oulebsir, *Les usages du patrimoine*, 38, 77–79.

60. Although the duc de Dalmatie, the minister of war, sought to further this goal, it had still not been accomplished by the 1840s. Archives Nationales de l'Outre-Mer (ANOM) 80 F 1587: *Rapport sur le projet de démolir l'arc de triomphe de Djémilah et de le transporter en France*, January 9, 1843; Février, *Approches du Maghreb romain*, vol. 1, 38.

61. *Bulletin officiel des actes du gouvernement* 4 (Algiers: Imprimerie du gouvernement, 1844), 64–65. ANOM 80 F 1589: Letter from the minister of war to the governor-general, July 29, 1853.

62. Monique Dondin-Payre, *Le Capitaine Delamare: La réussite de l'archéologie romaine au sein de la Commission d'exploration scientifique d'Algérie* (Paris: Imprimerie F. Paillart, 1994).

63. Oulebsir, *Les usages du patrimoine*, 48–69.

64. Dondin-Payre, *La Commission d'exploration scientifique d'Algérie*.

65. Archives de l'Académie des inscriptions et belles-lettres no. 359, Archives de l'Institut de France: Letter dated April 30, 1842, from the minister of war to Baron Walckenaër, the perpetual secretary of the Académie des inscriptions et belles-lettres.

66. Archives des Musées nationaux, Musée du Louvre A4, July 1842.

67. Archives de l'Académie des inscriptions et belles-lettres no. 359, Archives de l'Institut de France: Letters dated July 29 and September 6, 1842, from the minister of war to Baron Walckenaër, perpetual secretary of the Académie des inscriptions et belles-lettres.

68. Nadia Bayle, "Quelques aspects de l'histoire de l'archéologie au XIXe siècle: l'exemple des publications archéologiques militaires éditées entre 1830 et 1914 en France, en Afrique du Nord et en Indo-chine 1" (PhD diss., l'Université de Paris-Sorbonne [Paris IV], 1986), 146–154.

69. ANOM 80 F 1589: Letter dated December 31, 1843, from the minister of war to Governor-General Thomas-Robert Bugeaud.

70. ANOM 80 F 1589: Letter dated January 4, 1844, from the Colonel Commandant de la subdivision d'Orléansville to the Governor General Thomas-Robert Bugeaud.

71. ANOM 80 F 1587: Various correspondence between officials including the prefect of Algiers, Adrien Berbrugger, M. Demortière (responsible for extracting the mosaic from its original location), and the governor-general, dated between November 22, 1851, and February 9, 1852.

72. Léon Renier, "Deuxième rapport de M. Renier, en mission dans la province de Constantine pour la recherche des monuments épigraphiques," *Archives des missions scientifiques et littéraires* 2 (1851): 217–222; ANOM 80 F 1587: A series of letters was sent between the minister of war, the minister of public instruction, the minister of the interior, and various military authorities between July 1851 and April 1852.

73. The bibliography on these topics has grown enormously in recent decades, so some worthy contenders had to be omitted from this list. On French interventions overseas, see Sophie Basch, "Archaeological Travels in Greece and Asia Minor: On the Good Use of Ruins in Nineteenth-Century France," in *Scramble for the Past: A Story of Archaeology in the Ottoman Empire, 1753–1914*, ed. Zainab Bahrani, Zeynep Çelik, and Ehdem Eldem (Istanbul: SALT, 2011), 157–179; Michel Sève, "Les missions scientifiques française en Grèce du Nord et en Macédoine sous Napoléon III," and Christian Robin, "La mission d'Ernest Renan en Phénicie," in *Histoire et archéologie méditerranéennes sous Napoléon III. Actes du 21e colloque de la Villa Kérylos à Beaulieu-sur-Mer les 8 & 9 octobre 2010* (Paris: Diffusion de Boccard, 2011), 109–124, 125–154.

74. Effros, "Museum-Building in Colonial Algeria," 243–259.

75. Archives des Musées nationaux, Musée du Louvre A4: Letter dated June 14, 1845, from the duc de Dalmatie to King Louis-Philippe and letter dated June 19, 1845, from the duc de Dalmatie to the comte de Montalivet, quarter master general of the civil list.

76. Archives des Musées nationaux, Musée du Louvre A4: Letters dated July 15 and August 1, 1845, from the duc de Dalmatie to the comte de Montalivet, quarter master general of the civil list.

77. Archives des Musées nationaux, Musée du Louvre A4: Envoi par de Lagau, consul à Tunis, de mosaïques de Carthage, February 25, 1845.

78. *Bulletin officiel des actes du gouvernement* 4, no. 209, circulaire no. 32 (Algiers: Imprimerie du gouvernement, 1845), 181–185.

79. Archives des Musées nationaux, Musée du Louvre A4: Letter dated August 30, 1845, from the duc de Dalmatie to the comte de Montalivet, quarter master general of the civil list, the minister of war acknowledged the king's wish to unite this collection with that of Delamare at the Louvre.

80. Archives des Musées nationaux, Musée du Louvre A4: Letter dated April 25, 1851, from M. Royer to the inspector general.

81. Archives des Musées nationaux, Musée du Louvre A4: Letter dated September 10, 1851, to the director of national museums to the minister of the interior, division of Beaux-Arts.

82. Archives des Musées nationaux, Musée du Louvre A4: Extensive correspondence dated between November 27, 1850, and December 15, 1851, between Adrien Longpérier, curator of antiquities at the Louvre, the general director of Beaux-Arts, and the director-general of national museums.

83. Archives des Musées nationaux, Musée du Louvre A4: Letter dated February 2, 1856, from the minister of the imperial household to M. Pfeiffer, general agent of transports of war.

84. Archives des Musées nationaux, Musée du Louvre A4: Letter dated March 12, 1856, from the director general of imperial museums to the minister of foreign affairs.

85. Archives des Musées nationaux, Musée du Louvre A4: Letters dated between September 18, 1856, and June 3, 1857, between the director general of imperial museums, Adrien de Longpérier, and M. Lalaisse, who wrote on behalf of M. Rattier.

86. Archives des Musées nationaux, Musée du Louvre A4: "Notice sur un fragment de statue remarqué par S. M. l'Empereur dans sa visite aux ruines de Lambèse," 1865.

87. *Notice sommaire des principaux monuments*, 5.

88. ANOM 80 F 1589: Correspondence spanning from July 3, 1855, to February 27, 1856, involving the minister of war, the governor-general, and Adrien Berbrugger.

89. Archives des Musées nationaux, Musée du Louvre A4: Correspondence dated August 21, 1874.

90. Myriam Bacha, *Patrimoine et monuments de Tunisie* (Rennes, France: Presses universitaires de Rennes, 2013), 46–48.

91. *Notice sommaire des principaux monuments*, 2.

92. A. Judas, "Note sur les antiquités d'Orléansville," *Revue archéologique 5*, no. 2 (1848–49): 482–483.

93. Adrien de Longpérier, "À M. A. Leleux, éditeur de la *Revue archéologique*," *Revue archéologique 5*, no. 2 (1848–49): 570–571.

94. ANOM 80 F 1589: Letter from the minister of war to the governor-general, dated July 23, 1853; Archives des musées nationaux, Musée du Louvre A8: Letter dated August 12, 1847, from G. H. Delaporte, the consul general of Tunis, to the comte de Montalivet, quarter master of the civil list. Letters dated June 29, 1853, and December 7, 1853, between the minister of state and the comte de Nieuwerkerke.

95. "Procès-verbal de la séance du 2 Juin 1831," *Mémoires de la Société archéologique du Midi de la France*, 1 (1832–33): xi–xiv; Louis Peyrusse, "La connaissance par l'écrit et par l'image," in *Toulouse et l'art médiéval de 1830 à 1870. Musée des Augustins: octobre 1982–janvier 1983* (Toulouse: Le Musée, 1982), 27–28.

96. Georges Fournier, "Le 'Midi' des Toulousains de la fin de l'Ancien Régime au début du XIXe siècle," in *Identités méridionales: Entre conscience de soi et visions de l'autre*, ed. Pierre Guillaume, Congrès national des sociétés historiques et scientifiques v. 126, Toulouse, 2001 (Paris: Éditions du Comité des travaux historiques et scientifiques, 2003), 280–287; Caroline Barrera, *Les sociétés savantes de Toulouse au XIXe siècle (1797–1865)* (Paris: Éditions du Comité des travaux historiques et scientifiques, 2003), 64–68, 101–117, 232.

97. SHAT 1 H 9-3.

98. M. Poujoulat, *Études africaines: Récits et pensées d'un voyageur* 1 (Paris: Comptoir des Imprimeurs-Unis, 1847), 1–2.

99. Pierre Berthézène, *Dix-huit mois à Alger* (Montpellier, France: Chez August Ricard, 1834), 130–131.

100. Alexandre du Mège, *Description du musée des antiques de Toulouse* (Toulouse: Imprimerie de Jean-Matthieu Douladoure, 1835). On the French in Egypt, see Reid, *Whose Pharaohs?* 31–44. See also Chantal Orgogozo, "Le voyage dans le Basse et la Haute-Egypte,"

in *Dominique-Vivant Denon: L'oeil de Napoléon* (Paris: Réunion des Musées nationaux, 1999), 108–115.

101. ANOM 80 F 1589: Letter dated February 6, 1844, from the minister of war to Governor-General Thomas-Robert Bugeaud.

102. ANOM 80 F 1588: Letter to the minister of war, dated July 20, 1852.

103. On the tensions between center and periphery in French antiquarianism of the nineteenth century, see Stéphane Gerson, *The Pride of Place: Local Memories and Political Culture in Modern France* (Ithaca: Cornell University Press, 2003); Effros, *Uncovering the Germanic Past*, 237–274.

104. Margarita Díaz-Andreu, *A World History of Nineteenth-Century Archaeology: Nationalism, Colonialism, and the Past* (Oxford: Oxford University Press, 2007), 67–72.

105. André Laronde, "Claude Le Maire et l'exportation des marbres de Lepcis Magna," *Bulletin de la Société nationale des antiquaires de la France* (1993): 242–255. Françoise de Catheu, "Les marbres de Leptis Magna dans les monuments français du XVIIIe siècle," *Bulletin de la Société de l'histoire de l'art français* (1936): 51–74.

106. Joël Le Gall, *Alésia: Archéologie et histoire,* reprint edition (Paris: Fayard, 1980); Michel Reddé, *Alésia: L'archéologie face à l'imaginaire* (Paris: Éditions Errance, 2003).

107. Effros, "Museum-Building in Nineteenth-Century Algeria," 243–259.

PRETTY THINGS, UGLY HISTORIES

Decorating with Persecuted People's Property in Central Bohemia, 1938–1958

Cathleen M. Giustino

She was there before World War II and is there now. She is Ariadne, daughter of King Minos and wife of Dionysus, confidently reclining on the back of a panther and using the animal's head as an armrest. The alabaster woman and her feline companion, a chiseled copy of German sculptor Johann Heinrich von Dannecker's early nineteenth-century work, *Ariadne on the Panther*, have not vanished from the baroque Chateau Dobříš in central Bohemia.[1] A few other interior decorations found in this former aristocratic home before the war are there now, too, including Louis XVI chairs covered with fading, yet still eye-catching upholstery. Viewed on their own and without consideration of the past, the current presence of original furnishings in an imposing noble residence might suggest the silent stillness of objects that escaped the vicissitudes of history. These pages show, however, that Ariadne and the panther had no such escape. While the sculpted figures were relatively fixed in space, their life-span inside Dobříš included the extremely violent and mobile years during and after the Second World War. This was a time when millions of people and things were on the move in Central and Eastern Europe because of military battles, genocide, ethnic cleansing, and revolution, in addition to deeply intrusive, state-directed confiscations of private property.

The intense violence and mobility surrounding Ariadne and the panther in Dobříš between 1938, when the Munich Agreement was concluded, and 1958, the first year of a major new preservation law, are not visible on the object's polished stone surfaces. Severe hardship and suffering that resulted from racism, ethnic hatred, and social-class leveling marked these profoundly unsettling decades when three separate mobilization regimes followed one another in ruling over Bohemia, the westernmost province of Czechoslovakia (currently the Czech Republic). These regimes included the Nazi Protectorate of Bohemia and Moravia (1939–45), the Third Czechoslovak Republic (1945–48), and Socialist Czechoslovakia (1948–89). The three mobilization regimes carried out four far-reaching expropriations of private property in central Bohemia and elsewhere in Czechoslovak territory between 1938 and 1958. In all four cases, and similar to those that Alice Goff and Bonnie Effros discuss in this volume, many of the sequestered belongings were potentially status-enhancing cultural objects that could advance the power of individuals, groups, and the state. They included castles, chateaux, and interior decorations, some of them works of art and carefully crafted antique period furnishings. These cultural objects, especially interior decorations seized from private owners, are of central concern for this study.

During World War II, when the Third Reich controlled the Protectorate of Bohemia and Moravia, agents working for the Nazi-dominated administration carried out two extensive sequestrations of private property in the occupied lands. In one, they dispossessed the Protectorate's Jews, the great majority of whom perished in Terezín and other concentration and extermination camps.[2] In the other, they targeted the pro-Czech nobility of Bohemia and Moravia, whose belongings were taken while their lives were spared.[3]

Two additional large-scale seizures of private property occurred after the defeat of Nazi Germany, following one another sequentially rather than happening simultaneously like the wartime confiscations. The first postwar wave took place immediately following the Third Reich's collapse in May 1945 and before the communist coup in February 1948. In it, postwar decrees authorized the state-run expropriation of Czechoslovakia's

Germans, roughly three million of whom were expelled from their homes and the country, carrying very few things with them. The second postwar confiscation occurred after the February coup, when additional possessions were sequestered from groups labeled "enemies of the proletariat." They included members of the Czech aristocracy, the Czech middle class and religious organizations, thousands of whom experienced grim fates in political prisons and forced labor camps.[4]

Dobříš and the interior decorations inside it, including Ariadne and the panther, were entangled in all four confiscations, making these seizures of persecuted people's property and the human cruelty and suffering that they accompanied, part of the objects' increasingly unseen and forgotten histories. In 1941 Nazi officials took Dobříš and its contents from their aristocratic owners, transforming the status-rich chateau into a residence of Kurt Daluege, a high-ranking SS (Schutzstaffel) member and director of police forces active in the shooting of thousands of Jews in Eastern Europe during 1941. Shortly after the war ended, during the time of the ethnic cleansing of the Germans from Czechoslovakia, Dobříš and its contents were seized again, this time by the restored independent state, which approved the former noble home being used as a prestige-building retreat for the Union of Czechoslovak Writers. Following the 1948 communist coup, the chateau and the things inside it became the property of the socialist state, and they continued to serve the writers' association, which had become an official purveyor of Communist Party ideology.

With a focus on one built space and attention to a single object inside it, this study follows some of the intense movement of persecuted people's things in central Bohemia during and after the Second World War. It reveals similarities and differences between Nazi and Czechoslovak mobilizations of material culture across the May 1945 line, which was no mere "zero hour." Evidence analyzed in this study of objects as subjects shows that state officials in all three regimes in central Bohemia between 1938 and 1958 did not express moral misgivings or ethical qualms about benefiting from the property of persecuted people who lost their belongings, and often much more, due to war, genocide, ethnic cleansing, and revolution. All three regimes gained from the expropriations in similar ways, including through funds raised from the sale of dispossessed things and, very important for this study, through the use of confiscated cultural property, including the status-rich interior decorations at Dobříš, to advance the power of the state and leading individuals and groups within it. In each case, officials worked to develop standardized practices, with some reliance on expert knowledge, for the state takeover and use of persecuted people's things, at times competing with one another or other state actors for control over confiscated objects, rather than working in lockstep as older models of totalitarianism and dictatorship posit.

An important difference between the Nazi mobilization regime and the postwar systems lay in divergent attitudes and practices regarding the use of expropriated cultural property at Dobříš. During the war the managers of valuable interior decorations inside of and migrating to the chateau largely came from Third Reich police forces. These foreign occupiers more readily approved of people in positions of power sitting on, sleeping in, sipping from, writing at, and otherwise using potentially empowering sequestered things. After the Third Reich's collapse Czechoslovak officials responsible for furnishings at Dobříš included native historic preservationists who perceived sequestered works of art and antiques as national patrimony worthy of state protection. They worried that use caused material harm to expropriated-cum-heritage objects and strove to place them either in storage or on display in protective museum settings with barriers and admonitions of "Do not touch." Despite their best efforts, the postwar Czechoslovak preservationists were not always heeded. In sum, this study shows that regimes on both sides of the May 1945 line appreciated the symbolic power of valuable interior decorations taken from persecuted people but differed in their concern about the material vulnerability of these furnishings, with Czechoslovak managers of confiscated cultural property at Dobříš after the Nazi defeat more devoted to but not always successful at physically preserving pretty things with ugly histories.

Before the Nazi Invasion of Czechoslovakia, 1939

Dobříš was one of three well-appointed chateaux that the aristocratic Colloredo-Mannsfeld family owned for many decades prior to the Second World War. Their other properties included Chateau Zbiroh in western Bohemia, where Alfons Mucha painted his *Slav Epic*, and Chateau Opočno in eastern Bohemia, with its valuable collection of eighteenth-century paintings. Dobříš is a two-story baroque residence laid out along three tracts. Its roughly one hundred rooms sit about twenty-five miles south of Prague, the capital city of Bohemia, Czechoslovakia, and now the Czech Republic. Much of its appearance dates from the 1760s, when its noble owner, Prince Jindřich Pavel z Mannsfeldu, hired architects Jules-Robert de Cotte and Giovanni Niccolò Servandoni to rebuild the chateau after a fire. Spreading out behind the chateau's south tract is a stately French garden where a large cascading fountain is crowned with a statue of Helios watering his horses by the esteemed Bohemian sculptor, Ignaz Franz Platzer.[5] Exploitative serf labor that lasted until the middle of the nineteenth century helped make this built grandeur possible.

Dobříš's representational rooms, used for entertaining and impressing guests with a cosmopolitan assortment of luxurious interior decorations, are located in the southern tract. Some are smaller, including a bedroom adorned with delicate white furniture and hunting scenes painted on its four walls. The largest room is the twenty-five-meter-long, rococo Great Hall with wall paintings symbolizing the four seasons and an illusionist ceiling painting by the German artist Johann Peter Molitor (see figure 3.1). Another large representational space in the south tract is the once well-appointed Salon. In a 1907 inventory of the chateau's interior decorations, handwritten in German, Ariadne and the panther appeared among the Salon's furnishings, listed as item number 151 and with the less-than-accurate label "Alabaster Figure of 'Girl on Lion.'"[6] In a photograph of the Salon taken before World War I, the stone pair rested on an ornately carved console table that stood in a place of pride under a full-length portrait of Princess Lucy Sophie Yvonne Colloredo-Mannsfeld wearing a low-cut dress and a slightly visible ermine robe.[7] Very likely the princess's portrait disappeared from the room around the time of her and her husband's divorce in 1925, if not sooner.[8]

In 1938, the year in which Hitler demanded and received the Sudetenland, the Colloredo-Mannsfelds had Dobříš's interior decorations inventoried again and also appraised. The resulting "Register and Appraisal of the Art and Antique Inventory of the Dobříš Chateau," typed in Czech, treated only the representational rooms in the south tract and did not include rooms in the middle tract, where the family slept and carried out other daily activities. The "Register" recorded an abundance of distinguished and distinguishing interior decorations adorning Dobříš prior to the Third Reich's invasion of Czechoslovakia and the creation of the

Figure 3.1. The Great Hall before the Second World War. The wall and illusionist ceiling paintings are by Johann Peter Molitor. Interior decorations date from before the confiscations, when the Colloredo-Mannsfelds resided in the chateau. Photo used with kind permission of the National Heritage Institute, Directorate-General, Prague.

Protectorate in March 1939. Its twenty-three pages listed 591 items and ensembles, with some mention of materials, most notably bronze and mahogany. Notes added during the war to a copy of the "Register" indicated that some objects had moved between Dobříš and Opočno and even Paris (although in which direction is unclear) and recorded that a small number of bronze pieces were gone from the chateau due to wartime "metal gathering."[9]

Furnishings on both the 1907 and 1938 inventories complemented the chateau's baroque exterior and its rococo interior and spoke to the worldly taste of generations of noble owners. The 1938 list contained Louis XVI and Empire-style furnishings found in the Great Hall, along with Chinese vases, French bronzes, Venetian mirrors, and exotic animal hides (see figure 3.1). Additional status-rich furnishings were in the Salon. There a Louis XV vitrine, desk, and table rested among Louis XVI chairs and sofas, a painted piano, Sèvres porcelain, Limoges boxes, a Meissen tea service from 1790, and much more. Ariadne and her four-footed companion, identified in the 1938 "Register" as item number 371 and simply called "Statue from Alabaster," still resided in the Salon, although it is unclear precisely where.

The Protectorate Years, 1939–1945

In early 1942 the migration of persecuted people's things to and through Dobříš began, when Nazi authorities expropriated the chateau and all of its contents from the Colloredo-Mannsfelds, who were declared enemies of the Third Reich. Their other properties, including Zbiroh and Opočno, were seized, too. In 1938 and 1939, heads of the family had signed "Declarations of Members of the Historic Nobility," proclaiming support for the Czech nation.[10] Other aristocrats signed them, as well, including Schwarzenbergs, Lobkowiczs, Kinskýs, and Sternbergs. Protectorate officials, eager to weaken Czech elites and benefit from their property, sequestered the signatories' possessions, including dozens of castles and chateaux and the furnishings inside them.[11] This was one of the two deeply intrusive, state-organized confiscations of private property in the Protectorate, the other inflicting far more harm on the Jews of Bohemia and Moravia.

Kurt Daluege was a longtime member of the Nazi Party, a high-ranking SS leader and, beginning in 1936, chief of the Ordnungspolizei, the Third Reich's uniformed police and one of the groups that made up the Einsatzgruppen responsible for the mass shootings of Jews in Eastern Europe.[12] He worked with Reinhard Heydrich, acting Reich protector. On May 28, 1942, a day after assassins attacked Heydrich in Prague, Hitler named Daluege the new acting protector. Daluege and his rival Karl Hermann Frank were attracted to Dobříš and both hoped to make it one of their residences. Third Reich use of old noble properties, like the Wewelsburg Castle, and design of the Ordensburg schools to resemble medieval fortresses were part of Nazi efforts to make SS members a knightly elite within the racist state.[13] Hitler granted Daluege the coveted privilege of enjoying Dobříš as a reward for his many years of service to the NSDAP (the National Socialist German Workers' Party) and his active role in the murderous destruction of the towns of Lidice and

Ležáky in retaliation for Heydrich's death. Daluege had an apartment in the Prague Castle, itself a symbolic space with things on the move, where he carried out Protectorate business. Dobříš and its hunting grounds became a retreat for him and his family, and he wanted it redecorated to suit their tastes and needs, a fact that resulted in the migration of sequestered aristocratic and also Jewish furnishings from various parts of Bohemia to the chateau.

The Nazi takeover of pro-Czech noble property, like the Nazi dispossession of Jewish property, was generally not wild, spontaneous, or indiscriminate looting carried out by war-hardened soldiers eager to secure booty. While both enabled advantageously positioned individuals to profit from the cruel suffering of others, each also had elements of regularized bureaucratic undertakings with standardized procedures for sorting, storing, and using persecuted people's things. Daluege was a brutal man with much blood on his hands. He was also aware that valuable art and antiques existed in the Protectorate's many castles and chateaux and that some objects had disappeared, including etchings by Rembrandt and Albrecht Dürer taken from the chateau of the wealthy Jewish Gompertz family.[14]

To help stop further unauthorized movement of cultural objects within and from the Protectorate and to strengthen his control over confiscated property, in October 1942, Daluege created two Einsatzstäbe (special task forces). Einsatzstab I was responsible for securing objects of artistic worth held within the Protectorate's castles and chateaux; Einsatzstab II's primary charge was making available to Germans who were resettling housing furnished with expropriated belongings.[15] Both consisted, in large part, of police reservists from the Ordnungspolizei. Some Einsatzstab men were selected because they had studied art history.[16] They also had art-historical publications to aid their work and could call on leading experts, including Professors Karl Maria Swoboda and Josef Cibulka, art historians working for the Bohemian-Moravian Provincial Museum, which became part of the Czechoslovak National Gallery after World War II.[17] This brought some knowledge to their decision making. Their records and activities, however, did not reveal concern about the materiality of things—the thingness of things—and how confiscated interior decorations serving to symbolically strengthen NSDAP power could be physically weakened due to use.

Daluege's Einsatzstab men had warehouses for storing, selecting, and selling things expropriated from the pro-Czech nobility.[18] Frank acquired his opera glasses in one of them.[19] Czech directors of the Museum of Applied Arts and the Náprstek Ethnographic Museum, both in Prague, identified confiscated objects in them, including Japanese *kakemono*, that they each sought to "borrow" for their collections.[20] Daluege's secretary, Fräulein Knoblauch, expanded her possessions from the Einsatzstab storage sites, gaining "along with complete home furnishings for two bedrooms, one dining room, and one kitchen . . . , five Persian carpets and nine Persian rugs."[21] Berlin's chief of police obtained a Chinese vase, a Rosenthal figurine, coffee and liquor services, and crystal plates, among other nice objects callously seized during wartime.[22]

When processing the contents of castles and chateaux, the Einsatzstab men followed specific instructions that show NSDAP efforts to regularize the state takeover of aristocratic interior furnishings. Helmut Rinnebach, director of Einsatzstab I and a lieutenant in the police reserves, wrote them. "All rooms, from the attic to the basement," were to be gone through. "All art objects, all furniture, all pictures, table-silver, porcelain, sculpture, carpets, textiles, glass, and decorative-arts objects" were to be recorded with each item given a brief description and a unique inventory number. Further, each thing was to be evaluated and assigned one of three ranking numbers. The rankings were (1) cultural objects of museum quality; (2) less important but nonetheless valued artworks and antiques; and (3) objects without any artistic value that could be replaced "at any time."[23] Rinnebach's instructions did not include precise criteria for what qualified as a highly valued museum-quality work or one of the other categories. They required that at least two men be present when confiscated holdings were being inventoried and the regular submission of written reports to Rinnebach. Not all inventories were completed before the war ended, although thousands of interior decorations confiscated from pro-Czech nobles were on the move during the Second World War as were their former owners who were displaced from their homes.[24]

The homicidal Daluege assigned men in Einsatzstab II the job of redecorating Dobříš, leaving little evidence of what visions or expectations he had for this interior design project. In October 1942, after some alterations were done, men in Einsatzstab I completed two inventories of the chateau's interior furnishings.[25] One listed engravings and small paintings.

The other consisted of thirty-three typed pages devoted to furniture and three-dimensional decorations. Unlike the shorter and less descriptive prewar inventories, the NSDAP inventory included information about the colors of chairs and draperies, as well as the types of fabrics used. It also assigned quality rankings to the confiscated objects, per Rinnebach's instructions. Very few of the items listed among the 1,159 inventory numbers received a quality ranking of one, although many were assigned a two. The 1942 inventory indicated that Ariadne and the panther were still in the Salon. Now labeled "Nude on Lion," the sculpted pair was listed next to inventory number 207, along with other decorative objects including Meissen figurines and a bronze mantel clock with putti. Ariadne did not much impress the Einsatzstab men evaluating her, as they gave her a quality ranking of three. All other items on the page where she appeared had a ranking of two, except for a spinning wheel, which received a one.[26]

The 1942 Nazi-era inventory, unlike the Colloredo-Mannsfelds' 1938 "Register," listed objects in all three tracts of the chateau, including the middle tract where Daluege, his wife and their four children had bedrooms and other private spaces. No available records show what furnishings, if any, moved with the Dalueges into Dobříš in 1942. In 1939, for insurance purposes, Daluege had the contents of his Berlin home inventoried and appraised, but this was a relatively short list containing far more practical objects than luxury furnishings.[27] The Berlin inventory did not include the gilded, white-silk rococo sofa and chair ensemble, the Louis XVI table with a marble top, and the baroque secretary with intarsia in the Dobříš boudoir of Daluege's wife. It did not include the suede-upholstered bed with red silk blanket and matching red silk curtains in his Dobříš bedroom. Available evidence makes it impossible to state with certainty whether any of these striking furnishings had been in these rooms or elsewhere in the chateau prior to Daluege's arrival. Given the large number of confiscated objects that moved around and to Dobříš as part of the redecorating project, including a set of Chippendale chairs that appeared in the Great Hall, it is possible that some of these things had been elsewhere in the chateau before its expropriation from the Colloredo-Mannsfelds or were confiscated from other people persecuted by the Nazis during the war.[28]

A March 1944 report from Einsatzstab II provided some information about objects from other aristocratic residences in the Protectorate that moved to Dobříš.[29] It recorded that Daluege ordered two Einsatzstab

men, Peter Flory and Rolf Teichmann, to secure furnishings for the chateau from other confiscated noble properties. Flory and Teichmann, both
police reservists with art-historical training, had an array of places from
which to make their selections, including Zbiroh and Opočno, also seized
from the Colloredo-Mannsfelds, and the Konopiště Castle, the onetime
Bohemian home of Archduke Franz Ferdinand, which became Czechoslovak state property after World War I under the terms of the Treaty of St.
Germain. This report and others did not reveal any precise logic or taste
guiding their selections, moral qualms about taking property from persecuted people, or worry that the use of valued interior furnishings would
harm their symbolic power by compromising their material strength.

The 1944 report did clearly express concern that all the confiscated
interior decorations that moved to Dobříš had receipts or contracts showing proof of purchase. Some came from Zbiroh which, Einsatzstab men
reported, contained "various noteworthy pieces from the seventeenth
and eighteenth centuries."[30] These sequestered things were purchased for
82,604 crowns and paid for in an "orderly manner."[31] Specifics about
the objects were not provided. They were possibly the same items pen-
ciled onto an undated list of things, including two large and two small
pictures, a Renaissance-style table, and yellow curtains for the library; a
table, a chair, and two pictures for the hunting room; and one sofa, three
stools, an armchair, and two ceiling lights for an assistant's room.[32] They
were not the same furnishings transferred from Zbiroh to Dobříš in late
July 1942, including a Renaissance-style table and armchair, two rustic
painted cupboards, and a carved trunk from the weapons room.[33] Other
cultural objects sequestered from Zbiroh went to places in Prague, including the Castle, the Bohemian-Moravian Provincial Museum, the Military
Museum in the Schwarzenberg Palace, the Rudolfinum, and Einsatzstab
warehouses.[34]

A number of confiscated cultural objects traveled to Dobříš from the
Renaissance Chateau Opočno, the grandest of the Colloredo-Mannsfelds'
Bohemian homes.[35] The March 1944 report stated that interior decorations from Opočno were "on loan." Karel Kühn, a Bohemian-German art
historian working in the Protectorate monument office in Brno, disagreed
with the "borrowed" nature of the art and antique furnishings taken from
Opočno. He argued that their removal was illegal. Kühn's charges led to
an investigation, which revealed that men from Einsatzstab II had filled

a small number of trucks with valuable objects from Opočno, including five tapestries. Some of the things went to Dobříš and others to the Prague Castle. The Einsatzstab men did not record or document what they carried away. In fact, they tried to hide their culling of things from Opočno by rearranging the remaining furnishings in a manner intended to conceal the gaps left by the missing pieces. When questioned about this cover-up attempt, Lieutenant Targatsch of Einsatzstab II stated that "Oberstgruppenführer Daluege had ordered that necessary furnishings for the fitting out of the guest rooms in Dobříš should be taken from Opočno."[36]

Rinnebach protested the devious removal of cultural property from Opočno and wanted the missing objects found. He was reprimanded for his "richly grotesque proposal" that someone search Daluege's servant and guest rooms at Dobříš for things from Opočno. Still, under pressure, the Einsatzstab men returned some of the furnishings that they surreptitiously took, although in that process "a valuable console with a marble top" went missing.[37] The story of interior decorations taken from Opočno shows that the Protectorate was not a monolith with all state actors acting in conformity with one another. Some Protectorate officials strove to follow rationalized policies and practices for the expropriation of persecuted people's things; others did not.

At the same time that Protectorate officials were seizing family heirlooms and other belongings from pro-Czech aristocrats, they were also carrying out the dispossession of the Jews of Bohemia and Moravia, most of whom were murdered. Before being deported Jews had to sign over their belongings, including keys to their homes, to agents of the Nazi administration, who sorted through their things and decided how the state could benefit from them. Valuable interior decorations expropriated from Jewish homes were stored and sold in a large art nouveau apartment building in central Prague at 16 Dlouhá Street, among other places.[38]

The 1944 report stated that Daluege had ordered Einsatzstab men to secure "furnishings of all types for Dobříš" from the Dlouhá Street warehouse. It indicated that purchases resulting from this command totaled roughly 73,000 Reichsmark, for which receipts were written, and a "transfer of ownership" contract was concluded. No specifics about the items purchased were provided. A different document listed seventy-six dispossessed Jewish furnishings that Einsatzstab men bought from the warehouse on May 14, 1943. Fifty-eight were purchased for Dobříš, six were for the Prague Castle, and fourteen, mostly oil paintings, were for Daluege himself. Found among the sequestered Jewish belongings that went to Dobříš were seven category one items, including two damaged eighteenth-century Chinese vases and a carved, gilded clock; forty-two category two items, among them a seventeenth-century Italian library table, a Renaissance-style armchair, and an Empire-style commode; and eight category three items, including a Spanish screen and a damaged mountain landscape oil painting by Alfred Karl Julius Otto von Schönberger.[39]

The murderous Daluege did not stay for long among the status-enhancing comforts of Dobříš. In May 1943 he suffered his second heart attack, leading to his retirement on an estate in occupied Poland that Hitler gave him.[40] A postwar search for valuable carpets and tapestries suggested that he took some interior decorations from Dobříš and elsewhere in the Protectorate with him.[41] For unknown reasons, he left a few personal possessions in the chateau. They included several crates of objects moved in March 1943 from his Berlin home, one of which contained Allach porcelain figurines produced by Jewish and other prisoners in a sub-camp of Dachau.[42]

After Daluege departed, Dobříš was turned over to the new Reich protector, Wilhelm Frick. Photographs of Frick's wife in some of the chateau's rooms provide rare views of the results of Nazi interior decorating in the old residence. At least two were taken in the Salon. Ariadne and the panther were absent from the images and in both of them Frau Frick occupied the location where the stone pair had been before World War I. The protector's wife, wearing a broad-shouldered jacket and shoes with chunky heels, posed on a settee upholstered with fabric depicting dancing figures in Renaissance attire, which was seen earlier in the tapestry room. On the wall above Frau Frick, in the spot where the portrait of Princess Lucy Sophie Yvonne in her low-cut dress had hung, was a painting of a stiff-looking woman wearing a winged lace collar and wide lace cuffs like those of seventeenth-century English court dress.[43]

The Third Czechoslovak Republic, 1945–1948

After the Third Reich's defeat in May 1945 came the short-lived Third Czechoslovak Republic and the expulsion of more than three million Germans from their homes and the country.[44] Accompanying this postwar chapter in the history of forced migration and ethnic cleansing was a new wave of intrusive, state-directed confiscations. In it, Czechoslovak officials expropriated millions of German possessions, including castles, chateaux, works of art, and carefully crafted antique furnishings.

President Eduard Beneš led the liberated Czechoslovak state, helping to oversee the expulsions and implement a series of decrees, including three instituting the dispossession of the displaced Germans. Decree No. 5 (May 1945) authorized the restitution of property taken by Nazi officials after the Munich Agreement to those original owners whom the state deemed to be reliable, that is, loyal to Czechoslovakia. Decree No. 12 (June 1945) established the state seizure of all rural property owned by Germans and other groups categorized as unreliable.[45] It affected agricultural property ranging from small peasant farms to large aristocratic estates and all movable objects on them, including interior decorations. Sequestered rural property was under the jurisdiction of the National Land Fund, part of the Ministry of Agriculture. By February 1946 the National Land Fund had over a million hectares of land, along with 450 castles and chateaux and their contents.[46] Decree No. 108 (October 1945) legalized the seizure of all urban property from Germans and others labeled as unreliable. It affected villas, apartments, palaces, and all objects in them. The Fund for National Renewal was responsible for property confiscated under this decree.[47] In the context of these decrees and the expulsions, it merits noting that German-speaking Jews who survived the Shoah were categorized as unreliable Germans with some limited opportunities to prove their loyalty to the state.[48]

At the war's end, the Colloredo-Mannsfelds expected to resettle in their homes in Dobříš, Zbiroh, and Opočno. This was due to Decree No. 5, which stipulated that property seized by Germans after the Munich Agreement would be restituted to reliable owners. The family had signed the pro-Czech "Declarations of Members of the Historic Nobility" which, they argued, demonstrated their loyalty to Czechoslovakia. Still, Colloredo-Mannsfeld property was not returned. Instead, their Bohemian estates were treated as German agricultural property and transferred to the National Land Fund under the terms of Decree No. 12. Czechoslovak officials argued that they had grounds for treating the Colloredo-Mannsfelds as potentially dangerous Germans, rather than as reliable Czechs. In the autumn of 1940, in an attempt to protect their property from state seizure, some family members tried to obtain German citizenship. To this end, they filled out the so-called *Fragebogen* (questionnaires) that asked about nationality and ancestry, including Jewish parents and grandparents. NSDAP authorities did not believe the sincerity of the applications, turning them down and dispossessing the family. After the Third Reich's defeat, Czechoslovak state officials remembered the Colloredo-Mannsfelds' endeavor to secure German national belonging and used it to justify the postwar expropriation of their property, including Dobříš.[49]

In October 1945 the state turned Dobříš over to the Syndicate of Czechoslovak Writers, which was renamed the Union of Czechoslovak Writers.[50] In February 1946 the National Land Fund informed the writers' association that Colloredo-Mannsfeld family members living in France had made a restitution claim on furnishings in Dobříš that Daluege's Einsatzstab men had carried there from Zbiroh. No specific information about the objects was provided, and it is unclear whether they or any of the expropriated Jewish objects taken to Dobříš during the war were returned. In response to this restitution claim the Land Fund gave the writers' association specific instructions regarding Dobříš's interior furnishings, stating that "when using the chateau, the furniture [is to] be preserved, be left in its places and not be moved into other rooms, and that an inventory be drawn up as quickly as possible."[51] In March 1946 Land Fund officials, along with authorities from the Ministry of the Interior and National State Security, created a list of the chateau's interior decorations. Historic preservationists were not yet involved in postwar care of confiscated cultural property in Dobříš, but that was soon to change.

In May 1946, when the Czechoslovak parliament began to meet again, a law was passed creating the National Cultural Commission.[52] This was a new state agency responsible for the selection and preservation of cultural objects that were confiscated under the terms of the postwar decrees and deemed valuable enough to be protected as national heritage. With the establishment of the commission, preservationists became prominent managers of persecuted people's things in Dobříš and elsewhere. A large impetus for its creation were reports about the loss, through destruction, theft and export, of valuable works of art and antiques. For example, in the autumn of 1945 it was reported that Wilhelm von Medinger Jr., son of a prominent German politician, had managed at the war's end to move three paintings of "enormous artistic worth," packed with Persian carpets, from his Chateau Malá Skála, to Prague and then, it was guessed, to Munich.[53]

Zdeněk Wirth served as the commission's director from 1946 until 1951. Wirth, like others working there, was an art historian who special-ized in historic preservation. He was not a member of the Czechoslovak Communist Party but, while directing the commission, he received sup-port from his longtime friend, Zdeněk Nejedlý, a powerful communist.[54] Wirth and other commission employees filtered through the residences of Germans and other "enemies of the people" that the state had seized under the terms of the postwar decrees. They exhibited no misgivings or qualms about taking over the property of displaced Germans, not all of whom had supported the Nazis. Using a standardized ranking system sim-ilar to the Einsatzstab men's categories, they selected architecture, art, and antiques to be placed under the commission's care and helped to develop regularized procedures for inventorying, evaluating, and preserving heri-tage made out of persecuted people's things.

On May 1, 1947, forty-seven sequestered chateaux with their interior decorations were transferred from the National Land Fund to the National Cultural Commission.[55] Dobříš was among this first group of confiscated objects to receive protected heritage status. The turnover terms for Dobříš stated that the Union of Czechoslovak Writers would continue to use the chateau and its contents free of charge for a twelve-year period. These terms were in effect when the communist coup occurred in February 1948 and another wave of confiscations began, this one targeting Czechs out of favor with the new regime.

The First Socialist Decade, 1948–1958

In February 1948, called "Victorious February," the Communist Party gained control over the Czechoslovak state, unleashing Stalinist purges and harsh disciplining of "class enemies" in the name of proletarian rev-olution. This included expropriating the property of religious organi-zations, the Czech aristocracy, and the Czech bourgeoisie, members of which were cast as dangerous outsiders and thousands of whom suffered ruinous fates in political prisons and forced labor camps, including those in uranium mines.

During the late Stalinist period Wirth and other art experts at the National Cultural Commission sorted through more confiscated cultural property. They transformed some former aristocratic residences into estate-museums with aestheticized and protected displays of noble lifestyles made out of persecuted people's things.[56] Thousands of things continued to be on the move in central Bohemia, including objects from Dobříš which did not become an estate-museum. In 1950, the same year as the show trial and hanging of Milada Horaková, a box of family embroidery and other "bits of decoration" left Dobříš to be preserved in the Museum of Social Culture then being created out of confiscated cultural property in the nearby Chateau Jemniště, itself a seized object.[57] In that same year twelve chairs with leather seats and armrests, along with other Renaissance-style furnishings, traveled from Dobříš to the set of the movie *The Emperor's Baker*, after which time they were preserved in the expropriated Chateau Nelahozeves.[58] In 1951 coins taken from the Colloredo-Mannsfelds joined other confiscated things in the National Museum in Prague,[59] and two Canaletto landscapes depicting Venice went to storage in the sequestered Chateau Lnáře, along with other paintings.[60] In 1956 a selection of paintings, engravings, and colored lithographs moved from Dobříš to Prague's Kinský Palace, staying only for a short time before being stored in Chateau Mělník, sequestered from the pro-Czech Schwarzenberg noble family. Among them were two portraits of Colloredo-Mannsfeld family members, including one of a princess in rococo dress.[61] In 1957 lithographs and engravings, most with military content, made the shorter journey to the District Museum in the town of Dobříš.[62]

Many interior decorations also remained in the chateau, including Ariadne and the panther. This further relative fixedness in the midst of more intense mobility largely resulted from the Union of Czechoslovak Writers' continued use of the baroque edifice in the socialist period, which was confirmed in a new December 1949 agreement. Under the terms of the agreement, the commission had to supply Dobříš with furnishings. This included books for the chateau library, which were to be "obtained through the sorting of books in buildings acquired through article 12 of Decree No. 108."[63] The union's desire to benefit from the millions of publications taken from Germans was not new. In March 1948, a month after the communist coup, it asked for confiscated books, requesting that the commission enable "Czech writers to use the wealth which is lying fallow elsewhere in the hallways of abandoned chateaux."[64] The migration of print material also went in the opposite direction. In 1952 German and Czech forestry books and periodicals traveled from Dobříš to the State Agricultural Archive.[65] In 1953 unspecified books from the chateau moved to the Institute of History and the University Library in Prague.[66]

While supplying confiscated books for Dobříš posed little challenge to the National Cultural Commission, providing sequestered interior decorations was harder. The 1949 agreement stated that the commission remained responsible for "completing the decor in the social rooms of the Dobříš chateau with all possible period furnishings [*stylovým zařízením*]." Conflicts grew between the union and the commission over this term, not because anyone was uncomfortable about benefiting from persecuted people's things. Rather, commission officials worried that sequestered furnishings that had become protected heritage objects would be damaged if they were used, while union leaders wished to strengthen the status-heightening impact of Dobříš through rooms decorated with imposing objects. Conflicts over the use of displaced people's things at Dobříš show that even before Stalin's death in 1953, and similar to the Third Reich, the Czechoslovak socialist state was not a monolith of uniform opinions and practices. They also reveal that commission employees who were experts in historic preservation, in contrast to Daluege's Einsatzstab men, worried about the material vulnerability of symbolically significant things and damage that could result from them being used.

Friction between the union and the commission continued after the completion of the first socialist-era inventory of Dobříš's interior decorations in February 1950. Its 103 pages listed roughly three thousand confiscated works of art and antique furnishings, a quantity notably larger than in the 1938 prewar "Register." Ariadne and the panther were item number 463, this time called "Marble Statuette of Lion with Woman." They were in the Salon, although where exactly was not indicated.[67] Photographs from around 1950 included in an album belonging to Jan Drda, the union's communist chairman from 1949 to 1956, show nicely dressed people sitting on and gathered around confiscated period furnishings in the Salon, enjoying food, drinks, and cigarettes. One of the images provides a hazy glimpse of Ariadne back in her prewar location, now on top of a dark piece of furniture rather than the delicately carved console.[68]

Following the completion of the inventory and still in 1950, the
National Cultural Commission selected particularly valuable confiscated
objects "of museum quality" to be moved from Dobříš for preservation
purposes. Ariadne, again listed as item number 463 and called "Lion with
Woman," appeared among the thirty pages of special heritage objects.[69]
Union leaders protested with "determined opposition" plans for any interior decorations leaving Dobříš.[70] They wanted all objects to remain, and
they wanted more period furnishings to join them. In August 1950 they
requested that the commission send additional things. Their letter complained that Dobříš had been turned over to the union "with diversely
mixed furnishings, just as the German occupiers left them" and that
"some rooms are distastefully furnished; other furnishings are just very
poor." Union leaders wanted "befitting furniture" for their members and
guests, whom they wanted to impress.[71] They expressed no concern or
dismay that the things they desired had been expropriated from private
individuals and families, or that they could be damaged through use.

In early 1951 Tat'iána Kubátová, an art historian employed in the
National Cultural Commission, tried to satisfy the union's call for more
interior decorations. She located some suitable objects in Čimelice and
Orlík, two chateaux confiscated from the Orlík line of the pro-Czech aristocratic Schwarzenberg family.[72] Objects from Čimelice included a bedroom suite with a double bed, a closet and a toilet table, wicker chairs
and couches, and a baroque bed.[73] If the union was at all satisfied by
this mediation effort, it was not satisfied for long. In March 1951, the
commission again discussed removing valuable furnishings from Dobříš.
In an effort to convince the preservationists not to do this, in April the
union offered to create educational displays of period furnishings with
"stylistic unity" in the Great Hall and the Billiards Room that would be
open to the public. It also pointedly reminded commission officials that
they had stored some valuable furnishings in the attic where, the writers
maintained, the conditions were causing more material damage than if the
objects were being used.[74]

In 1951 a reorganization of state heritage care led to the dissolution
of the National Cultural Commission and the absorption of confiscated-
cum-heritage objects under its care into the State Monument Administration. Following this change and Stalin's death, struggles and negotiations
over interior decorations in Dobříš continued. Perhaps the Soviet leader's

demise made union leaders worried that any subsequent loosening of ideological control would weaken the standing of official writers and caused them to be more intent on employing Dobříš and its furnishings for status-enhancing purposes. In 1954 the rationale for preservationist worries about material damage to heritage objects resulting from use were confirmed when the writers' association asked for repairs to upholstery on some protected chairs. After looking into the matter, representatives of the State Monument Administration recorded that "this is an example of how things turn out when period furnishings are borrowed for the normal operations of accommodations." With the proviso that the union place the restored period furnishings only in rarely used rooms, the preservationists sought new fabrics for the damaged pieces including, among others, two armchairs with "pseudo-Renaissance" textiles, a copy of a seventeenth-century armchair with a pink, flower-patterned brocade, and two baroque gilded armchairs covered with brocade and velvet. Authentic period fabrics could not be found, so textile experts at state-run institutions, including the School of Decorative Arts in Prague, were asked to create suitable materials.[75]

In 1954 employees of the State Monument Administration photographed rooms in Dobříš's south tract. One black and white image revealed that while the Great Hall was not as lavishly decorated as it had been before the war, it still contained imposing period furnishings taken from the Colloredo-Mannsfelds. Ensembles of richly upholstered things to sit on, including a high-backed chair decorated with Botticelli's *Birth of Venus*, surrounded various tables that were arranged in a manner encouraging people to gather in small groups. Also now in the Great Hall was the settee with the dancing figures that Reich Protector Frick's wife had posed on in that spot in the Salon where Ariadne and the panther had been before the war. Another 1954 photograph showed the Salon. In it Ariadne was in her old location, this time resting on a Louis XIV cylinder desk with the stiff-looking woman in the winged lace collar hanging above her and two small marble busts of ancient Greeks standing on either side of her (see figure 3.2).

The 1954 photographs contain evidence that the Union of Czechoslovak Writers was still using Dobříš's grandest rooms and things inside them. In the image of the Salon, across the room from Ariadne, a loaded typewriter sat on a Louis XV table among sheets of paper and a book (see

Figure 3.2. The Salon in 1954. Sculpture of "Ariadne on the Panther" is in the background. Typewriter and papers on a Louis XV desk show the Union of Czechoslovak Writers' use of the room after the confiscations. Photo used with kind permission of the National Heritage Institute, Directorate-General, Prague.

figure 3.2). More striking is the photograph of the bedroom with the hunting scenes. The pillow on the double bed was wrinkled with the imprint of a head, one of the chairs had a towel thrown over it, and on the white dressing table there was an ashtray, a snack, and a purse. This photograph shows the ease with which some people could live with persecuted people's things and that the union did not share the preservationists' worries about the material weakness of symbolically strong things(see figure 3.3).

In 1958 the government of socialist Czechoslovakia approved the country's first comprehensive historic preservation law. One result of this landmark legislation was the completion in 1961 of another inventory of Dobříš's interior decorations. Ariadne appeared on this streamlined list with a new inventory number followed by her old number (157/463) and the very brief label "Statuette."[76] The report accompanying the inventory indicated that many objects in the chateau were damaged due to "frequent movements connected with the operation of the building."[77] A slightly

Figure 3.3. The bedroom with hunting scenes in 1954. The pillow wrinkled from use, the towel thrown over the back of a chair, as well as the plate of plums, the ashtray, and the purse on the white table show the Union of Czechoslovak Writers' use of the room. Photo used with kind permission of the National Heritage Institute, Directorate-General, Prague.

later report confirmed and further explained the damage. It stated, "The cause of these defects is frequent movement and that the given things have been in constant use since 1945 and are consequently worn out."[78] The preservationists had not secured control over things at Dobříš. They had some successes in heritage sites where they did not struggle so much with another interest group, but that is a topic for another study.

Conclusion: Restoring History to Things

It is fitting to close this study where it began, that is, with Ariadne and the panther. In nineteenth-century Europe, Dannecker's marble sculpture was a well-known work that was frequently written about, reproduced in a variety of materials, including ivory and marzipan, and sometimes found among interior decorations in upper-class homes.[79] In Frankfurt today the piece remains a celebrated work, currently exhibited in the Liebieghaus after having been seriously damaged during the Second World War and later expertly restored. Given its reputation, it is striking that none of the six lists of things examined here ever identified the object by its correct name or as a copy of Dannecker's work. Perhaps this inaccuracy resulted from the training or national biases of the different experts who created the inventories; perhaps it means that in central Bohemia the material strength of the object outlasted its symbolic power. This study has restored identity and history to the Dobříš copy of *Ariadne on the Panther*, the lifespan of which included the intensely violent and mobile years during and after the Second World War. It has laid bare the frequently overlooked and forgotten facts that pretty things can have ugly histories filled with injustice and cruelty and that much of what is considered heritage is intricately tied to war and other forms of violence.

Since the end of Communist Party rule in Czechoslovakia in 1989, the physical structure of Chateau Dobříš has been restituted to the Colloredo-Mannsfelds, while the interior furnishings seized between 1938 and 1958 remain national property, which the family rents for display purposes. The Great Hall, the Salon, and other rooms in the south tract are open for public tours with Ariadne and the panther recently seen resting on a bookcase in the Library. In the early nineteenth century, one observer of Dannecker's celebrated work wrote that it represented "wildness being tamed by beauty."[80] This study of interior decorating with persecuted people's things concludes with a less optimistic reading of the sculpture. Like the ugly histories of pretty things in Chateau Dobříš, which are not visible on the surface, a darker reality churns below the smooth finishes of Ariadne and the panther—one in which beauty or culture never have true control and the destructive power of nature, particularly human nature, is always potentially menacing.

Notes

1. Information on Dannecker's *Ariadne on the Panther*, popular during the nineteenth century and currently displayed in Frankfurt's Liebieghaus, is in Ellen Kemp, *Ariadne auf dem Panther* (Frankfurt am Main: Liebieghaus, 1979). I am grateful to Austin Spain for helping me to identify this work.

2. Studies treating the dispossession of the Jews during World War II include Götz Aly, *Hitler's Beneficiaries: Plunder, Racial War, and the Nazi Welfare State* (New York: Metropolitan,

2007); and Jan Gross, *Golden Harvest: Events at the Periphery of the Holocaust* (New York: Oxford University Press, 2012). Works discussing the dispossession of the Protectorate's Jews include Helena Krejčová and Otomar L. Krejča, *Jindřich Baudisch a konfiskace uměleckých děl v protektorátu* (Prague: Tilia, 2007); Jan Björn Potthast, *Das jüdische Zentralmuseum der SS in Prag: Gegnerforschung und Völkermord im Nationalsozialismus* (Frankfurt: Campus Verlag, 2002); Monika Sedláková, "Die Rolle der so gennanten 'Einsatzstäbe' bei der Enteignung jüdischen Vermögens," in *Theresienstädter Studien und Dokumente,* ed. Gabriela Kalinová, Jaroslava Milotová, Ulf Rathgeber, and Michael Wögerbauer (Prague: Institut Theresienstädter Initiative, 2003), 275–305; and Madga Veselská, *Archa paměti: Cesta pražského židovského muzea pohnutým 20. stoletím* (Prague: Jewish Museum in Prague, 2012).

    3. For information on the confiscation of noble propertyin the Protectorate, see Zdeněk Hazdra, Václav Horčička, and Jan Županič, eds., *Šlechta střední Evropy v konfrontaci s totalitními režimy 20. století* (Prague: Ústav pro studium totalitních režimů, 2011); Ondřej Vlk, "'Národ žije tak dlouho, jak dlouho žijí jeho kulturní památky': Konfiskace uměleckých předmětů na území protektorátu" (PhD diss., Charles University in Prague, 2008); and Jiří Záloha, "Zabavení majetku hlubocké větve Schwarzenberků gestapem r roce 1940," *Československý časopis historický* 39, no. 1 (1991): 65–77.

    4. Studies related to confiscated cultural property during the Third Czechoslovak Republic and the early socialist period include Cathleen M. Giustino, "Open Gates and Wandering Minds: Codes, Castles, and Chateaux in Socialist Czechoslovakia before 1960," *Socialist Escapes: Breaking Away from Ideology and Everyday Routine in Eastern Europe, 1945–1989,* ed. Cathleen M. Giustino, Catherine J. Plum, and Alexander Vari (New York: Berghahn Books, 2013), 48–74; Kristina Uhlíková, *Národní kulturní komise* (Prague: Artefactum, 2004); and Kristina Uhlíková, ed., *Šlechtická sídla ve stínu prezidentských dekretů* (Prague: Artefactum, 2017).

    5. An unpublished description of the eighteenth-century renovations is "Doberschisch," Národní archiv (hereafter NA), Úřad řísského protektora (hereafter ÚŘP), 114-8-32. Published descriptions are *Dobříš: Mansion, Gardens, Park* (Prague: State Center for the Preservation of Historical Relics and Nature Protection and the Czech Literary Fund, 1983); and *Zámek Dobříš* (Prague: Regulus, 1999).

    6. The 1907 inventory, "Schloss Dobřísch. Inventar. Stand am 22 Juli 1907," is in NA, ÚŘP, 114-8-28.

    7. A photo album with copies of these prewar photos is at Dobříš. I thank Pavel Krejcárek, director of the Dobříš Chateau, for kindly allowing me to study these visual sources. I also thank Tereza Vyhlasová, a tour guide at Dobříš, for sharing with me her knowledge of the history of rooms and objects in the chateau.

    8. The troubled marriage is discussed in Václav Horčička and Jan Županič, *Šlechta na křižovatce: Lichtenštejnové, Schwarzenbergové a Colloredo-Mannsfeldové v 1. polovině 20. století* (Prague: Agentura Pankrác, 2017), 619–631.

    9. A copy of the original Czech inventory, "Soupis a odhad uměleckého a starožitného inventáře zámku Dobříš," dated January 3, 1938, is in NA, ÚŘP, 114-8-28. The German translation is in NA, ÚŘP, 114-8-32.

    10. Details on the expropriation and the *Zwangsverwaltung* (forced administration) preceeding it are in Jan Županič, "Mezi dvěma ohni: Colloredo-Mannsfeldové ve čtyřicátých letech 20. století," in Hazdra, Horčička, and Županič, eds., *Šlechta střední Evropy,* 231–233. English translations of the declarations are in Eagle Glassheim, *Noble Nationalists: The Transformation of the Bohemian Aristocracy* (Cambridge: Harvard University Press, 2005), 237–241.

    11. A list of all chateaux in the Protectorate is "Register aller Schlösser im Protektorat nach den Angaben der Oberlandräte," NA, ÚŘP, 114-8-39. Chateaux confiscated from Jews were marked with a star of David.

12. No published study dedicated to Daluege exists. Ordnungspolizei participation in mass shootings of Jews is discussed in Christopher R. Browning, *Ordinary Men: Reserve Police Battalion 101 and the Final Solution in Poland* (New York: HarperCollins, 1992).

13. In 1942 Daluege joined the Vereinigung zur Erhaltung deutscher Burgen (Union for the Preservation of German Castles), for which Albert Speer served as protector. See "An den Herrn SS-Oberst-Gruppenführer und Generaloberst der Polizei," December 1, 1942, National Archive and Records Administration (hereafter NARA), T580, reel 220.

14. "Bericht über eine Dienstfahrt 10.3.43 bis 11.3.43," March 15, 1943, NA, ÚŘP, 114-8-39.

15. In April 1943 the director of Einsatzstab II reported that 134 furnished residences with a total of 360 rooms were ready for German families. Sedláková, "Die Rolle der so gennanten 'Einsatzstäbe,'" 287.

16. See, for example, Rinnebach's 1942 request, based on Daluege's order, that Willi Schimmelpfennig, an art historian in the police reserves, report to him in "Betrifft: Kunsthistoriker in der Polizeireserve," NA, ÚŘP, 114-8-42.

17. On activities of Cibulka and Swoboda, see Alena Janatková, "Museumspolitik im 'Protektorat Böhmen und Mähren': Die Prager Galerie alter Kunst/Nationalgalerie/ Landesgalerie," in *Kunstgeschichte in den besetzten Gebieten 1939–1945*, ed. Agnieszka Gasior, Magdalena Bushart, and Alena Janatková (Cologne: Böhlau, 2016), 47–70. A receipt for topographies of monuments in Bohemia and Moravia purchased for Einsatzstab I from the Prague bookseller André, an official dealer in confiscated property, is "Rechnung an den Einsatzstab Rinnebach," November 20, 1942, NA, ÚŘP, 114-8-42.

18. Sedláková, "Die Rolle der so gennanten 'Einsatzstäbe,'" 275–306.

19. On Frank's opera glasses, see "Opis No. 990," dated January 17, 1945, NA, Zemský úřad Prague: Oddělení církevní, nadační, a školské, 1911–1949 (hereafter ZÚ), carton 244.

20. "Letter of Director of Museum of Applied Arts to Rinnebach," March 18, 1943, and "Letter of Director of Náprstek Museum to Rinnebach," March 19, 1943, in NA, ÚŘP, 114-8-42. Jan Herain wrote the first letter and signed it "Heil Hitler."

21. Sedláková, "Die Rolle der so gennanten 'Einsatzstäbe,'" 288.

22. "Opis No. 701," November 24, 1944, NA, ZÚ, carton 244.

23. A copy of the instructions is in Sedláková, "Die Rolle der so gennanten 'Einsatzstäbe,'" 276.

24. "Tätigkeitsbericht des Einsatzstabes (I) Rinnebach," June 19, 1943, NA, ÚŘP, 114-8-39.

25. Information on Einsatzstab II's remodeling workat Dobříš is in Sedláková, "Die Rolle der so gennanten 'Einsatzstäbe,'" 291. Einsatzstab II men also decorated Daluege's apartment in the Prague Castle.

26. "Inventarverzeichnis von Schloß Doberischisch aufgenommen am 15.10.1942," NA, ÚŘP, 114-8-32. At some point after 1954 Ariadne lost a hand and a foot, but she was complete during World War II, so this damage does not explain why Nazi appraisers gave her the lowest possible quality ranking.

27. The June 1939 inventory of Daluege's home in Berlin at Faradayweg 10 is "Aufnahme vom 14. Juni 1939," NARA, T580, reel 218.

28. The 1942 Nazi inventory, "Inventarverzeichnis von Schloß Doberschisch," is in NA, ÚŘP, 114-8-32.

29. "Bericht," March 31, 1944, NA, ZÚ, carton 244. An undated draft of another report indicated that Einsatzstab II worked on redecorating Dobříš in 1942 and 1943, with the architect Eichhorn overseeing them and receiving 100,000 Reichsmark per year for the purchase of interior decorations. See "Zum 1. Umbau," NA, ÚŘP, 114-8-28.

30. "Schloß Sbirow," no date, NA, ÚŘP, 114-8-39.

31. "Bericht," March 31, 1944, NA, ZÚ, carton 244.

32. Some items transferred from Zbiroh to Dobříš are listed in "Aus Schloss Sbirow sind folgende Gegenstände entnommen für Schloss Doberschisch," NA, ÚŘP, 114-8-32.

33. "Vorläufige Bestätigung der nach Schloß Doberschish überführten Möbel, Bilder, Einrichtungsgegenstände und Diverse," July 28 and 30, 1942, NA, ÚŘP, 114-8-24.

34. Lists of things taken from Zbiroh and sent to various places are in NA, ÚŘP, 114-8-24.

35. In 1929 the Colloredo-Mannsfelds commissioned artist Hubert Landa to catalogue paintings in Opočno. Einsatzstab men used the catalogue, printed in German, when inventorying Opočno. See *Katalog der Colloredo Mannsfeldschen Gemälde-Galerie in Opočno* (Opočno: n.p., 1929) in NA, ÚŘP, 114-8-37.

36. See the three-page summary, "Betrifft: Entnahme von Bilden, Möbeln, Teppiche, usw. aus Schloss Opotschno," August 3, 1943, NA, ÚŘP, 114-8-39.

37. "Betrifft: Entnahme von Bildern usw. aus Schloss Opotschno," August 6, 1943, NA, ÚŘP, 114-8-39.

38. "An das Zentralamt für die Regelung der Judenfrage," May 14, 1943, NA, ZÚ, carton 244. Nazi procedures for confiscating property from Jews and the fate of some Jewish cultural valuables are discussed in Veselská, *Archa paměti*; and Potthast, *Das jüdische Zentralmuseum der SS in Prag*.

39. "Opis: Uebergabeverhandlung," May 14, 1943, ZÚ, carton 244.

40. After the Nazi defeat he was captured in the British zone of occupied Germany, sent to Czechoslovakia for trial, and hanged in Prague in October 1946.

41. "Letter of the Syndikát českých spisovatelů," April 16, 1946, Státní oblastní archiv, Mimořádný lidový soud Praha: Kurt Daluege, LS I-2043/46. The letter was resent on September 5, 1946.

42. The contents of nine boxes are listed in "Verzeichnis der nach Prag gebrachten Einrichtungsgegenstände und Bücher," NARA, T580, reel 218. That they came from Daluege's Berlin home is confirmed by an inventory of that residence completed in January 1943 for insurance purposes (his possessions had significantly grown since the 1939 inventorying of his household; see note 27 above). For the 1943 inventory see "Verzeichnis der privaten Kunstwerte, Möbel und Einrichtungsgegenstände in der Dienstwohnung des Chefs der Ordnungspolizei," January 7, 1943, NARA, T580, reel 218.

43. I am grateful to Petr Kadlec for allowing me to study this photograph and sharing his knowledge with me. He is author of *Dvakrát ukradený Dobříš: Letní sídlo říšských protektorů, 1942–1945* (Dobříš: Knihy-Kadlec, 2017).

44. A new study of the expulsions and their relation to property and the rebuilding of the Czechoslovak economy is David W. Gerlach, *The Economy of Ethnic Cleansing: The Transformation of the German-Czech Borderlands after World War II* (Cambridge: Cambridge University Press, 2017).

45. Karel Jech and Karel Kaplan, eds., *Dekrety prezidenta republiky, 1940–1945: Dokumenty*, vol. 1 (Brno: Ústav pro soudobé dějiny AV ČR, 1995), 276–283.

46. "Zápis o udržování rekeačních objektů," February 20, 1946, NA, Úřad předsednictva vlády (hereafter ÚPV), Sig. 217/16: "Objekty rekreační—udržování (Dobříš, Roztěž a Doksy), carton 101.

47. Jech and Kaplan, eds., *Dekrety prezidenta republiky*, vol. 2, 848–860.

48. The fate of German-speaking Jews in postwar Czechoslovakia is discussed in Kateřina Čapková, "Germans or Jews? German-Speaking Jews in Poland and Czechoslovakia after World War II," *Kwartalnik Historii Żydów* 246 (2013): 348–362.

49. Županíč, "Mezi dvěma ohni," 229–250.

50. On the union, see Michal Bauer, ed., *II. sjezd Svazu československých spisovatelů: 22–29. 4. 1956* (Acropolis: Prague: 2011); and Marci Shore, "Engineering in the Age of Innocence: A Genealogy of Discourse Inside the Czechoslovak Writers' Union, 1949–67," *East European Politics and Societies* 12, no. 3 (1998): 397–441.

51. "Věc: Zámek Dobříš, uplatňování vlastnických práv," February 20, 1946, NA, ÚPV, Sig. 217/18: "Dobříš: Přidělení objektů u velkostatku Dobříš," carton 101.

52. The best study of the National Cultural Commission remains Uhlíková, *Národní kulturní komise.*

53. "Věc: Ztracené akcie, odvezené originály obrazů, perské koberce z majetku Dr. W. Medingera," November 15, 1945, Archiv bezpečnostních složek, Sig. 2M 13530.

54. On Wirth, see Jiří Roháček and Kristina Uhlíková, eds., *Zdeněk Wirth: Pohledem dnešní doby* (Prague: Artefactum, 2010); and Kristina Uhlíková, *Zdeněk Wirth: První dvě životní etapy* (Prague: Národní památkový ústav, 2011).

55. The turnover's history is outlined in "Zápis sepsaný dne 9. prosince 1949 na zámku v Dobříši," NA, Státní památková správa (hereafter SPS), Dobříš, carton 139.

56. Giustino, "Open Gates and Wandering Minds"; and Uhlíková, *Národní kulturní komise.*

57. "Seznam," April 28, 1950, NA, SPS: Dodátky, carton 60.

58. "Dobříš: Inventář půjčený čs. st. filmu převezen do Nelahozeves," NA, SPS, carton 140.

59. "Věc: Odpověd na dotaz č. 5867/54-SPS," NA, SPS, carton 140.

60. "Věc: Zámky Dobříš, Hrádek u Nech., Hrubý Rohozec a Loučeň," NA, SPS: Dodátky, carton 60.

61. The thirteen-page list is "Z inventáře zámku: Dobříš/sklad Kinský palác," NA, SPS, carton 140.

62. "Seznam litografií s rytin, které správce státního zámku v Dobříši předal dne 27.4.1957 Okrenímu museu v Dobříši," NA, SPS: Dodátky, carton 61.

63. "Zápis sepsaný dne 9. prosince 1949 na zámku v Dobříši," NA, SPS, carton 139.

64. "Letter of the Syndicate to the National Cultural Commission," March 31, 1948, NA, SPS, carton 139.

65. "Věc: Předání odbor. knih hospodářských," April 24, 1952, NA, SPS, carton 140.

66. "IV. Odvozy," NA, SPS, carton 139.

67. The February 1950 inventory, "Zámek Dobříš: Seznam inventáře," is in NA, SPS: Dodátky, carton 60.

68. "Jan Drda při různých příležitostech se spisovateli na zámek v Dobříši: Album nedatovaných fotografií," Památník národního písemnictví, Fond Jan Drda, č. přír. 14/75.

69. "Seznam předmětů vytřídených Národní kulturní komisí v Praze podle zákona č. 137/46 Sb. z mobilního inventáře zámku Dobříše," NA, SPS, carton 139.

70. "Přehled spisů v záležitosti dobříšského zámku," NA, SPS, carton 140. This is a summary of disagreements and negotiations between the union and the commission over the use of period furnishings in the chateau.

71. "Věc: Stylové zařízení na Dobříši," August 4, 1950, NA, SPS, carton 139.

72. "Další postup práce v záležitosti Dobříš-Čimelice," January 24, 1951, NA, SPS, carton 140.

73. "Draft letter by Taťána Kubátová," January 31, 1951, NA, SPS, carton 140.

74. "Úprava interiéru, Dobříš," April 20, 1951, NA, SPS, carton 140.

75. "Věc: Stylové nábyt. Látky," April 9, 1954; and "Věc: O. Pechová, cestovní zpráva, st. zám. Dobříš," June 29, 1954, both in NA, SPS, carton 140.

76. "Státní zámek v Dobříši: Seznam předmětů schválených do kat. A," n.d., NA, SPS: Dodátky, carton 61.

77. "Protokol schvalovacího řízení subkomise pro třídění památkového mobiliáře na státním zámku Dobříši ve dnech 14.–16.3.1961," March 16, 1961, SPS: Dodátky, carton 61.

78. "Protokol předání z převzetí movitého majetku kulturní povahy instalovaného v zámku Dobříš," September 20, 1961, SPS: Dodátky, carton 61.

79. Kemp, *Ariadne auf dem Panther*, 40–41.

80. Kemp, *Ariadne auf dem Panther*, 29.

Part II

People and Things

Individual Use of
Things in Wartime

Leora Auslander and Tara Zahra

In part II of this volume we move from the wartime seizure and redeployment of things by the state to the uses made of things by soldiers,
prisoners of war, concentration camp inmates, and civilians. People who
found themselves in each of these wartime roles used things in ways both
familiar and novel. Men serving as soldiers came to have relationships
with their weapons they would have found unimaginable in peacetime.
Concentration camp inmates who had been quite indifferent to fashion
before the war became obsessed with it. Prisoners of war who had thought
that the arts of homemaking were only for women discovered unsuspected
skills and pleasures. Some of these relations to things were fostered by the
state, but many were quite contrary to them and reveal the capacity of
things to help people retain a sense of humanity in unhuman situations.

Modern armies attempted to regulate soldiers' relations to things,
creating a regime of goods appropriate to wartime. Rather than using
clothing to shape and reflect identity as in civilian life, for example, soldiers were to wear uniforms provided by the state that differentiated only

by regiment and rank and that eliminated individuality. Soldiers were allocated weapons and entrusted with their maintenance; they were, in fact, encouraged to develop strong emotional bonds with their guns. The restrictions imposed on what soldiers could plunder from conquered peoples and territories indicate a certain normalization of the normally abnormal practice of theft.

The first two essays in this section examine the use of things by individual soldiers in two very different contexts: the U.S. Civil War and the Second World War. These include the relationship of soldiers to the objects they used to kill and the objects they stole from battlefields, occupied territories, and other soldiers' bodies. Elite warriors had always been attached to their handcrafted weapons; in Brendan Schechter's article we see the transformation of that affect in relations among soldiers, the Soviet army, and their guns in the context of an industrialized, bureaucratic state. Each soldier received a mass-produced gun, whose serial number was carefully noted in his identity papers. Soldiers expressed love for those weapons, weapons so valuable symbolically and materially that their loss was a capital crime.

While trophy-taking, theft, and looting often served the interests of the state, individuals also engaged in these practices for their own benefit (and sometimes against military orders). Soldiers kept some of their booty but also shipped stolen goods home to their wives and families, sharing their experience of violence through everyday objects pillaged from the enemy. In the first chapter in this section Sarah Weicksel describes civilians' efforts to protect themselves against this loss, burying their possessions or, in the case of women in the U.S. South, going so far as to hide them under their hoop skirts in specially designed pockets. Next, Brandon Schechter's chapter shows German defeat materialized in the form of the bicycles, watches, and domestic goods sent or carried back to the USSR by Red Army soldiers. These trophies were extracted as reparations for wartime suffering and enabled soldiers to carry home the experience of Soviet victory. Revenge was exacted in other ways; in the United States, emancipated slaves participated in looting, taking from their former owners the things they needed to start a new life.

In the third and fourth chapters of this section, Iris Rachamimov and Noah Benninga each analyze the uses made of things by those whose involuntary voyages paused, or ended, in incarceration. Rachamimov examines

the prisoner of war camps of the First World War that became the temporary homes of officers. She demonstrates how POWs creatively sustained
(but also sometimes subverted) prewar class and gender roles through
the production and use of domestic objects and clothing in internment
camps. Benninga turns his attention to elite prisoners in Nazi concentration camps, where block elders and other elite prisoners appropriated
clothing and personal goods stolen from other inmates to instantiate their
social status in the camp.

As these essays make clear, not all camps were alike. There were huge
differences between the level of suffering and deprivation in a relatively
porous and comfortable officer's POW camp during the First World War,
refugee camps created with "humanitarian" objectives, and Nazi concentration camps, for example. Objects played different roles in each of these
contexts. For the POWs analyzed by Rachamimov, objects gained heightened significance as bridges across time and space. They linked people
inside and outside of camps, helped people to pass the time, and enabled
internees to maintain or subvert norms of domesticity, gender, and class.
For elite prisoners in the Nazi concentration camps described by Benninga, by contrast, "fashion" often constructed and conveyed new hierarchies within the social world of the camp. Clean or tailored clothing
enabled some individuals to retain a sense of their humanity in conditions
designed to dehumanize.

In both cases, however, prisoners used the stuff and meanings of consumer society to transform unrecognizable, brutal circumstances into
something that connected to the lives they had lived before their incarceration, into something that could allow them to imagine life after it. The
ability to pass time carving wood or bone into beautiful or useful objects
gave meaning to "empty time" for the prisoners of war discussed by
Rachamimov. And the reconstruction of norms of middle-class masculinity and domestic life within all-male camps helped prisoners to feel more
"at home," even as camp life also offered opportunities to transgress.

Elite prisoners in Auschwitz-Birkenau, in far more desperate circumstances, also used the stuff of everyday life to cling to their own humanity
as it was under assault. Benninga analyzes the significance of tailored,
high-quality clothing and boots for inmates who managed to acquire a
relatively secure position in the camp hierarchy. The visual and textual
images that form the evidentiary base of these essays are perhaps more

shocking than those of squalor and abjectness that we expect when reading of wartime incarceration. In both essays, what disorients is the very
ordinariness of the protagonists' relation to these consumer goods. Rachamimov and Benninga persuasively demonstrate that domesticity, the material signs of gender, and the fashion system had been so deeply internalized
in twentieth-century Europe that even people who found themselves violently displaced and forcibly immobilized sought to recreate them. These
essays force us to rethink the role of things in the making of humans in
the modern world.

"Peeled" Bodies, Pillaged Homes

Looting and Material Culture in the American Civil War Era

Sarah Jones Weicksel

In 1925, a Confederate veteran presented the Confederate Museum in Richmond, Virginia, with a tintype of C. C. "Charley" Wheat, a soldier who was "killed 19 April 1862."[1] Across the cardboard mat, Wheat's brother, Joseph, scrawled the photograph's history: "this Pictur was lossed in 61 was found on the Body of a Dead Yankey at Sharpes Bourge 62." Charley gave his photograph to a female relative, but it was "lossed" when Union soldiers stole it from her house in 1861.

Years later, a Confederate soldier stopped at this woman's home for dinner and showed her his collection of battlefield "relics." Imagine her shock at discovering the stolen tintype of Charley in the soldier's bag. The pleasure of having the tintype returned to her must have been dampened by the memories triggered by the knowledge that the tintype had been looted from the pockets of a dead soldier, for Charley's body, too, was looted when he died. His body was found "all muddy from the red clay, and stripped of everything but the underclothes."[2]

Figure 4.1. Tintype of Confederate soldier Charles C. Wheat, c. 1861. The inscription reads: "this Pictur was lossed in 61 was found on the Body of a Dead Yankey at Sharpes Bourge 62." Courtesy of the American Civil War Museum, Richmond, Virginia.

Charley Wheat and his tintype likeness both fell victim to theft during the American Civil War: The tintype was stolen by a Union soldier from a private house; it was taken again when a Confederate soldier rifled through the pockets of that dead Union soldier; and upon his death Charley himself was stripped of his clothing, shoes, and personal effects. This story is somewhat remarkable in terms of the series of coincidences that occurred, but the individual thefts themselves were not uncommon during the American Civil War, despite the fact that, while Army regulations permitted soldiers in both the Confederate and Union armies to forage for food and livestock, to "plunder and pillage" was explicitly banned.[3] As chapters in this volume demonstrate, plundering has been—and continues to be—a form of violation that has historically accompanied war.[4] It is, then, tempting to explain Civil War looting as simply a casualty of war and the soldiers' behavior a wartime aberration. Regardless of whether or not this was a temporary deviation from men's normal behavior, acts of theft, fear of looting, and the stolen objects themselves performed powerful cultural work in the United States during and after the Civil War.

Wartime looting connotes the theft and destruction of belongings, violently wrested away from the owners or ransacked in their absence. But as the story of Charley Wheat and his tintype suggests, not all wartime theft was accompanied by such drama. Soldiers rifled through the pockets of dead comrades and enemies; they took the shoes from dead men who no longer needed them. Soldiers, teachers, and relief workers occupied houses abandoned by their occupants, using the furniture as their own. Formerly enslaved people built homes for themselves using windows, furniture, and other items taken or salvaged from derelict and vacant houses.[5] As soldiers departed towns, local inhabitants took goods and furnishings from unattended houses and stores. Union and Confederate soldiers, along with white and black Southern civilians, were all culpable of, and fell victim to, such actions.

This chapter explores the threat and reality of wartime theft, expanding what constituted such theft to include the broad range of incidents in which personal belongings were taken or used without their owners' consent.[6] Unlike the looting that occurred as part of nation-building projects discussed by Alice Goff and Bonnie Effros in this volume, the American Civil War was not a conflict between sovereign nations. When eleven of the thirty-three United States seceded from the Union, the U.S.

government did not recognize these "Confederate States of America" as a nation but rather as Southern states in rebellion. At the heart of secession lay the institution of slavery, upon which the Southern economy and society was based. The roots of war lay in decades-long political arguments and compromises related to slavery and its expansion into new territories acquired by the United States. Cultural conflict, too, was brewing, as a growing, predominantly Northern antislavery movement vocalized moral and religious opposition to human bondage. In fiery speeches, secessionists emphasized the right to own human property, the right to expand slavery into new territories, the balance between free and slave states, resistance to a centralized government, and an ardent belief in states' rights. In the wake of an attack on federal Fort Sumter, President Abraham Lincoln called up Northern militia and volunteers to quash the rebellion in order to preserve the union. What many believed would be a short contest turned into a full-scale war—a war not only to restore the union but also to end slavery. Many Northerners viewed the South as an aggressor, expressing a desire to punish Confederates for having drawn the nation into this bloody war. Property—humans, land, and movables—took center stage.

Within this context, people grappled with the blurry boundaries of ownership, theft, and violation. Those boundaries were all the more muddled because the war itself entailed a redefinition of the relationship between people and property through debates over confiscation and the destruction of the institution of American slavery. As legal historian Daniel Hamilton shows, competing property ideologies were tested and negotiated within the broader context of the United States and Confederate confiscation programs that allowed for enemy citizens' private property to be seized.[7] In 1862, the U.S. Army firmly situated the emancipation of enslaved people within this context of property, declaring them "contraband of war" that could be confiscated from states in rebellion.

Human property and movable property were further linked because the looting of houses by Northern troops and enslaved people's self-emancipation often occurred in tandem. In such circumstances, slave-owning Southerners experienced the theft of their belongings as part of the larger loss of their economic status as slaveholders. The freeing of people likely influenced Union soldiers' perspectives on the theft of material objects. Indeed, some soldiers referenced "liberating" Southerners of their possessions, using language typically employed in describing the emancipation of enslaved people to reference material objects. In such a context, a stolen teapot was but one part of a much broader redistribution of Southern property and declining economic status.

Typically considered within a framework of disputes over "total war" and "hard war," studies that address Civil War–era theft focus on the destructiveness and after-effects of looting and loss.[8] More recently, that conversation has shifted to include the deleterious effects of war on Southern infrastructure and the environment.[9] As this chapter shows, however, looting is not always best described in terms of destruction or legality. The *threat* of looting had profound effects on the material world, resulting in not only the movement of thousands of people and their possessions but also the creation—and creative reuse—of objects that were designed to prevent the loss of one's monetary and emotional valuables. People built new lives using looted objects. They acquired luxuries that they could not otherwise afford. Some people used stolen objects to physically document slavery's horrors, while others donated objects to historical societies prior to the war's end. Soldiers on both sides disregarded military regulations that prohibited looting, and they were motivated by as many reasons as there were men: a quest to obtain battlefield souvenirs and relics; to boost morale by sending relics to loved ones; to destroy symbols of the planter elite; to exact revenge. Some simply saw objects that they liked and took them.[10]

Found. Taken. Obtained. Appropriated. The language looters used to describe their actions suggests that they were engaged in an effort to understand theft within this broader context of liberating and appropriating. Rarely did looters use terminology of theft or looting in describing the objects they stole. How then should historians reference actions that led to the redistribution of possessions during wartime? The use of the term *looting* suggests a moral condemnation of the act, yet referencing objects as having simply been "taken" denies the validity of the experience of violation felt by many who lost their possessions. Historical actors themselves offered no clear consensus, as their attitudes varied depending on their relationship to the objects taken. Some expressed ethical and moral opposition to the practice. People whose objects were stolen used language of violence—bodies were "peeled" or "stripped," houses were "ransacked" and "pillaged." Formerly enslaved people who took objects with them when they emancipated themselves did so with the understanding that they had earned the right to those objects through their forced labor, exercising the rightful claiming of property for which they had worked. The range of ways in which those who took objects and those whose objects were taken—the verbs they used to describe those actions—suggests that, in the midst of war, Americans were defining a language of looting that centered on the reassignment of property. Preserving the historicity of that experience requires employing the language of looting, appropriating, and taking as it pertains to the perspective of the historical actors.

Exploring the theft of objects from both bodies and houses, this chapter re-situates wartime theft in the context of the politics of everyday life and highlights the embodied experience of wartime looting and the ways in which material life was altered by such actions. This research draws on a broad range of material objects, including household decorative arts, clothing, accessories, tintypes, and scraps of fabric, examining them alongside photographs, prints, newspapers, diaries, correspondence, memoirs, and military records. The materiality of objects shaped their itineraries as hidden, looted, and destroyed objects. This is not to say that the objects were always causal forces or that they did things "instead of" humans but rather that their physical qualities enabled and placed limits on their portability, and the social value they created and stored contributed to their desirability.[11] Objects, as Leora Auslander argues, have effects in the world—communicative, emotive, expressive, performative, and, as this chapter shows, at times violent and dangerous effects.[12] In the context of looting, such objects ranged from the small portable tintype taken from a pocket to the bulky piano that was destroyed when it could not be shipped. Both bodies and houses were material sites through which nineteenth-century Americans confronted the ravages and opportunities created by war.

Bodies

On February 13, 1864, the New York City–based *Frank Leslie's Illustrated Newspaper* published a front-page illustration entitled, "Rebel Soldiers after Battle 'Peeling' (i.e. Stripping) the Fallen Union Soldiers—From a Sketch by an Officer." In the foreground, a soldier pulls the shirt off of a dying man, while another removes a man's boots. At the center, a man yanks the pants off of a dead soldier whose body is suspended in the air. One can imagine his lifeless body jerking as the Confederate tugs on the pant legs. The newspaper's assessment of this "pitiable scene" is evident in the portrayal of the Confederates—the visible faces are sinister; the man in the foreground to the right has an almost animal-like appearance. In the background, one man pulls on a soldier's pants, while another pulls off his coat, tugging the body between them as if it were any other object. Two other men converse while one is engaged in stripping a body, showing no emotion for the dead man.

After battles, officers in both armies commanded soldiers to gather items that would be useful to the army, including guns and ammunition. In the process, soldiers often stripped enemy bodies of uniforms, shoes, and personal effects. Historians have generally explained such acts as evidence of Confederate desperation for supplies and a breakdown of order.[13] Some Confederates were, indeed, poorly supplied and *did* require new clothing. However, as evidenced by the discovery of Confederate Charley Wheat's body—stripped to the underwear and covered in mud—Union soldiers, too, stole clothing from dead men. The broad range of objects taken from bodies defies an explanation centered on need. Among items donated to the Confederate Museum specifically identified as having been taken from a dead man's body were a tin cup, a pipe, a daguerreotype, a watch, a breastplate, and a holster.[14] While most of these items had practical uses, they were objects of convenience, rather than necessity. Furthermore, as the example of the daguerreotype suggests, not all objects taken from the dead had obvious uses for the living.

Relic hunting on Civil War battlefields began immediately after battles or significant events, such as the final surrender that ended the war. As historian Teresa Barnett so accurately points out, it is important to note the "sheer mass of objects the fighting left behind."[15] Both civilians and soldiers tramped through the field, picking up torn flags, tent cloth, artillery shells, canteens, pocket diaries, and *cartes de visite*.[16] Those bits and pieces of the battlefield were sent home in letters and packages to family members—as mementos of war, objects that stored its memory. This traffic in objects helped to shape collective memories of the war.[17] That Charley Wheat's tintype was ultimately donated to a museum is evidence of such memory at work.

Although they might have obtained the same objects, there was an important distinction between the actions of relic hunters who picked up items from the ground and those who obtained their finds by searching dead and dying men's pockets. Words describing such stripping do not capture its corporeality. To take a dead man's clothes did not simply involve retrieving an abandoned coat from the ground. It required pulling off the man's gear, unbuttoning the coat, pants, and suspenders; reaching into the pockets and sifting through letters, knives, and trinkets. It meant wrestling to remove clothing from a body whose limbs had begun to stiffen in the process of rigor mortis.

Battlefield looting had important cultural and political implications for the men involved, raising critical questions about the sanctity of the body. The manner in which dead and wounded bodies were treated was critical for cultural, emotional, and practical reasons. As Drew Faust suggests, when it came to treatment of the dead "humanity, not just particular humans, was at stake." For Protestants, "redemption and resurrection of the body were understood as physical, not just metaphysical realities, and therefore the body . . . preserved a 'surviving identity'" that required "sacred reverence and care."[18] Treating the dead with disregard was debasing for both the dead and the living. As one soldier wrote, "They were stripped to the skin by our Soldiers who have long since lost all delicacy on the subject."[19]

Stripping bodies threatened to blur subject-object relations. In describing acts of stripping and rifling through pockets, *Leslie's Illustrated* used the term *peeling*—a word that would have been read by contemporaries with a dual meaning in mind. On the one hand, *peeling* is a term historically used to refer to robbing a person of their possessions, or seizing goods by means of violence. On the other, the term described—and evoked the image of—paring away the skin of a fruit (as it would for us), peeling tree bark, or removing an animal's hide. Indeed, in describing the process of peeling the clothing from a dead body, soldiers themselves made comparisons to skinning animals. One Confederate admitted, "I can't imagine how to illustrate the scene, but it did present something similar to a fellow drawing the hide off of a squirrel to see them, one fellow holding him at the head and the other at his feet, drawing off his overcoat."[20] Such comparisons heightened the tangibility of stripping those men's clothing, but describing men in the context of skinning animals may also have been a subconscious effort to categorize the soldiers' bodies as nonhuman, to distance the peeled body from the man whose soul had departed.

The reduction of human bodies to objects was central to the 1940s total war described by Brandon Schechter and the extermination of Jewish prisoners discussed by Noah Benninga in this volume. Civil War soldiers, however, expressed a great deal of angst about the reduction of humans to objects, struggling with how to think of the battlefield dead. One soldier wrote: "All the Yank dead had been stripped of every rag of their clothing and looked like hogs that had been cleaned."[21] Some soldiers would not, or could not, relegate the dead human body to the status of a thing or object. Nevertheless, men described "wandering soldiers rifling their persons of all valuables."[22] While some sought out items of monetary value, others seized overcoats, canteens, pants, jackets, and shirts. One man bragged to those at home that he had "made a pretty good Hall off the Yanks," having "Captured . . . one pair of fine shoes pocket books & knifes."[23] Likewise, his brother was proud to have "captured a fine Yankey over coat" that he intended to wear.[24]

Few soldiers reflected on what it meant to wear a dead man's clothes. In the mud and mire of many soldiers' lives, it may have made little difference. Yet others seem to have been haunted or repulsed by the experience. As Noah Benninga shows of sartorial practices in Auschwitz-Birkenau, some prisoners commented on obtaining clothing through a material surplus created by the murder of other prisoners. Similarly, one imagines that when pulling on a dead man's coat, a Civil War soldier might have considered how he obtained it. Confederate Alexander Hunter, for instance, was proud of the coat he wore. So proud, in fact, that he later donated his coat to the Smithsonian Institution. The coat was that of a dead man, but Hunter did not steal it—the dead man's sister gave it to him.[25]

In contrast, another soldier was repulsed when he discovered that his secondhand pocket watch was looted from a dead man's body. Charles Pluemacher purchased a watch after the war and had his initials engraved in it. In describing the purchase, he explained: "I bought a watch without knowing where it came from, but was told later by comrades of the very thief that this time piece had been stolen from an officer . . . at the battle of Antietam." He inquired further about the officer's identity and how he died—he was shot down "only 16 paces from the cannons mouth."[26] Underlying Pluemacher's statement was the knowledge that the Virginia officer would have been severely wounded, possibly mutilated. The soldier who stole the watch likely rifled through the bloody pockets of a man whose inner organs were exposed. Disgusted, Pluemacher never wore the watch again, eventually attempting to atone for what he considered a disgraceful act by sending the watch to the governor of the state of Virginia, not knowing the original owner's name.[27] Although both Pluemacher and Hunter owned and used articles taken from a dead man's body, they had opposite reactions to that experience. That contrast suggests that what mattered to their sensibilities was *how* those objects of personal adornment had been obtained—whether they had been removed lovingly by a sister or seized from the bloody pockets of a soldier maimed by a cannonball.

Stripping or looting the pockets of bodies that lay on the battlefield had devastating consequences for many families. With the burial process often taking days after battle, many men's bodies had decayed beyond recognition. Some soldiers wrote their names inside their clothing, likely to make them easier to identify when they were laundered, but such names could also be relied upon to pass on information to family members about a soldiers' fate. Letters and papers in jacket pockets, knapsacks, and haversacks provided clues about a soldier's identity, addresses for loved ones, and mementos to send home. Insignia on hats identified the companies and regiments from which men hailed, if not their names. When these items were stolen—the letters, the coats, the knapsacks, the hats—a body could remain unidentified. One Fredericksburg woman reported that "all the clothes had been stripped from the bodies of the Union soldiers," and the only clothing that could be identified were "three soldier caps, bearing the numbers '131 P.V.'"[28] The burial party did not recover their remains for over a week. In circumstances such as these, families might never know the fate of fallen soldiers. The "peeling" of their bodies had erased their ability to be identified—and therefore their identities themselves.

Tramping through battlefields in search of dead men's possessions further blurred already dubious boundaries of war front and home front. Elite women's writing suggests that although they recognized that the Southern home front was often the battlefield, they nevertheless expected soldiers to exercise decorum when interacting with white, female civilians. But soldiers took the acts of looting to which they had become accustomed on the battlefield into the homes of Southern civilians. As historian Lisa Frank has argued, the methods soldiers employed in ransacking houses must be read as part of a "concerted effort to wage a gendered form of warfare" against Southern femininity and domesticity.[29]

The threat of looting affected women's corporeal experience of war. Southern women's belief in the sanctity of their own bodies meant that they used their persons to thwart looting soldiers. Many women hid their valuables on their persons and in their bedrooms, believing, as Frank argues, that the "feminine sphere was off limits to invaders" and assuming that "anything on their body would remain untouched."[30] The expectation that many elite Southern women drew upon in hiding valuables on their persons—that men would not violate the personal space of the body—had, however, proved moot when it came to men's bodies on the battlefield.

The experience of hiding valuables beneath skirts was class-based, both in terms of the items hidden and the manner in which it was done. The experience of clanking silver hidden under one's dress required both objects of value and the fashion to conceal them. Some women described tying objects to the steel hoops of cage crinolines, allowing the objects to dangle from the hoop. Although made from steel, these graduated hoops were necessarily thin and incapable of supporting a significant amount of weight. Hiding several objects required an alternative approach, such as that taken by Susan Blackford, who, at the news of the Union army's impending arrival, gathered up the family's silver into the legs of a pair of her husband's long underwear, "tying up each leg at the ankle and buckling the band around my waist" so that the objects hung under the crinoline.[31]

A material culture of improvisation and the repurposing of old dress practices emerged in response to the threat of looting. Some women turned to the use of an outdated article of women's dress: the pocket. A large, flat bag, the pocket was tied around a woman's waist and worn underneath the crinoline.[32] By the 1840s, dress patterns show the incorporation of pockets sewn into the seams of skirts, but working-class women continued to wear pockets that tied around the waist. Elite women's attempts to preserve the material trappings of their social status, then, involved both the resurrection of an old dress practice and the use of what was, by then, a largely lower-class accessory.

The physical weight of the pockets women hid under their dresses was a material reminder of the threat of looting and conflict; the experience was laden with emotion and often anxiety. Fear of discovery when walking in

the presence of soldiers with metal valuables beneath their skirts motivated women to devise ways to silence the clanking. Some women sewed
small pockets into the pocket, employing a long-used construction technique that offered extra protection for fragile objects.[33] One Richmond
family, for instance, had both a fabric pocket and a "money belt" made
from basic, unbleached utilitarian cotton fabric.[34] Circular rust stains of
various sizes and snipped threads evidence the sewing of coins of various denominations into the fabric.[35] In contrast, Susan Blackford's sister
unstitched "some flannel strips, which decorated her homespun linsey bal-
moran skirt" and sewed coins into the dress fabric itself.[36]

Anticipating the Union army's arrival, Emily LeConte was "hastily
making large pockets to wear under my hoopskirt" because she believed
that "they will hardly search our persons."[37] LeConte and other women
who donned pockets expressed a confidence in soldiers' adherence to gender conventions that privileged the sanctity of their white, female bodies.
White and black women were raped and assaulted during this war, but
these elite white women seem not to have widely assumed that bodily rape
would accompany war, as compared to later conflicts. Instead, they used
rhetoric of rape to reference the physical destruction and violation Sherman's army might bring.[38] Weeks before she asserted that soldiers would
not search her person, LeConte wrote: "Not one house, he [General Sher-
man] says, shall be left standing, and his licentious troops—whites and
negroes—shall be turned loose to ravage and violate."[39] When the army
passed through, another woman declared: "There was no place, no chamber, trunk, drawer, desk, garret, closet, or cellar that was private to their
unholy eyes."[40] While their gender may have protected many women from
the theft of objects on their bodies endured by men (both living and dead),
it did not exempt them from the experience of looting altogether. Fear of
violation and attempts to avoid such theft and destruction affected the
experience and aesthetics of everyday life—of both civilians and soldiers.

Houses

In the 1860s, the movement of people—elite and poor, black and white—
and their possessions throughout the South was vast, significantly altering
the material culture and daily routines of people's lives. Roughly 250,000

white refugees fled their homes to avoid Union invasion, often preceded by the forced relocation of enslaved people.[41] The ability to ship, store, and hide valuables—even to flee one's home—was significantly divided along class lines. Elite families could afford, at least for a time, to rent rooms or houses in locations further south or inland; they owned furniture, silver, and other luxury items unnecessary for daily life that could be turned into cash; and they had the connections and money to secure space for storage or shipment on trains and ships. Some had family and connections in Northern states willing to receive shipments of their belongings. One New Orleans woman shipped her carpets and curtains to New York and her silver and smaller valuables to other areas of the Confederacy, while she remained in occupied New Orleans.[42]

While many elites preemptively relocated, non-elite families fled the armies' path when their homes were under imminent or direct threat—by either Union or Confederate soldiers. Before they left, some buried their belongings on their property or entrusted their care and protection to those they enslaved, while others took as many items with them as possible. "Every train that leaves our depot for the interior" of South Carolina or Georgia, a Charleston observer noted, "is gorged with refugee families and their furniture and effects."[43] Writing from Macon, Georgia, another man described beginning "at night to pack our piano and furniture so as to be ready to pack our [rail] *Car* on Monday, having chartered a car to carry the whole of the house and store furniture" to Atlanta.[44] When the evacuation of towns and cities occurred with minimal warning, a glut of belongings and people were hastily crowded into train cars and crammed into wagons.[45] Some people could not escape quickly enough. When Union soldiers arrived in one port city, they found the town deserted, and yet "still there was much private property about, some in scows on the wharf, ready to be removed."[46]

A photograph entitled "Refugees Leaving the Old Homestead," depicts one family's departure, their belongings packed to a precarious height.[47] The house they are leaving has a broken window, the missing panes stuffed with a wad of fabric. A woman sits on the driver's seat of a wagon with broken boards, striped bedding beneath her. Ladder-back chairs with woven seats—one in need of repair—are piled into the wagon, as is a braided rug and a woven basket, all of which suggest that the family was of a lower- or middle-class background. Additional items made from cloth—which could be difficult and expensive to acquire in the blockaded South—can also be seen. The women wear multiple layers of clothing, perhaps for warmth but also as a means of carrying additional items. The photograph evidences both the type of belongings people chose to take with them as well as the mode of transportation at their disposal, pointing to the very real limitations the material objects themselves placed on the number and type of belongings that could be transported. What was deemed "valuable" depended largely upon one's economic circumstances. Elite Southerners, for instance, typically included silver, china, silks, and paintings among their valuables. In making choices about what they could take with them, people selected family heirlooms, items that retained the most monetary value and therefore could be sold and turned into cash if necessary, and items for survival and comfort, including clothing and bedding.

Lacking time or resources to move to another location, families devised a variety of ways to hide their belongings. Confederate nurse Kate Cumming described a hospital's flurry of activity when the arrival of Union soldiers appeared imminent:

> A wagon was loaded with all the valuables and sent to parts unknown. We had valises packed with a few clothes, and baskets filled with provisions, in case we should be compelled to take to the woods.[48]

Like these hospital workers, many families sought to hide their possessions in wooded areas, buried in the ground, hidden in logs, concealed in a spring, or carried away from the house by enslaved people who were tasked with guarding them.[49] Floorboards in slave cabins were pulled up and attic spaces opened, to be filled with items of value—sentimental and monetary. The Bradford family hid valuables with the help of two enslaved people—Adeline and Jordan—who "dug pits in unlikely places; secreted some small articles in hollow trees; hid the oil paintings under the floor of Adeline's own house; carefully wrapped the family portraits and put them in the loft above her head."[50] Items that could not be easily replaced were also hidden, as in the case of a bolt of cloth that was forgotten beneath the floorboards of a North Carolina house and rediscovered years later.[51]

The departure and arrival of vast numbers of people resulted in a marked change in the daily workings and appearance of towns, cities, and plantations. One man invoked the imagery of "stripping" Charleston of its inhabitants and possessions in referencing the departure of people: "The city is stripping for the terrible wrestle in which, sooner or later, if the war lasts, it must engage . . . Already one cannot walk in the streets without noticing the change that the last month has wrought."[52] Some towns were abandoned for the duration of the army's presence in a particular area, while the population of others remained limited until war's end. Such desertion meant a dramatic change in the appearance of some towns, not to mention challenges to the local economy, and resulted in a built environment of shuttered, vacant—although not always empty—houses.

In seeking out areas of safety for themselves, Southerners who could afford to do so attempted to place their valuables and furniture in storage. Columbia, South Carolina, doubled in population and became a central storage site for Charlestonians' possessions, including silver, jewelry, paintings, and books.[53] Indeed, so much furniture was stored in Columbia that one Confederate officer advertised: "Any refugee having furniture stored where it is liable to injury, will greatly accommodate a prominent officer residing in Columbia by allowing it to be removed to his residence, where it will be properly cared for and preserved."[54] Less than one month later, Columbia burned, likely destroying that officer's house, as well as the furniture stored throughout the city.

The threat of looting could be a daily, corporeal experience for inhabitants of areas through which armies frequently passed. While some families buried their valuables indefinitely, others hid them only when news arrived of soldiers' approach. Although not as disruptive as refugee life, hiding valuables resulted in a marked change in both the movement and aesthetics of everyday life. Walking through the halls after the family's valuables had been buried, Susan Bradford observed that the "walls look bare with only the big mirrors to break the broad expanse." Mealtimes were also markedly different at the Bradford plantation. "We will eat off of vari-colored plates and dishes," she wrote. "The set of French china and all the cut glass are boxed and buried." As the silverware was packed, her father "mournfully" announced: "Fingers were made before knives and forks," suggesting that the absence of fine tableware was a significant impediment to maintaining his sense of civility.[55] Such inconveniences seem trivial, but with furnishings removed, a house could seem foreign and thus serve as a daily reminder of the circumstances of war. As one woman wrote, "We have a most unsettled feeling—with carpets up, curtains down, and the rooms without furniture."[56]

When families retrieved objects hidden out of fear of looting, were those objects the same afterward? Or did the process of hiding and surviving change their meanings and associations? "Various methods were resorted to save jewelry & other valuables," Henrietta Macbeth wrote in a letter. "Among others, I just took a silver cup, filled it with rings, watches, etc., and buried it just below the middle of the bottom step as I sat there."[57] When she returned to her burned plantation, Macbeth found the buried jewelry and silver still intact, including a silver sugar bowl and cream pitcher made in 1799. Engraved with "FE," these London-made, Federal-style silver pieces were important possessions that stored and performed a familial history of wealth and refinement.[58] But how would the Macbeths have viewed these items and the jewelry hidden in them once they were retrieved from the ground? Although the Macbeths did not leave a record detailing their reactions, one imagines that the survival of the silver seemed remarkable amidst the ruins of their burned plantation; they must have registered relief that it had survived, and yet, each time the silver was used to serve tea, it was likely also a reminder of all that was lost in the war. Indeed, the story of the silver's concealment and reclamation has been passed down through generations.

Efforts to preserve valuables also resulted in the damage and even loss of material objects. In their hurry to conceal clothing, books, and silver, people did not consider the potentially damaging effects of soil and moisture. One woman recalled: "My aunts dug holes and put into them their silver and watches, which, when they took them up, they found seriously injured by being soaked in water."[59] In other instances, the location of valuables was lost when the person who had buried them died. Meanings developed during wartime could replace earlier associations due to the intensity of the experience of looting. In such circumstances, while the Macbeth's silver remained physically the same, the memories it bore shifted from wealth and genealogy to those of wartime struggle. Experiences were also encoded in the materiality of the objects themselves—in the watch that no longer kept time, the stain on a favorite dress, or the warped binding of a book. In such instances, a single object might carry both stories of survival and loss.

While the Macbeths returned to find their home demolished, those houses standing in key locations, including ports, battlefields, "contraband" camps, and occupied towns were frequently seized and re-appropriated. In many instances the houses were put to entirely new uses. Bedrooms became the living quarters for an entire family, a pair of schoolteachers, or multiple soldiers. The parlors and dining rooms in which white families had entertained and enslaved people were compelled to serve were used as hospitals, schools, and soldiers' quarters.[60] When elite white Southerners fled their houses, their homes and furnishings might be used without their consent.

Some Union soldiers asserted that by inciting the conflict, Southerners had brought upon themselves the destruction or occupation of their houses. Others implied that by vacating their houses, the owners proved their complicity in the rebellion. As Union soldier David Day wrote upon arriving in hastily evacuated Newbern, North Carolina: "We are nicely settled in the fine mansions of the lordly fugitives, who but yesterday ruled these spacious homes and paced the pictured halls. What strange infatuation, bordering on insanity, must have possessed these people, to bring this terrible calamity of war upon themselves, thus becoming voluntary exiles and strangers from their homes and property."[61] Using terms of "voluntary exile" and "strangers from their property" while also delighting at the newfound comforts of his quarters, Day implied that by choosing to leave and by their very identity as Southerners, the former inhabitants had nullified their ownership of this house and its furnishings. Similarly, Union soldier Edmund Miles wrote that he "could not but feel sorry for those deluded ones who had left such nice homes & for all I know their all, to go and fight against their best friends, and try and overthrow this government which has vouchsafed to them such property in the past."[62] Miles implied that rebelling against the United States government, which had previously protected property ownership, invalidated expectations for that property's protection. Both Miles and Day marveled at the social status forfeited when the families departed.

Many scholars have pointed out that slave owners were naive to assume that enslaved people would loyally remain on plantations to protect their masters' belongings. Although some did remain and defend that property, others emancipated themselves, frequently taking both their own belongings and those that they had been tasked to guard, ranging from furniture to architectural elements. Little attention has been paid to the contested nature of the material culture and the embodied experience of freedom enacted through it. Indeed, it is telling that one historian suggests that African Americans "occasionally took souvenirs from white people . . . even as most bondsmen were primarily concerned with escaping bondage."[63] Numerous soldiers commented on former slaves' use of their enslavers' belongings. "The negroes had removed and secreted in their quarters most of the furniture that had been left by their masters," observed one man.[64] A photograph of a barge filled with furniture and textiles has been described as former slaves with their possessions leaving Richmond, Virginia.[65] However, some of those belongings were likely newly acquired from wealthier homes, including two matching glass-paned cabinets—items that would have commanded a considerable price when they were initially purchased.

In Mitchelville, South Carolina, refugees built new lives for themselves with belongings carried from their enslaved homes, items taken from white Southerners' abandoned houses, secondhand Northern goods, and military castoffs. Objects depicted in the yard and found during archaeological digs suggest that refugees possessed a range of items that were likely taken from plantation houses. Among these may have been the sash and paned windows fitted into their self-built houses made from wood that was in part repurposed from slave cabins and plantation houses. The fancy jewelry, soup tureen, and colorful, transfer-printed ceramics uncovered during an excavation, as well as a slat back chair in the foreground of one photograph, may also have been owned by a former master.[66] Far from being "souvenirs," such chairs, cabinets, windowpanes, textiles, and ceramics were the pieces from which free life was, in part, being constructed.

Even as they fled, white refugees were anxious about their homes and their belongings, often hoping to hear news of them. Judith McGuire described the uncertainty and fear that accompanied leaving one's home, emphasizing not simply the monetary value of the furnishings left behind but also the historical and familial value of those things: "Oh, that I could know what is going on in those walls, all encompassed by armies as it is. With my mind's eye I look into first one room and then another, with all the associations of the past; the old family Bible, the family pictures, the library, containing the collection of forty years, and so many things which seemed a part of ourselves. What will become of them? Who are now using or abusing them?"[67] Bound up in these material goods were both memories and personal identity—"so many things," McGuire emphasized, "which seemed a part of ourselves." She expressed concern for the furnishings themselves, asking, "What will become of them?" But underlying this was a more pressing question: What would become of the identity she had bound up in those objects if they were lost? And even if they were not lost, how might the significance of, and memories stored by, those objects be altered knowing that others might have "used"—or "abused"—them?

In focusing on the destruction of looting, bonfires, and soldiers' quick abandonment of their loot, historians have passed over the less dramatic but perhaps more powerful stories looted objects have to tell. As objects change hands, the meanings and associations that they store also change. The manner in which the exchange happens—by theft, purchase, or gift— has important implications. As Alice Goff and Bonnie Effros show, such meanings could be instilled at the level of the state, but such appropriation also occurred at an intimate level. While the stolen, now absent object was no longer in the material possession of its owner, the owner continued to hold a memory of that object. As Judith McGuire described, possessions and houses could be revisited through the "mind's eye."

minds eye

Functional and decorative items that were buried, packed away, or lost entirely were removed from daily use, profoundly affecting everyday movements. Daily routines were in disarray when one dressed without a corset; ate on earthenware instead of china; sat on a foreign, wooden chair instead of an upholstered settee; or lacked a piano for entertainment. The absence of such objects affected the experience and aesthetics of everyday life. These small discomforts spoke to the depth of change then taking place in the war-torn South, forcing the elite to come to terms with declining social and economic status and the destruction of the institution of slavery upon which it had been based. But what did those objects mean to those who stole them?

The objects that made their way North via knapsacks, boats, and mailed packages have generally been categorized as the results of trophy hunting, which is itself an elastic term. However, while scraps of upholstery taken from the "Rebel senate chamber" were mementoes by which to establish one's presence at a particular event, other objects had much more than antiquarian meaning for recipients who incorporated them into their families' daily lives.[68]

Kate Cumming implicated Northern women's social aspirations in the looting of Southern homes, charging them with plaguing soldiers with insistent requests for looted objects. "I do not suppose the men would rob us as they do," she asserted, "if they were not incited by the importunities of their women." Elaborating, Cumming wrote: "Many letters, taken from dead Federals on the battle-fields, contain petitions from the women to send them valuables from the South. One says she wants a silk dress; another, a watch; and one writer told her husband that now was the time to get a piano, as they could not afford to buy one."[69] In each of these instances, the desire to improve one's social status through the possession of status objects was cited as a motivating factor in women's requests. Like the Red Army soldiers discussed by Brandon Schechter who seized hard-to-find consumer goods, Civil War–era soldiers and civilians were motivated to steal by the possibility of owning objects of luxury and status. While the Red Army invited soldiers to loot through parcel shipment policies, however, the U.S. Army attempted to prohibit such shipments of stolen goods.

The desire to obtain objects that would elevate the social status of their families motivated some soldiers to steal, package, carry, or otherwise plan for objects to reach their loved ones at home. In July 1863, Corporal Frederic Gibson arrived at the home of Elizabeth Miles in Cambridge, Massachusetts, carrying a small package with him sent by her husband who was then in Louisiana. Unwrapping the package, Elizabeth found a small, silver-plated vessel and a letter from her husband, Edmund, explaining that it was "a present for you. . . . I think you will prize it, as I obtained it from one of the rebel houses which we burnt up above Alexandria on our recent campaign" in Louisiana.[70]

In a style that suggests it was made in the 1830s or 1840s, the vessel has an elliptically shaped body and a distinctive cast pear-shaped finial. Although the spout and handle give it the appearance of a teapot, the handle lacks separators to prevent the conduction of heat, and the vessel itself is small compared to other American-made teapots from this time period. Altogether, it is a rather odd object that raises questions about whether it was altered at some point in its history or served a purpose other than that of a typical teapot.

Figure 4.2. Silver-plated teapot by an unidentified maker. Edmund Miles took
this small silver-plated teapot from a house outside Alexandria, Louisiana, in 1863.
Miles sent it to his wife, who had it engraved with the inscriptions "Taken from
a rebel's house in Louisiana" and her name, "Elizabeth Miles." Collection of the
Massachusetts Historical Society, Boston, Massachusetts.

Reading the Mileses' correspondence alongside the teapot suggests
possible reasons for the vessel's peculiar appearance, as well as insight
into Edmund's motivations for stealing it and the meanings ascribed to it
by Elizabeth. In his letter gifting the vessel to her, Edmund wrote, it is "a
silver tea pot, or cream pitcher, I don't care which you call it," suggesting that, he too, was confused by its size and intended function. With the
freedom to call it what she liked, Elizabeth chose to refer to the object
as a teapot. Miles's daughter acknowledged the receipt of the gift, writing, "Gibson brought Mother a letter from you and a very nice little tea
pot. Mother feels quite *big* because she has got a silver teapot." Feeling
"big" or swelled with pride, Elizabeth showed a visitor the teapot, who
offered to "get it all fixed up for her and get her name put on it for her."[71]
The suggestion that the vessel could be "fixed up" suggests that it was
in need of some repair. Elizabeth was glad to have the man take it with
him, and he returned the teapot as promised. Although there is no record
of what precisely was repaired on the vessel, it is reasonable to suggest

that the pot's eccentricities—the pear-shaped finial, the handle in need of separators—may have been added in a Massachusetts silversmithing shop. At any rate, Elizabeth Miles was clearly proud to be the new owner of a "silver teapot." Perhaps it was, as her husband suggested, once only a cream pot.

As the story of the stolen Louisiana teapot suggests, looters and the recipients of looted objects could imbue those stolen objects with new meanings and uses. Edmund Miles—a printer—was not a wealthy man. In 1855, he and Elizabeth lived with their three children in a house with eight adult men and one adult woman, all of whom appear to have been unrelated.[72] Elizabeth Miles, intent on asserting her ownership of the object, had it engraved: "Elizabeth Miles" on one side and "Taken from a Rebel's house in Louisiana" on the other. And she likely felt "big," as her daughter described, because owning a silver teapot was a mark of social distinction that she did not already possess. Indeed, the desire to own such an object may have been enough motivation for her to refute the possibility that it was a cream pot and have repairs made to it so that it would be recognized by visitors, as well as by herself, as a teapot.

Male soldiers are typically associated with looting, yet they were not alone in the search for high-quality possessions. When looting Union soldiers departed a city, Southern civilians, male and female, also took and salvaged objects thrown into the street. As sketches of looting in Fredericksburg, Virginia, suggest, opportunities to do so could be plentiful.

In one illustration, parasols and mirrors lie outside, while a soldier sits in an upholstered rocking chair and another leans against a bureau. It was in this context that a mantle clock was retrieved from a Fredericksburg street where it was left upon the Union army's retreat. Georgian William King suspected that a female acquaintance obtained a "very rich" elaborate marble and mahogany dresser in a similar manner: "a piece of furniture which was probably worth $75. a marked contrast with the rest of her plain & scanty furniture, it occasioned some painful suspicions of the manner in which she became possessed of it."[73] Finer than any of the woman's other furniture, this mahogany dresser spoke to both the woman's own social aspirations and the declining status of those who lost it.

When armies left material chaos behind, others might justify taking objects by asserting that the objects' destruction was imminent or its owners unidentifiable. As civilians salvaged mahogany bureaus, chairs, and

Figure 4.3. Pencil sketch by Arthur Lumley, "Halt of Wilcox's Troops in Caroline Street Prevous to Going in to Battle," December 13, 1862. Prior to the Battle of Fredericksburg in December 1862, Union soldiers looted houses, dragging furniture and other possessions into the streets. Courtesy of the Library of Congress Prints and Photographs Division, Washington, D.C.

clocks from the streets of looted cities and soldiers looted abandoned houses, the anonymity of former owners could make it easier to incorporate such objects into their own homes; they might consider their theft more as taking advantage of an opportunity and less as outright pillaging. Indeed, taking the silver-plated vessel from the "Rebel's house in Louisiana" likely seemed a small infraction—perhaps even an act of salvage—to Edmund Miles as he and his fellow soldiers set fire to the house itself and witnessed the emancipation of human property. In this context, the redistribution of people's possessions contributed to a broader unsettling of the social order and the prestige that those objects conferred within it.

The American Civil War raised important questions about what it meant to steal or own an object. When Judith McGuire left her home, she carefully packed away her belongings and furniture, locking them in bureaus and behind doors. She thought the locks were inviolable. Two years later, upon receiving word of the condition of her house from a friend, McGuire was irate. Her house was being used simultaneously as a hospital, quarters for surgeons' families, and the headquarters of a Union officer. The officer's wife, Mrs. Newton, "politely invited her [McGuire's friend] into her (!) parlour." Apologizing for the lack of carpeting on the floor, Newton explained that she was just preparing to lay down the carpets because she had only recently "found in a locked room some very nice ones." The parlor curtains were also "ready to be put up." McGuire was furious: "She found them, no doubt, while exploring the third story, for there we left them securely wrapped up to protect them from moths." McGuire implied that Newton had violated the space by exploring and trespassing beyond a locked door. But then she asked a confounding question: "Does she consider these carpets her own?"[74]

It might seem that, in the end, it did not matter whether or not Mrs. Newton considered the carpets her own or that she invited guests into "her (!) parlour," for McGuire would never see them again. But for McGuire, who traversed her former home through the "mind's eye," it *did* matter. The loss of her belongings was all the more bitterly borne as she attempted to imagine how they were being used and by whom. At war's end, she and her husband were looking "around for some other place, in which to build up a home for our declining years. Property we have none—all gone. . . . How few of us have homes!" Those who still did have homes often found that they bore the physical marks of war: shattered windows, bullet-riddled walls, and missing furniture. The floors of houses used as battlefield hospitals were stained from pools of blood that flowed off operating tables.[75] The memory of looting was also there: in the steps under which a woman buried her silver; in the once-buried tureen displayed in a cabinet; in the mahogany bureau that a woman had taken from the street when soldiers left the town.

Looting and the threat of such theft was experienced in a material way—whether through the comfort of sleeping in an abandoned elite house; the weight and clanking of carrying silver under one's skirts; or the discomfort of living without one's usual possessions. It was in this context that a tintype of a young Confederate soldier could be stolen from a stranger's house; be looted from a dead Union stranger's pocket; make its way back to the original owner; and then be described not as having been stolen or looted but rather as having been "lossed in 61" and "found" in 1862. In this single object, we see both Confederate and Union soldiers and civilians engaged in, deeply affected by, and struggling to come to terms with not only the peeling of bodies and the looting of homes but also the role of old, destroyed, and new belongings in their postwar lives.

Notes

I thank Leora Auslander, Tara Zahra, and the contributors to this volume for their helpful comments. A note of thanks is also due to Teresa Barnett for her insights and to Nancy Bercaw, Kathleen Conzen, Ellen Feingold, Thavolia Glymph, Jim Grossman, Katie Knowles, Meghan Titzer, and Margaret Vining. A Committee on Institutional Cooperation-Smithsonian Institution fellowship provided research support.

1. Tintype, C. C. Wheat, American Civil War Museum, Richmond, Virginia; Joseph N. Wheat, Robert E. Lee Camp Confederate Soldiers' Home Applications for Admission, 1884–1941, Library of Virginia, Richmond, Virginia.

2. The background of Wheat's death was recounted by his brother, Joseph Wheat, and later published in the "Do You Remember?" column of the November 7, 1941, issue of the Page County *News and Courier*. Robert H. Moore, "Sesqui'fying April 20, 1862—Luray Learns of Charley Wheat's Fate," *Cenantua's Blog*, April 20, 2012, https://cenantua.wordpress.com/2012/04/20/sesquifying-april-20-1862-an-unpleasant-surprise-in-luray/.

3. As Joan Cashin explains, "Article Fifty-two of the U.S. Articles of War, compiled in 1806 and still in effect during the Civil War, barred 'plunder and pillage.' The article did not define these terms, but common usage as found in the *Oxford English Dictionary* defines plunder as the taking of spoils, especially in time of war, and pillage as the robbing or sacking of a place or a person." Joan E. Cashin, "Trophies of War: Material Culture in the Civil War Era," *Journal of the Civil War Era* 1, no. 3 (2011): 341.

4. See James Q. Whitman, *Verdict of Battle: The Law of Victory and the Making of Modern War* (Cambridge: Harvard University Press, 2012).

5. I use the terminology of "enslaved people" in keeping with recent scholarship on American slavery. While some scholars continue to use the word *slave* to describe African Americans held in bondage, the term *enslaved* acknowledges the legal status of enslavement while maintaining that this status was only one part of an enslaved person's identity. It is particularly important to highlight this distinction when discussing the American Civil War, a moment of transition from enslavement to emancipation.

6. This chapter focuses on personal belongings and will not address the theft and destruction of utilitarian items, such as wagons, or those categorized as "forage," including provisions and livestock.

7. Daniel W. Hamilton, *The Limits of Sovereignty: Property Confiscation in the Union and the Confederacy during the Civil War* (Chicago: University of Chicago Press, 2007), 5.

8. Focusing on the conflicts between soldiers and the people who lived in the path of the armies, earlier studies have been driven in part by the question of whether or not the Civil War was a "total war." Accounts of looting recounted in scholarly works are primarily used as illustrative evidence of the process by which civilian property and morale were destroyed, highlighting the economic losses experienced during Union campaigns, the devastation of Southern agriculture, and the loss of infrastructure. The looting of household goods

is generally depicted as a wartime aberration and used to illustrate Union soldiers' sympathy for, or hostility toward, Southerners. An exception is Joan Cashin's article "Trophies of War," which takes seriously the looting of ordinary household objects. On looting, see Charles Royster, *The Destructive War: William Tecumseh Sherman, Stonewall Jackson, and the Americans* (New York: Knopf, 1991); Mark Grimsley, *The Hard Hand of War: Union Military Policy toward Southern Civilians, 1861–1865* (Cambridge: Cambridge University Press, 1995); Anne J. Bailey, *War and Ruin: William T. Sherman and the Savannah Campaign* (Wilmington, Del.: Scholarly Resources, 2003).

9. See Megan Kate Nelson, *Ruin Nation: Destruction and the American Civil War* (Athens: University of Georgia Press, 2012); Yael Sternhell, *Routes of War: The World of Movement in the Confederate South* (Cambridge: Harvard University Press, 2012).

10. On motivations for looting, see Cashin, "Trophies of War"; Teresa Barnett, *Sacred Relics: Pieces of the Past in Nineteenth Century America* (Chicago: University of Chicago Press, 2013).

11. Bruno Latour, *Reassembling the Social: An Introduction to Actor-Network-Theory* (Oxford: Oxford University Press, 2005), 80, 72.

12. Leora Auslander, "Beyond Words," *American Historical Review* 110, no. 4 (2005): 1017.

13. See, for instance, Drew Faust's description of stripping. Drew Gilpin Faust, *This Republic of Suffering: Death and the American Civil War* (New York: Alfred A. Knopf, 2008), 74–75.

14. *Catalogue of the Confederate Museum, Richmond, Virginia* (Richmond, 1905).

15. Barnett, *Sacred Relics*, 81.

16. *Catalogue of the Confederate Museum, Richmond, Virginia*; Henry Bowditch, "Bowditch Memorial Cabinet Catalog," 1877, Massachusetts Historical Society.

17. Cashin, "Trophies of War," 339.

18. Faust, *This Republic of Suffering*, 61–62.

19. Quoted in Joseph Glatthaar, *General Lee's Army: From Victory to Collapse* (New York: Free Press, 2009), 175.

20. Richard Lewis, *Camp Life of a Confederate Boy* (Charleston: New and Courier, 1883), 37.

21. Quoted in Glatthaar, *General Lee's Army*, 175.

22. Oscar Lawrence Jackson, May 28, 1862, in *The Colonel's Diary: Journals Kept before and during the Civil War by the Late Colonel Oscar L. Jackson* (Sharon, Penn.: Executors Estate of Col. Jackson, 1922), 58.

23. William McFall to Sister, October 9, 1864, William McFall Letters, Stuart A. Rose Manuscript, Archives, and Rare Book Library, Emory University, Atlanta, Georgia.

24. James McFall to Sister, November 21, 1864, McFall Letters.

25. Confederate Shell Jacket worn by Alexander Hunter, National Museum of American History, Smithsonian Institution, Washington, D.C.

26. "Letter from Charles Pluemacher, April 18, 1921" and "Undated statement signed by Charles F. Pluemacher, ca. April 1921," accession file, pocket watch, 0985.13.01468, American Civil War Museum, Richmond, Virginia.

27. "Letter from Charles Pluemacher, April 13, 1921," accession File.

28. Martha Stephens, quoted in Carol Reardon, "The Forlorn Hope: Brig. Gen. Andrew A. Humphreys's Pennsylvania Division at Fredericksburg," in *The Fredericksburg Campaign: Decision on the Rappahannock*, ed. Gary Gallagher (Chapel Hill: University of North Carolina Press, 1995), 106.

29. Lisa Tendrich Frank, "Bedrooms as Battlefields: The Role of Gender Politics in Sherman's March," in *Occupied Women: Gender, Military Occupation, and the American Civil*

War, ed. Lee Ann Whites and Alecia P. Long (New Orleans: Louisiana State University Press, 2009), 36.

30. Frank, "Bedrooms as Battlefields," 33, 40. On this gendered interpretation of male soldiers and female civilians, see Lisa Tendrich Frank, *The Civilian War: Confederate Women and Union Soldiers during Sherman's March* (New Orleans: Louisiana State University Press, 2015).

31. Susan Lee Blackford and Charles Minor Blackford, *Letters from Lee's Army,* ed. Charles Minor Blackford III (Lincoln: University of Nebraska Press, 1998), 281.

32. At the height of its fashion in the eighteenth century, this flat bag was accessed through slits along the seams of skirts and petticoats. Madelyn Shaw and Lynne Z. Bassett, *Homefront & Battlefield: Quilts & Context in the Civil War* (Lowell, Mass.: American Textile Museum, 2012), 154.

33. *The Workwoman's Guide,* 1838, 73.

34. Money Belt and Pocket, c. 1864, The Valentine, Richmond, Virginia.

35. Shaw and Bassett, *Homefront & Battlefield,* 154.

36. Blackford, *Letters from Lee's Army,* 281.

37. Emma LeConte, February 14, 1865, diary transcription, 1864–1865, Southern Historical Collection, University of North Carolina, Chapel Hill, North Carolina.

38. Frank, *Civilian War,* 46.

39. Emma LeConte, December 31, 1864, diary transcription.

40. Quoted in Frank, *The Civilian War,* 102.

41. Sternhell, *Routes of War,* 94, 100.

42. Julia LeGrand Waitz, March 27, 1863, in *The Journal of Julia LeGrand, New Orleans 1862–1863,* ed. Kate Mason Rowland and Agnes E. Croxall (Richmond, Va.: Everett Waddey Co., 1911), 273.

43. "Late Southern News," *New York Times,* June 15, 1862.

44. Samuel P. Richards, September 29, 1861, in *Sam Richards's Civil War Diary: A Chronicle of the Atlanta Home Front,* ed. Wendy Hamand Venet (Athens: University of Georgia Press, 2009), 69.

45. Sarah Morgan Dawson, July 24, 1862, in *A Confederate Girl's Diary* (Boston: Houghton Mifflin, 1913), 128.

46. S. W. Godon to Secretary of the Navy, March 10, 1862, *Report of the Secretary of the Navy, December 1862* (Washington, D.C., 1863), 208.

47. George Barnard, "Refugees Leaving the Old Homestead." (Hartford, Conn.: The War Photograph & Exhibition Co., 1862), Library of Congress, Prints and Photographs Division, Washington, D.C.

48. Kate Cumming, July 15, 1864, in *Kate. The Journal of a Confederate Nurse,* ed. Richard Barksdale Harwell (Baton Rouge: Louisiana State University Press, 1998), 210.

49. Memoir of Mrs. W. B. Dunlap, in *South Carolina Women in the Confederacy,* ed. Mrs. Thomas Taylor and Sallie Enders Conner (Columbia, S.C.: State Company, 1903), 232.

50. Susan Bradford Eppes, February 21, 1865, in *Through Some Eventful Years* (Macon, Ga.: J. W. Burke, 1926), 256.

51. Bolt of Rockfish fabric. North Carolina Museum of History Collections.

52. "Late Southern News," *New York Times,* June 15, 1862.

53. J. Grahame Long, *Stolen Charleston: The Spoils of War* (Charleston, S.C.: The History Press, 2014), 50.

54. "City Items," *The Daily South Carolinian* (Columbia, South Carolina), January 24, 1865.

55. Eppes, February 21, 1865, 256.

56. Judith McGuire, May 15, 1861, in *Diary of a Southern Refugee during the War* (Richmond, Va.: J. W. Randolph & English, 1889), 14.

57. Henrietta Ravenel Macbeth, quoted in Long, *Stolen Charleston*, 57.

58. Macbeth Silver, Charleston Museum, Charleston, South Carolina.

59. Margaret Crawford Adams, in Taylor and Enders, *South Carolina Women in the Confederacy*, 221.

60. Martha Schofield Papers, Southern Historical Collection, University of North Carolina, Chapel Hill, North Carolina.

61. David L. Day, *My Diary of Rambles with the 25th Mass. Volunteer Infantry* (Milford, Mass.: King and Billings, 1884), 47.

62. Edmund Miles Papers, Massachusetts Historical Society, Boston, Massachusetts.

63. Cashin, "Trophies of War," 340.

64. W. T. Truxtun to secretary of the Navy, January 13, 1862, 185.

65. Alexander Gardner, "Richmond, Va. Barges with African Americans on the Canal; Ruined Buildings Beyond," 1865, Library of Congress Prints and Photographs Division, Washington, D.C.

66. Brockington and Associates, "Archaeological Recovery at Mitchelville," December 2013, 163. For more on Mitchelville and the transition to freedom, see Dana Byrd, "Loot, Occupy, and Re-Envision: Material Culture of the South Carolina Plantation," in *The Civil War and the Material Culture of Texas, the Lower South, and the Southwest* (Houston: Museum of Fine Arts, 2012).

67. McGuire, September 12, 1861, in *Diary of a Southern Refugee during the War*, 54–55.

68. "Relics" from the Confederate Capitol, Massachusetts Historical Society, Boston, Massachusetts; Cashin, "Trophies of War," 340.

69. Cumming, July 17, 1864, in *Kate*, 211.

70. Edmund Miles to Elizabeth Miles, July 4, 1863, Miles Papers.

71. Annie Miles to Edmund Miles, July 24, 1863, Miles Papers.

72. Although they do not appear in the 1860 census, it is unlikely that the Mileses' economic status had changed dramatically by 1863; in 1870, they were living as a nuclear family of two adults and four children, but the value of their personal estate was only $500. *Massachusetts State Census for 1855*; "The Late Edmund Miles," *Cambridge Chronicle* (Mass.), January 21, 1899; *1870 Federal Census*.

73. William King, July 14, 1863, diary transcript, Southern Collection, University of North Carolina-Chapel Hill, Chapel Hill, North Carolina, 14–15.

74. McGuire, September 30, 1862, in *Diary of a Southern Refugee during the War*, 160–161.

75. A number of houses, including one at Carnton Plantation in Franklin, Tennessee, and another at Sailor's Creek, Virginia, have bloodstains on their floorboards.

5

EMBODIED VIOLENCE

A Red Army Soldier's Journey as Told by Objects

Brandon Schechter

Virtually everything we know about the man in the accompanying photograph (see figure 5.1) stems from his proficiency in violence. As a soldier in the Red Army's 27th Guards Novobugskaia Red Banner Order of Bogdan Khmel'nitskii Rifle Division, he would eventually become a Full Cavalier of the Order of Glory, a sort of Bolshevik knight, which brought him minor celebrity status that remains to this day.[1] His name is Bato Damcheev, a librarian from Sanaga, a small village in Buriatiia, an ethnic enclave in Siberia. The Soviet state would send him over vast distances during the Great Patriotic War to kill and kidnap its enemies. As the crow flies, he traveled roughly seven thousand kilometers from his hometown to Berlin, where he would be seriously wounded in the last days of the war. When one considers the various detours he took to Stalingrad, Donbas, Odessa, Poznań, and smaller trips such as missions behind enemy lines, to hospitals and the like, he must have covered several thousand kilometers more. According to a biography of Damcheev, as a sniper and later scout he killed nearly ninety German soldiers, took ten more

Figure 5.1. Guards Senior Sergeant B. M. Damcheev, most likely winter or spring 1945, http://www.ww2incolor.com/soviet-union/soviet_1.html.

as "tongues" (prisoners captured for interrogation), and destroyed three tanks and several enemy bunkers.[2] As a Buriat-Mongol, his entry into the heart of the Third Reich was the realization of the Nazis' race-based fears of Eastern "mongoloid hordes" conquering Germany. But Bato Damcheev was not a faceless member of a horde; he was a very skilled, highly decorated, and thoroughly modern Soviet subject serving in what had become a competent and professional army with some of the most effective equipment available.

His medals speak to his accomplishments, forming a text that would have been readable to both his colleagues and Soviet civilians. Decorations identified him as an elite scout, sniper, and Guardsman; showcased his ability to wield violence; and noted battles he had participated in as well as the number and severity of his wounds. These decorations crystallized moments of violence and celebrated the ability to kill and destroy. In a total war, medals were an embodiment of "great esteem," "respect," and "the people's love" that soldiers could only earn in battle, specifically through the act of killing.[3] The weapons and other equipment and the ability to wield them allowed Damcheev and his comrades to survive and preserve the Soviet Union in the largest conflict in world history.

The following chapter takes Bato Damcheev and examines several things that he would have used or acquired during the war in order to show how a particular violent subjectivity was made possible by key material objects (identity booklets, weapons) and embodied in the form of others (medals, trophies). Section one focuses on his body and a discussion of the massive mobilization in which he participated, the ways in which the Soviet state classified and laid claim to soldiers' bodies, specifically how Damcheev's biography may have impacted his fate. Section two examines the weapon Damcheev used to such effect as both a utilitarian and socially relevant object. Section three discusses the decorations that Damcheev and his unit earned, focusing on their multiple meanings and the moments of violence that they celebrated. Section four looks at some of the trophies that Damcheev and his comrades might have taken from their vanquished foe.[4] All of these objects enabled and embodied violence.

This chapter is an exercise in allowing objects to speak for people. Bato Damcheev is its subject because he seems to have left no personal writings, even though he was written about extensively as a war hero. This chapter utilizes recommendations written for his decorations from the Russian

Ministry of Defense Archives, the wartime press, personal writings by other Red Army soldiers about identical objects, and hagiographical texts about Damcheev. Each section draws on objects that were explicitly mentioned in his recommendations, present in his photograph, or so universal as to be unavoidable.[5] In examining these objects, and in objectifying Damcheev himself, we can see how people and objects were used and invested with meaning as well as how these meanings shifted during and after the war.

While there are universal elements to this story (for instance, a massive mobilization, ordinary people becoming war heroes and seeing the world), it is worth noting its particularly Soviet aspects. The Soviet Union nearly collapsed during the war and, in ways similar to its experience of crash industrialization, was forced to rely on volunteerism and coercion during a variety of dramatic shortages rather than on a well-supplied cadre of professionals. Furthermore, the Soviet state was neither a free market nor a democracy, meaning that rather than facing periodic elections and citizens who could mobilize economic resources independently of the state, it possessed the ability to impose legislation at the will of its top leadership and controlled access to goods for its citizens. The combination of shortage and a near-monopoly over distribution positioned the state from the very beginning as the bearer of favors to chosen categories of citizens, leaving others to fend for themselves. During the war, the Soviet leadership, needing defenders, bestowed privileges in direct relationship to one's contributions to the destruction of the enemy (whether by making munitions, commanding military formations, or active killing) and went to great lengths to mark and serve those who successfully did so. In this regard, the meaning of objects is quite different from the other works in this volume. Things are often much more utilitarian, and their distribution to individuals, whether issued by the state or taken as battlefield trophies, was, by 1945, the domain of the state. This stands in contrast to Sarah Weicksel's and Noah Benninga's contributions to this volume, where the violent redistribution of objects happened despite official censure. Unlike Alice Goff and Bonnie Effros's essays, Damcheev's odyssey is not the story of the movement of objects with great symbolic value from one polity to another but rather the creation of new symbols and selves during war.

In becoming an object of the state, mastering weapons, earning medals, and possibly taking trophies, Damcheev transformed from a low-level functionary to a war hero and after the war could use the social capital he had acquired to become a leader of his community. By looking at one soldier through a few of his things, this essay shows how objects constitute the story of Red Army soldiers' dramatic movement and participation in violence during the Great Patriotic War and hint at how these experiences impacted what it meant to be Soviet, detailing how one soldier from the hinterland attained status through successful mastery of violence. But before he could earn medals, the state had to draft Damcheev and millions like him, turning them into usable human capital for the army.

Mobilization

The massive movement of people in the ranks of the Red Army—first from all corners of the Soviet Union to battlefields spanning the Arctic Circle to the Caucus Mountains, then beyond Soviet borders into Europe—was unprecedented. While the period of the Civil War (1918–21) had seen massive displacement, mobility was dramatically curtailed as Bolshevik power solidified. The Soviet Union had been all but hermetically sealed in the 1930s with severe restrictions on the movement of its citizens and a variety of means of forcibly removing and resettling whole categories of people within its borders. Internal passports determined the locations people were permitted to live and the right to move around a complicated hierarchy of spaces requiring various levels of access (border zones, closed cities, capitals, and so forth). Peasants, including Damcheev, did not receive internal passports. The war gave many peasants their first major opportunity to leave the area near where they had been born and was later an absolutely unique opportunity to travel outside of the Soviet Union. However, this travel was far from touristic or idyllic.[6] Their purposes were specific and their itineraries tied to the fate of their unit.

The peripatetic nature of soldiers' lives often included not only travel with their unit but also moves between units. Soldiers often shuffled between units after being wounded, something that could be isolating and demoralizing.[7] The Red Army's concept of how to build morale and unit pride centered on the idea of a "backbone" of commanders and rear-area personnel that would maintain the "traditions" of a unit and integrate newly arrived soldiers, giving privileges, including increased social stability, to elite units and specialists. Damcheev, who was a scout and elite Guardsman, enjoyed these privileges.[8]

The growing presence of "non-Russian" soldiers like Damcheev, most of whom had not been subjected to the regular draft before the war, was in large measure due to the army's massive losses.[9] The expanding need for cadres also meant that déclassé elements and eventually even criminals would be allowed to join the army. For many of these people, serving in the military could mean a dramatic shift in their personal status and greater mobility for their families, as military service lifted restrictions on place of residence and led to the commutation of sentences.[10] For representatives of national minorities, military service meant further integration into the Soviet project.

This wide variety of people had to be turned into useful material for the army. The army reduced a soldier's prewar biography to military metrics. The first pages of the Red Army booklet, the official document that proved a soldier's identity and tied him or her to everything that the state had given them, recorded a soldier's name, place of induction, ethnicity, military specialization, education, occupation, blood type, next of kin, and address. It then listed the sizes and equipment soldiers had been issued and remarks about their service. This document, signed by a soldier's immediate commander and with the official stamp of their unit, stated clearly where a person belonged—the unit that was to serve as the soldier's home as he or she moved thousands of kilometers. It was supposed to have the bearer's photograph as well, but due to camera and film shortages they often did not. Additional pages could be stapled in as needed for those who had served for long periods of time or had distinguished themselves repeatedly, the unit's stamp converting a piece of paper torn from a notebook into an official document. These books turned soldiers into readable, usable components for the army and tied them to all their equipment, medals they had earned and weapons they had been issued, including serial numbers.[11]

Once catalogued and accessioned into the army, soldiers became subject to an extremely harsh disciplinary regime. Treason, which included desertion to the enemy, allowing oneself to be captured, and self-mutilation, was a capital offense; a soldier's punishment could even be extended to his or her family in the form of exile and confiscation of property. Cataloging and harsh discipline effectively allowed the state to take control

over soldiers' bodies, handing them over to their deputies, the commanders, to be used as material to wage war.[12] Losses of equipment such as
machine guns and mortars were tallied alongside human casualties in
battle reports.[13] Commanders gambled with soldiers' lives, risking them
for territory, the destruction of enemy resources, and information. The
objectification of soldiers' lives is universal to all armies, while the draco-
nian discipline of the Red Army and extension of punishment to families
was a Soviet particularity. This is not to imply that the Red Army won the
war because its soldiers were more afraid of their own commanders than
the Germans. Hatred of the enemy grew as Nazi crimes were revealed on
liberated territory and a core group of active supporters of the state, in
particular Komsomol and Party members, sustained the army throughout
the war.[14]

Damcheev was part of this core of active supporters, even if he was
far from the urban, Slavic person imagined as the ideal recruit.[15] He was
a representative of the Buriat ethnic minority that made up only 0.13
percent of the Soviet population, according to the 1939 Census.[16] However, Buriats, the largest indigenous group in Siberia, had been subject
to all of the same processes of social engineering as other Soviet citizens
that aimed to create a new Soviet person and society. Despite his apparent demographic peculiarity, Damcheev was thoroughly Soviet. While one
might have expected him not to speak much Russian given that he hailed
from a national enclave far from the country's center, most educational
instruction in Western Buriatiia was in Russian. Furthermore, quite rare
among Soviet citizens of his generation, he had received eight years of
education.[17] His education, ability to speak Russian, and trustworthiness
as a Komsomol member would all serve him well as the army figured out
what to do with him, as did the fact that he was so far from the front. His
ethnicity may have helped as well, as stereotypes about indigenous Sibe-
rians being excellent hunters could lead them into privileged positions.[18]
Instead of becoming a regular soldier, Damcheev served as an elite sniper-
scout, receiving additional training. Given the nature of their job, scouts
and snipers, who functioned autonomously and often behind enemy lines,
had to be trusted, well-vetted individuals. Ironically, given the overlap in
skill sets, many former criminals would also become scouts, making this
a branch of service in which elite and marginal elements of Soviet society
became intimate friends.[19] Scouts were seldom used as regular soldiers,

but rather primarily used to gather information and to strike high-priority targets in special operations. Their duties kept them near headquarters when they weren't on missions, while in emergency situations they could be sent into counterattacks or used as a last-ditch defense force for a key piece of territory.[20] As a result, their losses tended to be lighter than regular troops, and they helped form the "backbone" of a unit.[21]

His Weapon

Damcheev's special status meant that he was better armed than the average soldier. After brief service as a sniper, Damcheev became a scout, using the most iconic weapon of the war, the PPSh-41 submachine gun.[22] This weapon helps to explain how he became so successful at killing and why he survived. Chances of survival and social status were determined by the position and the weapons used, with soldiers' social lives organized around their weapons. Many Red Army soldiers learned on the job, receiving minimal training before being sent into frontline units during periods of crisis. While soldiers were supposed to be slowly integrated into combat collectives before being sent into battle, they were often sent into combat without basic skills.[23] Massive shortages that came with the Wehrmacht's thrust deep into Soviet territory and the attenuating losses and dislocations of factories, mines, and other resources key to making weapons, ammunition, and everything else soldiers need contributed to heavy losses.[24]

One of the ways that the Soviet state made up for its lack of heavy equipment and training was by fostering volunteerism and emphasizing soldiers' responsibility to master their art. This included a cult of the individual weapon. A soldier's weapon was his or her central tool, often described as his or her "honor and conscience."[25] The *Red Army Booklet* tied soldiers to their weapons, and they could be executed for the loss of their firearms. Many soldiers attributed considerable agency to their weapons. Despite being mass-produced, nearly identical objects, soldiers had very close relationships with their weapons. Each had its own "caprices," and veterans felt uncomfortable with a weapon they had yet to fire.[26] The mechanical failure or incompetent use of a weapon could get a soldier and their comrades killed, while skillful use gave one a chance to survive the terrors of mechanized warfare. Weapons were purpose-defined tools that did more than simply destroy, they allowed for the taking or defense of territory and for the imposition of one's will on the enemy (for instance, pinning them down, forcing them to retreat or surrender).

Soldiers felt immense affection for their arms, writing about them as living beings with personalities and agency. Some remembered the serial numbers of their weapons and wrote about them after the war, one soldier mourning the loss of a submachine gun that took a piece of shrapnel and saved its user's life as if it were a fallen comrade.[27] Another recorded in his diary that his submachine gun was "bored from idleness."[28] Tender words for one's weapon were very common, and many soldiers wrote home about their arms, using terms of friendship or even romantic love, as one soldier coyly wrote that he had met "a pretty special someone"— his submachine gun.[29] Wounded veterans were encouraged to pass their weapons on to a newly arrived soldier in a highly ritualized fashion. An example of this ritual can be seen in the following attempt to inscribe a longer history into a weapon from a propaganda article in which a soldier passes on his submachine gun to a comrade: "Paramonov killed 114 Germans with this weapon. Savushkin killed 121 Germans with it. I vow not to release this weapon from my hands until complete victory over the enemy."[30] These "named weapons" were just one example of the state engendering a sense of responsibility to kill the enemy. The absurdly high number of enemy soldiers that the two previous owners reportedly killed were part of a conscious policy to use shame as a motivating force.

Around the time that Damcheev took his first shot in battle, a major propaganda campaign was underway, titled: "I have killed a German, and you?" In this program, soldiers were encouraged to keep competitive tallies of enemy dead, recreating the "Socialist competitions" that had become a hallmark of Soviet labor practices.[31] This propaganda made it abundantly clear that one showed love for the state and those at home by killing the enemy and that no man would be loved if he did not have an impressive tally. In effect, there was immense shame attached to not having killed. A special propaganda letter for Buriats serving in the Red Army stated, after invoking the landscape of Buriatiia: "when you step over the threshold of your own beloved house, we will ask each of you: how did you fight? How many enemy soldiers did you destroy? Keep this in mind dear *mergeny* [sharpshooters in Buriat], and mercilessly destroy the evil enemy, kill more enemy-brigands."[32] Killing was a productive action that earned love and respect and was to be celebrated, with tallies of dead Germans replacing figures of industrial production as the measure of individual contribution. Weapons were the tools that allowed a soldier to claim membership in the Soviet community through killing as well as a means to survive.

The submachine gun that Damcheev used for most of his service was the perfect weapon for a state struggling to arm and train soldiers. The PPSh-41, the most widely used submachine gun of the war, was a short-range weapon that could be used effectively with minimal training.[33] The Red Army ultimately made the most extensive use of submachine guns of any belligerent, in part to offset the lack of heavy machinery.[34] These weapons were stamped, rather than machined, meaning that even modest workshops could produce them. They were also easy to maintain. The compact size, rapid fire, and high capacity of the submachine gun made it ideal for both urban combat and for trench warfare and an absolute necessity for scouts, who needed a weapon that provided lots of firepower if they got into trouble behind enemy lines.[35]

These weapons often came packaged with other benefits. Scouts were among the very few elite troops who were issued camouflage overalls in a variety of colors and patterns that changed with the seasons and evolved in the course of the war. Elite formations also received special rations, and scouts and snipers had many more chances to distinguish themselves.[36]

Decorations

Damcheev earned his first of many medals ("For Valor") near Stalingrad on September 27, 1942, for throwing a grenade into a bunker, silencing a machine gun, personally killing two German soldiers, and helping to capture two more. Damcheev's decorations and tell a rich story of their bearer's history, as do those of his unit. A wartime article reminded soldiers that "you have the whole history of your life at the front on your chest."[37] Medals, orders, badges, and other decorations composed a readable text that spoke of the bearer's status, feats, skills, geographical movement, and injuries. There was an established hierarchy of decorations with its own grammar that dictated placement.[38] Similarly, a unit's title spoke to its accomplishments as each unit's decorations were affixed to its banner.[39] Damcheev served in the "27th Guards Novobugskaia Red Banner Order of Bogdan Khmel'nitskii Rifle Division." The division's rather clunky title chronicles such exploits as when it earned the title "Novobugskaia" and the Order of the Red Banner liberating the city of Novyi Bug and the Order of Bogdan Khmel'nitskii for liberating Odessa. These decorations served a variety of political purposes and gave specific material and social benefits to their bearers.

Despite dramatic shortages during the war, the Soviet state was dedicated to manufacturing large numbers of decorations, instituting dozens of new ones in 1942–45, all of which were made of semi-precious or precious materials ranging from brass and enamel to platinum and diamonds. The official statute of each new decoration was printed in both military and civilian press, clearly defining what one had to do to earn it.[40] Unlike most other armies, Red Army service personnel wore their decorations in combat, taking them off only if sent to infiltrate enemy lines or as part of their punishment if arrested.[41] Medals were given out extensively in the Red Army, with foreign observers noting that Red Army soldiers wore more medals than other armies.[42] The dedication of resources to this seeming frivolity speaks to the importance placed on decorations, which served a number of purposes. First, they distinguished soldiers and units who had excelled in combat, creating new hierarchies that came with social and material benefits. Second, they acted as a stimulus for soldiers. Soldiers were supposed to draw inspiration from those who had earned medals and emulate them. According to propaganda: "We must teach others using the example of heroes."[43] Conversely, those who failed to earn at least one decoration were shamed. An officer complained in his diary that without a medal: "I have no reputation. . . . The earth crumbles beneath my feet."[44] Third, the creation of new decorations highlighted the historical significance of the war itself and allowed the Soviet state to make connections with the pre-Soviet past.

Medals were supposed to tell stories, and Damcheev's tell us a remarkable amount about both his service and the state's logic in instituting and distributing decorations. In the photograph we can see Damcheev's campaign medal "For the Defense of Stalingrad" (far right). This medal was issued to over 760,000 people for being present at the battle. He later earned similar medals for the Warsaw-Poznań Operation, Taking Berlin, and Victory Over Germany, the last of which was issued to all soldiers in the Red Army's ranks on May 9, 1945 (over fifteen million people).[45] These medals documented the geographical movement of soldiers and their presence at crucial battles. Interestingly, the use of the words "defense," "liberation," or "taking" in the titles of medals betrayed editorial choices in how the war's history was inscribed. If a city was in the Soviet Union, then the medal would read "For the Defense of . . ." regardless of whether that city had been successfully defended or not, while cities outside of the Soviet Union read "For the Liberation of . . ." for friendly cities or "For the Taking of . . ." for enemy cities. There were no medals for liberating Soviet cities, as this would draw attention to the shameful fact of their occupation. So despite having participated in battles to liberate major Soviet cities in Ukraine (for instance, Odessa), Damcheev did not receive any campaign medals documenting these battles.

However, while Damcheev did not receive a medal documenting the liberation of Odessa, his unit did, and a most interesting one at that. His division earned the Order of Bogdan Khmel'nitskii ("Bohdan Khmel'nyskyi" in Ukrainian) for its role in retaking Odessa, the Black Sea port famous for its Jewish and criminal subcultures, in 1944. This decoration was part of a series of orders named for heroes of the Old Regime, such as Aleksandr Nevskii and General Suvorov, all of whom had films made about them before or during the war. The Ukrainian Hetman (Cossack military leader) Bogdan Khmel'nitskii was the only hero from outside the Great Russian nation to be so honored. Instituted as the Red Army entered Ukrainian territory, this medal was a clear nod to the Ukrainian people, the second-largest nationality in the Soviet Union.[46] It was in fact the result of lobbying by Ukrainian Party Leadership and Intelligentsia to include a figure from their own gallery of medieval heroes into the greater Soviet historical narrative. Khmel'nitskii swore fealty to the tsar in 1654, uniting Ukraine and Russia. Fittingly, the announcement of the order was timed to coincide with the recapture of Pereislavl, where the historic agreement had been reached.[47] The Hetman was famous for leading a rebellion against the Poles, which was accompanied by anti-Jewish pogroms of such ferocity that his name was synonymous with trauma among Jews. This led some to believe that the decoration's purpose was to signal a new war against Poland.[48] The Soviet narrative of Khmel'nitskii, effacing his anti-Semitism, helped underline the hierarchy of nationalities in the Great

Friendship of Peoples, emphasizing Russian leadership through a Hetman who voluntarily joined Russia.

Creative borrowing from the past mobilized institutions as well as individuals. The most remarkable example was the reestablishment of elite "Guards" units, an Old Regime tradition. In the fall of 1941, several units earned this distinction for their exemplary service in combat, and by 1945 over two hundred formations had become Guards. In May 1942, a series of privileges was instituted for Guards units that included higher priority in the allocation of weapons, rations, equipment, and personnel (and the right of return after being wounded), the title "Guards" attached to their rank as well as a special badge. (Damcheev's Guards badge can faintly be seen on his pocket on the left side of the photograph.) Guardsmen received much higher pay, with soldiers earning double and officers 150 percent of the base pay for their rank. These concrete benefits helped cement the elite status of Guards units, which often performed better in combat. Reestablishing "Guards" was the most expansive adoption of Russian Imperial practices in the Red Army, which was increasingly positioning itself as the inheritor of Russian military traditions. The Bolsheviks were eager to create new forms of hierarchy based on accomplishment at the front, which had become the new litmus test of what it meant to be Soviet.[49] The Guards badge was a clear external marker of those who had been deemed worthy of receiving extra resources in a time of desperate shortage. Campaign medals and Guards badges were symbols of corporate identity, but most of Damcheev's medals were tied to personal accomplishments.

Among those accomplishments was survival. On the left side of the photograph a small square with a bright stripe is visible between a badge and his buttons. This is a square of cloth onto which his wound stripes are sewn. Starting in mid-July 1942, wound stripes were to be awarded to all personnel who had been injured since the beginning of the war. A dark red stripe indicated a "light injury" (one that was not life threatening), while a gold or yellow stripe indicated a "heavy injury" (broken bones or compromised arteries).[50] Every time a soldier was wounded, he or she received the appropriate stripe. Damcheev would earn his first stripe in August 1943, the same day he earned a medal for helping to reestablish contact with a neighboring unit. He would earn his next wound stripe crossing the Vistula in 1944. He earned a final one in the last days of the war, in Berlin, after being hit with an anti-tank rocket on May 2, 1945.[51]

Wound stripes were to be used as a pedagogical tool to show that soldiers could survive the enemy's fire. Soldiers were encouraged to tell stories to new recruits about how they had survived, creating a macho culture that minimized fear and pain.[52]

Other badges celebrated competence rather than fortitude. Damcheev earned both the Excellent Sniper and Excellent Scout badges (left side of picture). In the summer of 1942, the army introduced a number of badges to promote the mastery of skills, everything from Excellent Baker to Excellent Machine Gunner. These badges were in theory among the least prestigious, carrying no monetary prize. However, a scout serving in a neighboring division, Galina Golofeevskaia, told a historian that excellent badges were "prized more highly than any order" precisely because they were *not* issued for exceptional deeds. An excellent badge "shows how you handle yourself in reconnaissance, what kind of scout you are in total."[53] Damcheev earned both this badge for professionalism and a number of decorations for exceptional acts. We know a great deal about Damcheev because of the latter.

Bato Damcheev became a Full Cavalier of the Order of Glory, a reincarnation of the St. George's Cross, one of the most prestigious decorations of the Old Regime. Established in 1769, the St. George's Cross existed in four classes and could be earned only for combat deeds. Despite its origins in the regime that the Bolsheviks had toppled, it was sometimes worn by veterans of the Great War in Red Army service and carried by the sons of those who had earned it as a good luck charm.[54] The Order of Glory was reportedly devised by Stalin himself as a soldier's award to offset the expansive number of awards that only officers could earn. It was announced alongside the platinum and diamond-studded Order of Victory, which could only be earned by generals.[55] Stalin's new decoration replaced the St. George's Cross with a star and the engraving of the saint slaying a dragon with the Kremlin. It retained the orange and black color scheme of the old regime decoration, which would also later be the motif for the Victory Over Germany Medal. As opposed to many other orders where rank alone determined which class one could earn, soldiers had to earn three classes of this medal in succession by repeated acts of heroism to become Full Cavaliers.[56] The third-class order was made of silver, the second of silver with a gold circle around the Kremlin, and the first of pure gold.[57] The Order of Glory First Class was so prestigious that it could only be given by the Presidium of the Supreme Soviet, formally the highest legislative body of the Soviet government.

The list of things a soldier could do to earn this order was expansive and at times very specific, such as fighting from inside a burning tank, using a tank to run over enemy artillery or machine guns, or destroying specific numbers of enemy planes, tanks, or ships with an airplane. It explicitly mentioned scouts' duties and could be awarded for capturing an enemy officer or attaining particularly useful intelligence while on reconnaissance. It could also be attained for saving the life of one's commander or destroying an enemy bunker and its garrison "with definitive action."[58] In short, it was given for effective killing and destruction. Damcheev earned his first Order of Glory for disrupting the date of three German officers with Polish women near the Pilica River on the night of October 6–7, 1944. According to the recommendation written on his behalf, as his group of scouts approached three Germans escorting Polish women deep behind enemy lines, the scouts were spotted. Damcheev killed one German and seized another. One of the Polish women came with him and gave useful information.[59] He earned his second Order of Glory in the taking of Poznań, where on January 29, 1945, the scouts were ordered to destroy a group of German soldiers in a house that had pinned down a battalion. Damcheev crawled up to the house and destroyed a machine gun with a grenade, then entered the house and killed nine German soldiers. This allowed the battalion to advance, and Poznań fell shortly after.[60] His final Order of Glory was earned on April 27, 1945, on a hill near Berlin, where he and a handful of scouts and submachine gunners held off a large German counterattack. Damcheev rallied panicking soldiers and killed eight Germans.[61] Each order crystallized a specific date and actions, providing proof of a soldier's exceptional status and immense social capital.

Each order also carried with it very concrete benefits. The Order of Glory garnered its bearer a five- to fifteen-ruble raise in his or her monthly pay. It was also supposed to carry with it an instant and dramatic rise through the ranks, although it appears that this did not happen in Damcheev's case. The order also garnered its bearer a 50 percent raise in his or her pension and free basic and higher education for his or her children.[62] In addition to the privileges specific to the Order of Glory, there was a package of benefits given to all order recipients. This included a free round trip once a year by rail or boat to anywhere in the Soviet Union, free use of tramways, a significant tax break, reduction of time until retirement by one third, and reduced utility bills, all of which were transferrable to spouses and dependents such as children or elderly parents.[63] In a society where resources were based on state-recognized status, order recipients were a special class who could use their medals not only for official privileges guaranteed by law but also as social capital in letters to various authorities asking for assistance solving problems from securing a cow or enrolling in university to finding an apartment for themselves or relatives.

Trophies

Success on the battlefield has been connected to more immediate rewards for soldiers from ancient times, such as the taking of trophies. Scouts took parts of German uniforms such as belt buckles or overcoats and wore them; they would also use German weapons. Looted uniforms were both trophies and camouflage, and using enemy weapons made resupply behind enemy lines easier. Enemy prisoners of war were often themselves treated as trophies. Their lives were entirely in the hands of their captors, who could kill them at will. German POWs were frequently paraded through the streets of Soviet cities as early as the fall of 1941 (Leningrad) and in a particularly spectacular parade in Moscow in 1944.

Prisoners had special relevance for Damcheev and his scout comrades because their primary task was the capture of enemy soldiers for interrogation. These "tongues" counted even more highly in the tallies and accolades than enemy soldiers killed. The reduction of humans to objects that this term implies betrays a reality of total war. War turned human beings into resources. This could take on a macabre tone, such as when soldiers knocked gold teeth out of the jaws of those they had just killed.[64] The soldiers themselves were components of a massive military machine, while enemies became tally marks, prisoners to be interrogated or bodies to be looted.

Alongside the reduction of people to objects was the liquidation of the property of living enemy soldiers. Eager to monopolize all major resources on the battlefield, the state developed increasingly sophisticated methods for the collection and distribution of everything left on the battlefield. This did not prevent soldiers from consuming captured food and or using captured weapons and vehicles, but it did ensure that the state was the biggest player in divvying up the loot. While the Red Army officially had a strict policy against robbing POWs, it was mostly unwilling to stop it. Of particular interest were watches. Galina Golofeevskaia, a scout serving in another division, described the proliferation of watches after the battle of Stalingrad: "As a rule, when we would lead a column [of prisoners] the soldiers would take watches before anything else. Therefore every soldier had 8–12 watches. I had 8 watches. On the road I traded these watches."[65] Watches were ideal trophy items for people on the move. Small, lightweight, potentially useful, and of relatively high value, they quickly became a sort of currency for soldiers who had largely forgotten the value of money.[66] They had also been rare before the war, among the objects that marked one as urban. Given his status, record, and duties, Damcheev would have had ample access to watches throughout his service.

The looting of prisoners of war would expand to include enemy civilians as the army went abroad. Without ever explicitly telling soldiers to engage in looting, in the last months of the war the army invited them to do so. On December 26, 1944, the army announced that soldiers in the active army (already beyond Soviet borders) would be allowed to send parcels home monthly, with weights and costs dependent on rank. Soldiers were prohibited from sending home parts of their uniform, print material in any language, or perishable food--in other words they were not permitted to send anything that was already *theirs*. While initially leading to confusion, it soon became clear to all that this policy indeed called on Red Army soldiers to expropriate enemy property.[67]

This policy served several overlapping purposes. It relieved some of the tensions that arose from the observable material wealth of average Eastern European and particularly German civilians. The fact that even rural people had access to goods that in the Soviet Union were scarce and only available to urban people could be deeply disturbing and lead to acts of destruction as well as looting.[68] This was officially explained away by highlighting that much of this wealth came from plunder, and indeed objects from all over Europe and the Soviet Union were found in German homes inside and outside of the pre-1939 borders of the Reich, particularly consumer items such as soap, clothing, and alcohol.[69] The Germans came to stand in for class as well as national enemies, and their character was heavily associated with bourgeois philistinism, which, according to

Soviet propaganda, helped explain the crimes of the Third Reich. In this interpretation, mindless obsession with material objects and comforts and jealousy of what neighbors possessed had led naturally to Hitlerism and its drive to murder and steal.[70] This is key to understanding the second purpose of this policy. The confiscation of property was a common addendum to criminal prosecutions in the Soviet Union and had occurred regularly during intensified campaigns against class enemies during the Civil War, the First Five Year Plan, and the Great Terror. In allowing soldiers to loot, the Soviet state was underlining the criminality of the Third Reich. Looting also served to highlight the total nature of the Red Army's victory. Finally, this could be seen as compensation for soldiers and their families, many of whom were living under desperate material conditions due to the war's privations and previous decades of social experimentation.

All manner of objects were moving from the Third Reich to the Soviet Union. The state took machinery and whole factories, while soldiers had a rare opportunity to get hard-to-find consumer items.[71] Many soldiers took writing materials. Cameras suddenly became common, and it is likely that Damcheev's picture was taken with a trophy camera on trophy paper. Intimate items such as chamber pots could be taken.[72] Clothing was particularly popular, and some women at home wrote to their loved ones reminding them of their sizes once word got out about parcels.[73] Soldier's looting was often utilitarian but could also have a symbolic component. For example, a Komsomol organizer took a tuxedo as a trophy. That a young communist could take the finest clothes from the vanquished foe embodied the eminent victory of the Red Army. He was, however, worried about the effect the taking of trophies was having on the troops: "It seems that it was a mistake to allow these parcels. It's a good thing that the Germans don't booby-trap anything, or we would lose a lot of people. In general this has a demoralizing effect."[74]

The seizure of intimate items such as clothing, sometimes off the backs of German civilians, could be accompanied by more severe forms of humiliation and violence, particularly rape. Many observers at the time saw these actions as the result of a process of brutalization of soldiers and linked the invitation to loot enemy property with sexual assault.[75] Not only did these forms of assault often occur simultaneously, they were both the result of a dramatic loosening of control that could be seen as a reward for the forthcoming victory. Contemporaries claimed that these actions were overwhelmingly the province of rear-area personnel who had the time, freedom of movement, and relative safety to steal and rape.[76]

It is unclear what Damcheev would have taken, given that he left no observable personal writings; further, the author could find no information about his family. We have no reason to believe that Damcheev participated in rapes. Damcheev is important here not because of what he did or did not do but rather because of what he represented to the Germans. German women frequently translated the racial stereotypes that had been ubiquitous in the Third Reich onto their assailants. Racial enmity could run so deep that it denied both the humanity of the assailants and their agency as perpetrators, often reducing them to the status of beasts.[77] Damcheev was literally the face of German fears, and his presence on the streets of Berlin undeniable proof of German defeat.

Conclusion

The fact that Damcheev fought from Stalingrad to Berlin and survived is exceptional, as is his demographic information. His record was extraordinary, which is why we know so much about him. He was a salient example of the success of the Soviet state in crafting a new type of modern subject to defend the Soviet experiment. Damcheev's postwar life was more typical. After recovering from his wounds he returned to occupation duty in Berlin and was demobilized in December 1946, surrendering his weapon and retaining his medals. He returned home as a war hero and as a member of the Communist Party, which allowed him to receive additional education and become first a propagandist and later the head of the local "house of reading," head of a rural club, and eventually chairman of the rural soviet of his home town.[78] His wounds dramatically shortened his life, and he died at a sanatorium in Crimea in 1965.[79] His postwar opportunities were largely determined by his status as a decorated veteran, who as a group would dominate management positions in the Soviet Union long after Damcheev's death.[80] However, even if his elite status as an order recipient could garner him access to limited resources such as sanatoria, Damcheev was relegated to positions of power in the rural periphery. Nonetheless, a street in his hometown bears his name, a boxing competition was started in his honor in 1980, and Damcheev's internet presence is quite impressive for a person who passed away decades before the web became available.[81]

A word about the afterlife of some of Damcheev's objects is also in order. Many of the chapters in this volume are stories of changes in meaning over time, and Damcheev's things are no exception. The orders that Damcheev had earned lost their pecuniary value in 1948, when the Soviet government curtailed all benefits associated with them. This was explained by the dire budgetary straits faced by the Soviet state after the war. It came as a shock to many, who felt that they were losing guaranteed, lifelong privileges that they had earned in battle. For many, it seemed that the state was trying to dramatically reduce their status.[82] Veterans would eventually see their status and benefits returned, a process that took decades.[83] After their recipients passed on, decorations took on a variety of meanings. During the war, they were often the only remains family members would receive. For the unknown dead unearthed today, serial numbers on medals are one of the few means of identification. Many medals ended up as family reliquaries or public objects of veneration in museums around the former Soviet space. However, with the collapse of the Soviet Union, they also became commodities alongside uniforms, equipment, and weapons used by Red Army soldiers. At the time of writing, an Excellent Sniper badge can fetch a few hundred dollars, while Order of Glory can be bought from $125 to $11,500.[84]

The marketing of these objects is taking place in the political as well as economic sphere. Damcheev's most remarkable decoration, the Order of Glory, has become a major symbol in Russia. The Order of St. George has officially returned as a decoration, while a distinction known as "St. George's Ribbons" has become a symbol of pride in the participation of ancestors in the Great Patriotic War; it has been distributed around Victory Day (May 9) every year since 2005. The ribbon was subsequently utilized as a symbol of support for Putin, in contradistinction to the white ribbons worn by anti-Putin activists beginning in late 2011. Finally, the ribbon became a common symbol worn by separatist fighters in Ukraine, where the rhetoric casts the conflict as a replay of the Great Patriotic War, with the post-Maidan Ukrainian state and the West in general cast as the fascists.[85] Conversely, Ukrainian soldiers fighting against separatists continue to be awarded the Order of Bohdan Khmel'nytskyi in its Ukrainian national edition.[86] The meaning of the objects and symbols from the war is in constant flux.

Damcheev's unexpected journey and transformation from rural librarian into a highly decorated scout was an abrupt rupture with the rest of his life. It forced him to master the tools of killing and later provided him with decorations that captured moments of violence. His war experience gave him opportunities for distinction and personal advancement but also scars. It allowed him to travel the Soviet Union and see the world outside of its borders, where he earned immense social capital and a sort of immortality as a Full Cavalier of the Order of Glory. The objects he used and may have obtained were ubiquitous, while the medals he was awarded made him a man of distinction. These medals and his photograph freeze moments of the massive, violent movement of people and things that was the Great Patriotic War at the scale of a single human being. This is of course but one version of events, written in a language provided by the Soviet state to serve its own purposes, but the continued survival of the story and the afterlife of the objects that constitute it show that the power of this telling has outlived the regime that authored it.

Notes

The author thanks Zain Lakhani, Mirjam Voerkelius, Ivan Sablin, Bair Irincheev, Tatiana Linkhoeva, Xenia Cherniaev, Milyausha Zakirova, Tara Zahra, Leora Auslander, Yuri Slezkine, Victoria Frede-Montemayor, and the participants in the 2016 Davis Center Fellows Seminar (in particular Kelly O'Neill, Jillian Porter, Alexander Diener, and Jackie Kerr) for their feedback and ideas in writing this text.

1. Due to multiple shifts in the alphabet used by Buriats and the fact that documents were often filled out via dictation, multiple variations of Bato Damcheev's name exist.

2. D. M. Tsyrenov, *Nashi zemliaki—polnye kavalery ordena Slavy* (Ulan-Ude, USSR: Buriatskoe Knizhnoe Izdatel'stvo, 1988), 39–48. Here and elsewhere, the author acknowledges that the body counts may be inflated.

3. B. Gorbatov, "Orden Slavy," *Krasnoarmeets* 1 (1944): 14. On killing in the Red Army, see Amir Weiner, "Something to Die For, A Lot to Kill For: The Soviet System and the Brutalization of Warfare," in The Barbarisation of Warfare, ed. George Kassimeris (London: Hurst, 2006), 114–115.

4. This chapter draws from my manuscript, "Government Issue: The Material Culture of the Red Army 1941–1945," under contract with Cornell University Press.

5. My understanding of material culture draws from Bruno Latour's Actor-Network-Theory, Elaine Scarry's concepts of material culture as embodied knowledge and attention to the symbiotic relations between people and objects, and Nathan Joseph's exploration of clothing as communication. See Latour, *Reassembling the Social: An Introduction to Actor-Network*

Theory (New York: Oxford University Press, 2005); Scarry, *The Body in Pain* (New York: Oxford University Press, 1985), 151–152, 303, 310; Joseph, *Uniforms and Nonuniforms: Communication through Clothing* (New York: Greenwood Press, 1986).

6. For an excellent overview on the issues of mobility in the Soviet Union, see Lewis H. Siegelbaum and Leslie Page Moch, *Broad Is My Native Land: Repertoires and Regimes of Migration in Russia's Twentieth Century* (Ithaca: Cornell University Press, 2014).

7. See, for example, Valentina Chudakova, *Ratnoe schast'e* (Moscow: Voenizdat, 1980), 9.

8. I. Mints, "O traditsiiakh Krasnoi armii," *Agitator i propagandist Krasnoi Armii* 13 (1944): 6–18, 7; N. Markovich, "Ofitserstvo—kostiak armii," *Agitator i propagandist Krasnoi Armii* 9–10 (1943): 9–16; K. Kulik, "Vospitanie na boevykh traditsiiakh," *Agitator i propagandist Krasnoi Armii* 15 (1943): 14–22.

9. "Non-Russians" was a blanket term for people from ethnic enclaves. See Brandon Schechter, "'The People's Instructions': Indigenizing the Great Patriotic War among 'Non-Russians,'" *Ab Imperio* 3 (2012): 109–133.

10. A. I. Barsukov et al., *Prikazy narodnogo komissara oborony SSSR 1943–1945gg.: Dokumenty i materialy. Russkii arkhiv: Velikaia Otechestvennaia*, vol. 13 (2–3) (Moscow: TERRA, 1997), 109–111.

11. Barsukov et al., *Prikazy narodnogo komissara oborony SSSR 22 iiunia 1941 g.–1942 g.: Dokumenty i materialy. Russkii arkhiv: Velikaia Otechestvennaia*, vol. 13 (2–2), 111–112; N. I. Borodin and N. V. Usenko, *Glavnye Politicheskie Organy Vooruzhennykh Sil SSSR v Velikoi Otechestvennoi Voine 1941–1945 gg.: Dokumenty i materialy. Russkii arkhiv: Velikaia Otechestvennaia*, vol. 17–6 (1–2) (Moscow: TERRA, 1996), 78–79.

12. Brandon Schechter, "*Khoziaistvo* and *Khoziaeva*: The Properties and Proprietors of the Red Army, 1941–1945," *Kritika: Explorations in Russian and Eurasian History*, vol. 18, no. 3 (Summer 2017), pp. 487–510, 497–499.

13. Nauchnyi arkhiv Instituta Rossiiskoi istorii Akademii nauk Rossiiskoi Federatsii (NA IRI RAN) f. 2, r. I, op. 230, d. 1, l. 12. This appears to be a more general military, rather than Soviet practice. See Scarry, *Body in Pain*, 21.

14. Roger Reese, *Why Stalin's Soldiers Fought: The Red Army's Military Effectiveness in World War II* (Lawrence: University Press of Kansas, 2011), 260–261, 306–314.

15. See, for example, Sergei Kudriashov, *Voina: 1941–1945* (Moscow: Arkhiv Prezidenta Rossiiskoi Federatsii, 2010), 124.

16. Melissa Chakars, *The Socialist Way of Life in Siberia: Transformation in Buryatia* (Budapest: Central European University Press, 2014), 2; Iu. A. Poliakov, ed., *Vsesoiuznaia perepis' naseleniia 1939 goda: Osnovnye itogi* (Moscow: Nauka, 1992), 57. For ethnographies of the Buriats, see L. L. Abaeva and N. L. Zhukovskaia, eds., *Buriaty* (Moscow: Nauka, 2004); and G. R. Galdanova, *Zakamenskie Buriaty* (Novosibirsk, Russia: Nauka, 1992).

17. Chakars, *Socialist Way of Life in Siberia*, 71–80. According to the 1939 Census, 7.78% of the Soviet population had graduated from high school. *Vsesoiuznaia perepis' naseleniia 1939 goda*, 49.

18. See, for example, Dem'ian Bednyi, "Semen Nomokonov," *Krasnoarmeets* 12 (1942): 16.

19. See, for example, NA IRI RAN f. 2, r. X, op. 7, d. 13-a and NA IRI RAN f. 2, r. X, op. 7, d. 13-b.; Gabriel Temkin, *My Just War* (Novato, Calif.: Presidio, 1998), 124–125.

20. Damcheev earned his first medal in just such a situation near Stalingrad, his last one under similar circumstances near Berlin.

21. Temkin, *My Just War*, 124–125.

22. The full title is *7,62 mm Pistolet-pulemet obraztsa 1941 goda sistema Shpagina* (Machine pistol model 1941 of the Shpagin system).

23. *Programmy uskorennoi boevoi podgotovki strelkovykh podrazdelenii* (Moscow: Voenizdat 1941); Kudriashov, *Voina*, 142.

24. Anna Krylova, *Soviet Women in Combat: A History of Violence on the Eastern Front* (New York: Cambridge University Press, 2010), 30, 175–183.

25. *Frontovoi tovarishch* (n.p.: Voenizdat, 1942), 37–38.

26. NA IRI RAN f. 2, r. I, op. 16, d. 1, l. 21ob.; Krylova, *Soviet Women in Combat*, 251–252.

27. Khazratkul Faiziev, *Ognennye versty* (Dushanbe, USSR: Irfon, 1980), 158–169.

28. Lidzhi Indzhiev, *Frontovoi dnevnik* (Elista, Russia: Kalmytskoe Knizhnoe Izdatel'stvo, 2002), 26.

29. Rossiiskii gosudarstvennyi arkhiv sotsial'noi i politicheskoi istorii (RGASPI), f. M-7, op. 1, d. 6387, l. 118.

30. Nikolai Bogdanov, *Beregi oruzhie, kak zenitsu oka* (Moscow: Voenizdat, 1942), 19–20.

31. *Frontovoi tovarishch*, 89–91; *Metkuiu puliu v serdtse vraga* (n.p.: n.d.), 34; Jochen Hellbeck has pointed out that this volunteerism was a major part of Soviet strategy. See Jochen Hellbeck, *Stalingrad: The City That Defeated the Third Reich* (New York: Basic Books, 2015), 35, 47–50.

32. *Nakaz naroda* (Moscow: Voenizdat, 1942), 124–125.

33. RGASPI f. 74, op. 2, d. 121, l. 5. D. N. Bolotin, *Sovetskoe strelkovoe oruzhiie* (Moscow: Voenizdat, 1983), 114; A. I. Yeremenko, *Dnevniki, zapiski, vospominaniia* (Moscow: ROSSPEN, 2013), 144; *Deistviia roty avtomatchikov v boiu* (Moscow: Voenizdat, 1942).

34. David M. Glantz, *Colossus Reborn: The Red Army at War, 1941–1943* (Lawrence: University of Kansas Press, 2005), 192.

35. Bolotin, *Sovetskoe strelkovoe oruzhiie*, 118–120, 126–128, 134. They also had chromed barrels, which made them much easier to keep clean. A later version, the PPS-43, was adopted with scouts in mind, borrowing elements from German submachine guns.

36. Veshchikov et al., *Tyl Krasnoi Armii v Velikoi Otechestvennoi voine 1941–1945 gg.*, 148, 414.

37. Vasilii Subbotin, "Soldatskaia dusha," *Krasnaia zvevda*, February 19, 1943.

38. "Pravila nosheniia ordenov, medalei, ordenskikh lent i znakov otlichii," *Krasnaia zvevda*, June 20, 1943.

39. V. F. Loboda and I. P. Kergal'tsev. *Pravila nosheniia ordenov, medalei SSSR, nagrudnykh znakov i ordenskikh lent* (Moscow: Voenizdat, 1948), 26.

40. See, for example, "Orden Otechestvennoi voini," *Pravda*, May 21, 1942, 1.

41. Barsukov et al., *Prikazy narodnogo komissara oborony SSSR 22 iiunia 1941 g.–1942 g.*, 315; Mansur Abdulin, *160 stranits iz soldatskogo dnevnika* (Moscow: Molodaia gvardiia, 1985), 77.

42. Alexandra Orme, *Comes the Comrade* (New York: William Morrow & Co., 1950), 255.

43. "Nagrada v boiu," *Krasnaia zvevda*, March 6, 1943.

44. Diary entry from August 5, 1944, Vladimir Gel'fand, edited and with an introduction by Oleg Budnitskii, *Dnevnik 1941–1946* (Moscow: ROSSPEN, 2015), 317.

45. Aleksandr Kuznetsov, *Entsiklopediia russkikh nagrad* (Moscow: Golos Press, 2001), 370–373, 287.

46. "Orden Bogdana Khmel'nitskogo," *Pravda*, October 11, 1943.

47. Serhy Yekelchyk, *Stalin's Empire of Memory: Russian-Ukrainian Relations in the Soviet Historical Imagination* (Toronto: University of Toronto Press, 2004), 35–37, 96–97.

48. RGASPI f. 17, op. 125, d. 242, l. 2; Jan Gross, *Neighbors: The Destruction of the Jewish Community in Jewabne, Poland* (Princeton: Princeton University Press, 2001), 123.

49. NA IRI RAN f. 2 r. III op. 5 d. 2a l. 7ob.–8; Amir Weiner, *Making Sense of War: The Second World War and the Fate of the Bolshevik Revolution* (Princeton: Princeton University Press, 2000), 43–81.

50. "Vvedenie otlichitel'nykh znakov dlia voennosluzhashchikh, ranenykh na frontakh Otechestvennoi voini," *Krasnaia Zvevda*, July 16, 1942.

51. Tsyrenov, *Nashi zemliaki*, 42–43, 47; "Prikaz podrazdeleniia No. 30/n ot: 02.09.1943 Izdan: 27 gv. sd Iugo-Zapadnogo fronta." Tsentral'nyi arkhiv Ministerstva oborony Rossiiskoi Federatsii (TsAMO RF), f. 33, op. 682526, d. 696, No. zapisi: 16393597, *Elektronnyi Bank Dokumentov "Podvig Naroda v Velikoi Otechestvennoi Voine 1941–1945 gg,"* http://podvignaroda.mil.ru/?#id=16393597, accessed May 21, 2017.

52. See, for example, Subottin, "Soldatskaia dusha"; NA IRI RAN f. 2, r. II, op. 103, d. 6, l. 3.

53. NA IRI RAN f.2 r. X op.7 d. 13-b l.130.

54. Vasilii Grossman, *Gody voiny* (Moscow: Pravda, 1989), 172.

55. M. A. Izotova and T. B. Tsareva, *Polnaia entsiklopediia ordenov i medalei Rossii* (Rostov na Donu, Russia: Vladis, 2008), 248–249; "Orden Pobedy," *Izvestiia*, November 19, 1943.

56. See, for example, "Orden Bogdana Khmel'nitskogo," *Pravda*, October 11, 1943.

57. "Statut Ordena Slavy," *Izvestiia*, November 19, 1943.

58. "Statut Ordena Slavy."

59. "Prikaz podrazdeleniia №: 99/n ot: 25.10.1944 Izdan: 27 gv. sd 1 Belorusskogo fronta." TsAMO RF, f. 33, op. 690155, d. 5443, No. zapisi 33704393, *Elektronnyi Bank Dokumentov "Podvig Naroda v Velikoi Otechestvennoi Voine 1941–1945 gg.,"* http://podvignaroda.mil.ru/?#id=33704393, accessed May 21, 2017.

60. "No. 544/n ot: 26.03.1945 Izdan: VS 8 gv. A." TsAMO RF, f. 33, op. 686196, d. 3278, no. zapisi: 25488410, *Elektronnyi Bank Dokumentov "Podvig Naroda v Velikoi Otechestvennoi Voine 1941–1945 gg.,"* http://podvignaroda.mil.ru/?#id=25488410, accessed May 21, 2017.

61. Tsyrenov, *Nashi zemliaki—polnye kavalery Ordena Slavy,* 46–47.

62. "Statut Ordena Slavy."

63. Barsukov et al., *Prikazy narodnogo komissara oborony SSSR 1943–1945 gg.,* 100–101.

64. Veniamin Tongur, *Frontovoi dnevnik (1941–1945)* (n.p.: Simferopol', 2006), 102.

65. NA IRI RAN f. 2, r. X, op. 7, d. 13-b, l. 88.

66. Boris Slutskii, *O drugikh i o sebe* (Moscow: Vagrius, 2005), 32.

67. Barsukov et al., *Prikazy narodnogo komissara oborony SSSR 1943–1945 gg.,* 344–347; Veshchikov et al., *Tyl Krasnoi Armii v Velikoi Otechestvennoi voine 1941–1945 gg.,* 639–640. On confusion, see, for example, Temkin, *My Just War,* 200.

68. See, for example, B. G. Komskii, "Dnevnik 1943–1945 gg.," in O. V. Budnitskii, ed., *Arkhiv evreiskoi istorii,* vol. 6 (Moscow: ROSSPEN, 2011), 66–67; Vladimir Stezhenskii, *Soldatskii dnevnik* (Moscow: Agraf, 2005), 208.

69. See, for example, NA IRI RAN, f. 2, r. X, op. 6, d. 1, ll. 3-4; NA IRI RAN f. 2, r. I, op. 30, d. 23, ll. 2ob–3.

70. See, for example, M. Nechikina, "Velikii russkii narod," *Agitator i propagandist Krasnoi Armii* 13 (1945), 21–29.

71. Austin Jersild, "The Soviet State as Imperial Scavenger: 'Catch Up and Surpass' in the Transnational Socialist Bloc, 1950–1960," *American Historical Review* 116, no. 1 (2011): 109–132.

72. Temkin, *My Just War,* 221.

73. See, for example, letter from January 9, 1945, Vladimir Gelfand, *Pis'ma*, http://gelfand.de/1941-1946/Brife/BriefeRUS.html, accessed May 21, 2017.

74. Vladimir Bushin, *Ia posetil sei mir: Iz dnevnikov frontovika* (Moscow: Algoritm, 2012), 89. The symbolic component was particularly critical when soldiers destroyed things. See Brandon Schechter, "Trophies of War," in *Government Issue: The Material Culture of the Red Army 1941–1945* (PhD diss., University of California at Berkeley, 2015), ch. 6.

75. See, for example, Vladimir Stezhenskii, *Soldatskii dnevnik: Voennye stranitsy* (Moscow: Agraf, 2005), 211. See Norman Naimark, *The Russians in Germany: A History of the Soviet Zone of Occupation, 1945–1949* (Cambridge: Harvard University Press, 1995); Schechter, "Trophies of War," 221–223.

76. Slutskii, *O drugikh i o sebe*, 100; Anonymous, *A Woman in Berlin* (New York: Metropolitan Books, 2005), 143–144.

77. Atina Grossmann, "A Question of Silence: The Rape of German Women by Occupation Soldiers," *October* 72 (1995): 42–63.

78. Mark Edele, "Veterans and the Village: The Impact of Red Army Demobilization on Soviet Urbanization, 1945–1955," *Russian History* 36 (2009): 159–182.

79. Tsyrenov, *Nashi zemliaki*, 48.

80. Weiner, *Making Sense of War*, 331.

81. See, for example, "Damcheev Bato Mikishkeevich," *Geroi strany*, www.warheroes.ru/hero/hero.asp?Hero_id=12063; "Damcheev Bato Mikishkeevich," *Ministerstvo oborony Rossiiskoi Federatsii. Entsiklopediia*, http://encyclopedia.mil.ru/encyclopedia/gentlemens/hero.htm?id=11461883@morfHeroes; entry for "Damcheev Bato Mikishkeevich" on Russian Wikipedia.

82. Grigorii Pomerants, *Zapiski gadkogo utenka* (Moscow: Tsentr gumanitarnykh initsiativ, 2012), 130.

83. Mark Edele, *Soviet Veterans of the Second World War: A Popular Movement in an Authoritarian Society, 1941–1991* (New York: Oxford University Press, 2008), 192–195. As veterans dwindled in numbers and became more organized, the benefits associated with orders were extended to all veterans. See Edele, *Soviet Veterans*, 206–210.

84. See, for example, "Order of Glory," *Collect Russia: Medals-Militaria-Antiques*, www.collectrussia.com/showcat.htm?cat=glory2, accessed May 21, 2017.

85. See Serguei Alex. Oushakine, "Remembering in Public: On the Affective Management of History," *Ab Imperio* 1 (2013): 269–302.

86. "President Awarded the Order of Bohdan Khmelnytskyi to Maksym Myrhorodskyi," April 25, 2015, www.mil.gov.ua/en/news/2015/04/25/president-awarded-the-order-of-bohdan-khmelnytskyi-to-maksym-myrhorodskyi/, accessed May 21, 2017.

SMALL ESCAPES

Gender, Class, and Material Culture in Great War Internment Camps

Iris Rachamimov

Artifacts and Prewar Modes of Life

On March 3, 1917, an interned German officer sent home a postcard from the POW Officer Camp of Khabarovsk, in the Russian East-Asian Maritime Province (Primorskaia oblast). "We live here in three two-storied barracks," he reported, "which lie within a large fenced yard. I live on the first floor and have a view of the surrounding landscape. We arranged our beds so that every two or three beds form a corner, in the middle of which stands a table. Cloth curtains [Stoffvorhänge] are hung up to enclose this corner so it would not be possible to look from the outside in. In addition to the living spaces we also have a classroom and a music room."[1] This postcard was incorporated into a newsletter compiled from POW correspondence by Ilse Raettig, a family member of a German POW officer in Khabarovsk, and circulated among the families of the prisoners interned there ("solely for the private use of family members").[2]

Compiled during the war by relatives for a number of Siberian and Maritime Province camps, family newsletters attest to the efforts of interned German officers to bridge the geographic distance between themselves and their families by describing in considerable detail objects, spaces, and places. German officers interned in the camp of Omsk in Siberia portrayed in their letters what they perceived as the painterly beauty of the place and highlighted the dramatic seasonal transformations of the area. After the conclusion of the first violent summer storm of 1916, one of the officers wrote to his family about the "sun coming out in the east through a wildly fissured black and gray sky, lighting up the yellow barracks of the rank-and-file [POWs] and their red roofs. A grand picture!"[3] Another described the habit of the local population in Omsk to wear automobile protective glasses "during the warm part of the year" to guard their eyes from "the sandstorms sweeping in from the endless steppe." It is a "comical sight" (*ulkiger Anblick*), he reported.[4] By using vivid and evocative language, POW officers attempted to draw their addressees closer and elicit a yearned-for emotional response.[5]

As recent studies in cognitive science suggest, humans rely from infancy on the dichotomy "proximity/distance" to undergird certain structures of cognition and feeling.[6] These two antithetical notions govern the locomotion of toddlers in the world—whether for example an object is within tactile reach or not—and are abstracted at a very early age to create a mental map of our universe. "Proximity" and "distance" organize our sense of time (something taking place just now as opposed to an event that happened in the past or will occur in the near/remote future); they color our perceptions of the social world ("better is a neighbor who is near than a brother far away," Proverbs 27:10); and they are crucial in linking the temporal, spatial, and social facets of our existence. In the words of psychologists Nira Liberman and Yaacov Trope, "temporal, spatial and social distances . . . are associated, affect each other and are inferred from one another."[7] The various forms of distance have a "common meaning (psychological distance) that is accessed even when not related."[8]

If indeed various kinds of distance are all processed by individuals as "psychological distance," then it is not surprising that certain objects and artifacts acquire a central role in the lives of people who feel themselves displaced from a previous identity. Refugees, migrants, internees, and prisoners are particularly inclined to value certain objects, to use them to offset an inner sense of psychological distance, and to re-enact with them subjectively meaningful scripts. As Gerdien Jonker and Sandra Dudley suggest in their contributions to this volume, personally meaningful objects carried by displaced people help in maintaining a sense of internal integrity at times of upheaval.

The Khabarovsk prisoners, located ten thousand kilometers away from Germany, in a part of the earth they "had imagined as a huge snow wasteland [occupied] by barbarian tribes," keenly described to their families the surprisingly familiar material world of the camp and its region—"big cities . . . electrical lights, huge stores, banks, hotels and restaurants, theaters etc."[9] One officer reported ordering a silk suit from a Chinese tailor, while another told his wife he is stocking up on silk and will have something to bring home upon repatriation.[10] "Our [barrack] hall is pretty colorful," wrote a third prisoner. "Everywhere there are these small quarters created by hanging curtains for every 3–4 gentlemen [*Herren*]: one chooses white for his wall, another flowers, the third light blue and together they create the most wonderful color effects."[11] By providing detailed material descriptions, prisoners attempted to de-alienate their world for their families, inviting them to imagine it and to partake in it sensually.

Prisoners also utilized artifacts to bridge the temporal distance between their present existence and their previous one by recreating a sense of prewar modes of life. Letters of the POW officers portray almost without exception the attempts to structure daily activities according to civilian patterns: to delineate clear boundaries between "private" and "public" spaces with the aid of bedsheets, blankets, and written signs; to create cozy households for small groups with the aid of cloth and wood; to establish educational facilities such as libraries, schools, and vocational instruction frameworks; to tend garden allotments for practical and aesthetic purposes and to designate zones for business, entertainment, and sporting activities.[12] Whenever and wherever possible, POW officers seem to have been determined to give their daily life in captivity a civilian texture. The family newsletter from the officer's camp in Omsk described the habit taken up by POW officers of wearing sporting clothes instead of the required daytime military uniforms, using the pretense that they were always "on the way" to the sporting grounds.[13] Many had such clothes made especially for them by other camp inmates, while others ordered them from tailors in the city of Omsk.[14]

These attempts to create affective links to prewar civilian identities—most POW officers were civilians in uniform, not career officers—helped inmates imagine a future release from captivity to a yearned postwar existence. It was an attempt to construct bridges on both ends of a seemingly everlasting present and to defy time. With repatriation nowhere in sight, time in internment camps seemed—in the words of one inmate—to "stand still," devoid of any clear purpose or direction.[15] "What does this terrible enemy, Time, have in store for us?" wondered one Khabarovsk prisoner. "All that is personal recedes behind completely, and I have hardly the desire to write about it."[16]

Escape stories are staples of captivity literature and of twentieth-century cinema. However, in wartime, few prisoners actually attempt a "great escape"; most try to overcome the constraints of time and space indirectly and imaginatively. Material objects are essential for the success

Figure 6.1. First World War civilian internees inside an internment hut, Knockaloe Camp, Isle of Man. Courtesy Manx National Heritage, Douglas, Isle of Man. Photographic archive ID number: PG/7870/39421. Licensed from Bridgeman Art Library.

Figure 6.2. First World War civilian internee drinking tea in a robe and tie.
Note the small "Home Sweet Home" sign in the background. Knockaloe Camp,
Isle of Man. Courtesy Manx National Heritage, Douglas, Isle of Man. Photographic
archive ID number: PG/7870/38524. Licensed from Bridgeman Art Library.

of these "small escapes," and they played an essential role in military
camps in Russia and other belligerent countries during the First World
War. This was the case also in many of the Great War civilian internment camps (referred to varyingly in English as "civilian POW camps,"

"alien detention camps," or "concentration camps"). Inmates in both types of camps relied heavily on objects to navigate the unfamiliar world of captivity. At times the protracted and dedicated labor invested in making an object—rather than its use—gave internees much-needed sense of direction and purpose. In some cases they were allowed and even encouraged by authorities to create objects and keep themselves busy in productive activity. They established workshops of various kinds (woodworking, shoemaking, weaving, basket-making, printing, and so on) and constructed toys, decorations, and clever gadgets. In the British camp of Knockaloe (Isle of Man), the biggest civilian internment camp of the Great War, James Thomas Baily, a master woodcarver from Kent and a Quaker pacifist by conviction, was entrusted with organizing workshops for the internees. He stated with pride that over 70 percent of the estimated twenty-seven thousand internees worked in one productive activity or another, overcoming "the evident signs of mental and physical deterioration."[17]

The production and multifaceted usage of objects in Great War internment camps are at the heart of this chapter. Amidst the uncertainties and dislocations of captivity, POW officers and civilian internees relied on artifacts to perform meaningful social scripts and deployed them to articulate a range of emotions and identities. Although these scripts had multiple collective and personal meanings, many of them were aimed at sustaining prewar notions of "normalcy," "respectability," and productive masculinity. However, because these social scripts emanated from the prewar bi-gender world, recreating them in one-gender (homosocial) settings often led to transgressions of respectable masculinity.

Following the insights of anthropologist Alfred Gell, I argue in this essay that the prisoners—alongside camp personnel and administrators of relief—were the "intentional agents" who set in motion "the causal chains which . . . c[a]me into being as states of mind."[18] The artifacts in camps did not possess intentional social agency of this kind, but they were nonetheless indispensable in providing what Gell called "physical mediation" required to produce these sought-after states of mind. They were essential in bringing forth a certain ambience—in this case being part of a prewar urban world—and had in Gell's theoretical framework "secondary agency."[19]

World War I Internment: A Two-Tiered World

According to prevailing estimates there were around 8 to 8.5 million military prisoners during World War I and about 750,000 civilian internees ("civilian POWs," in the terminology of the time).[20] The great majority of prisoners were able-bodied men between the ages of 18 and 50, and some remained in captivity until 1922.[21]

One way to divide this immense group of prisoners is according to their legal status (or lack thereof): Military prisoners were covered by the Hague Conventions of 1899 and 1907, while civilian prisoners were not covered by any international convention. Whether the Hague framework proved to be an effective guarantor of POW survival and well-being during World War I is a matter of dispute among historians (and beyond the scope of this essay).[22] Suffice it to say that mortality rates during the First World War never reached the appalling figures of the Eastern Front during the Second World War.[23]

A second way to divide this immense group is according to whether or not they were forced to perform labor for their captors during the war. According to the Hague Convention of 1907, captured officers were not required to perform any labor duties while in the hands of the captor power, a provision that was universally respected during the First World War.[24] During their internment, these POW officers received pay (from the captor state) equal to that of an officer of similar rank in the army of their captor—in Russia, for example, staff officers (majors and above) received a monthly salary of 125 rubles, captains received 75 rubles, and lower-grade officers 50 rubles. In some belligerent countries, captured noncommissioned officers (NCOs) also enjoyed this exemption from forced labor (though without receiving pay), and so did some injured men.[25] In addition, an estimated group of about 150,000 civilian men of military age, who were found on enemy territory at the outbreak of war and locked away in internment camps, also enjoyed such an exemption.[26] They might decide to work for their own reasons—as the majority of Knockaloe inmates did—but they were not obliged to do so. The group that was exempt from labor constituted perhaps 10 percent of the overall World War I prisoner population, and the present discussion focuses on them. The essay focuses on a number of the big internment camps in Russia (Khabarovsk, Krasnoiarsk, Omsk, and Rasdolnoe), Germany (Ruhleben) and Great Britain (Knockaloe and Douglas), though examples from a few other camps are also discussed.

The second and much larger group of prisoners, namely the rank-and-file military prisoners and interned civilians from occupied territories in Western and Eastern Europe, had to perform forced labor in the service of the captor state and its economy. This does not necessarily mean that forced laborers always faced much harsher conditions than those exempt from labor—in many cases they clearly did—but in some cases, especially in countries that suffered from food scarcity during the war, agricultural laborers were often better fed than inmates who remained in camps.[27]

The crucial point in the context of this essay is whether prisoners had control over their daily schedule and whether they lived in a world that was segregated from the outside world. The forced laborers (both military and civilian) were integrated to a much greater degree into the spatial and temporal world of their captor societies, while officers, NCOs, and civilian internees of military age—those exempt from forced labor, that is—usually lived apart from the outer society, following the distinctive daily rhythms of their own camps. They could obtain various goods and raw materials through official supply lines, through relief organizations, or by purchasing them with their own money, but they usually had to stay in camp. Camp boundaries could thus be described as being "semi-porous": open to a certain extent to objects and supplies, yet restricted the movement of people to a much greater degree. Prisoners might be moved from camp to camp—and many indeed experienced several places of internment during their captivity—yet when in camp they had to stay inside. However, within camp they enjoyed a great deal of autonomy as long as they remained within physical and disciplinary bounds. In the words of J. Davidson Ketchum, a civilian internee at the camp of Ruhleben (near Berlin) and later a professor of psychology at the University of Toronto—"the men created for themselves a unique social world so complete and many-sided that its existence in a prison camp is almost unbelievable."[28]

"I Am Very Busy Always"

As early as November 1914 prisoners in Ruhleben realized that internment was a long-term affair.[29] Ketchum reported that internees had begun in the late autumn of 1914 to describe Ruhleben as a "town" and a "city," a designation they would continually use until November 24, 1918, when "they packed their bags, said their farewells and . . . left for home."[30] Converting a prewar racetrack (many of the lodgings were disused stables) into something that actually felt like a civilian town involved continuous efforts and playful inventiveness, which were expressed by such things as giving Ruhleben pathways London street names, creating professional-looking business ads in the camp newspaper, or giving sleeping quarters a domestic feel.[31] These all followed models of prewar urbanity with a broad pathway dubbed "Bond Street" serving as the "Shopping Centre," which offered among other amenities a department devoted to "tinned foods, fruits and greengrocery," an "outfitter," a "tailor," a "watchmaker," and a "refreshment bar."[32]

The project of creating a feel of prewar urbanity involved what Ketchum described as an "explosion of activity."[33] The prisoners "discovered numberless things to do, and set themselves eagerly to organize and perfect the doing of them. And in the process they created a network of social activities so extensive and absorbing that the camp became a world in itself—sometimes *the* world."[34] A German POW officer, writing on November 23, 1916, from the camp of Krasnaia Rechka in the vicinity of Khabarovsk, tried to impress upon his family how busy he was by providing detailed schedule:

> Around 9–9:30 one completes the morning washing, then breakfast: interchangeably tea, cocoa or coffee; honey, self-made jam but seldom butter as a spread. Then a stroll or playing fistball [*Faustball*]. Then Spanish or Russian lessons, then lunch. After eating I play bridge in order not to go to sleep otherwise I would become too fat. Afternoons strolling, bowling or fistball, from 5:30–6:30 English conversation, then dinner usually of our own cooking. Evenings, for entertainment bridge, skat or lectures. Around 11 pm off to bed.[35]

Keeping very busy could be of course a personal preference, but it also carried with it a reassuring communal message of combatting the lethargy of camp life and remaining mentally sound. "I cannot lay too much stress upon the serious mental condition of the civilian prisoners," wrote to *The Times* of London Sir Timothy Eden, the older brother of Sir Anthony Eden and a Ruhleben internee.[36] "Suddenly snatched from their peaceful occupations these men have been herded into a racecourse . . . the men have nothing to think of save their ruined prospects and the hopelessness of their position."[37] Major Pál (Paul) Stoffa, an Austro-Hungarian artillery officer, had the curious distinction of being imprisoned twice during the Great War, in two different countries and under two different legal categories: first as a captured enemy officer in the Russian/East Asian camp of Shkotovo, and then—after managing an unlikely escape with false documents—as an enemy civilian in Britain. Arriving in Knockaloe on the very last day of 1916, he wrote:

> The incessant drizzle outside supplied the key-note of our existence. In a sense it was exactly like Shkotovo: it gave one the same feeling of utter isolation, a complete severance from the outside world. No wonder that so many men degenerated here by degrees into something like a state of savagery: the decent majority struggled hard to keep afloat in a sea of hopeless despondency, many went under, insanity claiming not a few.[38]

This pervasive concern for the sanity of prisoners permeates also the diary of James Thomas Baily, a devout Quaker pacifist and a master carpenter by trade who was summoned by his church to provide craft instruction to interned enemy aliens in Britain. Upon arriving at his first camp—Lofthouse Park near Wakefield, Yorkshire—Baily discovered that "moral rot had already set in. Immediate steps were taken . . . to provide woodworking tools and timber, and leatherworkers' and bookbinders' equipment; tailors and shoemakers soon got busy with repairs, working for their fellow prisoners; even the most unskilled began turning out simple objects such as blotter pads and writing-cases from scrap cardboard."[39]

In August 1915 Baily arrived in Knockaloe and stayed there for four years, first as an "industrial adviser" and then from 1918 as "industrial superintendent," overseeing the efforts in what he called intermittently as "the black prison town" or "the malignant city."[40] As was the case in Lofthouse Park, he concluded that "signs of mental and physical deterioration among the internees" were largely a result of "lack of occupation" and that the surest way to battle "moroseness, avoidance of others and aimless promenading up and down the barbed-wire boundary of the compound like a wild animal in a cage . . . was to banish idleness."[41] As industrial superintendent of Knockaloe, Baily organized workshops in all twenty-three compounds of the camp using "tools and equipment loaned by the Friends Emergency Committee (FEC) [a Quaker wartime aid organization] and materials supplied at cost price."[42]

In a report written immediately after the closure of Knockaloe in 1919, Baily took pride in the various workshops he had established. He highlighted in particular the basket-weaving enterprise, which employed over a hundred men and produced all kinds of baskets, and the bone-carving workshop.[43] "Long leg bones," he reported, "were transfigured into slender flower vases decorated with carvings of tulips, lilies or a human figure [see the ornamental vase behind seated prisoner in figure 6.2]. The shorter bones were made into pin cushions, ashtrays, match and cigarette stands, table cruets, serviette rings, paper knives and brooches, very delicately carved."[44] The extensive reliance in Knockaloe on bone as raw material was connected at first with the availability of animal remains in the kitchens of all four sub-camps. "Large marrow bones were collected, boiled and bleached," reported Baily, and "were beautifully carved, the larger kinds having often sprays of flowers in bold relief standing out of the surface."[45] But the popularity of bone-carving had to do also with the materiality of the bone itself. When the camp switched its meat supply in December 1915 from animal carcasses to a salt-cured product called bully beef, Baily began to import animal bones to Knockaloe, "so off went the Industrial Adviser to Liverpool to search for bone, and succeeded in purchasing two tons of this smelly importation from the Argentine [sic] and had them transported into Douglas."[46] Transforming a material that signified death and decomposition into a tangible object of beauty seems to have had an engaging quality for the internees. Bone-carving channeled anxieties onto utilitarian and aesthetic artifacts and remained a widely practiced craft in all four sub-camps until 1919. These carvings became sought-after objects outside camp well after the war ended and remained so for many years. Leslie Baily, who in 1959 published a biography of his father, called them a "big industry" and reported that "Manx POW bone-work found its way to buyers from all over the world. The most exquisite pieces were carved by the brothers Lang of the Oberammergau Passion Play fame."[47]

Woodcarving also developed into a prevalent pursuit, especially in camps that housed interned sailors. The sailors seem to have brought with them an activity practiced on ships during long sea voyages, and from them it rapidly spread to other inmates. Anna Braithwaite Thomas of the Friends Emergency Committee described how the sailors "began to produce all sorts of curious and interesting models and ornaments, and many other inmates appealed for a chance for like occupation."[48] When Baily visited Handforth Camp in Cheshire in 1915, he inquired whether any of the prisoners was engaged in woodcarving: "my purpose being to encourage them to pursue their craft and also to find potential leaders to teach others."[49] He was introduced to R. Wildmann who had worked as valet in Scotland before the war and was married to a Scottish servant. Impressed by the lovely white holly boxes Wildmann had carved, Baily requested to be shown the tools Wildmann used:

> Not having tools he had improvised some which showed much ingenuity, for a saw he had serrated the back edge of his dinner knife with a file, for a hammer he had salvaged a disused stock lock, taken out the bolt, and seized it by means of wire to a piece of wood which he shaped it into some semblance of a shaft; various sizes and shapes of chisels were made with broken pieces of knife blades fitted into pieces of stick and bradawls from different sized nails inserted also into pieces of stick. From a small block of wood he had, with much patient labour, modelled a small plane.[50]

Most inmates clearly lacked such ingenuity but enjoyed nonetheless making wooden artifacts. Braithwaite Thomas emphasized that many of these "quite unskilled men" relied on wooden objects for practical and affective purposes: "as gifts to their wives and children; they improved the fittings of the camp and prepared boxes in which to carry home their little belonging, and keepsakes for the future."[51] These self-made wooden artifacts helped to bridge the various forms of psychological distance by allowing prisoners to recreate a sense of domestic comfort, reconnect imaginatively with their loved ones and with their past selves, and envision a future after the hoped-for release. Anthropologist Jane Dusselier, who studied the crafts done by Japanese-Americans interned in concentration

camps during the Second World War, identified woodwork as a quintessentially "manly medium"—Japanese-American women attempted to
ameliorate "oppressive living conditions by crocheting, sewing, weaving,
embroidering and knitting"—and "as a tool of recuperating a sense of
place."[52]

In some cases woodwork evolved into a full-scale carpentry workshop. Charles Matt, a former foreman of a furniture factory in London,
made wooden furniture in Knockaloe for war-devastated areas in Europe
assisted by the Quakers, while also constructing high-end furnishings
based among others on the designs of the famous Art Nouveau designer
and architect Charles Rennie Mackintosh. The work was commissioned
by W. J. Bassett-Lowke, a patron of Mackintosh and the proprietor of a
toy company specializing in model trains, boats, and ships. Bassett-Lowke
contracted Mackintosh in the years 1916 and 1917 to renovate his house
at 78 Derngate in Northampton in the modernist style. "It was the first
'modern' house to be built in England," wrote Lesley Baily, "and it was
furnished with the beautiful Knockaloe furniture of Charles Matt and his
colleagues . . . to see so many untutored amateurs find an unknown craft
at their finger-tips confirmed his [that is, Baily's] peacetime experience in
schools, that craft-ability is natural to more people than realize it."[53]

As mentioned, the acknowledged aim of the workshops was primarily
occupational therapy: to provide a remedy for the seemingly deteriorating
mental health of prisoners, described by German speakers as *Stacheldraht-
krankheit* and by English speakers as "barbed-wirelitis" or "barbed-wire
disease."[54] Baily stated with pride that employment in one productive
activity or another "arrested the 'barbed-wirelitis' to such an extent that
the ex-internees testified that no man who became busily occupied fell a
victim to it."[55] In Knockaloe, workshops also became "commercial and
utilitarian" over time with manufactured goods sold through the international network of Quaker organizations in countries such as "Great
Britain, the United States of America, Holland, Denmark and Sweden."[56]

This gradual commercialization of production also characterized a
number of officer camps in Siberia. Whereas during the first three years
of the war artifacts were created mostly to fulfill personal and communal
needs, the breakdown of central government in Russia in 1917 and the
rapid devaluation of the ruble created an incentive to sell in bulk outside the camp. From the spring of 1918 until the collapse of the Admiral

Kolchak's White government in January 1920 the workshops in the officer camp of Krasnoiarsk made brisk trade with the surrounding region. "Their coveted products," according to one memoirist, "managed to fetch high prices."[57] In addition to the woodworking and metalworking workshops, commonplace in many camps, the camp of Krasnoiarsk distinguished itself with its unique tobacco industry, which catered to the needs of its mixed Siberian clientele. Importing tobacco leaves from Manchuria, the Krasnoiarsk camp produced a range of tobacco products: coarse tobacco (*makhorka*) for local peasants and for soldiers in the White Armies; pipe tobacco, chewing tobacco, and snuff for general consumption; and fine cigars and cigarettes, manufactured mostly by Turkish internees on self-devised machines. "Hundreds of prisoners found rewarding employment in the tobacco business, the pounding knives merrily drumming in the hacking containers of the 'makhorka men.'"[58]

Thus, the labor of the prisoners inside camps had two distinct aims: to assist inmates with coping with the mental travails of internment and to raise revenue for the prisoners (and on many occasions for relief organizations and for camp authorities where they received a cut).[59] The products and artifacts produced by these prisoners became part of two separate value systems: an experiential-performative value system that placed an emphasis on the (re)enactment of meaningful roles and scripts and a monetary value system that commodified the artifact and augmented the material resources available to the internees. Both of these value systems reduced the feeling of psychological distance experienced in camps and helped inmates retain the sensations of "being productive," "living in a proper home," "having private spaces," "going shopping," "being civilized," and other subjectively meaningful scripts, as well as increasing the financial means at their disposal and assisting their material well-being.

Displaying Artifacts

Although the preservation of sanity was presented as the *raison d'être* of all productive activity, it was an understanding of sanity that was firmly rooted in the social and gender norms of the fin-die-siècle. B. E. Sargeaunt, the government secretary of the Isle of Man during the First World War, made the connection explicit by arguing that the "remedy for such a mental malady is, of course, a healthy occupation . . . the prisoners were in considerable danger of falling into habits of gambling and other vices more reprehensible still."[60] He did not specify what these more reprehensible vices might be, but the commandant of Knockaloe was quoted as having "the familiar unsavory tale to tell, of the sexual perversities of an all-male society, of the mischief of idle minds and hands, and of the 'barbed-wire disease.'"[61]

Loss of mental soundness should therefore be understood as a code for a spectrum of actions and dispositions. These could include severe cases such as suicide attempts, memory loss, or mental breakdown or encompass forms of behavior deemed reprehensible by contemporaneous mores such as gambling, laziness, and same-sex relationships. Incomplete sources make it very difficult to estimate the number of prisoners who had suffered complete mental collapse, but W. R. Hughes of the FEC in Ruhleben and Knockaloe stated that "the number of complete mental breakdowns was less than has been feared."[62] According to a memorandum written in Ruhleben at the end of 1917, out of four thousand internees, there were "fifty cases of 'insanity' and fifty cases of 'total nervous collapse' up to December 1, 1917."[63] By March 1916 seventy internees had been transferred for convalescence to the Weiler Sanatorium in Charlottenburg, not far from Ruhleben, while those exhibiting clear psychotic symptoms were committed to a psychiatric institution in Neuruppin in Brandenburg. Ketchum reckoned that three internees committed suicide during the whole internment period in Ruhleben, and three additional prisoners attempted to do so without succeeding.[64]

As a result, work and productivity were highly valued not only for the mental balance they may have fostered or the revenues they had generated, but also as reminders of middle-class masculine prowess and probity. Self-produced goods reflected the efforts, resolve, and skills required to be industrious men and were displayed and photographed as such. In some camps internees held industrial, agricultural, and art exhibitions intended for inmates, camp personnel, and outside visitors (mostly representatives of relief organizations). These exhibitions imitated the big industrial and horticultural exhibitions that so fascinated western urban spectators throughout the second half of the nineteenth century and the early years of the twentieth century. Like grander expos, camp exhibitions aimed to highlight ingenuity, dexterity, sophistication, and national technological expertise.

The Ruhleben Horticultural Society (RHS), for example, wrote a letter in September 1916 to the Royal Horticultural Society (also RHS) "requesting to become affiliated to the Royal Horticultural Society. Under the circumstances we are unable to remit the usual fee but trust this will be no hindrance to our enjoying the privileges of affiliation. . . . During this, our second summer, the magnificent show of flowers and tasteful decorative schemes which were carried out have done much to alleviate our lot."[65] Ruhleben horticulturalists organized a second "Flower Show and Competition" in August 1917 that included the display of miniature table rock gardens—modeled on rock gardens in the Royal Society exhibitions—as well as a sweet pea competition displaying fifty-one different cultivars—"the show was well patronised by the Camp and was honoured by a special visit by members of the Netherlands Legation."[66] Brent Elliott, the historian of the Royal Horticultural Society, points out that "sweet peas were the pre-eminent floral craze of the Edwardian period" and that Ruhleben internees viewed them as "our almost national flower."[67] From this perspective, Ruhleben horticulturalists were displaying not only their work ethic but also a patriotic dedication to a flower they perceived as quintessentially English. With much toil and effort—Ruhleben was built on sandy soil—members of the affiliated RHS managed to construct in camp a synecdoche of England that their parent organization—the London RHS—could be proud of. One German official was quoted by a memoirist as saying vis-à-vis the gardening efforts: "You English seem to set to work as if you were founding a new colony."[68]

As mentioned, these exhibitions were organized with a clear cultural script in mind: industrious men displaying their creations before a visiting crowd of urbane spectators. In Knockaloe industrial exhibitions placed on view hundreds and often even thousands of different items, ranging from the luxurious to the functional and to the mundane (see figure 6.3). After their repatriation to the United Kingdom in the winter of 1918–19, former Ruhleben inmates held a concluding exhibition at Westminster Hall opened by King George V.[69]

The exhibitions held in camps were visited by a large number of prisoners, and a judging committee from among the inmates handed out awards for the best-crafted pieces. At first glance these industrial exhibitions seem

Figure 6.3. Industrial Exhibition Knockaloe Camp IV with internee Otto Gross, head of the Industrial Committee. J. T. Baily scrapbook, J. T. Baily Papers MS 10417. Courtesy Manx National Heritage, Douglas, Isle of Man.

indeed to conform to prevalent middle-class conceptions of manliness in fin-de-siècle western and central Europe: Self-pride and social esteem are acquired through productivity and useful pursuits. By previously denying inmates productive outlets internment camps had destabilized their sense of gender equilibrium, which was restored by carrying out constructive work.

However, a closer inspection reveals that something more ambivalent had been taking place in these industrial exhibitions. "I remember," wrote Baily in his private scrapbook, "Camp IV having as an adjunct to a most excellent exhibition a café which was very popular, with some of the good looking young men impersonating female waitresses."[70] The female impersonators were photographed extensively (see figure 6.4) but "as a precautionary measure to avoid unpleasant misunderstanding outside the camp, these postcards were strictly forbidden to be sent beyond the camp boundaries."[71]

Although female impersonation is not the focus of the present essay, it is worth mentioning that it was a pervasive part of everyday life in Great War internment camps in all belligerent countries.[72] Gender

Figure 6.4. Wiener Café at the Industrial Exhibition Knockaloe Camp IV. J. T. Baily scrapbook. J. T. Baily Papers MS 10417. Courtesy of Manx National Heritage, Douglas, Isle of Man.

transgression is usually discussed in conjunction with theatrical produc-tions on the camp stages, but it actually took place in a wide variety of settings such as industrial and horticultural shows, camp dancing schools, camp promenades, and in the privacy of one's barrack home. Impersonation could fit snugly within the central script of camp life, that is, to create a subjective feeling of a prewar urban society. The theater in Krasnoiarsk officer camp, for example, had a four-barrack theater com-plex that included also a buffet, a coffee shop, and "one of the barracks converted by a group of German and Austrian architects into an elegant restaurant with all the amenities, decorated in a modern style by the art dealer Lieutenant Kunft."[73]

In performing diverse scripts of urban life, prisoners navigated between domestic and commercial settings, between leisurely and edu-cational pursuits, and between activities coded as "masculine" and those coded as "feminine." They worked, studied, competed in sports, made baskets, mended clothing, and nurtured younger inmates in vari-ous ways. Hungarian civilian internee Aladár Kuncz described in his camp memoirs *Black Monastery* how a thirty-eight-year-old prisoner, Dr. Herz, fussed over a young Czech internee, "cooked for him, sewed

for him and washed for him. He cared for him like a mother."[74] Each
of these everyday activities offered different emotional rewards, and
each came with its own material articulation, some of which was self-
created. As long as gender transgression constituted a part of this over-
arching script it could be viewed as acceptable. Some interwar studies
even argued that in the all-male environment of camp, impersonators
preserved the "image of woman" and served as necessary reminders
of the bi-gender world.[75] Theater scholar Hermann Pörzgen wrote in
his seminal 1933 study *Theater without Woman (Theater ohne Frau)*,
"he was what he impersonated. He was the only woman that they saw
through these long years, the only human being that could show them
the grace of the other sex."[76] Describing the impersonators was at times
a grammatical challenge for memoirists, who alternated between the
masculine pronoun *him* and the feminine pronoun *her*, with or without
quotation marks. A female impersonator described in loving detail the
lovely clothes s/he was wearing in Knockaloe while emphasizing "Bin
weder Fraulein, weder schoen" (I am not a damsel, nor am I pretty; see
figure 6.5).

In her essay "Beyond Words" Leora Auslander argued that in twentieth-
century Europe "objects did not reflect as much as *create* social position (as
well, some would argue, the self itself)."[77] Objects helped Europeans—and
doubtless also non-Europeans—consolidate from early childhood a sense
of personal distinctiveness that was socially bound with an array of meaningful frameworks such as family, class, gender, sexuality, religion, region,
political party, nation, and many others. Wooden spoons, silver forks,
black-felt berets, porcelain plates, and family jewelry were all employed
alongside many other objects to perform socially legible and individually
evocative scripts.

As this essay has attempted to show, these meaningful scripts did not
vanish into thin air when millions of men found themselves interned in
camps during the First World War. Although placed far away from home
and in an environment that was unfamiliar and disorientating, World
War I prisoners attempted to bridge psychological distance and retain a
connection to their prewar sense of selfhood. Certain categories of privileged inmates—mostly officers and some of civilian internees—had access
to funds and the relative freedom to structure the everyday as they saw
fit. In many cases, they chose to create artifacts and perform meaningful

Figure 6.5. "Bin weder Fraulein, weder schoen: Theaterplauderei" (I am not a damsel, nor am I pretty). *Quousque Tandem* magazine, November 1915, Collection of WWI Internment Camp Magazines. Courtesy of Manx National Heritage, Douglas, Isle of Man.

scripts through their usage and display. Many of these scripts were tied to the performance of what sociologist Raewyn Connell termed as "hegemonic masculinity,"[78] while others had socially transgressive elements that sanctioned—at least partially—nonconforming forms of masculinity and being.

German-Jewish painter and journalist Paul Cohen-Portheim described in his memoirs the "complete bliss" he felt when, after almost three years of internment, he was finally allotted a small cubicle (six feet by four) for himself and could experience at last a much-desired sense of privacy.[79] To

convey "how marvelous a place" his cubicle was, Cohen-Portheim provided a detailed description of its interior:

> There was a bed on the sleeping-car system, which went up against the
> wall in daytime, when a curtain hid it, and a couch, which was a box with
> cushions on it, was revealed underneath it. The curtain also hid a washing-
> basin and like paraphernalia. Above the bed was a long shelf for books, quite
> a library, before the window a small collapsible table (again on sleeping-
> car principles), and along the other long wall a cupboard for clothes and
> belongings, only a few inches deep but six feet long. There were two tiny
> tabourets, vestiges of my stage activity, and a deck-chair which could be
> hidden behind the curtain. But that cubicle was not only practical but
> also handsome as well. The walls were papered in grey-blue, the wood-
> work stained brown, the curtain an Indian print, a red-silk handkerchief
> made a lampshade, and there were paintings on the wall where any space
> remained.[80]

By having a private, richly decorated cubicle Cohen-Portheim felt at last
that his individuality had been restored and that he "had surmounted all
prison troubles, and was going to be quite happy and contented there for
any length of time."[81] A week later he was moved to another camp.

Notes

This essay was written with financial support from Israel Science Foundation (ISF) grant number 1152/12. I wish to thank the foundation for its generous support of my research.

1. Ilse Raettig, *Bericht 9 über das Offiziersgefangenenlager Chabarowsk (Nur für den
Privatgebrauch der Angehörigen)*, June 1917. BA/MA Msg 200/20.

2. Raettig, *Bericht 9.*

3. *Bericht 1 über das Offizierlager Omsk* (Druck "nur für den privatgebrauch der Angehörigen") Bundesarchiv: Militärarchiv N 448/3, 1

4. *Bericht 1.*

5. *Bericht 1.*

6. Nira Liberman and Yaacov Trope, "Traversing Psychological Distance," *Trends in
Cognitive Sciences* 18, no. 7 (2014): 364–369; Nira Liberman and Yaacov Trope, "The Psychology of Transcending the Here and Now," *Science* 322 (2008): 1201–1205.

7. Liberman and Trope, "Traversing Psychological Distance," 364.

8. Liberman and Trope, "Traversing Psychological Distance," 365.

9. Ilse Raettig, *Bericht 10 über das Offiziersgefangenenlager Chabarowsk (Nur für den
Privatgebrauch der Angehörigen)*, August 1917. BA/MA Msg 200/20.

10. Ilse Raettig, *Bericht 7 über das Offiziersgefangenenlager Chabarowsk (Nur für den
Privatgebrauch der Angehörigen)*, March 1917. BA/MA Msg 200/20.

11. Raettig, *Bericht 9*.

12. On domestic spaces, see Iris Rachamimov, "Camp Domesticity: Shifting Gender Boundaries in WWI Internment Camps," in *Cultural Heritage and Prisoners of War: Creativity behind Barbed Wire*, ed. Gillian C. Carr and H. Mytum (London: Routledge, 2012), 291–305.

13. *Bericht 2 über das Offizierlager Omsk (Nur für den Privatgebrauch der Angehörigen)*, April 1917, Bundesarchiv: Militärarchiv N 448/3.

14. *Bericht 2*.

15. Paul Cohen-Portheim, *Time Stood Still: My Internment in England 1914–1918* (New York: Dutton & Co., 1932), 5.

16. Raettig, *Bericht 9*.

17. J. T. Bailey, "Report to the Government Secretary, Douglass," September 30, 1919, 1; J. T. Bailey Papers MS 10417, box 1, Manx National Heritage, Douglas and Knockaloe Camps Library.

18. Alfred Gell, *Art and Agency: An Anthropological Theory* (Oxford: Oxford University Press, 1998), 20.

19. Gell, *Art and Agency*, 20–21.

20. For estimates of the numbers of prisoners during World War I, see Heather Jones, *Violence against Prisoners of War in the First World War: Britain, France, and Germany 1914–1920* (Cambridge: Cambridge University Press, 2011), 19–27; Iris Rachamimov, *POWs and the Great War: Captivity on the Eastern Front* (Oxford and New York: Berg Publishers, 2002), 31–66; Niall Fergusson, *The Pity of War: Explaining World War I* (New York: Basic Books, 1998), 369, table 42. Matthew Stibbe, *British Civilian Internees in Germany: The Ruhleben Camp, 1914–1918* (Manchester: Manchester University Press, 2008), 4–5; Matthew Stibbe, "Civilian Internment and Civilian Internees in Europe, 1914–20," *Immigrants and Minorities* 26 (1–2): 49–50; Heather Jones, "A Missing Paradigm? Military Captivity and the Prisoner of War, 1914–1918," in *Captivity, Forced Labour, and Forced Migration in Europe during the First World War*, ed. Matthew Stibbe (London: Routledge, 2009), 25; Heather Jones, *Violence against Prisoners of War in the First World War*, 19–27.

21. Iris Rachamimov, "Military Captivity in Two World Wars: Legal Frameworks and Camp Regimes," in *The Cambridge History of War, Volume 4: War and the Modern World, 1850–2005*, ed. Roger Chickering, Dennis Showalter, and Hans van de Ven (Cambridge: Cambridge University Press, 2012), 214–235. See Rachamimov, *POWs and the Great War*, 31–44, 191–196, 221–222.

22. Rachamimov, "Military Captivity," 214–235; Heather Jones, *Violence against Prisoners of War*, 1–8; Rachamimov, *POWs and the Great War*, 67–132.

23. Rachamimov, "Military Captivity," 222–229.

24. Rachamimov, "Military Captivity," 214–235.

25. Rachamimov, *POWs and the Great War*, 97–107.

26. Stephane Audoin Rouzeau and Annette Becker, *14–18: Understanding the Great War* (New York: Hill and Wang, 2002), 72.

27. Rachamimov, *POWs and the Great War*, 109–110.

28. J. Davidson Ketchum, *Ruhleben: A Prison Camp Society* (Toronto: University of Toronto Press, 1965), 3.

29. Davidson Ketchum, *Ruhleben*, 79.

30. Davidson Ketchum, *Ruhleben*, 339.

31. See for example the issues of the *Ruhleben Camp Magazine* at the "John C. Masterman collection of Ruhleben Prisoner of War camp material 1914–1918. Hollis 12512521. Harvard Law School Library. Harvard University, https://iiif.lib.harvard.edu/manifests/view/drs:13136016$185i, accessed April 15, 2017.

32. John C. Masterman collection of Ruhleben Prisoner of War camp material 1914–1918. Hollis 12512521. Harvard Law School Library. Harvard University, https://iiif.lib.harvard.edu/manifests/view/drs:13136016$505i, accessed April 15, 2017.

33. Davidson Ketchum, *Ruhleben*, 192–210.

34. Davidson Ketchum, *Ruhleben*, 192, emphasis in the original.

35. Raettig, *Bericht 7*.

36. Davidson Ketchum, *Ruhleben*, 167.

37. Davidson Ketchum, *Ruhleben*.

38. Pàl Stoffa, *Round the World to Freedom: Being the Escapes and Adventures of Major Paul Stoffa (of the Hungarian Army)*, ed. and trans. L. Harta (London: John Lane, 1933), 232–233.

39. Diary quoted in Leslie Baily, *Craftsman and Quaker: The Story of James T. Baily* (London: George Allen & Unwin Limited, 1959), 88.

40. J. T. Baily, MS10417, 600; Baily, *Craftsman and Quaker*, 95,

41. J. T. Baily, "Report to the Government Secretary, Douglass," September 30, 1919, 1; J. T. Baily Papers MS 10417, box 1, Manx National Heritage, Douglas and Knockaloe Camps Library; Leslie Baily, *Craftsman and Quaker: The Story of J. T. Baily* (London: George Allen and Unwin, 1959), 93. Quoted in Yvonne Cresswell, ed., *Living with the Wire: Civilian Internment in the Isle of Man during the Two World Wars* (Douglas: Manx National Heritage, 1994), 19.

42. J. T. Baily, "Report to the Government Secretary, Douglass," September 30, 1919, 1; J. T. Baily Papers MS 10417, box 1, Manx National Heritage, Douglas and Knockaloe Camps Library; see also Baily, *Craftsman and Quaker*, 98–107.

43. J. T. Baily, "Report to the Government Secretary, Douglass," September 30, 1919, 1; J. T. Baily Papers MS 10417, box 1, Manx National Heritage, Douglas and Knockaloe Camps Library.

44. Baily, *Craftsman and Quaker*, 100.

45. J. T. Baily Papers MS 10417, box 1, scrapbook, Manx National Heritage, Douglas and Knockaloe Camps Library, undated report, 2; see also Baily, *Craftsman and Quaker*, 100.

46. J. T. Baily Papers MS 10417, box 1, scrapbook, undated report, 2. See also the diary of Karl Schönwälder, a German subject who grew up in Holland and came to Britain as a teenager: "we had bully beef today as 11,000 lbs. of beef had to be desztroid [sic]." Diary of Karl Schönwälder, Manx National Heritage, Douglas and Knockaloe Camps Library, MS 12028, entry December 2, 1915.

47. Baily, *Craftsman and Quaker*, 100.

48. Anna Braithwaite Thomas, *St. Stephen's House: Friends' Emergency Work in England 1914 to 1920*, London: Emergency Committee for the Assistance of Germans, Austrians and Hungarians in Distress, 1920), 61.

49. J. T. Baily Papers MS 10417, box 1, diary, 546.

50. J. T. Baily Papers MS 10417, box 1, diary, 546–547.

51. Braithwaite Thomas, *St. Stephen's House*, 61.

52. Jane Dusselier, "The Arts of Survival: Remaking the Inside Spaces of Japanese American Concentration Camps," in *Cultural Heritage and Prisoners of War: Creativity Behind Barbed Wire*, ed. Gilly Carr and Harold Mytom (London and New York: Routledge, 2012), 83, 85, 94.

53. Baily, *Craftsman and Quaker*, 102.

54. J. T. Baily Papers MS 10417, box 1, scrapbook; A. L. Vischer, *Barbed Wire Disease: A Psychological Study of the Prisoners of War* (London: Oxford House, 1919); Cresswell, ed., *Living with the Wire*, 26.

55. J. T. Baily Papers MS 10417, box 1, scrapbook. American Embassy inspectors even estimated at one point that 85 percent of the inmates were employed in such a manner. See Cresswell, *Living with the Wire*, 28.

56. J. T. Baily, "Report to the Government Secretary, Douglass," September 30, 1919, 1; J. T. Baily Papers MS 10417, Box 1, Manx National Heritage, Douglas and Knockaloe Camps Library.

57. See Leopold Kern, "Lagerindustrie," in *Feindeshand: Die Gefangenschaft im Weltkriege in Einzeldarstellungen*, vol. 1, ed. Hans Weiland and Leopold Kern (Vienna: Göth, 1931), 123–128.

58. Kern, "Lagerindustrie," 124

59. See letter by B. E. Sargeaunt, Government Secretary and Treasurer of the Isle of Man, to Baily: "I am to convey to you the thanks and appreciation of Lieutenant Governor for the very valuable work which you conducted at Knockaloe Camp during the period of the War, resulting as it did in the manufacture of many thousands of articles for the making of which British labour was not available, and contributing to the revenue of a sum of £1,363 by way of reduction of prisoners' wages towards their maintenance." B. E. Sargeaunt to J. T. Baily, October 9, 1919, J. T. Baily Papers MS 10417, box 1.

60. Quoted in "Behind the Barbed-Wire: The Quakers' Splendid Work at Knockaloe, Immense Quantities of Goods Made in Camp, Prisoners Saved from Despair and Madness," *Isle of Man Examiner*, September 24, 1926.

61. Baily, *Craftsman and Quaker*, 93.

62. "Behind the Barbed-Wire."

63. Davidson Ketchum, *Ruhleben*, 167.

64. Davidson Ketchum, *Ruhleben*, 168.

65. Brent Elliott, "A Tale of Two Societies: The Royal Horticultural Society and the Ruhleben Horticultural Society," *Occasional Papers from the RHS Lindley Library* 12 (2014): 42–43.

66. Elliott, "Tale of Two Societies," 51.

67. Elliott, "Tale of Two Societies," 51–52.

68. The quote is from J. C. Masterman, *On the Chariot Wheel: An Autobiography* (Oxford: Oxford University Press, 1975), 103. See also Elliott, "Tale of Two Societies," 61.

69. On the Ruhleben Exhibition in Westminster Hall, see Matthew Stibbe, *British Civilian Internees in Germany: The Ruhleben Camp 1914–18* (Manchester and New York: University of Manchester Press, 2008), 163; Davidson Ketchum, *Ruhleben*, 174.

70. J. T. Baily Papers MS 10417, box 1, scrapbook, K98, Manx National Heritage, Douglas and Knockaloe Camps Library.

71. J. T. Baily Papers MS 10417, box 1, scrapbook, K98, Manx National Heritage, Douglas and Knockaloe Camps Library.

72. On that see Iris Rachamimov, "'Er war . . . , was er darstellte,' Geschlechterüberschreitungen in den Internierungslagern des Ersten Weltkriegs," in *Mein Kamerad—Die Diva. Theater an der Front und in Gefangenenlagern des Ersten Weltkriegs*, ed. Julia B. Köhne, Britta Lange, and Anke Vetter (Munich: edition text + kritik 2014), 115–127; Rachamimov, "The Disruptive Comforts of Drag: (Trans)Gender Performances among Prisoners of War in Russia, 1914–1920," *American Historical Review* 111, no. 2 (2006): 362–382; David A. Boxwell, "The Follies of War: Cross Dressing and Popular Theatre on the British Front Lines, 1914–1918," *MODERNISM/modernity* 9, no. 1 (2002): 1–20; Hermann Pörzgen, *Theater ohne Frau: Das Bühnenleben der Kriegsgefangen Deutschen 1914–1920* (Osteuropa Verlag: Königsberg und Berlin, 1933).

73. Franz Rehor, "Das Offizierstheater in Krasnojarsk," in *In Feindeshand: Die Gefangenschaft im Weltkriege in Einzeldarstellungen*, vol. 1, ed. Hans Weiland and Leopold Kern (Vienna: Göth, 1931), 203.

74. Aladár Kuncz, *Black Monastery*, trans. Ralph Murray (New York: Harcourt, Brace and Company, 1934), 141.

75. See Rachamimov, "Disruptive Comforts of Drag," 377–381.

76. Pörzgen, *Theater ohne Frau,* 78.

77. Leora Auslander, "Beyond Words," *American Historical Review* 110, no. 4 (2005): 1018, emphasis in the original.

78. R. W. Connell and James Messerschmidt, "Hegemonic Masculinty: Rethinking the Concept," *Gender and Society* 19, no. 6 (2005): 829–859.

79. Cohen-Portheim, *Time Stood Still,* 193.

80. Cohen-Portheim, *Time Stood Still,* 191–192.

81. Cohen-Portheim, *Time Stood Still,* 193–194. Cohen-Portheim was moved to be interned in neutral Holland, where invalid English and German prisoners (both civilian and military) were to be held until the end of the war. This would seem as an improvement, but Cohen-Portheim reported feeling "thoroughly miserable and frightened. I felt I had been cheated out of the fruit of all my effort."

THE BRICOLAGE OF DEATH

Jewish Possessions and the Fashioning of the Prisoner Elite in Auschwitz-Birkenau, 1942–1945

Noah Benninga

According to survivor Benedikt Kautsky, social differentiation in Auschwitz was greater than in free society: "the prisoner camp-eldest . . . stood higher above a Muselmann than a wealthy industrialist or the steersman of a democratic state stands above a penniless, unemployed man sleeping on a bench in the open."[1] Kautsky's 1946 memoir even claimed that fashion was a feature of prisoner society: "fashion . . . would suddenly dictate plus-fours and people would get clocks sewn on their hose, or would have their jackets and coats tailored, or would wear black cloth caps."[2] In this, Kautsky was not alone: Survivor Hermann Langbein, for example, claimed that the adage "the clothes make the man" had greater significance in a concentration camp than in free society.[3]

But if the notion of "fashion in Auschwitz" strikes us as strange, I argue, this reflects our postwar desire to see all victims as equal before their oppression more than the sources or the historical reality. Differences among prisoners existed and were integral to the Nazi socio-racial planning and running of the camp. To survive, prisoners had to "make a career," that is, to achieve success in the terms of the camp. Despite the abnormal situation, success was reflected along lines familiar to us from "normal" life. Using survivor accounts, this chapter explores the ways in which fashion and dress manifested in a social world on the precipice of immediate death.

What was the significance of such "fashion" in Auschwitz? We begin by substantiating that indeed this term is not a misnomer. Following this we will take a closer look at what (short of escape) we might call the objects of the prisoners' desire: their hand-altered wardrobes. While these two sections might seem surprising, we then deal with the material basis, of which fashion was a symptom; in other words, how it was possible for there to be such a thing as fashion in a concentration and extermination camp. The conclusion attempts to gauge the factors that drove prisoner fashion.

Introducing Fashion in Auschwitz

Our imagination is quick to equate Auschwitz and other extermination centers with the grays of smoke, ash, and steel; it is hard to imagine that fashion—in the sense of caring about one's appearance and the accruement of superior goods—even had a place in the everyday life of prisoners. However, one questions whether fashion as a semiotic system based on differences can ever be truly absent. In the hypercompetitive world of Auschwitz, where the purpose of the competition was to survive, looking "better than" someone implied a degree of power and often ensured not being picked on as the weakest in the pack.[4]

As is well known, the SS developed a system of classifying prisoners based on reason for arrest, country of origin, and racial background.[5] This system, used with minor variations in all of the Nazi concentration camps, was expressed in marking on the prisoners' uniforms. The uniform was a text meant to be read from the front, the side, and sometimes the back. In addition to the *Winkel* (the colored cloth triangle denoting the information mentioned above), the uniform displayed the prisoner's number; the sequential nature of these numbers disclosed seniority at a glance, and experienced prisoners and guards knew how to read these numbers and identify with which group or transport a prisoner had arrived. These details were worn at the breast and along the seam of the leg. In cases of flight risk, a red dot was sometimes added on the back of the uniform (the part of the fleeing prisoner most prominently visible). Members of the penal company had a black dot below their *Winkel*, a token of their fate. Additional signs could be appended as the need arose, including bands on the arms to denote senior prisoners, foremen, and Kapos.[6]

Though the systematic nature of prisoner categorization and marking is well known, what has received less attention is the surprising degree of latitude which the prisoner elite had regarding the fashioning of their uniforms. The word *uniform* denotes uniformity and sameness, but the prisoner elite were allowed—to a certain degree even expected or encouraged—to alter and ameliorate their uniforms. This could only be accomplished through, and therefore became a mark of, the personal power of prisoners within the system.

According to prisoner testimonies, the SS generally reacted favorably to the improved appearance of the prisoners—up to a point. Finding out again and again where this point lay and arriving at and maintaining an appearance that was deemed proper made up a large part of the strategies prisoners used in an attempt to earn grudging respect from camp authorities and to emanate an aura of power. It was a strategy of survival, and it was not a science but an art:

> [This was] one of the most torturing uncertainties: one never knew how the mood of the Germans "ran"—whether, if one was *seen* shaving or cleaning one's boots, that it wouldn't get one killed. It was an incredible daily roulette; . . . one SS might consider a man looking after himself in this way as making himself "conspicuous"—the cardinal sin—and then another might not. The *effect* of being clean always helped—it even created a kind of respect in them. But to be seen doing it, might be considered showing off, or toadying, and provoke punishment, or death. We finally understood that the maximum safety lay in looking much—but not *too* much—like the SS themselves and the significance of this went even beyond the question of "safety."[7]

With which materials were these appearances were built and maintained? In Auschwitz-Birkenau and the other extermination camps, the material was provided by a vast surplus created by the murder of the Jews. Limited to the amount of baggage they could carry with them, the deportees, unknowingly condemned to death, chose to bring the most valuable possessions they had left, among them objects that would be important for starting a new life or had a high monetary value and would be useful for barter (among them, by all reports, hard currency and jewels).[8] Upon arrival in Auschwitz, Jews were told to leave their baggage on the train and were immediately subjected to a selection after which all the *unarbeitsfähig* (unable to work)—the elderly, children, and the sick—were killed. Meanwhile the luggage was cleared from the ramp by the Kanada-Kommando (the storage hangers used to house the Jewish goods were nicknamed "Kanada" in camp parlance), and the contents began their "illegal" journey into the camp, "sticking" to the hands of prisoners and guards in a myriad of ways. The principles behind these practices are addressed below, but a full exposition of this subject in Auschwitz remains a desideratum. The fact that these goods were accessible to the camp elite meant access to luxury—both in relative and at times even in absolute terms. And this was occurring literally in the shadow of the crematoria, while other prisoners starved to death and the rest of the world was experiencing wartime rationing.

In addition to the material resources of the murdered Jews, the SS selection system—which famously gave primacy to manual labor skills while disavowing higher learning and "intellectual" professions—ensured that the camp was well stocked with experienced tailors and cobblers. Auschwitz, like other camps, had workshops for the production of textile goods, stocked not only with sewing machines but also with the best of Warsaw's Jewish tailors.[9] These resources were used also to engage in *schwarzarbeit* (the production of goods by prisoners for trade). They were the basis for a bricoloric production indigenous to the camp itself. Claude Lévi-Strauss, who popularized the concept of bricolage in his 1962 book *The Savage Mind*, considers it a form of creative ability expressed within a limited repertoire. Forced to use a set repertoire, the "bricoleur" nonetheless proceeds to produce something new with whatever tools and materials that are at hand.[10]

This chapter attempts to expose the phenomenon of "camp fashion": to show evidence that in fact the phenomenon existed and to attempt to read this evidence in terms of signification in the camp. I claim that to understand the meaning of a crease, an angle, a color, a fabric—to recognize what is ubiquitous and what is rare—we need the sensitivities of a camp's inmate. I use witness testimonies and memoirs in a manner similar to what Roland Barthes termed "written clothing": textual descriptions that include both word-pictures of the objects and directions on how to read these pictures and where to lay the emphasis.[11]

The "voice of the survivor" is integral to this study, which is part of an ongoing effort to show how the voices of survivors can contribute to our understanding of past events. The "fieldwork" undertaken as part of my doctoral research involved an open-ended process of meeting survivors, which sometimes resulted in a closer relationship over many meetings.[12] In this context I became aware of seemingly marginal anecdotes in which survivors told "incongruous" stories about Auschwitz; elsewhere I argue that these anecdotes provide us with uncanny glimpses into the past.[13] But such anecdotes are present not only in the living and recorded speech of survivors but also in their writings and narrative fragments. Memoir after memoir, testimony after testimony, and recording after recording provide us with a wealth of "apocryphal" details in which survivors remark on and describe their everyday life and sufferings in the camp. But such wealth must be worked into a concrete form and reflected upon, or else it remains part of the archive but not of history. To allow these voices, their anguish and irony, into historical writing, this chapter attempts, where possible, to preserve the authentic voice of survivors by using their words (technically: their anecdotes) to expose the historical reality.

The Upper Cut: Prisoners in Tailored Suits

We are all familiar with the extreme suffering of prisoners in the SS concentration camps: In most scholarly descriptions and survivor testimonies prisoner uniforms are described as rags, and proper shoes were replaced by wooden clogs—rationed because rubber was a rare wartime resource, necessary for tires and the boots of soldiers.[14] Together with starvation rations, slave labor, and the lack of hygienic conditions, prisoners' dress was intimately related to death. Yet within this general situation, descriptions stemming from witness testimony from "career prisoners" in Auschwitz-Birkenau and other extermination camps depict the prisoner elite as dangerous peacocks. This section describes only the most rudimentary forms of prisoner fashion, and that concerning only one segment of the prisoner population, the male inmates. "While the clothes were still being distributed, I noticed two young Polish prisoners, talking together," Rudolf Vrba reports. "It was their clothes which first attracted my attention."

> They looked as if they had been tailored. The caps had a definite shape and were worn at a jaunty angle. The trouser legs were impeccably creased. Their jackets fitted them perfectly; and the whole outfit was worn with an air of confidence that bordered on arrogance. There was something else, however, which made them stand out from most of the others. They were sturdy, well-fed. . . . Here, I decided, were men who knew the secret of survival . . . two camp aristocrats.[15]

A tailored suit is a time-honored symbol of western male power, respectability, and professionalism and, according to Michael Zakim, even political rights.[16] Of course, practically all of the actors on site at Auschwitz were familiar with this symbol from their prewar lives. The shapelessness of the common prisoner "rags" was likely the result of several factors, including design, neglect, and deliberate humiliation. At Auschwitz, a prisoner's first set of clothes was distributed in the initial reception and registration process, which included the removal of all bodily hair, delousing, and tattooing. The mass of people treated at the same time meant that clothes were distributed under pressure. Finding suitable clothing was impossible.

Afterwards, worn camp clothing could theoretically be replaced. Primo Levi writes with bitter sarcasm about the camp practice of *Wäschetauschen* (laundry replacement).[17] He recounts the scrambles to trade in shoes and shirts, of which there were never enough. Any "abominable, ragged, dirty shred of a shirt which . . . has three holes suitable to fit more or less over the heads and arms . . . at the time of the *Wäschetauschen* is valid as a shirt and carries the rights of an exchange."[18] But though equipment could rarely be replaced through official channels, survival required that other channels be found. In Auschwitz, the lack of a prisoner jacket button was treated as a punishable crime.

The conduct of the prisoner elite contrasted starkly with the sorry lot of prisoners scrambling to appear fully formed at roll call. Robert Waitz,

Figure 7.1. Prisoner wearing a tailored "three-piece suit" uniform. Israel Gutman, Belah Guterman, and Lili Meier, *The Auschwitz Album: The Story of a Transport* (Jerusalem: Yad Vashem, 2002).

a French hematologist consigned to Buna-Monowitz who testified at the Nuremberg trials, includes the following passage in his 1947 account:

> [The Greens] are very proud of their custom-made striped suits; they have the barber give them a facial massage, rub their faces with cologne and treat them with hot napkins. They obtain meat, sausage, and fruit in return for the blankets, sheets, pullovers, shirts, jewelry, and money that they steal from Kanada. Then alcohol and foodstuffs are brought into the camp from the factory in which the barter is made. On return to the camp certain labor details are completely safe from frisking of the guards because their Kapo knows how to grease the palms of the SS.[19]

The result was that a prisoner could try to improve his or her clothes, for which some capital was generally needed. In this context a tailored suit that fit perfectly, despite the prisoners' stripes, set its wearer apart from his environment. By chance, a German camera, used to document the "processing" of the Hungarian Jews, caught just such a well-dressed prisoner in its lens in the summer of 1944 (see figure 7.1 above). He is walking away from an unloading ramp, and the guard lets him pass. Clearly, he has some autonomy, and he comes off as "sharply dressed," with his cap at an angle, in comparison with the armed guard, who must remain onsite at what appears to be sentry duty. We will probably never know who the young prisoner in the photograph is. However, his suit tells us something about the class he belonged to inside the camp. This passage, from the memoir of an anonymous prisoner in Auschwitz, describes one of the linkages connecting tailored suits, corruption, and power:

> The most privileged were the Block-Seniors. They wore first class tailored suits made of the finest cloth. . . . Our good king was a good business man too. Among the prisoners in our block there were some good tailors and shoemakers. He set up two workshops for them and made them work for the SS and his colleagues. The SS men delivered cloth and leather and paid for the making up. The least part of these payments went to the tailors and shoemakers. The Block-Eldest threw parties for his friends every night, his band provided the music and his court jester the fun.[20]

The biting sarcasm of this anonymous narrator paints a dark world in which the common prisoner is a subject of a seemingly all-powerful god-king—not the SS but the Block-Eldest ("our good king"), who is in business with the SS. In these very few sentences we see a whole picture: both the SS and the Block-Eldest are breaking camp law by producing illegal work. In this case the SS men are supplying the raw materials and the Block-Eldest is supplying the manpower and perhaps access to the tools. As our anonymous writer points out, the fruits of this illegal trade hung brazenly on the person of the Block-Eldest himself, in the form of a tailored suit. How impressive a few well-cut pieces of cloth can be is wonderfully rendered in Rudolf Vrba's account:

> Standing, surveying us with the quick professional eyes of a butcher in a slaughter house, was a stocky man in well-creased prisoner's trousers, a blue military jacket that buttoned up to the neck and a black biretta; a Kapo, but not an undisciplined clown-Kapo like those we had known in Majdanek. Here was a man of authority, an old-timer; I saw from the green triangle on his jacket, too, that he was a professional criminal, a murderer, in fact, I learned later.[21]

This image of the well-dressed "man of authority" returns in Vrba's memoir like a mirror image, once the narrator has "come of age" and received his own "command" as the registrar in the Theresienstadt Family Camp, section BIIb. In Vrba's memoir this is also the locus dramaticus for his first (ill-fated) love affair: the lovers are forced to part as the family camp is liquidated. This is Vrba's description of his own appearance at the height of his camp power and manly prowess: "Sartorially speaking, of course, I jumped almost into the Saville Row class. Instead of my zebra trousers, I wore a pair of riding breeches, superbly tailored by a Polish prisoner. My riding boots would have done justice to a cavalry officer and, though I was not allowed to discard my striped tunic, I saw that it was neatly cut. I was, perhaps, a little over-dressed for my lowly rank."[22] The cap, of course, etymologically stems from the Latin *caput* for head. The details noted by Erich Kulka and Otto Kraus in their book *The Death Factory* on the semantic significance in the way a beret was worn are noteworthy. In a disciplining ritual, removal of the cap symbolized deference and obedience.[23] The manner in which caps were worn—the material from which they were made, their color, and their mode of use—constituted a language through which prisoners signaled their camp experience:

> The cap was the most expansive sign of the prisoner's "level" and his position in the camp. Newcomers . . . wore their caps "stuck" anyhow on their heads. Older prisoners . . . were very particular as to the shape and color of their cap, and especially regarding their own way of wearing them. The type of cap and its position on the head testified to the spiritual and physical suffering its wearer had been through, and his determination to endure the worst.[24]

The use of the cap to warm the ears or to protect the head from the elements was thus a sign of a new recruit to the camp as well as the *Muselmann*. The term *Muselmann*—sometimes written as "Mussulman" or "Muslim"—and the plural term *Muselmänner* denoted in camp language a prisoner so emaciated and exhausted that he or she had given up on life, becoming apathetic and unresponsive and declining to participate in the social world; the sole remaining focal points in this state were acquisition of food and protection from the elements.[25] The source of the word is uncertain, although many survivor accounts claim that the word referred to the resignation to fate commonly attributed by Europeans to Muslims or the typical Muslim prone praying posture; *Muselmänner* were generally too weak to be able to stand for long periods. According to survivor Władysław Kuraszkiewicz, it represented "the ultimate [state of] wretchedness in the camp. Prisoners feared this decay . . . more than any disease, because it was in fact the most widespread camp disease. Most people died precisely as Muselmänner. These men attracted all the curses and harassments of those in power."[26]

In contrast to the *Muselmänner*, experienced and powerful prisoners used their caps for emphasis and decoration, by placing them tilted or askew on the side of their head, advertising as it were their position and power. What made the cap, a rather negligible piece of material, such a symbolic marker? This question is perhaps better approached from an anthropological or psychoanalytical perspective than from a historical one, in which Auschwitz-Birkenau is only a case in point. One may hazard that the relative location of the position of the cap on the skull—the back, the front, off to one side, or flatly in the middle—permits the expression, consciously or not, of the wearer's emotional condition. For an example from a different context, Alexandre Orme describes at length what he calls the "language of the Red Army cap."[27] The salient point is not that there is a "universal language of caps" but rather that the juxtaposition of the circle of the cap and the sphere of the head can be used to express nuanced details.[28]

But regardless of the semiotics behind the "language of caps," the different color, material, and quality of the elite's caps were evidence of material surplus, a small detail that disclosed a prisoner's social standing, connections, and ultimately his or her relation to food (that is, whether he or she was obtaining above or below survival-rate nutrition).

A prisoner could obtain a better cap "under the counter," for there were tailors who would sew them clandestinely and sell them for food. Prisoners holding positions in the camp were distinguished by caps made of blue material which no other prisoner was allowed to wear. The more food a prisoner had, the more he would push his cap to one side. Starving and half-starved prisoners—the so-called Muselmanner—used to wear their caps hard down over their ears in the winter.[29]

While caps were a showy way of advertising social status and camp experience, shoes were even more important as the foundation upon which all life and work must stand. The image of the abysmal Dutch-style wooden clogs is familiar from testimonies and museum displays the world over. These clogs, and the festering sores they induced in the feet of prisoners, are the main reason behind Primo Levi's statement that death begins with the shoes. "For most of us, they show themselves to be instruments of torture," the first link in a chain which inevitably leads to a diagnosis of the incurable *dicke Füsse*, or swollen feet.[30] However, the prisoner's shoes in Auschwitz-Birkenau were not uniform. Privileged prisoners found better footwear. Rudolf Vrba points to shoes as one of the benefits of serving in the Kanada Kommando:

> Then and only then did the Kanada Kommando move off and, as we marched, I noticed a strange new sound. The clack of clogs was missing and in its place was the soft pad of leather. I glanced down and saw that nearly every man was wearing shoes, some in suede, some in crocodile, and all a world away from wood. Laco noticed the look of amazement on my face and said with a grin: "It's one of the perks. Somehow they don't seem to mind if we lift shoes. Maybe they think it adds tone to the command—or perhaps that clogs slow us up!"[31]

Exactly how "non-uniform" the footwear of prisoners in Auschwitz-Birkenau could be can be seen in other passages in witness testimony, such as that from Robert Waitz. His account shows not only the latitude given to high-ranking prisoners concerning dress but also some of the ways in which they went about obtaining different objects:

> The Block-Eldest desires a pair of ski boots a new arrival brought with him. He refuses to hand them over. One night the Block-Eldest calls a surprise roll call, announcing that he is going to control the state of our shoes. The prisoners must file past him, deposit their shoes, then, still in line, walk around the block, and return to take their shoes. Low and behold, a pair of shoes are missing; those coveted by the Block-Eldest. "You see," the Block-Eldest says to their dispossessed owner, "you are an idiot. They've been stolen. You would have been better off giving them to me."[32]

By contrast, in the penal company prisoners were not allowed to wear anything but wooden clogs, which they had to wear without socks.[33] The importance of footwear was both practical and a matter of image. Sturdy shoes were imperative to survive manual labor. But for the aspiring career prisoner, boots were also an object of desire, a sign of success by which prisoners attempted to place themselves "on equal footing" with the SS:

> Boots, the dream of every good German aspiring to be a soldier. If you saw a prisoner wearing boots, the chances were that he was a room orderly or a barber, someone who never had to wade through mud, or else a Kapo or the foreman of a ditch gang. Prisoners who toiled with water and mud seeping through their shoes never received any, which was, of course, in accordance with camp law: "to him that hath shall be given, from him that hath not shall be taken away."[34]

Finding suitable boot shining material was an Auschwitz-Birkenau growth industry: the product, which could be used for the leather of the wooden-soled clogs, for this reason became a tradable resource on the market.[35] Ideally, it seems, the boots would be completed by a set of riding breeches or creased pants. In fact, a well-turned-out suit had the capacity not only to reflect power but to create it, which is the essence of Primo Levi's story of Alfred L., a "prominent" (Levi's term for the camp elite) before his time. He knew that "the step was short from being judged powerful to effectively becoming so, . . . especially in the midst of the general levelling of the Lager, a respectable appearance is the best guarantee of being respected":

> he had the rare self-denial to wash his shirt every fortnight, without waiting for the bi-monthly change . . . finding soap, time and space . . . adapting himself to carefully keep watch on the wet shirt without losing attention for a moment, and to put it on, naturally still wet, in the silence-hour when the lights are turned out . . . he owned a pair of wooden shoes to go to the shower, and even his striped suit was singularly adapted to his appearance, clean and new. He had acquired in practice the whole appearance of a prominent considerably before becoming one . . . his spruce suit and his emaciated and shaved face in the midst of the flock of his sordid and slovenly colleagues in order to convince both Kapo and *Arbeitsdienst* that he was one of the genuinely saved, a potential prominent.[36]

The bricoloric prisoner's fashion was significant for relations not only with the SS but also with other prisoners. As mentioned earlier, Hermann

Langbein felt that clothing was more important in a concentration camp than in free society.[37] Langbein's example concerns a friend who dressed so as to impress the other prisoners with his supposed position of power, which enabled him to extend protection over a friend who found himself in a dangerous situation:

> Georges Wellers [was] serving as a nurse in the Monowitz infirmary, he wanted to help a friend who was still on the lowest rung of the camp hierarchy. Wellers dressed carefully and visited him in his block. He behaved like a big shot, smoked ostentatiously, though this was strictly prohibited to an ordinary inmate, and stood in the middle of the corridor so that everyone who wished to pass had to beg his leave—in short, he made sure that those in charge of the barracks noticed what acquaintances his friend had, for he knew that a bit of the glamour he exuded as a VIP would be reflected on his poor friend. As a matter of fact, the latter's standing rose markedly after that visit.[38]

It should be clear by now that the idea that clothes played an important role in the concentration camps is not a flight of fancy of the author, but originates in the experience of camp prisoners. But all we have done so far is to show that "even in Auschwitz" there was a phenomenon recognized by prisoners as "fashion." But whatever its precise forms, prisoner fashion cannot be understood without the context in which it functioned. It was enabled by the SS system, which used inequality as a tool to divide and conquer the camp inmates, and by the specific conditions at Auschwitz-Birkenau, which put the possessions of a million murdered Jews within reach of over a hundred thousand starving inmates. In order to understand this phenomenon fully, we must begin by understanding the material basis of life for prisoners in the Auschwitz-Birkenau camp archipelago.

The Socio-Material Basis

To appraise the significance of fashion, as evidenced above, we must try to understand it not by our own standards but in terms of the society in which it took place. We must show where, how, and why it grew just as it did. With this end in mind I propose that fashion was bound up with a three-tiered system: On the basis of the sharply sloping plane of everyday existence, designed to bring about the death of prisoners through starvation and work within several months, some prisoners had access to "pockets" of resources; these petty thefts were part of a culture of embezzlement and attempts at wartime self-enrichment that went far beyond prisoner society, into the camp command, up to and including the commandant of the camp, Rudolf Höss.

Unequal by Design: *Divide et Impera*

The lot of the common prisoner (after 1942 these prisoners were overwhelmingly Jewish) was starvation. But fashion was a marker that differentiated a certain group from this common lot. In this way both starvation and fashion served the interest of the SS, who desired a weak and splintered prisoner society. The base rate caloric rationing in Auschwitz was calculated for starvation. They understood high death rates among the population either as a goal or as an unavoidable side effect of the working conditions: "Within 15 months of arrival, the normal prisoner had become a Muselmann. Average life expectancy was six months. In 1944 nutrition improved by about 250 calories [a day per prisoner] in comparison with 1943. Correspondingly, life expectancy increased by about two months."[39] The downward slope of an individual's caloric trajectory—a limited caloric intake and particularly the relative absence of fat—coupled with strenuous heavy labor were likely designed to "squeeze" the surplus labor value out of a prisoner as quickly as possible, leaving only the empty "husk" of the Muselmann. Impressed by the manpower-to-subject ratio of the British colonial empire, the SS strove to rule an ever-expanding army of starving prisoners at Auschwitz-Birkenau with as little direct German involvement as possible.[40] After Stalingrad this became even more pressing: the guard force of able-bodied men was needed on the front, but the camp, whose massive extermination facilities opened between March and June 1943, was drastically expanding the scope of its "human processing." Chief among the tools through which the SS sought to rule was the notion of "prisoner self-government" (*Selbstverwaltung*).[41] The SS envisioned a dog-eat-dog society made up of the worst "mongrels" in Europe and the "Wild East," as Carroll P. Kakel has termed the Nazi colonial frontier.[42] These radical elements were not to be allowed to coalesce. Their tactic therefore was *divide et impera*, encouraging national divides and class antagonisms: Rivalries among groups of prisoners were "passionately maintained by the camp administration and constantly fanned in order to prevent any strong movement of solidarity among the prisoners. . . . The more groups fighting each other and the more intense the power struggle among them, the easier it was to control the camp."[43] Competition among prisoners was the fertile ground in which the fetid tree of prisoner fashion grew.

The caloric vise was loosened only slightly in the wake of Stalingrad, under the auspices of Reich Minister of Armaments and War Production Albert Speer. This "reformed" period can be summed up as the victory of the *Arbeit* (work) element over the *Vernichtung* (extermination) element in the practice of the SS concentration camps. A period marked by the more efficient utilization of human slave power in Auschwitz was ushered in by an increase in the bread ration, which achieved a level of 125 grams per day. Starvation persisted both before and after these "reforms," providing an incentive to participate in the camp sport of "organization," which denoted theft that did not harm any individual prisoner but targeted "anonymous" goods belonging to the camp. The surprising thing is that in Auschwitz such organization was also "tolerated" by the SS, up to a point. Where exactly this point was located was a delicate matter that cannot here be explicated. In 1964, Hauptsturmführer Franz Hofmann testified at the Auschwitz trials at Frankfurt that prisoners were "allowed" to organize "something to eat," provided that they eat it on the job and not bring it back into the camp.[44]

In other words, "small" thefts were permissible—thefts within the "normal" range, from the general stores, and not connected to any specific prisoner's property. In Auschwitz there were many unwritten norms governing theft and its accountability. Primo Levi names boot grease as one of the products that compliance with SS standards demanded but was paradoxically never present or officially distributed. The demand created a supply, and grease from Buna could be bought and sold in Auschwitz, traded for other items.[45] He writes:

> During the war it was impossible to exist without some sort of extras . . . to succeed in some kind of theft or hoodwinking now and again showed that you had your wits about you. At Auschwitz everybody stole and worked

a racket. It was a camp rule that block seniors, room orderlies, Kapos and foremen received bigger helpings of hot meals, but they were not content with that. The scope for stealing was practically endless. Corruption began in the kitchen, where the most valuable foodstuffs (fats, sugar, meat, sausages and so on) were stolen and traded to civilians for cigarettes and schnapps. Prisoners, especially the Aryan Poles, were as bad as the SS.[46]

Aside from this, from November 1942 non-Jewish prisoners could receive packages from home, thereby allowing the entrance of more "private," or non-issue, goods.[47] The goods in these packages made it into the camp, although not necessarily directly to the prisoners to whom they were addressed. The value of their contents generally depended on the financial situation of a prisoner's family, providing of course that said prisoners were not Jewish, although in this case they were also not likely to have a family member in a position to send parcels.[48] Though food was often consumed by prisoners and guards handling the distribution of mail, warm clothing was mostly of less interest and arrived at its destination. From an economic point of view, these resources in fact all arrived in the camp—what was not consumed or used by their recipients was either hoarded (in the case of SS guards, sent home by mail) or traded (in the case of prisoners, the likely eventuality). The black markets of Auschwitz-Birkenau were part of a lively traffic in goods and services in the camp; the subject comes up in many passages of Primo Levi's *If This Is a Man*. Levi considered it an act of desperation bordering on suicide for a common prisoner to attempt to trade his daily ration of bread for a few cigarettes, in order to attempt later to convert them back to bread and gain from the transaction.[49]

The system was designed to be unequal, and some prisoners were by design more privileged than others. Many survivors expressed a sense that in Auschwitz death was inevitable. Otto Dov Kulka terms this the "immutable law of the Great Death": even as all the rivers flow to the sea, the property of life in Auschwitz was to die.[50] Yet prisoners were subject to different life expectancies in Auschwitz, based on their racial category. A saying among prisoners, reported as part of the testimony at the 1964 trial in Frankfurt, was that "in Auschwitz Jews *must*, Poles *should*, and Germans *can*—die."[51] We should be leery of perceiving all prisoners as equal, because this amounts to turning a blind eye to elements of Nazi social planning and the reality of the camp, in which prisoner "society" was fragmented; the upper echelons, regardless of which faction was on top, bent to the will of the SS and collaborated out of necessity but not only for this reason. To survive, prisoners had to "make a career" and be successful in local terms. Whereas the SS were at least nominally accountable to their own judiciary system, prisoner functionaries were not accountable for the death of their workers—who were incarcerated under strenuous conditions during wartime and could be expected to suffer fatalities.

As a result, the social polarization in Auschwitz soared. It was the home both of the Muselmann and of a highly corrupted "localized surplus"—a result of processing the baggage of a million gassed Jews. We have already seen that according to Kautsky, Auschwitz was characterized by acute polarization between prisoners.[52] Differences in access to material goods directly reflected a prisoner's power in the social hierarchy. Naturally, this power was also expressed in clothing and related paraphernalia and behavior, which are in fact all too familiar to us from normal social reality. The driving logic of many of them can be classed as a particularly vulgar form of "conspicuous consumption," to use Thorstein Veblen's term:

> The SS delegate their power to the prisoners. . . . In exchange for their services these prisoners benefit from advantages which are not to be looked down upon: less painful work, better food, clothing and sleeping conditions. The SS turn a blind eye to their excesses. They authorize them at times to grow their hair, and—the supreme recompensation—in exceptional cases, to wear riding breeches and riding boots made to measure. This is the highest recompensation which a prisoner could ever imagine. The SS try hard to set many groups [of prisoners] against each other. They encourage informants. They try their best to divide and conquer.[53]

How are we to make sense of the various articles of clothing described? What was *most* coveted and, moreover, why? These questions are important because they beckon us to proceed into the realm of what we might call the prisoners' "cultural imagination," one in which they perceived themselves not (or at least not exclusively) as oppressed victims but as actors with agency, albeit an agency that involved victimizing other prisoners. A full picture of the social antagonisms between prisoner groups in Auschwitz-Birkenau and its reflection in prisoner dress and "style" has yet to be written. The waters are muddied because in Auschwitz (as opposed to the regular prison system in Nazi Germany and in the concentration camps within the Third Reich) there was never a full distinction between "civilian" articles and prison uniforms. This was beyond the resources of the camp and did not suit its "spirit."

After Stalingrad, the Eastern Front became increasingly dark from the Nazi perspective. Hoping to win at least one war, the Nazis stepped up the process of exterminating the Jews. In Auschwitz-Birkenau, as the crematoria incinerated the cadavers of the old and the young, the prisoner population boomed. The supply of uniforms could not keep up, and the camp had to "convert" clothes taken from the gassed Jewish victims into "prison clothes" by marking them with stripes, but this was not enough.[54] The camp term "Mexico" for the third sub-camp in Birkenau, which was under construction and was used to put many Hungarians and others "on ice" in 1944, is also connected to the lack of official resources from which these temporary residents of Auschwitz suffered.[55] In fact, for this reason there was room for quite a bit of "leeway" in the manner in which a given prisoner might look while still following the same set of formal rules.

How different prisoners could look from the way we might expect can be seen in a key passage in Rudolf Vrba's memoir that deals with the author's successful escape from the camp. Vrba consciously exploited the sartorial latitude of his position so as to be ready to blend in to free society once outside. But he overstepped the boundary. On the way to his hiding place between the two sets of fences, he was stopped because of his clothes:

> Fred and I were almost ready to go. Our clothes—expensive Dutch suits and overcoats and heavy boots—had been delivered from the Kanada Command departmental store. . . . It is true that I looked remarkably like a prosperous Dutch gentleman . . . however, a more experienced SS man . . . would have known that as a Registrar, I had a great deal of sartorial latitude. My elaborate outfit, indeed, would have been regarded merely as an eccentricity.[56]

The latitude which Vrba claims should have been his, due to his position, was the result of SS planning, a delegation of power which mirrored SS *Führerprinzip*.[57] "In every camp such a privileged layer was created among the prisoners," Anonymous from Auschwitz explains, "but nowhere did it attain such a high material standard as in Birkenau. Here they lived in real luxury, not only compared to the miserable existence of the ordinary prisoners, but also to the conditions of normal civilian life."[58] According to historian Falk Pingel, as many as 15 to 20 percent of prisoners had "positions" that provided them with relatively safe and privileged working conditions.[59] But what was the basis upon which they could build this kind of normality inside a concentration and extermination camp?

Localized Surpluses

Despite the conditions of extreme privation just discussed, Auschwitz-Birkenau was riddled with "localized surpluses"—a surplus that exists as a separate entity within a larger restricted situation characterized by lack. On the grounds of Auschwitz-Birkenau, storehouses were accessible to prisoners who worked there. Access to these resources was not ensured—it fluctuated with their fortunes and power and, in the case of Auschwitz-Birkenau, with the fortunes of the war. It is in the nature of a "localized surplus" to be restricted to a given time, place, and group—for once these limits have been broken, the wealth either "dissipates" to all participants and "disappears" or it finds a way to break into normal everyday life and becomes regular capital.

The Jewish goods taken to the storehouse complex (*Effektenlager*) known in camp parlance as Kanada—a term that, according to Vrba, denoted a dangerous land of milk and honey where men died violently after barely sipping its nectar—were meant to be sorted and shipped "back" to the Reich.[60] This process was carried out by the Kanada Kommando, beginning with the offloading of a transport's baggage at the ramp and ending with sorting and registry back at the warehouse itself.[61] "Kanada," Kulka and Kraus explain, "played an extremely important role in the camp. It was the source from which the prisoners obtained the wherewithal to make their life to some degree bearable."[62] Nonetheless, the rest of their description shows the darker side of the same reality: "Many of the 'Canadians' were very tough with the other prisoners and thought only of themselves. Their one aim was gold and wealth, even in the shadow of death. No doubt they were goaded by the thought it might ultimately buy them their freedom and life."[63]

Descriptions of the wealth of Kanada as well as other nodes of surplus within the Auschwitz system are often hyperbolic, yet one gains
the impression that the hyperbole was part of the historical reality of
that place, an oasis of death's harvest within a desert of starving prisoners. Survivors describe it as a "dangerous paradise" whose nectar both
preserved and killed.[64] "The place was like a huge open-air jumble sale
with silk underwear, eau de cologne, expensive soap, furs, shoes, cigarette lighters, knives, ladies' handbags."[65] Vrba's reports paint a vivid
picture of mess and plenty: "It was an incredible sight . . . a mountain
of trunks . . . Nearby was another mountain of blankets, 50,000 of
them, maybe 100,000. . . . hundreds of prams . . . Then I saw women.
Real women . . . young well-dressed girls with firm ripe figures and
faces made beautiful by health alone . . . [it] seemed sometimes to verge
on lunacy."[66] These impressions show that the female prisoners working at Kanada, like the men in his own work kommando, were enjoying
a material surplus as well as official leniency (for instance, the women's
hair was allowed to grow back).

Rudolf Höss is particularly instructive on the workings of Kanada and
its legitimate and illicit connections with the economy of the concentration camp. According to Höss, clothing and footwear were "handed over
to the camp to supplement the inmates' clothing. Later on they were also
sent to other camps" and various Nazi welfare organizations.[67] Valuables
were sorted by experts. Höss notes, "The jewelry was usually of great
value, especially when its Jewish owners came from the West." After that,
"when the sorting process . . . had been completed, the valuables and the
money were packed into trucks and taken to the Economic Administration Headquarters office in Berlin and then finally to the Reichsbank" and
from there, most likely via Switzerland, as a conversation with Eichmann
revealed, to the global market.[68]

Or at least this is the way everything was supposed to function.
Such heights brought with them their own dangers: Prisoners and SS
guards of all ranks, up to and including the commandant, dipped their
hands into the Reich's new wealth.[69] Prisoners were a necessary part
of this chain of self-enrichment because there were very many of them
who came into contact, one way or another, with the looted Jewish goods. The camp SS, by contrast, were mostly kept to minimal
contact with the Jewish possessions, in an (unsuccessful) attempt to

curtail looting. One of the easiest access points to this property was the unloading ramp. It was here, during and after the Jewish transports had been cleared, but before they had been registered, that "trinkets" could easily be picked up. One can find ample evidence of what kind of objects were to be had and were of interest in the entries in Dr. Kremer's diary, especially those that describe his participation in "special actions" and the contents of the packages he is sending home (all very meticulously noted).[70]

It seems that prisoners were the (often silent) intermediaries in such transactions. Baretzki, an SS Block-Leader, describes doing business at the ramps: "If I ever needed something, all I had to do was say to the Kapo 'I need ten dollars,' and he did it."[71] A prisoner's "pay" could take the form of an averted glance, which allowed them to wolf down a morsel of food or to stuff something away, at their own risk of course. "Steal only what someone else drops. Snatch fast beneath the cloak of another man's beating. By noon," Rudolf Vrba reports of his first day in Kanada, "my hunger had gone, and somehow I had steeled myself to heed Laco's warning, to eat only dry bread the first day."[72]

As the contents of the transport rolled on to their final destinations, slivers of material wealth were shaved off by multiple actors: the camp administration, individual SS men and women, prisoners of different types and nationalities, civilian workers, railway personnel, and the police.[73] By each according to his ability, dependent on possibility, desire, and need. At the end of a liquidation, Tadeusz Borowski's narrator relates the following scene. "The Kanada men [the sorting and storage warehouse], weighed down under a load of bread, marmalade and sugar, and smelling of perfume and fresh linen, line up to go. For several days the entire camp will live off this transport. For several days the entire camp will talk about 'Sosnowiec-Bedzin.' 'Sosnowiec-Bedzin' was a good, rich transport."[74] So despite the sharply sloping plane of everyday life at Auschwitz, as we have seen above, some prisoners did have access to "pockets" of resources. And these resources—traded at what prices, for what services, all of this detailed elsewhere—made it back into the general population or could be purchased in the camp. But the theft and "organization" occurring on one side of the barbed wire was nothing but a reflection of a greater culture of embezzlement and wartime profiteering that went far beyond prisoner society.

SS Corruption

Prisoner "fashion" was a result of the "trickling down" of big corruption to the world of the common prisoner. The scope of corruption at Auschwitz was massive, in line with the death toll and its material benefits. "In Birkenau, in the shadow of the crematoria, lay the center of corruption," Langbein remarks as the editor in his compendium of testimonies from the Frankfurt Auschwitz trial. "It was so dire," he continues, "that SS headquarters had established an investigatory committee." The former SS-Hauptsturmführer Doctor Morgen headed the committee and gave the following testimony:

> The investigation against the SS men of the concentration camp Auschwitz was set off by a postal package sent from the field. It was impounded due to its conspicuous weight. . . . It turned out to be high carat dental gold, which a medical orderly, who had seen service in Auschwitz, had shipped to his wife. On the basis of my own calculations, this amount of gold was equivalent to about 100,000 bodies.[75]

Rudolf Höss's pre-execution notes repeatedly raise the subject of corruption in the camp; his transparent attempts to minimize his personal responsibility by painting the matter as "beyond his control" should be dismissed.[76] As noted earlier, Höss seems to have profited personally from the Jewish goods.[77] Attempting to shift the focus elsewhere, his pre-execution memoir confirms that "an immense amount of property was stolen by members of the SS, the police, also by the prisoners, civilian workers, and by railway personnel."[78] Morgen's report agrees:

> I went to the SS guardroom in Birkenau. . . . Whereas guardrooms generally were Spartan in their simplicity, here SS men were lying on couches and dozing with glassy eyes. Instead of a desk there was a hotel-type oven; four or five young Jewish women of oriental beauty were making potato pancakes and feeding them to the men, who were served like pashas. The SS men and the female prisoners addressed one another as if they were relatives or friends. . . . During the ensuing check of the lockers, it turned out that in some a fortune in gold, pearls, rings, and all kinds of foreign currency was stored. In one or two lockers we found genitals of freshly slaughtered bulls that were supposed to enhance a man's sexual potency. I have never seen anything like it.[79]

The use of several different types of forced labor at the industrial site of Buna-Monowitz placed together civilian companies, concentration camp prisoners, POWs, and, above all, paid and conscripted workers from across Nazi-occupied Europe. Not all groups were subject to the same restrictions, concerning movement and post. According to Kautsky, this camp turned into "one vast brothel": "female forced laborers from Poland and the Ukraine, sex-starved men from all over Europe, German engineers, Nazi guards, and a handful of prisoners of war who with the chocolate and cigarettes received in their Red Cross packages were the undisputed kings of this market."[80] This was decidedly still "small-scale" in comparison with the power of large-scale operators, figures of legendary status in the world of the prisoners:

> Senior Kapo Reinhold . . . was in charge of all construction work in Birkenau and thus of all building material, 800 prisoners, and half a dozen capos. . . . Members of the SS, from top to bottom, ordered furniture and furnishings for their apartments from him. . . . It was rumored that he dined more opulently than the commandant. The best French and German wines, liqueurs, and whole liters of pure alcohol were at his disposal. When I questioned the former Block-Leader Baretzki about this his only reply was, "He had everything."[81]

Material riches in Auschwitz were of a different order from the normal material world. A survivor (Moshe Yaakobovitch) once told me of finding a suitcase full of thousand-dollar bills in Auschwitz.[82] At the same time, the camp was abuzz each day with deals and opportunism: "The Block-Seniors swindled prisoners out of their daily rations. The men in the kitchen traded in meat. . . . These Kapos . . . cooked steak and chips on their stoves, while the smell wafted through thin partitions to starving prisoners, and they washed it down occasionally with slivovitz stolen from victims of the gas chambers."[83] These are the figures with whom we are concerned, if we are to have anything to say at all about "fashion in Auschwitz": the middle and upper class of Lager citizens—the "white-collar" element of the Metropolis of Death.

The "Why" of Prisoner Fashion

It might be expected that prisoners in extermination camps suffered from extreme privation, as indeed they overwhelmingly did. Yet office-holding prisoners were exempt from death-inducing conditions. Witness testimonies indicate that practically all the prisoners who were involved in the administration of the camp achieved a level of dress far removed from what we normally associate with Auschwitz-Birkenau. Some among them,

Figure 7.2. The Kapo, at work (left) and during "leisure time" (right). Note the boots and riding breeches in the "work" picture. Agnieszka Sieradzka, ed., *The Sketchbook from Auschwitz*. (Oświęcim: Państwowe Muzeum Auschwitz-Birkenau, 2011). The sketchbook was found in 1947 hidden inside a bottle buried in the foundations of one of the structures in Birkenau.

surely, were like Primo Levi's nameless Alfred L., piecing crumb to crumb to be able to buy a suit. For others, dress and other objects of power were the trappings that went with greater positions in the camp and privileges over life and death. "Fashion in Auschwitz" is the sartorial range that begins with such prisoners as Vrba and his equivalents and moves upwards from there. It was concomitant with success: "The longer I survived the nearer I drew to the hard core who had learned not only to live, but to prosper. I became recognized as a semi-permanent fixture . . . and once I was accepted by the older hands, I earned promotion."[84]

The elite prisoners in Auschwitz-Birkenau used a localized material surplus to maintain appearances approximating "normal life." This was not done, however, as a measure of mental hygiene or in any attempt at "edification" but rather in the interest of their own survival and, by extension, as an expression of their power in the camp. The tyrannical nature of this power was bitterly apparent to those who did not share it. Note the Kapo's two-toned shoes and the variety of luxury goods depicted on the right-hand side of figure 7.2 above: The Kapo holds what might be a sausage or leg of ham in his hand, while spread out in front of him are a large loaf of bread, a rectangular wedge of butter or perhaps cheese, and a glass jar partially filled with liquid, possibly some slivovitz. The facial expression seems to impart an almost erotic satisfaction such as a rich man might have with his private treasure.

As opposed to the world of the POW Officers' Camp, where a prisoner's physical safety was ensured (Iris Rachamimov's chapter in this collection, for example), the prisoner elite in Auschwitz-Birkenau were literally faced with death, in the form of the smoke over Birkenau and in the face of the Muselmann. The elite lived far better than the dying manual laborers, yet they too teetered on the brink of a sudden and mortal downfall. The SS expected Kapos to rule their prisoners with an iron hand on their whip, and fulfilling the expectations of the SS bound their fate to their overlords. At the slightest displeasure meant a Kapo would be demoted to the ranks, with the intended result that their former underlings would then kill them during the night.[85]

We do not yet know enough about the intricate relations that took place at Auschwitz between guards and prisoners, a social field that Primo Levi immortalized as the "Gray Zone."[86] It seems clear that part of what emerged from these clandestine transactions was the phenomenon of prisoner fashion. In contrast to the alterations made by soldiers in the Red Army to their uniforms (see Brandon Schechter's chapter in this collection), those performed by Auschwitz prisoners on their suits were not formally directed from above. What may have originated as a survival measure became part of the culture of the camp.

The similarity of appearance between some prisoners and the SS has been remarked upon by both survivors and scholars.[87] The image most prisoners seems to have cultivated was a subservient, efficient-looking, and professional posture, a "clean cut" pose near enough to the SS itself to command their respect but not close enough to evoke their ire.[88] After Treblinka, Richard Glazar related this position as follows: "One was very concerned with the way one looked; it was immensely important to look clean on roll-call. One thought of small things all the time, like, "I must shave; if I shave again, I have won another round. . . . I always had a little shaving kit on me. I still have it. I shaved up to seven times a day."[89] Glazar's existential anxiety was not limited to Treblinka and recalls strongly Benedikt Kautsky's formulation of the "Law of the Lager."[90] This for him is the exemplar of "master race mentality,"[91] with which in the end, to his dismay, he cannot find fault:

> Briefly, the argument ran: In the camp only a few, and the strongest at that, have a chance of survival. Everybody who is old, weak or sick, is condemned to death. The chances of helping are slight; what I give to one, I must take from another. If I give to someone who is weak, I shall help him stay alive longer, but I cannot save him in the end; at the same time it means taking from someone who is strong, so that he too becomes sick and weak. What happens in the end is that I send both to their doom.[92]

This was how the prisoner elite gained power. Prisoners who could get their hands on life-preserving nutrients or material resources were preserving their own life and creating for themselves a semblance of normality. Helping the strong meant that "normality" signified "life," and life (help, lenience) was given to those who appeared more normal. This squared with SS designs and allowed for a semiautonomous prisoner elite that bore more physical and sartorial resemblance to its oppressors than to the prisoners they were designed to control. Even though it developed autonomously, prisoner fashion was ultimately one of the tools with which the SS created a "ruling class" of prisoners who acted in their stead. It was the prisoner elite that reflected these negative ideals and values into the depths of the camp, from which the SS tried to keep a healthy distance.

But was the phenomenon of fashion in Auschwitz unique to the camp? Survivors seemed to think that Auschwitz was more a "distillation" of normal life—an extreme expression of it. In a strikingly direct discussion on prisoner functionaries, survivor Tadeusz Hołuj stated, "It was simply a normal struggle for power, for life, for a position. That is, exactly as it is in the everyday social life."[93] If any generation was in a position to judge how similar such power struggles were to everyday life, it was that of the survivors—for they had the experience of before, during, and after the war. However, their complicity in the events complicates matters. It could be that Hołuj and his comrades were expressing their own partisan position.

The connections between "Auschwitz fashion" and our everyday experience of the same phenomenon must await further consideration. Was Auschwitz qualitatively different or "just" a clearer, more extreme example of the role that fashion plays in social competition and power struggles? How can we understand a fashion system that functioned outside of a traditional market economy, and what does it tell us about the human condition, both in the concentration camp and outside, in "normal" life? The phenomenon of "Auschwitz fashion" is of value because it raises these troubling questions even as it obliges us to face the full complexity of the everyday life of prisoners at Auschwitz-Birkenau as it emerges in the figure of the "morally repugnant victim."[94]

Notes

1. Benedikt Kautsky, *The Devils and the Damned*, trans. Kenneth Case (London: Digit Book, 1960), 145–146. Kautsky was an Austrian social democrat who spent seven years in concentration camps; he was first detained as a political opponent, but his Jewish ancestry led to categorization as a Jew. However, in January 1943, Kautsky was transferred to Auschwitz-Birkenau. Here he was lucky enough to be re-categorized as Aryan, a bureaucratic oversight that saved his life: "To my great surprise I was 'Aryanized' and classed not as a Jew but as a political prisoner of German nationality. I could now lie quietly in sick bay and regain my health without fear of being sent to the gas chambers, for no German nationals were ever gassed." See Kautsky, *Devils and the Damned*, 35.

As an Austrian social democrat, Kautsky was not affiliated with the far more numerous German-speaking communists. Perhaps in light of his experience of being incarcerated both as a Jew and as an Aryan, his memoir bears signs of an acute eye for social differences among prisoners. Yet Kautsky's 1946 book on the concentration camps was not well received: The title was read as a demonization of the SS and prisoner society, and the text was overshadowed by Eugene Kogon's *Der SS-Staat: Das System der deutschen Konzentrationslager* (1946; repr. Munich: Kinder, 1974). The latter was adopted in West Germany as the standard narrative. Bruno Bettelheim, who differed with Kautsky (on the basis of an entirely different experience in the camps), contributed to the book's critical reception. See Bettelheim, "The Concentration Camp as a Class State," *Modern Review* (1947), 628–637. This is a grave injustice to Kautsky's account.

2. Kautsky, *Devils and the Damned*, 225.

3. Hermann Langbein, *People in Auschwitz*, trans. Harry Zohn (Chapel Hill: University of North Carolina Press, 2004), 70.

4. It is important to bear in mind the "urban-industrial" nature of the Auschwitz-Birkenau camp archipelago, which at its height comprised three main camps as well as some forty-two satellite camps. The large camps were subdivided as well, several times over. Birkenau, for example, was divided into BI and BII; BI was divided into BIa (the women's camp) and BIb; BII held, at its height, five entire camps (BIIa–e) and one hospital camp (BIIf). Numbers fluctuated, but most of these camps held around fifteen thousand prisoners, and at times as many as twenty thousand. See Irena Strzelecka and Piotr Setkiewicz, "The Establishment and Organization of the Camp," in *Auschwitz 1940–1945: Central Issues in the History of the Camp: The Establishment and Organization of the Camp*, vol. 1, ed. Wacław Długoborski and Franciszek Piper, trans. William Brand (Oświęcim, Poland: Auschwitz-Birkenau State Museum, 2000), 63–131.

5. The details of the SS prisoner uniforms system are well known, evidenced in museum exhibitions and secondary literature. Deeper analyses can be found in Falk Pingel, *Häftlinge unter SS-Herrschaft* (Hamburg: Hoffmann und Campe, 1978). See also Maja Suderland, *Inside Concentration Camps: Social Life at the Extremes*, trans. Jessica Spengler (Cambridge, U.K.: Polity Press, 2013). For an early description that pays special attention to local "inflections" of the system at Auschwitz-Birkenau, see also Kautsky, *Devils and the Damned*, 104–155.

6. Kapos, from the Latin *caput* (head), were in charge of work parties (*Arbeitkommandos*). Kautsky, *Devils and the Damned*, 107.

7. Richard Glazar, cited in Gita Sereny, *Into That Darkness: An Examination of Conscience* (New York: Vintage Books, 1983), 197–198, emphasis added.

8. With black sarcasm Kautsky writes: "These Jews were not told where they were going . . . just that they were being sent to eastern Europe for building work in Jewish settlements and ghettos." They also received the good advice that "as there was no underwear, clothing, furniture, tools and so on . . . they should load up everything they could possibly take. This very plausible story induced the deportees to bring with them mountains of clothing, medical instrument and supplies, special tools, and valuables in the form of banknotes, gold and jewelry. Some of it was carried openly, some concealed." Kautsky, *Devils and the Damned*, 74–75.

9. The "Anonymous of Auschwitz" memoir mentions the illegal employment of tailors inside the living quarters by a Block-Eldest and the SS. See *My Journey to Hell and Back*, Leo Baeck Archive, ME 496, 1969.

10. Claude Levi-Strauss, *The Savage Mind* (London: Garden Press, 1966), 16–17.

11. Roland Barthes, *The Fashion System* (New York: Hill and Wang, 1983), 13–18.

12. "Fieldwork" is set in quotation marks to denote that this is a borrowed term from anthropology. In "history" proper, opposed in its very name to "oral history," the antimony between the spoken word and the written text is still very strong.

13. For my exposition of this concept and its application to the juxtaposition of Holocaust testimony and cultural history, see Noah Benninga, "Anecdote as Method, or: Holocaust Testimonies as Sources for a Cultural History of the Holocaust," *Kwartalnik Historii Zydow* [Jewish history quarterly] 246, no. 2 (2013): 414–432.

14. William G. Clarence-Smith, "The Battle for Rubber in the Second World War: Cooperation and Resistance," in *Global Histories, Imperial Commodities, Local Interactions*, ed. Jonathan Curry-Machado (New York: Palgrave Macmillan, 2013), 204–223. On the failed attempt to produce synthetic rubber in the IG Farben plant in the Auschwitz sub-camp of Buna-Monowitz, see Peter Hayes, *Industry and Ideology: IG Farben in the Nazi Era* (Cambridge: Cambridge University Press, 2001).

15. Rudolf Vrba, *I Escaped from Auschwitz* (London: Robson Books, 2006), 83–84. Vrba (born Walter Rosenberg) escaped together with Alfred Wetzler on April 7, 1944. In the SS system, Auschwitz security was considered particularly bad. According to Henryk Świebocki, there were 802 successful escape attempts. Of these, 327 were recaptured, 144 successfully escaped and survived the war, and in the remaining cases there is no conclusive evidence. See Henryk Świebocki, "Escapes from the Camp," in *Auschwitz 1940–1945: Central Issues in the History of the Camp: The Establishment and Organization of the Camp*, vol. 4, ed. Wacław Długoborski and Franciszek Piper, trans. William Brand (Oświęcim: Auschwitz-Birkenau State Museum, 2000), 191–236.

16. Michael Zakim, *Ready-Made Democracy: A History of Men's Dress on the American Republic, 1760–1860* (Chicago: University of Chicago Press, 2006).

17. Primo Levi, *If This Is a Man; and, The Truce*, trans. Stuart Woolf (London: Abacus, 2005), 87, 92–93.

18. Levi, *If This Is a Man*, 92.

19. The "Greens" are the prisoners interned on criminal grounds, called in this manner after the color of the triangle (*Winkel*) used on their prisoner uniforms to display the reason of incarceration. Other categories included: political opponents (red), "asocial elements" (black), Jews (yellow), homosexuals (pink), and Jehovah's Witnesses (purple). See Robert Waitz, "Auschwitz III: Monowitz," in *De l'Universite aux Camps de Concentration Temoignages Strasbourgeois* (Strasbourg: Societé d'Edition Les Belles Lettres, 1947), 479–499. Translation from Langbein, *People in Auschwitz*, 180.

20. Anonymous, *My Journey to Hell and Back*, 29.

21. Vrba, *I Escaped Auschwitz*, 75.

22. Vrba, *I Escaped Auschwitz*, 184.

23. As evidenced for example in descriptions of Camp-Eldest Franz Danisch. See Erich Kulka and Otto Kraus, *The Death Factory* (Oxford: Pergamon Press, 1966), 248–250; Langbein, *People in Auschwitz*, 148–150.

24. Kulka and Kraus, *Death Factory*, 34.

25. According to Jean Améry, such a prisoner "no longer had room in his consciousness for the contrasts good or bad, noble or base, intellectual or unintellectual. He was a staggering corpse, a bundle of physical functions in its last convulsions." Jean Améry, *At the Mind's Limits: Contemplations by a Survivor on Auschwitz and its Realities* (Bloomington: Indiana University Press, 1980), 9.

26. Zdzisław Ryn and Stanisław Kłodziński, "An der Grenze Zwischen Leben und Tod: Eine Studie Über die Erscheinung des 'Muselmanns' im Konzentrationslager," in *Die Auschwitz-Hefte: Texte der Polnischen Zeitschrift "Przeglad Lekarski,"* vol. 1, ed. Jochen August (Hamburg: Rogner & Bernhard, 1987), 89–154.

27. Alexandre Orme, *Comes the Comrade!* (New York: William Morrow & Co., 1950), 19–21. My sincere thanks to Brandon Schechter for pointing out this excellent reference, which goes into the subject at a level of detail I am unfamiliar with among Auschwitz survivors. But such a text concerning Auschwitz may well yet await discovery within vast archives of witness testimony and narratives.

28. The connection between spherical geometries and the subject and what he calls the self is an integral part of Carl Jung's interpretations of the eastern circular art of the mandala. See Carl Gustav Jung, *Nietzsche's Zarathustra: Notes of the Seminar Given in 1934–1939 vols. I and II*, ed. James J. Jarrett (Princeton: Princeton University Press, 1988), 181.

29. Kulka and Kraus, *Death Factory*, 34.

30. Levi, *If This Is a Man*, 40–41.

31. Vrba, *I Escaped Auschwitz*, 134.

32. Waitz, "Auschwitz III: Monowitz," 473, translation by the author.

33. Kulka and Kraus, *Death Factory*, 65.

34. Kautsky, *Devils and the Damned*, 225.

35. Levi, *If This Is a Man*, 95.

36. Levi, *If This Is a Man*, 107–109.

37. Langbein, *People in Auschwitz*, 70.

38. Langbein, *People in Auschwitz*, citing Georges Wellers, *De Drancy à Auschwitz* (Paris: Éditions de Centre, 1946).

39. Meticulous report by Dr. Hans Münch, formerly of the SS Hygiene-Institut Auschwitz (Raijsko), who was acquitted in the Krakow trials in 1947. Auschwitz-Birkenau State Museum, Bl. 4606, 44, translation by the author.

40. On the connection between Nazism and colonial practice, see Carroll Kakel, *The Holocaust as Colonial Genocide: Hitler's "Indian Wars" in the "Wild East"* (New York: Palgrave Macmillan, 2013).

41. Two tools were the non-German militias (the Trawniki) as well as the use of guard dogs. Höss, in particular, seems to have been a fan of the guard dogs. For the prisoner self-government the best sources are H. G. Adler, "Selbstverwaltung und Widerstand in Den Konzentrationslagern Der SS," *Vierteljahrshefte Für Zeitgeschichte* 8, no. 3 (1960): 221–236; Eugeniusz Brzezicki et al., "Die Funktionshäftlinge in den Nazi-Konzentrationslagern: eine Diskussion," in *Die Auschwitz-Hefte: Texte der polnischen Zeitschrift Przeglad Lekarski*, vol. 1, ed. Jochen August (Hamburg: Rogner & Bernhard, 1987), 231–239. For a still-relevant overview of the sources and problems, see Pingel, *Häftlinge,* 164–170.

42. Carroll P. Kakel, *The Holocaust as Colonial Genocide* (New York: Palgrave Macmillan, 2013).

43. Rudolf Höss, *Death Dealer: The Memoirs of the SS Kommandant at Auschwitz,* ed. Steven Paskuly, trans. Andrew Paskuly (New York: Da Capo Press, 1996), 131.

44. Yet in the same breath he acknowledges that these unofficial "rules" were not kept and that prisoners were smuggling alcohol into the camp. Hermann Langbein, *Der Auschwitz-Prozess: Eine Dokumentation* (Frankfurt: Verlag Neue Kritik, 1995), 252–253, translation by the author.

45. Levi, *If This Is a Man,* 95–98.

46. Kautsky, *Devils and the Damned,* 218–219.

47. Tadeusz Iwaszko, "Contact with the Outside World," in *Auschwitz 1940–1945: Central Issues in the History of the Camp: The Establishment and Organization of the Camp,* vol. 2, ed. Wacław Długoborski and Franciszek Piper, trans. William Brand (Oświęcim: Auschwitz-Birkenau State Museum, 2000), 419–427.

48. Kulka and Kraus mention that Jews could receive parcels, but in practice this did not happen. Kulka and Kraus, *Death Factory,* 50.

49. "Here scores of prisoners driven desperate by hunger prowl around, with lips half-open and eyes gleaming, lured by a deceptive instinct to where the merchandise shown makes the gnawing of their stomachs more acute and the salivation more assiduous. In the best of cases they possess a miserable half-ration of bread." Levi, *If This Is a Man,* 88–89.

50. Otto Dov Kulka, *Landscapes of the Metropolis of Death* (Cambridge: Harvard University Press, 2013). The term appears twenty-five times in the text; see examples on pages 40, 60, 101.

51. Langbein, *Der Auschwitz-Prozess,* vol. 1, 67.

52. See note 1.

53. Waitz, "Auschwitz III: Monowitz," 478.

54. Höss reports: "The textile shortage brought about cuts and more cuts for the prisoners. The mandatory clothing quota could not be met as far back as 1940. Not even using the clothing and footwear from the extermination of the Jews could sufficiently improve the clothing shortage." Höss, *Death Dealer,* 315.

55. See for example Irena Strzelecka and Piotr Setkiewicz, "Establishment and Organization of the Camp," 99–102.

56. Vrba, *I Escaped Auschwitz,* 237–238.

57. Heinrich Himmler, "Sonthofener Rede," June 21, 1944 (IfZ, MA 315, Bl. 3949ff.), cited in Pingel, *Häftlinge,* 164–165 and note 144.

58. Anonymous, *My Journey to Hell and Back,* 29.

59. Pingel, *Häftlinge,* 168.

60. Vrba, *I Escaped Auschwitz,* 127. In 1967 Vrba moved to Canada, where he remained until his death in 2006.

61. The warehouse was moved and expanded as the camp itself expanded.

62. Kulka and Kraus, *Death Factory,* 143.

63. Kulka and Kraus, *Death Factory.*

64. See, for example, Kitty Hart, *I Am Alive* (London: Abelard-Schuman, 1961).

65. Kulka and Kraus, *Death Factory*, 143.

66. Vrba, *I Escaped Auschwitz*, 131.

67. Höss, *Death Dealer*, 40.

68. Höss, *Death Dealer*, 40–41. See also Nikolaus Wachsmann, *A History of the Nazi Concentration Camps* (New York: Farrar, Straus and Giroux, 2015), 376–391.

69. In his edited publication of Höss's memoir, Jerzy Rawicz, a Polish former prisoner, has supplied some collected memories regarding the person of Höss and his family. According to Rawicz, Höss enjoyed his "Paradise in Auschwitz" organizing things though his caretaker, a German "Green" (professional criminal) who had been released from the camp and offered employment in a local leather factory. Through this connection, among others, the Höss family was able to accumulate a sufficient amount of personal possessions to require several freight cars to clear their property out when then left. See his foreword in Adwiga Bezwinska and Danuta Czech, eds., *KL Auschwitz Seen by the SS: Höss, Broad, and Kremer* (Oświęcim: Auschwitz-Birkenau State Museum, 1978), 7–27.

70. His diary is reproduced in Bezwinska and Czech, eds., *KL Auschwitz Seen by the SS.*

71. Langbein, *Der Auschwitz-Prozess*, vol. 1, 291. Presumably the cash was available to prisoners because this kommando was working on the ramp; as they cleared the luggage of incoming transport from the platform, they would pilfer from the contents (which according to German law were property of the Reich). Baretzki, who was formally in charge and wielded the power of life and death, knew what was going on and, as is evidenced here, was taking a cut. The reference to "dollars," not a currency used in the Third Reich, appears in the original text.

72. Vrba, *I Escaped Auschwitz*, 143.

73. See Höss, *Death Dealer*, 40.

74. Tadeusz Borowski, *This Way for the Gas, Ladies and Gentlemen* (London: Penguin Books, 1976), 49.

75. Langbein, *Der Auschwitz-Prozess*, vol. 1, 143. For a corroboration of Morgen's computations, see Andrzej Strzelecki, "Utilization of the Victim's Corpses," in ed. Długoborski and Piper, *Auschwitz 1940–1945*, vol. 2 (Oświęcim: Auschwitz-Birkenau State Museum, 2000), 399–419.

76. Höss, like many of those involved in the atrocities of World War II and the Holocaust, argues for personal "non-involvement" in the daily details of the atrocities as he was just an administrator.

77. See account of Jerzy Rawicz, in note 71. Rawicz, who as a prisoner was stationed in the Höss family home as a domestic worker, reports that the latter built a "Paradise in Auschwitz." The Höss family was able to accumulate personal possessions which, according to Rawicz, required several freight cars to clear when then left Auschwitz. See his foreword to Bezwinska and Czech, eds., *KL Auschwitz seen by the SS*, 19–23.

78. Höss, *Death Dealer*, 40.

79. Langbein, *Der Auschwitz Prozess*, vol. 1, 297.

80. Kautsky, *Devils and the Damned*, 209–210. On the British POWs in Buna-Monowitz, see Joseph Robert White, "Even in Auschwitz Humanity Could Prevail: British POWs and Jewish Concentration-Camp Inmates at IG Auschwitz, 1943–1945," *Holocaust and Genocide Studies* 15, no. 2 (2001): 266–295. Many similar reports about trade between prisoners can be found in the camp archipelago of Auschwitz-Birkenau.

81. Rene Coudy and Simon Laks, *Musiques d'un Autre Monde* (Paris: Mercure de France, 1948), cited in Langbein, *People in Auschwitz*, 153.

82. Moshe Yaakobovitch, "Unpublished Recordings," recording 1, June 11, 2009. Again we have the mention of dollars as a currency.

83. Vrba, *I Escaped Auschwitz*, 93.

84. Vrba, *I Escaped Auschwitz*, 137.

85. As stated explicitly in Himmler's "Sonthofener Rede," June 21, 1944 (IfZ, MA 315, Bl. 3949ff.), cited in Pingel, *Häftlinge*, 164–165 and note 144.

86. Primo Levi, *The Drowned and the Saved*, trans. Raymond Rosenthal (New York: Vintage Books, 1989), 36–69.

87. See Pingel, *Häftlinge*, 160n152.

88. The values and self-perceived image of the SS emerged in competition with the SA, to which it had originally been subordinated. In contrast to the swashbuckling lower middle-class, working-class image of the SA fostered by Ernst Röhm, Himmler developed the SS as an "order of knights" based around his own versions of roughly middle-class morality. See Peter Longerich, *Heinrich Himmler*, trans. Jeremy Noakes and Lesley Sharpe (Oxford: Oxford University Press, 2012), esp. chs. 6, 13.

89. Richard Glazar, cited in Gita Sereny, *Into that Darkness*, 197–198. Glazar had a "private" shaving kit, whereas Kulka and Kraus report that in Auschwitz a blunt straight edge razor was used to shave the entire body once a week, on Sundays. See Kulka and Kraus, *Death Factory*, 40. Nonetheless, it stands to reason that a private shaving kit would not have been difficult to come by for privileged prisoners.

90. See note 34.

91. Kautsky, *Devils and the Damned*, 148.

92. Kautsky, *Devils and the Damned*, 143.

93. Eugeniusz Brzezicki et al., "Die Funktionshäftlinge," 237, translation by the author.

94. My thanks to Michael Geyer for this useful adjective.

Part III

Afterlives

From Things to Memories

Leora Auslander and Tara Zahra

The three chapters in the last section of this volume address the afterlife of things that were set in motion by war or persecution. Tragically, war's end can bring as much devastation as its practice, as victors seize the spoils to which they feel entitled. Upon reaching new destinations, whether temporary or permanent, those things are redeployed by prisoners, refugees, and war widows in novel ways. Some objects are physically transformed in the context of displacement, and their meaning and use are altered as well. An item that once had purely practical value (like a tea towel) can become a precious reminder of a lost family member; a stolen cream pitcher can become a teapot.

In the longer term, in the years and decades following peace, things displaced in wartime move again. They are reclaimed through restitution processes or given new homes in museums, having gained public value and meaning through their experiences in wartime.

In one case, analyzed by Gerdien Jonker, those things have remained in the private sphere, kept within the family of their first owner. The suitcases are filled with the relics of German/Jewish/Muslim/South Asian bourgeois life and reflect one woman's efforts to make sense of her displacement by collecting objects from Germany and South Asia that "matched" or mirrored one another. The carefully preserved intimate items are the material traces of a quite extraordinary migration story. This story is echoed in the objects given to the Jewish Museum Berlin analyzed by Jeffrey Wallen and Aubrey Pomerance. The domestic items that have returned to Germany after having been sent into forced exile with their Jewish owners in the 1930s and early 1940s have now settled into their new home. They have been definitively taken out of the private, domestic sphere and moved into museum space. That move, however, poses as many questions to them, and their keepers, as it answers. Which, of the many stories each of these objects could tell, is the one to be told? How can these things best be allowed to act in the present and future world they now inhabit? These same questions are raised by our final contribution, that of Sandra Dudley. In this case, however, one of the Karenni skirt-cloths that are the object of her analysis is still being used by the woman who made it, while the two others are in museums, one in England and one in the United States. Produced by a community long in exile, each of these skirt-cloths has had a distinct trajectory. Dudley sees the job of the museum not to narrativize these things but rather to allow them full reign to act, in unpredictable ways, on those that come to visit them.

8

LISA'S THINGS

Matching German-Jewish and Indian-Muslim Traditions

Gerdien Jonker

In the summer of 2013 I flew to London to meet two people whose mothers had converted to Islam in Berlin before the Second World War. Back then I was doing research on the Muslim reform movement of the Ahmadiyya and their mission activities in interwar Europe.[1] Group photographs I had come across made me conclude that the Ahmadiyya mission not only functioned as a facilitator for Indian-German marriages but also catered to the children born out of those relationships. My search for them was fueled by the hope to find material remains that could throw light on the mission from a family perspective.

As a matter of course, the people I was going to see bore Muslim names. Suhail Ahmad, born in 1949 in Karachi, was the son of the Berlin painter Lisa Oettinger and hotel proprietor Nazir Ahmad, member of the Ahmadiyya in Lahore. Suhail's cousin Anisah Christina Rani, born in 1933 in Berlin, was the daughter of Lisa's sister Susanna, a professional head of office, and the Indian N. T. Gulrajani from Karachi who in the 1930s conducted export business in Berlin. In the mosque archive and files in the registration office I had come across Lisa's and Susanna's names many times. From these sources I also knew that their mother Emilia Oettinger in 1930 cofounded the Deutsch-Moslemische Gesellschaft (German-Muslim Society), the convert organization of the Ahmadiyya mission. When Ahmadiyya elders informed me that there were still Oettinger descendants living in the vicinity of London, I did not think twice and organized a plane ticket.

Little was I prepared for what I found. Anisah safeguarded papers that seemed to hold the story of the Oettinger family in a nutshell. Among them were the documents that proved her mother's and grandmother's conversion to Islam; the documents of her grandfather Friedrich Oettinger, telling us that he converted to Christianity in 1885 and exited from the Jewish community in Berlin some time after; the marriage contract between Friedrich's parents Louis Oettinger and Johanna Lewinsohn, which revealed much about Jewish marriage in Prussia in the late nineteenth century, and the document, issued in 1866 by the Prussian local administration, that granted Louis permission to leave Marienwerder in western Prussia, where he was registered as a member of the Jewish community. The Oettingers, these documents told me, were of Jewish descent and had quit Judaism prior to their conversion to Islam.

Initially, Suhail Ahmad presented me with the five photo albums his mother Lisa had put together in 1957 to explain to him her early life in Berlin, the life of her first husband Azeez Ur-Rahman Mirza, their social life in the Berlin mosque, their honeymoon to India, and her life in Lahore.[2] The next time I visited him, he also showed me two large trunks that had stood padlocked in his mothers' bedroom since 1957 and that he had left untouched after she died in 2006. When we opened them, they appeared to be full of fragile things from Marienwerder, Berlin, and Lahore, placed in the trunks in a jigsaw pattern, each of which Lisa had wrapped in tissue and provided with a note exhorting him to safeguard the contents. "MUST remain in the family!" she wrote on each of them.

Talking to Suhail Ahmad and Anisah Christina Rani, I realized that I had found two cousins who tried to make sense of a religious legacy that in many ways surpassed the jigsaw puzzle we uncovered in the trunks. Their own relation to the Oettinger family was intense. As a child, Anisah had been hidden in Nazi Germany, an experience from which she came away with disturbing memories, and which uprooted her relationship to her mother Susanna. From her perspective, youth in Germany had been traumatic, yet "home." From Suhail's perspective, the past took a very different shape. Born in Karachi, he lived with his mother until she died at the age of ninety-eight. Their lives together had been peaceful. Lisa painted and was proud of her Prussian (Jewish) roots but urged her son to acknowledge the importance of having inherited two wholly different roots, German culture and Islamic civilization, so that he was filled with a sense of responsibility. As a result, he became the guardian of his mother's legacy.

Because their mothers had fallen out with each other after the war, the two cousins had not been aware of any family treasures or memories the other possessed. My entry into their lives brought the two parts together again. Seated in Anisah's drawing room, they perused each other's things, exchanged reminiscences, compared experiences, and looked at me for help whenever the German past threatened to slip beyond comprehension. This became my role in the proceedings. During those visits—I went back six times—I became involved in the memories and anecdotes of a family that was not mine yet had entrusted me with the family treasures, had trusted that I would turn them into a story that would explain to them what it was all about. Together we unraveled a religious history that in retrospect seemed strange, yet appeared to have been quite common at the time of its occurrence.

Apparently, in the timespan of four generations, the Oettinger family transitioned from traditional Jews to German-Jewish citizens with a secular outlook; baptized their children to give proof of their German loyalty; experimented with the Lebensreform (Life Reform), a fin-de-siècle movement about which the reader will learn more on the pages ahead, as a way to adopt individual lifestyles; experimented with Islam, became devout Muslims, and produced Muslim children who, in their turn, opted to become Christians. In the end, I wrote a book in which I assigned to every generation its role in the slow movement over decades: the great-grandparents in Jewish Marienwerder, the grandparents in Jewish-secular Berlin, the mothers Susanna and Lisa in the Ahmadiyya mosque, and the two cousins in England who inherited a religious past that puzzles them to this day.[3]

In this contribution I propose to focus on Lisa Oettinger and her trunks. It starts from the suspicion that the collection she bequeathed in

1957 to her son carries a meaning and that the things she selected were meant to serve as its carrier. I therefore ask what kind of collection she procured and why it was created. While undertaking this task it became clear that there was more to it than meets the eye. Different than the rest of the Oettinger archive, the contents of Lisa's trunks forced this observer to unravel not one but two family stories, which Lisa purposefully joined: her own German-Jewish past and that of her husband's family, which is rooted in reformist Islam.

At this point in the narrative, a short biographical note may orient the reader. Born in 1908, Lisa Oettinger belonged to the very first generation of women to enter the Art Academy in Berlin. An independent artist, in 1929, she joined the quickly growing Ahmadiyya community and in 1933 embraced Islam. She adopted the name of Zubaidah and became engaged to Imam Azeez Ur-Rahman Mirza, whom she married in 1937 in the Sarajevo mosque. From this city the couple launched into an extended voyage to the East, with Lahore as their final goal. But when they finally arrived, Azeez died within weeks. In 1939, Lisa remarried a wealthy hotel owner named Nazir Ahmad, who also was a supporter of Ahmadiyya. Giving birth to a child out of wedlock in 1949, she eventually traveled to England to take care of her new son's education, leaving India and her husband behind. Mother and son settled in Woking in 1956 in the vicinity of another Ahmadiyya mosque and remained together for the rest of her long life until, in 2006, Lisa Zubaidah Ahmad died peacefully in her bed.

This contribution has four steps. Since the objects that Lisa selected from her mother's household in 1937 to prepare for life in Lahore recall a discussion in the Ahmadiyya mosque during that time, the first step will be to recapitulate that discussion and trace it to the contents of her suitcases (Berlin, 1937). In the second step, the text addresses the trunks, which she arranged in Woking, England, twenty years later (Woking, 1957). Once that has been established, the trunks will be "unwrapped" and their contents systematically ordered and traced back to the families for whom they serve as a memory: the Oettinger family (the German Connection) and the Ur-Rahman Family (both the Mirza Connection and the Lahore Connection).

This much can be said already: Lisa Oettinger's collection saved two families from being forgotten: the Oettingers from Marienwerder and the Ur-Rahmans from Lahore. The collection allows them not only to live on in their things but also to join their family traditions in one box. For that reason, her collection is neither specifically Jewish nor specifically Muslim. It is in-between. If anything, that has been Lisa's legacy to her son.

Berlin, 1937

Lisa Oettinger was a painter with a long artistic pedigree. Her father, her grandfather, and her great-grandfather had all been businessmen who believed in the beauty of things. Back in Marienwerder, the family designed and produced lace artifacts and trimmings. Once in Berlin, they switched to art deco glassware. When it was her turn to choose a profession, Lisa studied industrial design and specialized in interior design. Her choice was a timely one. When Lisa entered the Berlin Art School in 1927, German homes were experiencing something of a revolution. Instead of the heavy furniture and draperies of the German fin-de-siècle, the younger generation preferred white lacquer furnishings, which they combined with oriental carpets and African art.[4] In Lisa's portfolios one meets with Chinese dragons, Japanese women, Egyptian sphinxes, apes, dancing mice, birds of paradise, and flowers in every possible color. They give ample witness to the fact that she believed in and catered to the oriental turn as her contribution to the popular movement of Lebensreform (improvement of one's personal way of living).[5]

Lisa believed in the power of artistic language. She took things seriously. She was not the only one. When in 1933 she converted to Islam in the Ahmadiyya mosque in Berlin, she met with a group of like-minded people who were looking for ways to live like a Muslim and furnish their homes accordingly. Their animated discussions about "Future Man" fired her imagination on how to apply her art to habits and expectations she was not yet familiar with. To understand the things that later ended up in the trunks beside her bed, we will therefore have to make a little detour into that mosque and look at the train of arguments that entered the debate and her mind.

When Germany realized it had lost the Great War and was stamped as the guilty party, the country was in a turmoil. Berlin became the scene of paramilitary organizations and uncontrolled street fighting.

Food and fuel were scarce. People starved. Missionaries from around the globe were quick to notice that the German people were on their knees. As one of them noted: "Among all the countries of the world, there does not appear to be so much scope for the propagation of Islam as there is in Germany."[6] Christian, Muslim, Baha'i, and Buddhist missionaries soon set up mission posts in Berlin and other German cities, and many Germans, Lebensreform proponents especially, but also Prussian officers who had experienced the nerve gas and the trenches, thankfully received them.[7]

Missionaries from the Ahmadiyya Reform movement in Lahore, British India, set up shop in Berlin in 1923. Their message was a peaceful Islam that urged people to stay away from politics and start working on themselves if they wished to improve the world. The missionaries, themselves the highly cultured descendants of the landed gentry in northern India, embodied what they preached. The press marveled at their "elegance" and "exotic flair."[8] In their version of Islam, good manners and a thorough knowledge of Persian poetry took the place of honor.

What the Ahmadiyya sought was intellectual exchange and the establishment of an interface between European modernity and Muslim quests to modernize Islam. Towards that aim, they built a mosque in Berlin, itself a little marvel of Moghul art and, when opening its doors, offered a platform for a broad-minded discussion on the future of mankind. Reform-minded Germans, both Jews and Christians, attended the lectures in great numbers, and the sympathetic public soon dubbed Islam a modern, democratic religion that was "up with the times." In the course of the mission's existence (when, in 1939, German armies invaded Poland, the last missionary left Berlin), some five hundred visitors actually embraced Islam, a number that was exceeded by those who became "friends of Islam," the official term for the supporters of the Ahmadiyya quest. And in 1930, missionaries, their friends and converts, and some Indian, Persian, and Tatar Muslims joined hands to initiate the Deutsch-Moslemische Gesellschaft (German-Muslim Society), the society for the propagation of Islam and the concluding of friendships between "East and West."

When Lisa joined the Ahmadiyya mosque, discussions about the "Man of the Future" held the German-Muslim Society in its grip. In the Berlin of the 1920s and 1930s, the Communists, the Nazis and the followers of the Lebensreform movement had already proposed their ideal of the coming generation. German followers of the Lebensreform movement for instance believed in the individual fashioning of the self through bodily exercise. As a consequence, they celebrated the body as "a holy temple," charging it with "the holy duty" to remedy "the social disturbances that we and the whole world experience at present." In their perspective, to rescue the world, one needed to return to an "original, healthy state." Once that stage was reached, it was believed that the current problems would disappear in no time at all.[9]

The "new man" touted by the Nazis, too, carried a notable bodily aspect. Adolf Hitler, when speaking to the German youth in Nuremberg in 1935, unfolded his vision that they should be "swift like chase dogs, tough like leather and hard like *krupp* iron."[10] More, he invited them to become the "living tools of the *Führer*," ready at all times to give proof of their "manliness, courage, and firmness."[11] In the reality of the war that followed, these youngsters were thrown in as suicide fighters and sacrificed for his aims.

In between these two extremes, the missionary organization in the Ahmadiyya mosque adopted a "new man" position that borrowed from both, yet differed in decisive ways from the speculations of the others.[12] Most German converts to Islam were Lebensreform enthusiasts. But, while they embraced bodily exercise, they strove to alter their lives through experience of the divine, an exercise in which the body was treated as the main gate of access to God. Hugo Marcus, president of the German-Muslim Society, himself of Jewish descent and an out-of-the-closet homosexual, suggested an opening that centered upon the body. Writing in 1930 in the tumultuous political and societal entanglement leading up to the era of National Socialism, he observed that "in the present situation" the best one could do was to keep a sober head and an objective mind. Only those who had the courage to hold on to both, Marcus postulated, were properly prepared to encounter the sacred. In his perspective, the "new man" was going to be "a sober man with a glowing heart" who did not shun from the adventure to "melt" the extremes in his soul and forge them into something new. Hinting at "the sacred experience of eroticism," Marcus suggested that having sex was the place to accomplish the impossible.[13]

The German-Muslim Society seethed. Nonetheless, many members responded to their president, offering alternatives to his provocative vision.

Among them was Omar Rolf von Ehrenfels, a young baron from Austria who had just been appointed editor of the *Die Moslemische Revue*, the Ahmadiyya mission journal edited in Berlin. Instead of eroticism, he proposed looking at the way German Muslims moved their bodies, dressed themselves, and furnished their homes. Ehrenfels considered the oriental way of living on the floor as a way to progress. First, he argued, this was an expression of solidarity with nature and thus a feature of advanced civilization—more natural and therefore better than European culture. Instead of putting chairs and tables in their houses, the baron urged, German Muslims should consider sitting, sleeping, and praying on the floor and also serve their meals there. Second, or so he thought, "the floor perspective" was the way to enhance the beauty of daily life. Only people who mastered the perspective "from below" were able "to design their home through and through in artistic beauty" and through this "live in beauty," he said.[14]

This text with its direct implications for modern interior design went right to Lisa's heart. As a consequence, when in 1937 she became engaged to be married to Azeez Ur-Rahman Mirza, assistant imam of the Berlin Ahmadiyya mosque[15] and the two of them prepared to travel to Lahore in British India, she singled out an abundant amount of lace from the family treasure. There were handmade table settings; many kinds of trimmings, lace, and fillet; and pieces large enough to cover a room. To this she added the family album with photographs reaching back into nineteenth-century Jewish Marienwerder; landscapes that used to hang in the dining room at home; a much-used book of German poetry and songs; Schubert's *Erlkönig* as the apotheosis of German culture; a greasy, handwritten recipe book; her grandmother's collection of Romantic poetry and ivory profiles of Goethe and Schiller; her mother's collection of German songbooks and piano pieces for four hands; albums filled with postcards for cultured conversation; her father's first tooth, lock of hair, and worn leather baby shoes; and many more smallish things with a family story.

Those were the things with which Lisa Oettinger planned to furnish her own future household. The collection shows that she projected to live on the floor, cover it with the lace of the grandmothers, and thus adapt to oriental culture in a manner that she deemed civilized. The collection also intimates that she considered herself a bearer of German culture and was planning to exhibit that knowledge in Lahore. Other German women in the Ahmadiyya mosque confirmed her vision. Some even wrote in the mission journal that "out there" was a task waiting for the "European woman," namely to mix with other civilizations and religious traditions while upholding and spreading European, specifically German culture.[16]

Comparing the contents of Lisa's suitcases with the lists of household furniture other migrants from Germany drew up before the war, there seems to have been a lack of the more conservative household goods. Even when taking into account that, during her move from Lahore to London in 1954, she must have left some of her possessions behind[17] and that the two trunks she rearranged in 1957 for her son offered only a limited space, what is in there amply demonstrates that it was her artistic understanding of an "Islamic" life that governed her original choices.[18]

In her groundbreaking essay "Beyond Words," Leora Auslander suggests that there is an interplay between the objects of the past and the narratives that accompany them.[19] Words may express *what* happened in the past, but only things may convey a feeling of *how* it was. Things are never mute. Quite the contrary, they serve as a tool in many different communications. Their presence in the home, for instance, enforces certain routines. Things are exhibited, polished, admired, hated, broken, and thrown away. They get lost and are found again. The very sight of them provokes images, memories, and emotions. In daily dealing with them, things sometimes become the memory they embody. They are considered spirited objects that are thought to bring the past back to life.

When Lisa gathered things from her mother's household in Berlin, she did not know yet what the future held in store. And indeed, once she arrived in Lahore, her husband died and she was left alone with a family that was utterly foreign to her. We may assume that, in her new surroundings, the lace and trimmings, Friedrich's shoes and her grandmother's cookbook assumed different roles, speaking to her from the past in moments of despair but also encouraging her when she tried to regain her bearings and create independence, thereby triggering the interplay Auslander speaks about. In the Lebensreform language of her time, Lisa strove to restore the links connecting art, aesthetics, and religion in Muslim Lahore, and she believed that things—both old and new—could help her establish that relation. In the end, she managed. That too is the legacy she wanted to convey to her son.

Woking, 1957

In the spring of 1957, exactly twenty years after she left Berlin, Lisa Oettinger, now living as Mrs. Louise Zubeidah Ahmad in the vicinity of the Ahmadiyya mosque in Woking, England, took stock of her life. Among other things, she filled two large trunks with objects that were meaningful to her, wrapping them in tissue paper and plastic bags, and adding little slips of papers to each of them on which she explained to her son which of the grandmothers had stitched which piece of lace, where they stood in the family home in Berlin, and which things she picked up in India, and why. Underneath she invariably added the sentence "MUST remain in the family!" To these she added the books and music sheets that originally had been dedicated to her as a girl and that she now re-dedicated to him. Breakable things she put in boxes and metal caskets and locked them. Then, she ordered everything in a pattern that designated each thing its place in the trunks. Finally, on April 8, 1957, trusting that he would read it only much later in life, she wrote a letter to her son in which she explained to him what had gone wrong in the past and why this was so. The sealed envelope she put on top of the collection. Once she was ready she padlocked the trunks and put them next to her bed, where they remained until her death in 2006 (figure 8.1).

When the trunks were opened in 2014, the "reading" of the contents began. But a trunk full of things is not a chronological table. Lisa's trunks were packed with objects that pointed in various geographical directions, covered different cultural traditions, and informed about historical periods that were sometimes spread far apart. Forms, textures, and smells may have hinted at their origin but without the story behind them, it was impossible to identify the objects with their original bearers, let alone disclose the memories they encapsulated.

The written instructions Lisa left behind provided us with a minimum of information, but they nonetheless showed the way. Some of the words she used betrayed family relations: *Muttchen* (mother), *Groß-muttchen* (grandmother), *Großvater* (grandfather), "your great grandmother," "auntie," etc. Name places like Berlin, Lahore, Karachi, and Woking established geographical relationships. It was enough to make a first ordering in which the things initially became separated again:

Figure 8.1. The padlocked trunks in the Woking bedroom in 2014.
Photograph by author.

Germany and the Jewish family on the one side, Lahore and the Muslim family on the other.

Where the trunks were silent on the Oettinger past, Anisah's stack of family documents came to the rescue. Taking my lead from those, I traveled to Marienwerder, today Kwidzyn in Poland, to establish their origins, then proceeded to visit cemeteries and archives to trace the family history to Berlin.

The political situation in Pakistan proved to be too precarious to conduct similar family research in that country. To gain knowledge about the Ur-Rahman family, I consulted the photo albums, which Suhail Ahmad still keeps in his care. The "Lange Mandi" album especially offered some three hundred photographs of home interiors, festive occasions, picnics, hikes, and boat outings on the river Ravi near Lahore, the bungalow in which Lisa established her life as an artist. For the rest of her stay in Lahore, after all another 15 years, she made it her home and her station. Even when marrying Nazir Ahmad, the hotel proprietor next door who also became the adopted father of Suhail, she insisted on living a solitary life in her atelier.[20] Each of these photographs Lisa painstakingly provided with an explanatory caption. Here too, words like *Amajee* (mother), *Abajee* (father), "my brothers," "my sisters," and so on helped to disentangle the intricate web of relationships. In addition, Ahmadiyya elders provided me with background information. Where everything else failed, there was still the letter she wrote to her son.

In the trunks we also encountered traces of Azeez Ur-Rahman Mirza, Lisa's first love and her legitimate husband. However short-lived their relationship may have been, the five years in which they got to know each other, fell in love, and finally married deeply influenced her further life course. The things she safeguarded as his memory were almost all of a textual nature: his declarations of love, the books and dedications he presented to her, his notes on a Hafiz translation, his collection of aphorisms of German poets, and the lectures he gave at the Berlin mosque. Besides, there was his prayer mat and the medals and badges he acquired in Berlin. Together with the photo albums she filled with his pictures, this was enough to grasp the nature of their friendship. They offer the key to understanding her decision to join their respective families in one and the same collection.

In the following, an attempt will be made to order the contents of the trunks and figure out how they were put to use. We will start with the oldest layer containing the Oettinger family treasures that were selected in Berlin. They are followed by Azeez's possessions and his gifts to Lisa, which tell us something about their life in Berlin and the nature of their friendship. Lastly, we take account of the things she collected in Lahore, which communicate her emotional ties to the Ur-Rahman family and a deeply felt respect for the beauty and handicraft of Moghul tradition.

The German Connection

When placing together all the things that were selected in Berlin in 1937, it becomes clear that they derive from a pool of objects that had survived three households. When great-grandmother Bertha Oettinger died in Berlin in 1906, her things, or at least part of them, wandered into the household of her son Louis and his wife Johanna. When Johanna died in 1914, her own son Friedrich, who after all lived with his parents until the age of 34, would have selected what was dear to him, what was still of use or represented the family memory. Whatever there may have been among the debris—gold-rimmed porcelain crockery, fruit bowls with copper adornments, porcelain dogs and shepherds, plaster and ebony figures from faraway countries, mantelpiece clocks, silver salt sprinklers, sunset paintings, and other knickknacks that used to adorn the Prussian home and can been glimpsed on the family photographs. Lisa took none of that; even her father's art deco glass collection she neglected. Instead, when it was her turn to choose, she exclusively picked artifacts of the family's lace production and other things that represented her father's family and their representation of German culture.

Remarkably, none of these objects represented the Läwen family, the family of Lisa's mother. In fact, if there was ever a story attached to this family branch, it was never collected or even mentioned. The things Lisa packed together unerringly bore the markings of German-Jewish culture as given shape by three generations of Oettinger women. The list contains:

- At least one suitcase filled with lace and trimmings[21]
- A suitcase full of tablecloth and napkins
- The family photo album (1871–1914)
- The handwritten family cookbook (1871–1957)
- Five albums filled with postcards (1880s–1937)

- Several framed color photographs of the landscapes around Berlin (ca. 1910)
- Several framed color prints of the streets of Berlin (ca. 1850)
- Books from the family library
- Sheet music with pieces by famous German composers
- Carved profiles of Goethe and Schiller (ca. 1850)
- A padlocked box with family jewelry
- Baby Friedrich's lock of hair, baby teeth, and shoes

The way in which she intended to employ these objects has already been clarified. The lace, tablecloth, and napkins were chosen to prepare for a life of beauty from the floor perspective. The postcards, the landscapes, the Goethe and Schiller profiles, the books, and the music she selected to sustain her knowledge of German culture. The family photo album was taken to give witness to her cultured origin. The cookbook would remind Lisa of home and all the pleasant hours she had spent in the kitchen and also encourage her to continue the family tradition of exploring new recipes. Friedrich's baby things seem to have represented the quintessence of family reminiscences. Back in Berlin, the future of the departing couple was still open. Their hint at Lisa's own fertility seems to have been be straightforward enough.

This is what can be established with some certainty. What is practically beyond reach is knowledge of how these things were actually put to use. A study of the family pictures in the "Lange Mandi" album, however, helped provide some idea of how the Ur-Rahman family lived and how Lisa, once she gained independence, furnished her own home.

The very first pictures in the album tell us that the Ur-Rahman family were actually in the habit of living on the floor. When they prepared to receive the couple, they covered the reception rooms with white sheets. But in daily life, the floors were covered with a nondescript brownish material. None of the photographs exhibit the lace that Lisa imported. Five weeks after their festive reception, Azeez died of appendicitis. In the family photos, Lisa visibly loses weight. Her brothers-in-law Khalid, Hamid, and Habib, who surrounded the new family member with loving care, carried a table and chairs to the roof in order to eat "European-style." It was probably an attempt to make her eat anything at all.

A year after her arrival, in the summer of 1938, Khalid Ur-Rahman arranged for a bungalow where Lisa could live on her own and teach in the nearby Islamia high school for girls. Frequent shots show the family in the bungalow garden, where they can be seen chatting and spreading a tablecloth on the grass to prepare for the inevitable picnic. Meanwhile, wicker chairs on the veranda demonstrate that Lisa, when alone, took refuge in a more comfortable seating position. Two pictures of her painting studio confirm this. After she married Nazir Ahmad in July 1939, a studio was built on the side of the bungalow. The photographs, which bear the caption "The studio house-warming party," exhibit a large studio table and some low, comfortable chairs.

Apart from these glimpses, the way in which Lisa put the treasures of the Oettinger family to use—the lace, the books, and the music—remains largely beyond our observation. Nonetheless, many objects in the trunks show telling signs of use, demonstrating that she actually surrounded herself with them. Four examples have been singled out to explain this.

The first one is a heavy package containing large photographs in golden frames that were tied together with a string. On the paper slip she attached, she states: "Mum's home country. Pictures of walks and lakes in and around Berlin. Colored photographic prints dated around 1900, which hung in our dining room and were taken by me to India, where I put them into the present frames. Mum."

The next example includes numerous plastic bags, each with a little slip of paper in a corner stating "For Suhail only" or "MUST remain in the family," contain the stiff linen napkins, tablecloths, and handkerchiefs, with filet inlay work and embroidered at the rim, that once made up the stock of her household. Other plastic bags contain specimens of embroidery and bone lace. Accompanying messages read: "Done by your Great Great Grandmother," "This was made by *Urgrossmuttchen*," or "*Grossmuttchen* made these embroideries and designed them also!" Clearly, this was a part of the heritage Lisa treasured most.

The cookbook especially shows many signs of wear and tear. Begun by Lisa's grandmother Johanna in 1871, it collects recipes from around the world. Instead of following the Jewish tradition of *kashrut*, the kosher kitchen that forbids combining meat with milk or preparing pork and crab, Johanna entered recipes for "hash of wild boar," "goose-liver pate," and "stuffed crab," reaching out to a universe far beyond the tradition of her ancestors.[22] Lisa's mother Emilia continued the tradition and also used the booklet to teach her daughters how to cook. In India, Lisa entered kebabs, chutneys, and chappatis; in Woking, scones and lemon curd. The many grease stains on the pages speak a language of their own.

The only item in the trunks that serves as a memory of all the Oettingers since they came to settle in Marienwerder in 1836 is the family photo album. It is a brown leather case with copper feet, a heavy copper lock, and copper corners to shield the pages, and it was started in 1871 by Johanna Lewinsohn on the occasion of her marriage to Louis Oettinger. The photos are studio pictures, representing family members in stilted poses. The pride of place is given to the engagement photographs of Isidor Oettinger and Bertha Lewinsohn (married in 1838), followed by Louis Oettinger and Johanna Lewinsohn (married in 1871), followed by Friedrich Oettinger and Emilia Läwen (married in 1907). Pictures of their siblings, children, and cousins amply show that this was a wealthy family with a great appetite for costly materials and the latest fashions. This album was once an expensive asset, the quintessence of the family pride, and was meant to stand on a separate table to be shown to visitors on festive occasions. When Johanna died in 1914, the tradition was discontinued. But after a gap of almost forty years, we once again discern a baby. It is Suhail on a bearskin, a studio portrait that was made in Karachi in 1949.

From the snapshots of the Ur-Rahman family and the objects introduced above we gain a picture of Lisa's life in Lahore. First of all, this family took care of Lisa in her distress, surrounded her with love, and designed a way that she could live an independent "European" life yet remain part of the family. For her part, as many of the captions in the "Lange Mandi" album show, Lisa dearly loved her husband's family and received them whenever she could. When she established her own household in Lahore, she unpacked her suitcases, reframed the pictures of Berlin and hung them on her walls, put the cookbook of her grandmother to intensive use, probably (there is no absolute certainty that she did) spread her great grandmother's lace on the dining table, and certainly used the tablecloth and napkins for the many picnics she organized; it is almost certain that she often opened her family photo album to show to the Ur-Rahmans where she came from, who was who, and what they looked like.

The Mirza Connection

To understand how the Oettinger family got entangled with the Ur-Rahman family at all, we have to return to the Oettinger home in Berlin. Lisa's mother was a cultured woman of Christian descent, a declared "agnostic" and a convinced follower of the Lebensreform movement. Moreover, she was a woman with money on her hands, which she amply spent on the bio-dynamic foodstuffs that were grown in the Lebensreform settlements around Berlin and on nature outings with her daughters. But in 1923, her husband lost his money in what came to be known in Germany as the first bank Crash, after which he fell seriously ill. And while he was in hospital, Emilia had to reorganize their lives in order to safeguard (some of) the family income. Like many bourgeois families, she rented rooms to students with ample foreign currency, Susanna, not yet out of school, taught them German, and Lisa sold her designs to studios specializing in interior decoration.[23]

Once they were on that track, a quick succession of events changed their lives decisively. In 1928, Sheikh Muhammad Abdullah, newly appointed imam of the Ahmadiyya mosque in Berlin, rented a room in the Oettinger apartment. Susanne taught him German, mother Emilia took him on hikes in woods around Berlin, the family befriended the circle of Indians in the mosque; already in the next year, all three Oettinger women participated in the *Eid-al-Fitr* celebrations at the end of the fasting month Ramadan.[24] When in 1930 converts and "friends of Islam" founded the German-Muslim Society, Emilia joined the board as a non-Muslim member.

Friedrich, observing the proceedings from his hospital bed, was more than supportive. Since it was the aim of the Society "to stimulate the understanding of Islam . . . through lectures, intensive community life . . . , and the breeding of friendships between Muslims and their friends in Europe,"[25] the Muslim connection seemed to have sat well with his own experience in circumventing his Jewish roots. In his time Friedrich too had been a Lebensreform practitioner, and conversion to another religion fit that philosophy well. Besides, the mosque seemed to offer a proper environment for his daughters to look for suitable husbands. The Indian Muslim elite that supported the Ahmadiyya Reform Movement and had come to Berlin to complete their studies usually belonged to the *Zamindar*, the landed gentry of Northern India, arriving in Europe as cosmopolitans with a culture of their own. Their understanding of Islam was rational and highly interiorized, serving as a compass for them to polish and refine their inner selves.

In this cultured environment rich with possibilities, Lisa soon encountered her future husband. Azeez Ur-Rahman Mirza (1906–37) was heir to a long pedigree of Muslim scholars and landowners.[26] Originally, he was sent to Berlin to write his dissertation in physics, as the Berlin faculty was considered among the world's best. But after he received his degree in 1935, he lingered on as assistant imam, lectured on Islam in several institutions, accepted a part in a movie in the Babelsberg film studios, was frequently seen on the tennis courts, acquired journalism credentials with which he covered the Berlin Olympics in 1936, and received training as a volunteer fireman in the Nazi organization Luftschutz Tut Not (Air protection is needed), which prepared Germans for future firebomb attacks.[27] Azeez was waiting, no doubt, to marry his "Lischen," a wait beset with problems for which he eventually found the winning solution.

The journalism credentials are an indication that Azeez did not shy away from contact with the Nazi regime. Azeez was an admirer of the Olympic games that the Nazis organized, and he acquired a press badge from the Indian Embassy that allowed him to attend on a daily basis. He also volunteered to be trained as a fireman in case the mosque and the adjacent mission house were firebombed in the war everyone expected. Those acts speak of a resolute and pragmatic attitude, of compliance with the German government, not disgust for it. Like other Muslims in Berlin, Azeez looked at the Germans with curiosity, as they were expected to help Indians and other colonized peoples to gain their independence. That Lisa held on to his badges tells us that he must have been proud of them.

His books, badges, and presents; his texts, prayer mat, and photo album documenting his role in the mosque's proceedings—these were among the things Lisa brought to Lahore. Together, they paint a portrait of this young Indian intellectual. Endowed with a little beard and a dark complexion, always solemnly rising to the occasion—a tuxedo for lectures, a multicolored turban for ritual occasions, a camel-hair coat with silk cloth for nature hikes—he must have stood out as a stranger in Nazi Berlin. What did this young man do to smooth the differences and explain Islam as their common ground?

During their courting period, Azeez presented Lisa with delicate little treasures, among them a pearl necklace, a small green jade bowl, and a star pendant with quartz inlay—these were part of the Ur-Rahman heritage, and after her death they were returned to the Ur-Rahman family.[28] Also, as soon as he arrived, he started to buy books, which mark his explorations into European culture. Among his first purchases was Max Henning's translation of the Koran, which he dedicated to Lisa, noting, "Important things are never considered enough. Goethe. Azeez 23.3.33." His curiosity enveloped Goethe's *Faust*, Rousseau's *Emile*, Nietzsche's *Also Sprach Zarathustra*, Greek and Roman culture, European philosophy, and the debate in the mosque on the "New Man." His own views on the matter have been documented in two speeches he gave in the mosque in 1933, in which he condemns the creation of an iron-hard, inhuman superhero whose body must express his power. Instead, he draws a picture of *jihad* as a way to obtain inner refinement. Ahmadiyya teaches that the more people speak of war, the more they commit barbarous acts, the more one must retreat into one's self and focus on "polishing" the soul. Azeez too made an effort to be a good person and "breathe" a cultured atmosphere. Because of his criticism of the Nazi ideology, those speeches were never published. But Lisa held on to two copies, typewritten on long sheets that no longer fit our standard paper formats, tied together with an official-looking colored band and two iron stitches, bearing witness of the mosque's treatment of texts that it considered central to its mission.

Azeez took seriously the attempt to bring together European and Muslim cultures in the things and attitudes of daily life. Taking Lisa's infatuation with the German romantic poets as a starting point, he made her multiple presents of Sufi poetry, among them Al-Hallagh, Rumi, the *Rubaiyat*, and the songs of Mirza Schaffy. They seem to have touched a nerve in her religious feelings, which she shared with large parts of the Ahmadiyya mosque community.[29] Seen from a Muslim perspective, German romanticism prepared the way for Sufi love poetry, much in the same way that Sufi poetry prepared the way for the core tenets of Islam. And indeed, romantic Germans do not seem to have had much trouble understanding them. For the German-Indian couples in the Ahmadiyya mosque, Azeez and Lisa included, poetry functioned as a bridge between Eastern and Western mentalities, preparing the ground for a meeting that was rooted in aesthetics and emotions rather than in religious rule and theology.

The trunks also contained Azeez's prayer mat. One can easily imagine that Lisa used it after his death. If so, it offered a continued emotional communion between the lovers, which came to an end only when she added the mat to her collection of things.

Incidentally, more than the other objects, the decision to store the prayer mat betrays her mindset while making that collection in 1957 for her son. In 1957, she had settled in England for good and was looking ahead to a quickly changing future, devising ways to combine her painting with earning money and providing her son with a proper British education. At that time, the Ahmadiyya mosque in Woking still offered her a rich community life (it was discontinued when, in 1965, Pakistani migrants undertook an inimical takeover), but the times were already changing. In the near future, Lisa would attend yoga classes and venture into meditation together with Suhail. Although she remained a Muslim and was eventually buried in the Muslim cemetery in Woking, her attitude toward religion remained informed by the ideology of Lebensreform. To her, religion signified experiment and synthesis, rather than holding on to one particular tradition.

Lisa's own synthesis bore the name of Bo Yin Ra.[30] Until the end of her life, she held on to a slim volume in linen, *Das Buch vom Glück* (The book of happiness), decorated with art deco vignettes and set in Gothic German script. It tells the story of a return to nature, of deep romantic feeling and the power to create out of scratch. On the front page she noted, "This book is a very great talisman and a *mysterious treasure. . . .* Please respect it as irreplaceable." More than the Koran translation, more even than the language of the Sufi masters, this was her understanding of what religion was about and another legacy to her son.

The Lahore Connection

Knowledge, the historian Peter Burke notes, is "cooked." It is processed, codified, tested, interpreted, handed down, and heightened as the very essence of tradition and "who we are"—and then, finally, forgotten.[31] In the case of the Oettinger family, knowledge central to their upward mobility was gathered through the art of stitching (and creating fashion and one's home), the art of cooking (and enlarging one's horizon), and the art of reading and making music (and forging individual access to German culture) as well as through the art of conversion (and fleeing the constrictions of one's social condition). From Marienwerder to Berlin, a multitude of family things carried this knowledge down the generations, using the lace, the linen, the embroideries, the cookbook, the photo album, the postcard collections, the music sheets, and the poetry books as its vehicle.

Rummaging through Lisa's trunks, we also encountered a string of objects that were crafted in the cultural tradition of Mughal northern India, conveying a knowledge that was very different from the European German-Jewish tradition. From these treasures, Lisa seems to have gleaned the kind of knowledge that helped her sustain life in a foreign country. Among those were the things she wore (saris, Indian blouses, mantillas, straw shoes, Mughal jewelry) and the things with which she decorated her home (precious glassware, ingeniously crafted play figures, masks, thin paper cutouts with intricate patterns). Prior to their storage in the trunks, the saris had been carefully folded, wrapped in cotton, and tied with a string. The accompanying explanatory note states: "Saris, gold blouse *Gharara*, petticoats & other blouses worn by Mum in Lahore."

In Lahore, Lisa became Zubeidah *Begum*. The title was given to her not only on the strength of her having been the wife of a *Mirza*, a nobleman, but also because she had become a genuine Muslim, adapting herself to the oriental way of life and siding with the Muslims against the colonial government. She was much respected, a person from whom people expected advice and wisdom. In return, she tried to live up to the expectations by dressing herself elegantly in Indian saris. There exists no specimen any more of the elaborate Mughal jewelry she used to wear, but nonetheless, her photographs convey a good impression of her status. They show a distinguished woman with a conscious posture, straight-backed and standing apart from the others. In England, her memory lingered on. When she died in Woking a good sixty years later, Ahmadis from all over the country gathered at her grave to pay respect.[32]

The things with which she used to decorate her bungalow in Lahore she carefully embedded in straw baskets prior to assigning them a place in the trunks. This time, there is no accompanying note to explain what their function is, but looking at those tender little clay figures and glass bottles, wooden masks and paper cutouts, it becomes evident that Lisa was deeply interested in the crafts and patterns of the Mughal culture and that she let herself be inspired by them. One of the photographs in the "Lange Mandi" album shows her at work in her studio in Murree, a hill station up in the mountains where rich Lahoris sought refuge from the summer heat. She is painting a pattern on the fringe of a tablecloth, much like the way she used to design patterns for industrial cloth production in Berlin. The difference is in the quality of the pattern, which is not "oriental" any more but of an exquisite graphic design that recalls the Mughal art tradition.

Concluding Remarks

Things are never mute, and yet they cannot speak. The knowledge Lisa gathered in Lahore served its purpose of survival. This shows in the ways she dressed, lived up to societal expectations, adapted her art to a different culture yet managed to live on her own in a country where women were not expected to do so. In this respect the Lahore collection did not differ much from the German-Jewish collection that was handed down in the Oettinger family. It was this knowledge she wanted to give to her son. But what she assembled for him he received with a very different perception than hers, and they triggered other memories that the ones Lisa had intended them to conserve.

History is contingent. In the sealed letter Lisa placed on top of the collection before closing her trunks, she explained to her son how lonely she had been in Lahore and how much she had longed for her mother. Yet, when she went to look for her family after the war, they refused to come with her to India. The reason was that she fell in love with a much younger marine officer from Karachi in the Woking mosque and rashly had a child with him: Suhail. Alas, the marine officer had been promised to her sister Susanna so that she would be able to enter India (then Pakistan) without much fuss. On account of Lisa's "betrayal," the sisters had a falling out, and in the end Lisa had to return to India alone. Her husband Nazir Ahmad graciously took her back, adopted the child as his own and protected her against slander. But his family objected, and eventually they both agreed that Lisa would better be off in England. And so, this is where she took her son in 1954, although the dispute with her sister continued to exist. Only when the two sisters passed away, Susanna in 2005, Lisa one year later, did their children come together to contemplate the heritage their mothers had left behind. The trunks and the documents provided them with a key, but the memories these things provoked differed significantly from the messages they once inhabited. From the perspective of the heirs, the heritage brought memories of Anisah's and Suhail's own unhappy youth, of the endless disputes between their mothers, their biting arrogance, rejection of fat or unhappy people, and obsession with German culture. Thus, Lisa's legacy, invested with the experience of generations of Oettingers and matched with the cultural knowledge of northern India, imbued with manifold emotions and intended to transfer the precious knowledge of how to survive, had finally reached the end of its memory cycle.

After the Second World War, the enthusiastic mood in which people in East and West in the interwar period embraced mixed marriages, amid speculations about the future of the globe as a common quest, utterly evaporated. Instead, Europe found itself in a shambles. Perpetrators denied their atrocities. Survivors counted their losses. The enormity of the Shoah slowly sank in. The Middle East saw the creation of Israel, and the colonial empires one by one gave way to the Muslim nation-states that rejected their dominance. This was not the time any more to think about connecting Indians and Europeans, or for that matter Indian Muslims and German Jews, as a way to peacefully create one world, nor was there an occasion or a place to accomplish that. As a result, the mood was forgotten and the history of Eastern missions in Western cities in the interwar period—when Muslims were perceived as highly cultured and Islam a rational, democratic religion, when Germans and Muslims intermarried with a view to becoming cosmopolitans or "citizens of the world," as is sometimes written on their graves, when people seriously contemplated modes to merge the different cultural traditions—has yet to be written. It is no coincidence that during my research into Ahmadiyya mission in Europe in the interwar period, I encountered many private archives, of which the Oettinger archive is only one. Germans who engaged in the mission strongly felt that they were witnessing a highly significant movement, one that could very well prove to be *the* turning point in world history.

Therefore, they started to collect the documents, letters, and articles; the objects and the photographs that gave witness to the *momentum*, if only to be able to tell their children. Lisa Oettinger eventually created a curated private collection and urged her son never to forget. Other participants too held on to their mementos or wrote their memoirs. Their collections allow a view on a highly significant moment in history, providing a clue that may speak to us today.

Notes

1. Gerdien Jonker, *The Ahmadiyya Quest for Religious Progress: Missionizing Europe 1900–1965* (Leiden: E. J. Brill, 2016).

2. Oettinger Archive in Woking (GB): "Lisa's Berlin Album"; "Azeez' Album"; "Mosque and Friends" Album; "The Journey to India" Album; "Lange Mandi (Lahore)" Album.

3. Gerdien Jonker, *Zwischen Juden und Muslimen: Eine europäische Familiengeschichte (1836–2016)* (Göttingen: Wallstein, 2018).

4. Enno Kaufhold, *Berliner Interieurs 1910–1930: Fotographien von Waldemar Titzenthaler* (Berlin: Nicolai, 2013).

5. Oettinger Archive in Woking (GB): Three Portfolios (Berlin 1927–1931).

6. Abdul Sattar Kheiri (1885–1944), founder of the *Islamische Gemeinde Berlin* (Islamic Community Berlin) in 1922. Quotation in Jonker, *The Ahmadiyya Quest*, 63; cf. Suzanne L. Marchand, "Eastern Wisdom in an Era of Western Despair: Orientalism in 1920s Central Europe," in *Weimar Thought: A Contested Legacy*, ed. Peter E. Gordon and John P. McCormick (Princeton: Princeton University Press, 2013), 341–361.

7. The German movement of Lebensreform came into being around 1900. Originally, it presented a blend of protest (pervading society and school education alike) against the Prussian military spirit; a romantic yearning for "nature" and a more natural way of living; and the wish to shape one's life for the sake of individual fulfillment. Building on this foundation, the movement produced the generation of scholars, artists and writers that left their imprint on the Weimar republic. See Kai Buchholz, Rita Latocha, Hilke Peckmann, and Klaus Wolbert, eds., *Die Lebensreform: Entwürfe der Neugestaltung von Leben und Kunst um 1900* (Darmstadt: Haeusser-media, 2001).

8. Jonker, *The Ahmadiyya Quest*, 78–79.

9. Bernd Wedemeyer-Kolwe, *"Der neue Mensch": Körperkultur im Kaiserreich und in der Weimarer Republik* (Würzburg: Königshausen & Neumann, 2004), 13–14.

10. Martin Roddewig, "Flink wie Windhunde, zäh wie Leder, hart wie Kruppstahl," Deutsche Welle, www.dw.com/de/flink-wie-windhunde-zäh-wie-leder-hart-wie-kruppstahl/a-16373027, accessed May 31, 2017.

11. Franz Albert Heinen, *Ordensburg Vogelsang: The History of the NS-Elite Training Centre in the Eifel* (Berlin: CH Links, 2014), 53.

12. Jonker, *The Ahmadiyya Quest*, 111–113.

13. Hugo Marcus, "Die Religion und der Mensch der Zukunft," *Moslemische Revue* 2 (1930): 68–69, 74; 3 (1930), 97; 1 (1931), 24–31. On Hugo Marcus, see Jonker, *The Ahmadiyya Quest*, 109–113, 144–145, 199–205.

14. Baron Omar R. Ehrenfels, "Der Islam und die junge Generation in Europa," *Moslemische Revue* 3 (1931): 85. See also Jonker, *The Ahmadiyya Quest*, 111.

15. Jonker, *The Ahmadiyya Quest*, 60–61.

16. Hildegard Scharf, Irma Gohl, and Hudah J. Schneider, "Drei Europäerinnen bekennen sich zum Islam," *Moslemische Revue* 1 (1931): 53–59; Latifa A. Roessler, "Ein Arbeitsfeld für die muslimische Europäerin," *Moslemische Revue* 1 (1934): 13–16; Jonker, *The Ahmadiyya Quest*, 113–119.

17. Suhail Ahmad recalled that there had been a notebook in which his mother wrote down the things that were left behind or sold, each with a short description and date. Although never thrown away, the notebook remained lost during the time of research.

18. Johannes E. Everlein, "Erste Dinge—Reisegepäck im Exil: Eine phänomenologische Lektüre," in *Dinge des Exils*, ed. Doerte Bischof and Joachim Schlör (Munich: edition text + kritik, 2013), 23–35.

19. Leora Auslander, "Beyond Words," *American Historical Review* 110, no. 4 (2005): 1015–1045.

20. *Mandi* means market in the Urdu language. Lange Mandi is a Muslim bazaar within the city walls of old Lahore. The Ur-Rahman family lived in one of its ancient merchant palaces (*havalis*).

21. Suhail Ahmad remembers that, when settling in England after the war, his mother sold a whole suitcase full of lace to British museums in order to cover their expenses.

22. Gerdien Jonker, "Setting the Table in Prussia and Lahore: A Jewish Recipe Book in Exile," *DisplacedObjects.com*, January 12, 2015, https://displacedobjects.com/2015/12/01/the-recipy-book-gerdien-jonker/, accessed May 31, 2017.

23. Jonker, *The Ahmadiyya Quest*, 63–85, 113–119.

24. Oettinger Archive in Hassocks (GB): Photo collection of Emilia Oettinger 1928 to 1939.

25. Statute of the DMG and Protocol No. 1, Vereinsregister Berlin-Charlottenburg, No. 8769, April 10, 1930.

26. *Mirza* means "nobleman" in the Persian language and points to a high Persian lineage.

27. Anonymous. "Dr. Azeez Mirza," *Moslemische Revue* 1 (1938): 1–3.

28. Oettinger Archive in Woking (GB): "Family heirlooms belonging to Suhail Ahmad, August 2006," unpublished document.

29. By the mid-1930s, Hosseyn Khazemzadeh Iranshär (1884–1962), Berlin's most popular speaker on Eastern mysticism, was regularly invited to speak for packed audiences in the Ahmadiyya mosque. His books and speeches synthesize Sufi poetry with romantic poetry and Christian suffering. Jonker, *The Ahmadiyya Quest*, 94–125.

30. This is the pen name of the Austrian painter Josef Anton Schneiderfranken (1876–1943), who taught that happiness lies in the use of one's ability to create with one's hands.

31. Peter Burke, *A Social History of Knowledge* (Cambridge: Cambridge University Press, 2012), 5.

32. Interview with Nasir Ahmad, eldest of the Ahmadiyya Lahore community in England, September 15, 2016. With in-house publications such as "A brief history of the Berlin Muslim Mission and the Berlin mosque" (Berlin: Berlin Muslim Mission, 2006), Ahmad kept the memory of the German heritage alive.

CIRCUITOUS JOURNEYS

The Migration of Objects and the Trusteeship of Memory

Jeffrey Wallen and Aubrey Pomerance

As visitors to the Jewish Museum Berlin walk through the various segments of its permanent exhibition, they encounter all kinds of objects: an old walking stick in the section on rural Jewry, a Kiddush cup in the module on the Enlightenment period, a top hat in the area devoted to tradition and change, a child's toy in the family segment, a bullet in the section on World War I.[1] What these objects all have in common is not apparent to the viewer, nor is it revealed in the accompanying labels: Jews took these objects with them when leaving Germany between 1933 and 1941.[2] Sixty or seventy years after having been taken to Shanghai, Palestine, the United Kingdom, the United States, South Africa, South America, or elsewhere, the objects have made a return voyage upon being donated to the museum, usually by their original owners or by their descendants.

What we see *now* in the museum—a set of tableware, a Kiddush cup, a piano, a painting, a World War I medal, a schoolbag—conveys insights about life *then*. The tableware, for instance, can give insights into German-Jewish bourgeois life in the late nineteenth and early twentieth centuries.[3] Objects of material culture in a museum transport us from one era to another, from a public display back to the life of the individual, the home, the family, or the group in which these items were embedded.

In order for these objects of German Jewish life to be available to us today, their owners had to decide to take these items with them when they were forced to migrate. After Hitler came to power in January 1933, Jews were faced with increasing discrimination, exclusion, oppression, and persecution by the National Socialist state. About 280,000 Jews, a little more than half the number of Jews who were in Germany in 1933, were able to leave the country before emigration was officially prohibited in October 1941. The overwhelming majority of them left legally—that is, they undertook all of the necessary administrative means required of them, and what they took with them depended on the laws in place at the time, their financial means, their destinations, and other factors. Restrictions on the goods that people were able to transport out of Germany increased gradually; initially, they were limited to objects of value, such as artworks, precious antiques, and items made of gold and silver (restrictions on transferring money and financial assets were much more severe). The later one left Germany, the less one was able to salvage from one's assets and belongings.

The collection of the Jewish Museum Berlin (JMB) is a highly unusual one; it is a unique resource for studying migration and material culture. Many of the objects in its collection are things that were taken out of Germany and then sent back only after an interval of several decades. The moment of migration was a crucial and illuminating point in the individual history of these objects and in a trajectory that eventually ended at the museum. It was a moment of both discontinuity and continuity. Taking an object out of Germany—displacing it from what had been its "home"—presents a stark break from the contexts that help us to understand its meaning in relation to Jewish life in Germany. Migration also involved a decision to maintain possession of these objects on the part of their owners and required conscious acts of selection, even for people who were able to ship a large portion of their possessions to their new country. Taking along items that convey ties to a land and a state that has declared that significant numbers of people longer have a right to live there freely as a citizen might also be seen as an act of assertion—as a decision to maintain certain connections, even while severing others.

The gaps opened up by migration, between living in Germany and living elsewhere, invite if not compel us to consider the temporal dimensions in the life of the object. What can we learn by looking at the object through multiple moments in time: as an object used in Germany but also as one selected for migration and preserved for decades afterwards? In addition to the crucial moments of migration, we will also consider the act of living with these objects over time and across generations, with the subsequent moves and dislocations. How were they embedded in the lives of their possessors? How were they kept—were they displayed in a parlor or living room? Or were they stored away in a drawer or attic? Also, do these objects have different meanings for the individuals who donated them to the museum than for the people who took them along when migrating (or for the archivist, curator, or museum visitor)?

Our aim is to expand our understanding of the objects we will be discussing by reflecting on their having been taken along during forced migration, rather than having remained in Germany. Our assumption is that there is much to learn by drawing attention to the migration history of these objects and by considering multiple points of time between "then" and "now," between the context of the object in a Jewish home in Germany before 1933, for example, and its being housed in the museum today. Our starting point, however, is our engagement with particular objects, specifically those that grabbed our attention when we were going through the collections of the Jewish Museum Berlin.

This chapter arises out of a collaboration between authors with different professional backgrounds and perspectives. Aubrey Pomerance, head of the archives of the Jewish Museum Berlin since 2001, has over the last fifteen years met with hundreds of German Jewish emigrants, refugees, and survivors as well as descendants who have expressed a willingness to support the collection efforts of the museum. The majority of these encounters have taken place in their homes to look at the materials that have been preserved pertaining to their individual and family histories. These materials usually consist mainly of papers and photographs that reflect a broad spectrum of the lives of the families: family, religious, social, educational, military, professional, and economic life as well as their fates during the period of National Socialism. In the course of these meetings, Aubrey has always raised questions regarding three-dimensional objects that the families were able to take with them when leaving Nazi Germany, which depended largely on the circumstances under which people left. Although most families and individuals were able to take objects, very few of these have survived to the present day. These conversations have brought to the fore fascinating things that their owners never imagined would be of interest to the museum, such as children's toys, army medals, medical tools, or musical instruments, most of which were indeed subsequently donated. Some of them will be addressed here.

Jeffrey Wallen, professor of comparative literature in the United States, has often taken students to the JMB while directing a study abroad program in Berlin and has done research on Jewish life in Berlin as well as on archives, museums, and collecting.[4] The catalyst for our discussions has been our own *encounters* with particular objects and the curiosity or fascination aroused by considering and talking about them. Why does this object impel us to want learn more about how it was used, about the meaning it had for its owner(s), about the transformation of its meaning in its new setting after migration? Did it have any significance for the children of the emigrants? What might this object tell us about Jewish life in Germany, and what was its manufacturing history? What is its visual power, and in what context and for what purposes is it displayed in the museum? In discussing such questions, the stories connected with these objects are often central for provoking us to think further about them, yet our point of departure in each case is specific objects, not a text or a symbol or a representative category (such as "education" or "Jewish culture"). That is why the topic of "migration and material culture" has been such a rich framework for us.

In the exhibitions of the Jewish Museum Berlin, the migration history of the object often goes unmentioned or is noted only briefly, unless it is being displayed in a section that is specifically devoted to the 1933–45 period. The exhibitions, which strive for narrative coherence, sensibly do not emphasize the many different moments and journeys in the history of any particular object. Although we will on occasion refer to the rubric under which an object is (or has been) displayed, we are not offering a critique of the presentation of these objects in the museum. Our concern here is not principally with how the JMB uses or has presented these objects but rather with what we can learn by exploring the migration history and the temporal dimensions in the life of these objects and by considering these objects from multiple perspectives (as a personal possession, as a commodity, as an object of utility, as a representation of Jewish life in Germany). By doing so, we hope that the questions raised and the lines of thinking developed here will serve as an invitation for others to view the collection of the JMB as a uniquely rich resource for exploring migration and material culture. More generally, we hope that our multidimensional approach—attending to multiple moments in time and the multiple contexts in which these objects have been embedded—will stimulate an analysis of the materials in other museums, collections, and archives as well.

Forced migration, being pressured to leave one's home and country for a new and foreign land, necessarily provides a different optic on the things that are taken along. Not only does it bring about a changed relation of people to their possessions (amidst new surroundings, without one's previous place in society), it also brings out multiple perspectives on these objects as they pass through the hands or under the scrutiny of others. First, we will consider some examples that highlight contrasting perspectives and ways in which the view of the object is transformed during the forced migration of Jews from Germany. Next, in order to help think about the continuity and discontinuity of life before and after migration and to illuminate the temporal dimensions in the life of these objects, we will ask questions about the extent to which an object was taken *prospectively*, with an eye toward its future use in the new country, or *retrospectively*, more for its connections to one's identity and past life. "Migration" during these years might mean a relatively short journey to England or Sweden (places where Jews could safely stay throughout the war, in contrast to those who settled in the Netherlands, France, or other places later conquered by the Germans), or it might connote a multi-year journey, with stops in several countries and entailing very harsh living conditions. We will also look at objects that draw attention to the *durée* of migration, where a familiar object might be one of the few fixed points during an open-ended and stressful period of trying to reach a new, safe, and permanent residence. In probing the changed relation to context and place brought about by migration, we will also consider the "return home" to Germany and the recontextualization of these objects within the Jewish Museum Berlin.

Uprooted Objects: Between Commodity and Singularization

Objects that people kept for years after migrating often had special meanings and associations for them, but the process of migration involved looking at objects as radically estranged from their connection to everyday life, as mere commodities and objects of basic utility. Jews migrating from Germany during the Nazi period were subjected to the perspective that treats possessions only as items to be listed on an inventory sheet. Starting in May 1938, in an effort to prevent the transfer of assets through the expansion of household possessions before emigration, Jewish migrants were required to provide detailed lists of all their belongings, indicating whether they were purchased before 1933 or after, and in the ensuing months restrictions continued to be increased. The list of absolutely forbidden objects was extended to include high-quality items that could be resold; exceptions might be granted when the emigrant could prove that the items were necessary for the practice of his or her profession.[5] There is a violence in this bureaucratic perspective, which forced people not only to write down but to open up for the inspection of others their most intimate and personal of items; it is an important stage in the process by which these items are ripped away from their context, from their "home" in Germany, and stripped of personal significance.

The museum has copies of some of the lists of items filed with the German authorities, and in a few cases some of individual items mentioned therein. These inventory lists forcefully highlight the contrast between an external, bureaucratic view and an internal view that attaches particular emotional value to certain items. They also provide a way to situate the specialness of the particularly "meaningful" item amidst or against the entire array of what people took with them. The "*Umzugsliste*" of Sally and Ruth Stiefel, dated January 31, 1939, contains two items that were later donated to the museum: his top hat and her dress from their wedding, which took place on July 8, 1938 (the museum also has a photo of the ceremony, looking down the aisle of the synagogue).[6] On the *Umzugsliste*, there is an entry under items purchased after January 1, 1933, for "3 Hüte" (three hats), and the wedding dress might be among the "8 Kleider" (eight dresses) or perhaps "4 Kostüme" (four outfits).[7]

Igor Kopytoff, in his well-known essay "The Cultural Biography of Things: Commoditization as Process," provides insightful ways for thinking about the dynamic relation between these perspectives. He contrasts the commodity (common, saleable, widely exchangeable) with the singular (unique, un-exchangeable) and explains that in different settings things shift between being culturally marked as a commodity and as singular ("decommoditization") and that this shift can go in both directions: sometimes there occurs a "later recommoditization." The "biography of things," which examines the processes by which something is "culturally marked as being a certain kind of thing," as a commodity, or as singularized and unique, offers the opportunity for gaining *cultural* insights and for making "salient what might otherwise remain obscure."[8] A top hat worn in a wedding is a quintessential example of how "commodities are singularized by being pulled out of their usual commodity sphere."[9]

For Sally Stiefel, his top hat becomes less ordinary and common, "singularized," when worn during his wedding in a synagogue in Duisburg. In the months between the wedding and their departure, that synagogue was destroyed during the Kristallnacht pogrom. The top hat and wedding dress are almost all that remain of what was captured in the wedding photo. As a remnant, the top hat is singularized in a different way— as one of the few remaining material objects that attest to the life and customs of the Duisburg synagogue—and it also evokes what is no longer possible for the Stiefels (a successful, communal life in Germany) and what no longer exists (a synagogue, a vibrant Jewish community in Germany).

The top hat and dress were displayed in the "Tradition and Change" section of the museum devoted to the life cycle and religious practice, exemplifying a central moment in German Jewish community life—the wedding.[10] As well as being "singular" to the Stiefel wedding, they also stand in for all the other top hats and dresses worn at (bourgeois) Jewish weddings in Germany. The view of the museum visitor opens up a third perspective, which is neither that of the possessor (personal, familial, sentimental, attached to a place) nor that of the impersonal gaze of the bureaucrat. The encounter with the object triggers multitudes of questions about the contexts that give it meaning and significance. To what extent and in what ways does Jewish life in Germany provide a context for the overwhelming majority of objects that were also owned and used by many non-Jews? The top hat intersects with many Jewish and German spheres of usage and meaning but does not belong exclusively to either. Seeing the top hat in the museum also raises questions about manufacturing (we know who made the hat; was it a Jewish-owned company? what were the roles of Jews in this segment of the clothing industry?), about class status and about Jewish customs (in which Jewish congregations did the men wear top hats, and on what occasions?), and about the broader cultural significance of the top hat in the 1930s (is there a connection to the Fred Astaire movie of that name, which came out in 1935?).[11] *This* top hat, when viewed at different moments in its "biography"—when it was manufactured, worn at a wedding, packed for migration, preserved and passed on to their children, and displayed in the JMB—brings out the interactions of these dimensions of commodity and of singularization, of individual history and of cultural representativeness.

We would like to suggest that taking things along when migrating from Germany in the Nazi period can be thought of as another moment of "singularization" in the biography of things. Forced migration implies that there is no longer the possibility of the same connections to the world—to a place, to a local context, to the nation, to home—as existed previously. Sandra Dudley's chapter in this volume helps us to understand that things are singularized by migration through their *changed* relation to place, context, and home. More strongly, she emphasizes their displacement, their decontextualization (and recontextualization), their no longer "being at home." She insightfully explores the ways in which Paku Karen skirt cloths raise very complex questions about "place" and "home," as some move from Burma to museums in Britain, while others are produced and remain in refugee camps. She writes that "displacement":

> conveys both a changed connection to place and an associated sense of movement. An active process, it tends to result in breaks between past and present, there and here; at the same time, the displaced persons or things work both to bridge gaps with the past and to create a new niche. Which of these dynamics appears more dominant may depend on both the position from which we look and the capacity of the displaced to make things happen and to change how people feel.[12]

Her approach, emphasizing an active process and the ongoing work of connection to place—of rupture, bridging, and creating—argues that displaced objects have the capacity to *change* the contexts by which we would seek to interpret them. She activates this approach through an extremely attentive engagement with objects, which goes as far as seeking "to take the artifact's point of view." Attending to migration can change our interpretation of earlier and later points in the biography of the object as well.

The Sommerfelds too had an *Umzugsliste*. They hurried their departure and left for England in late August 1939, but the container with their belongings was appropriated in Hamburg after the war began. All that remained from these possessions are the keys for the chests and suitcases in which the goods had been packed (figure 9.1) and the *Umzugsliste*,

Figure 9.1. The keys to the trunks of the Sommerfeld family that never reached them in England. Jewish Museum Berlin, inventory numbers 2005/139/28/001–028, gift of George and Peter Summerfield.

which is ten pages long.[13] If the container had arrived at its destination, we would not have this set of dozens of keys in a museum. They become important *during* transit, during the period between packing and locking up the family's possessions and the awaited unlocking, when the goods would arrive at the end of the journey. They draw attention to the ordinary mechanics of migration—to some of the steps that are required to bring about a changed connection to place—and years later, they serve as striking reminders of dispossession. Dispossession is a key theme with regard to the treatment of Jews during the Nazi period. The Holocaust is often narrated as a progressive series of dispossessions: More and more is stripped away, including finally people's lives. An ordinary or inconsequential object is often all that remains from that period and stands in for all that has been lost.

Yet if we do not move immediately from the keys to what they represent—to the story of the Sommerfelds' lost objects and to their forced migration from Germany—what do we see? The keys are very flimsy and offer little practical protection against theft. They epitomize the social conventions of transport, the premise that possessions are locked up when out of our hands. The belief that this minimal protection against the violation of one's possessions will be respected is a central thread from an entire worldview of presuppositions and mutual understanding that will be cut to pieces by the war. These keys belong to a horizon of expectations about migration that quickly becomes outdated within the relatively brief period of the Sommerfelds' own migration to England.

A set of keys is also an alternative to one of the most stereotypical symbols of migration and of the Holocaust—the suitcase. What sets of thoughts and associations do we take from these keys, in contrast to suitcases? Some Sephardic Jews kept the keys to their homes for generations after they were expelled from Spain in 1492. Keys have also become the symbol of the Nakba, of dispossession from the homes that Palestinians left in 1948, and are highly symbolic for many others who have undergone forced migration as well.[14]

By engaging with a particular object, such as this set of keys, we can open up lines of thinking about forced migration and dispossession rather than viewing the object, as often happens with Holocaust-related material, as merely a stand-in for and a necessarily inadequate representation of all that has been lost.

The towel that Paul Kuttner took with him when leaving Berlin on a Kindertransport in 1939 and that he donated to the museum more than sixty years later is a clear example of an object whose significance is thoroughly transformed by migration (figure 9.2). *Kindertransport*

Figure 9.2. Hand towel with the monograph of Margarete Kuttner. Jewish Museum Berlin, inventory number 2000/144/0, gift of Paul Kuttner.

was the informal name for the rescue efforts that following Kristall-nacht brought several thousand Jewish children from Nazi Germany (including Austria and parts of Czechoslovakia) to Great Britain between December 1938 and the start of the war in September 1939. Parents or guardians could not accompany the children (to be more precise, there were group guardians who accompanied the children but who had to return to Germany), and many never saw their parents again. We do not have an inventory list for Paul Kuttner, but we do have lists for other children who left on Kindertransports, with nota-tions such as "6 Handtücher" (six hand towels; the list distinguishes between three linen and three terry cloth towels). Kuttner never used, nor did he ever unfold this towel, which is monogrammed with his mother's initials. He describes the towel (in fact the two towels he took with him) as "the only remaining possession I still had from her," and elaborates:

> The night before I left Nazi Germany, my mother had once more washed and ironed the two towels for me; they actually were her own personal towels, identified with a large red-embroidered MK—for Margarete Kuttner—but I had deliberately never used them, because I wanted to keep something of hers that still had her fingerprints on it, with both towels being folded the way she had ironed them the night before my departure in 1939.[15]

Rather than using it to dry his own hands, as perhaps his mother intended, the towel is for Kuttner the one thing that still bears her imprint, the con-tact of her hands (which he was never to feel again; she was murdered in Auschwitz). Mona Körte, a German scholar, describes this towel as an "object of the last moment," which is "larger than life in the memory" of the former Kindertransport child, because it embodies "the last link to loved ones."[16]

For Paul Kuttner, it was important that the towel be "in a museum, where it will be an 'eternal' reminder of his mother," and "not simply be discarded after his death."[17] He also wanted the towel back in Ber-lin, after his own journey from Germany to England and later to the United States (he gave the other one to the United States Holocaust

Memorial Museum, where it has not been on display),[18] "so that one can say to Hitler, not everything from the Kuttner family has been annihilated. The towel should represent a small victory over the Nazis."[19] It was displayed in the museum for many years along with a picture of his mother and figured in the press coverage of the opening of the Museum (it is hard to imagine that displaying the second towel, in the United States, would have a similar impact, either for him or for the viewer).[20]

Why is the tea towel so striking as an emblem of the trauma of separation between mother and child? Its power derives from Kuttner's cathexis to it; would just any object serve that function, not only for him but for us? This object is ordinary, yet personalized and of a quality that differentiates it from a cheap, contemporary disposable towel. We can see it from an external viewpoint as a commodity or an item on a list and from an intimate perspective as something that belonged to one's mother. It is a manufactured good and was packed in his suitcase to be used. Yet it was ironed—a symbol of care (and of another lifestyle; who irons their tea towels today?)—and hand embroidered with his mother's initials, probably part of her trousseau. The intense pain of separation and loss are displaced onto a material object (it would be years before he would be certain that he would never see his mother again). Never unfolding the towel preserves it as if part of her remains are tucked into the creases.

The donation of this object to the museum further transforms it, bringing Kuttner's story to a wide public. But the display of the towel does not bring about a simple shift of meaning, in which the rich, private, personal significance of the object triumphs over the bureaucratic perspective of the inventory list. We do not fully adopt Kuttner's perspective. Whereas he describes the towel as representing "a small victory over the Nazis," most museum visitors will probably see it as embodying extreme loss, mourning, and permanent separation rather than as an emblem of outlasting the Nazis. Migration sets into play competing perspectives and multiple moments in the biography of the object, and our aim throughout is not to unify or reconcile these perspectives but to draw attention to them so as to sharpen and to unsettle our understanding and to provoke further interpretation.

Same and Yet Different: Using Things Elsewhere

The vantage point of migration changes how we look at and understand the objects that people took with them. An object's "Germanness," for example—its quality of manufacture, its typicalness for being found in a German home or business, its identification with a particular place or region—now stands out in a way that it did not before. When people brought things with them to be used for their career in a new land, the meanings connected to these things come not just from the past, from their use in Germany, but from the future after migration as well. These possessions helped shape, at least in a minor way, who the person would *become*. If the material culture of Jews in Germany played a role in constituting their identity—and we argue that it did—the work of identity formation performed by these objects did not end when they left Germany along with their owners. The piano that Helga Bassel took with her when migrating from Berlin to South Africa in 1936 provides an example of how our frameworks for interpreting these objects change when we also consider migration.

Helga Bassel's Blüthner grand piano is on display in the section "In the Bosom of the Family, 1850–1933." In the museum it connotes the affinity for high culture of German Jews and the importance of classical, German music in their lives. A very high percentage of middle-class German Jewish households in the late nineteenth and early twentieth centuries had a piano. Helga Bassel bought hers in 1930 (we have a record of how much she paid for it, as well as of the installment payments she made). She was a budding professional musician when Hitler came to power. After 1933, when Jews were increasingly excluded from professional life in Germany, she converted to Christianity and became engaged to someone who was not Jewish. Her conversion made little difference, and she was expelled from the Reichsmusikkammer in 1935 (membership in which was necessary to have a professional career in Germany at the time), the same year that the Nuremberg laws made marriage to her fiancé illegal.

In contrast to Rachmaninoff, who supposedly said (when leaving Scandinavia in 1918, a year after fleeing Russia in the wake of the revolution), "There are only two things which I took with me on my way to America . . . my wife and my precious Blüthner" and then received a new piano from Steinway upon his arrival in New York,[21] Helga Bassel had no such bright economic prospects upon her arrival in South Africa. For her, taking the piano was not only a matter of personal attachment. It was her means of livelihood and was a high-quality German manufactured product that she could not otherwise easily obtain after migration.

In South Africa, Helga Bassel used the piano to give lessons, and she also taught her daughter Tessa to play. Tessa Uys became a highly accomplished pianist, and the Blüthner piano was a strong link between mother and daughter. It also provided a connection to her mother's previous life. Helga never spoke to her children about her Jewish past. Only decades after her mother's suicide in 1969 did Tessa look through her mother's papers and find documents that confirmed family rumors that her mother was indeed Jewish. Returning the piano to Berlin was a means to reconnect with an unacknowledged past and to situate the piano again in a German Jewish context.

The piano is also one of the very few items in the museum that has retained its original function after being transferred to the museum—Tessa Uys has herself performed several times on this piano at the Jewish Museum Berlin. The piano straddles the realms of collected material and of things still serving the purpose for which they were created.[22] It is a dramatic example of an argument that could be broadly extended, that the museum need not be thought of as a place in which objects that have already reached the end of their purposeful lives are housed. To cite Sandra Dudley again, "the potentialities, or inherent possibilities, of things" do not necessarily come to an end in the museum. Moving the piano back to Germany also involved decisions about the condition in which it would be displayed. On its way to Berlin it was sent first to be restored and refinished at the Blüthner factory in Leipzig, where it had been manufactured in 1913. The refurbishing resulted in the erasure of some of the marks of its earlier use. Tessa's brother, the well-known satirist, actor, and playwright Pieter-Dirk Uys, employed the piano as a writing surface when he was growing up. The marks of his apprenticeship as a writer disappeared when the piano's case was refinished. A decision that enables some dimensions of the material history of the piano to be brought forth to the public results in diminishing others.

Pieter-Dirk Uys too has performed at the Jewish Museum Berlin, using the piano as a prop and talking about his history with the instrument. For both of Helga Bassel's children, the donation of the piano has connected them to their mother's birthplace and to her Jewish origins in a manner that otherwise would have been unthinkable. Like many of the objects we discuss, the piano can be viewed as powerfully evocative of displacement and separation, as well as of connection or reconnection (the museum has photos of Helga at the piano in Berlin with her fiancé, whom she left behind); of discontinuity as well as continuity. The piano was intimately linked to the vicissitudes of Helga Bassel's identity, influencing her sense of self throughout her life.

As a possession taken along during migration, the piano could also be classified as a "tool of the trade." In 1938, "tools of the trade" become a category under which Jewish migrants could take out of Germany certain valuable or otherwise restricted items necessary for their future employment that would otherwise not be permitted. Although Helga Bassel did not need that particular rubric in order to take her piano because she left Germany in 1936, we can nevertheless consider the piano alongside other professional items such as Samuel Antmann's tailor's shears and medical instruments such as Edith Weber's syringe (figure 9.3).[23]

Figure 9.3. Samuel Antmann's shears. Jewish Museum Berlin, inventory number 2010/67/3, gift of Fred Antman.

The ordinary object becomes less ordinary with migration. The tailor's shears, like the piano an excellent German product, are no longer easily replaceable outside of Germany, especially in Shanghai, the place to which Antmann was able to emigrate. Also like the piano, the user's hands become suited to it; the tape on its finger ring draws our attention to its repeated use. These objects also have a strong visual impact. They are almost sublime (arousing awe, fascination, and dread), leading the viewer to stop and consider them. Looking at the piano together with these other instruments may denude it of its bourgeois cultural associations, but it highlights the urgency, for their future employment and status, of what one could and could not take when migrating.

Those who had sufficient money and had obtained all the right papers could ship many of their belongings in a container. This is what Edith Weber was able to do when leaving for Palestine in 1935. In contrast, Antmann was able to take much less with him. He had had a successful business making women's coats in Berlin but was deported to the Polish border in October 1938 along with thousands of Jews who did not have German citizenship. His wife, a German citizen, and two sons remained in Berlin. Samuel Antmann wanted his wife and family to come to Poland, but she wanted to leave Europe. She liquidated his clothing business and succeeded in getting emigration documents for Shanghai. He was allowed to pass through Germany for twenty-four hours on their way to Shanghai. Along with the two pairs of shears he (we could also say "she," as it was women who usually did the packing, and probably much of the selecting as well)[24] also brought his fashion design sketchbooks and the head covering he had worn while serving as a cantor in Berlin, in its own right a tool of trade. The shears and sketchbook were crucial for rebuilding his business from scratch, first working as a tailor in Shanghai and later after moving to Australia in 1946 and founding a clothing business there with one of his sons.

Looking closely at objects grouped under the category "tools of the trade" also offers an excellent point of departure for exploring the milieu these people had been a part of. What was the role of Jews in garment production in Germany before 1933 or in music or in medicine? A high percentage of the doctors in Germany were Jewish, especially in the major cities. How did Jews' professional formation in Germany position them later when in a very different environment (as culturally advantaged? as fish out of water? both?). The display of an object in a museum exhibition can seemingly freeze it in an imagined moment in time. Yet it can also be the opportunity for following up many different moments in the actual and potential life of the object.

An artifact that forcefully leads us to think about how it might have been to use the same object before and after migration is Susanne Schlome's school satchel (figure 9.4). Susanne left Germany on a Kinder-transport in 1939, when she was eight years old, and never saw her parents again. They had given her this leather satchel before her first day of school in 1937, and it was one of the items her parents sent to her after her arrival in England. She used it during all the years of her secondary education and it was, in fact, the only school bag she ever had. Later in life it was used to keep letters in. It was not, however, something that Susanne was at all sentimental about, and she gladly donated it to the museum.

Figure 9.4. Susanne Schlome's school satchel. Jewish Museum Berlin, inventory number 2009/10/1, gift of Susanne Woodin.

In the museum, the satchel was on display together with a photograph of Susanne wearing it on her first day of school and carrying a *"Schul-tüte"* (a cone filled with candy, given to children on their first day of school).[25] Both the satchel and the *Schultüte* will be very familiar to German museumgoers. How was it for her to go to school every day with the same satchel but in radically different circumstances (in a foreign country, apart from her parents)? The signs of wear, along with the prompting of the photograph, remind one that the satchel was in frequent contact with and shaped by her body as she was growing up. Did this familiar object mark her as different and foreign to others, to her classmates? Would its display in an exhibition in England (or the United States or Israel) provoke very different associations than its display in Germany, where it is a recognizably *German* object, with no particular connotations of Jewishness?

The satchel is powerful because it connects living in different places and leads us to imagine Susanne's repeated, frequent contact with it, before and after migration. Other objects draw attention to life during the period of migration itself. Children's investments in their possessions can be particularly intense in this regard. The Käthe Kruse doll that seven-year-old Ingrid Esslinger took with her when leaving Germany with her parents in 1936 opens a window onto the *durée* of the ten years of the family's odyssey until they finally arrived in the United States in 1946. The doll could serve to anchor the narration of the frightening events and the twists and turns of their journey and to illustrate the uncertainty, hazardous choices, and difficulty of migration during these years. But as a familiar object with which she frequently interacted, the doll provokes us also to consider the "ordinary" activities and daily life that took place during the course of these extraordinary events—Ingrid's playing with it in the different places, circumstances, and times of her journey.

Alfred and Lieselotte Esslinger left Bremen, Germany, for Antwerp with their only daughter Ingrid in September 1936 after Alfred was dismissed from his job as a bank director. Ingrid took along her favorite doll, which she had received a few years before. Ingrid had always called this doll "Käthe Kruse," after the company that made it, singling it out from the other dolls she owned (figure 9.5).[26] While in Belgium, she sewed new clothes and knitted a blue beret for her doll. After the German occupation of the country, the family's experiences were harrowing. Alfred was

Figure 9.5. Ingrid Esslinger's doll, which accompanied her on her ten-year migration odyssey. Jewish Museum Berlin, inventory number 2008/123/9, gift of Ingrid Altman.

arrested by the Belgians and deported to southern France. Mother and daughter attempted unsuccessfully to flee to England, then traveled south to find Alfred but were betrayed at the border between occupied France and the Vichy south. Lieselotte Esslinger was imprisoned, Ingrid brought to a cloister. Mother and daughter were reunited and stayed for six weeks in a hotel in Châteauroux, and then left for the Gurs internment camp, to which Alfred had been transferred. Several months later the three of them sailed from Marseille to Oran in Algeria, from where they took a train to Casablanca, and then a ship to Cuba, being detained for a week by the British in Camp Gibraltar on Jamaica. They reached Cuba in 1942 but were not permitted to enter the United States until May 1946.

Ingrid was seven when she left Germany and seventeen when she entered the United States, still accompanied by "Käthe Kruse." The stresses, anxieties, and perils of her experiences can be read into the doll's blotched, damaged, and seemingly exhausted face. Her worn shoes aptly symbolize its arduous journeys, in contrast to the bright blue of the pants and beret, which were later washed by Ingrid. After her daughters were born, Ingrid tried to interest them in the doll, but like most children, they were far more attracted to newer things. For Ingrid, an only child, the doll remained transformed and imprinted by the years of constant companionship. In a recent conversation she remarked that it was the one constant in her life during those turbulent ten years. Yet for the daughters, their mother's emotional investment in "Käthe Kruse" did not significantly affect their relation to the plaything; it was just an old doll of their mother's. Ingrid donated the doll to the museum, where it again is, but now for others too, dramatically singular, unique, and an object attracting great interest.

Evoking Place, Transmitting Identity

Jewish migrants brought many things whose value resided in a powerful connection to the place they were being pressured to leave. Migration brought to the fore ambivalent feelings about Germany, and there are individual stories of men throwing their World War I iron crosses overboard from the ships taking them away from Germany. Far more frequently, however, people took with them medals and papers documenting military service, along with many other items that testify to a strong attachment to the place people were being forced to leave. They have kept to the present day these material reminders of having participated in a communal activity, having belonged to a group or club, or having been intimately familiar with a particular place or region. These objects are connected to the formation of identity and provide a wealth of information about Jewish life in Germany before the Second World War. Looking at them through the lens of migration enables us to see that the work of identity formation performed by these objects is ongoing and varies over time. The significance of these objects is not purely in the past. By considering several types of articles together we can ask comparative questions: about whether they convey a strong or weak connection to Germany and to the local community or to the nation; about their importance for the identity of the person who took them when migrating; about their power to transmit German-Jewish identity to the next generation; about how they were displayed after migration (openly and proudly or ignored or hidden away); and about their potential uses in the museum.

Among the most German of things that refugees took with them are World War I artifacts: photographs, letters from the front, diaries, award certificates, service and salary booklets, prayer books, iron crosses and other medals, dog tags, epaulets, helmets, swords, even a bullet extracted from the arm of a German-Jewish soldier. The presence of such items in countless collections entrusted to the museum testifies to the widespread importance that former soldiers and their families had placed on these material records of their commitment to the Fatherland. Many hoped and expected that official recognitions of their service and particularly medals such as iron crosses would protect them from the worst of the persecution directed at Jews. The vantage point of migration—thinking about their having taken these things with them when leaving Germany—helps us grasp that whatever their feelings about the Great War twenty years later, these artifacts still resonated strongly with their identity and sense of self. They demonstrate a deeply ingrained sense of Germanness, of patriotism and sacrifice. With a little investigation these objects can sometimes reveal the camaraderie between Jews and non-Jews and also the exclusion and prejudice that Jewish soldiers were subjected to.

For Jewish veterans of World War I such artifacts generally signify a connection to the nation more than a bond with a select group, and although taken into exile and preserved, they are highly ambivalent and complicated objects of remembrance, often heightening the bitterness that the refugees felt. Later, during, and after the Second World War, it was nearly impossible to display a sense of pride in having served in the German army, or indeed in having been German at all. None of the donors reported that a picture of their father or grandfather in uniform or at the front hung in the family home, nor were iron crosses or other medals displayed openly in cabinets or on shelves. Materials pertaining to the First World War were often found only after the passing of a parent, kept in a cupboard or closet and never shared with the family members. After migration, these objects had little power to transmit aspects of German Jewish identity or a feeling of personal connection to the past to the next generation.

The Jewish Museum Berlin has collected many objects from migrants that pertain to participation in Jewish religious and communal life, charitable organizations, student fraternities, sports clubs, and other associations. Occasionally the range of objects reflects the changes that took place in the 1930s. Earlier sporting trophies might indicate membership in a "German" club, whereas later ones won by the same person will have been bestowed by a Jewish sport association such as the Turnverein Bar Kochba Berlin or Makkabi Deutschland. Many items are connected to activity within Jewish organizations such as B'nai B'rith lodges, German-Jewish fraternities, and Jewish veterans and women's associations. These types of objects range from dedicatory cups, platters and goblets, pins, badges, pennants and flags, trophies and medals to the interesting array of fraternity paraphernalia, such as beer steins, ribbons, rings, and caps. They are for the most part commemorative in nature and testify, more than other items kept by the emigrants, to the Jewish collective in German society.

What sorts of attachment did people have to these mementos of youth and active participation in Jewish organizations, and did the importance of their involvement with these groups continue to have meaning for them once they were no longer situated within a German Jewish context? The plethora of objects relating to membership in Jewish fraternities is an interesting and probably exceptional example of the intensity of the bonds formed by the members of these groups. The Jewish student fraternity movements in Germany, both those that emphasized their adherence to the Fatherland (Kartell Convent, or KC) and those promoting a Zionist ideology (Kartell Jüdischer Verbindungen, or KJV), adopted the material culture and rituals of the non-Jewish fraternities of the majority university student body: beer ribbons, fraternity caps, and sashes as well as an array of objects dedicated and gifted to fellow students and members such as beer steins, glasses, pipe bowls, and photo albums. The crests and symbols and to a lesser extent the colors identified them as objects of Jewish fraternities.

The majority of the men who belonged to the fraternities and their alumni organizations (*Altherrenverbände*) and who managed to leave Germany took with them items that manifested their connection to these groups. For example, among the wealth of documents and photographs that Fritz Manasse gave to the Museum, the only three-dimensional objects were seven ribbons and pendants from the Sprevia and Thuringia fraternities (figure 9.6). Membership in the fraternities was seen as a lifelong bond, and these objects embody both individual and shared identity (ever more so due to the fact that so many of these are gifted objects that display the names of the givers) that transcends the time of residency in Germany. Following the war, the Kartell Convent was reestablished with chapters in the various countries where larger numbers of members had settled, and a successor organization of the KJV was founded in Israel. These associations met regularly, and the members donned the beer ribbons, sashes, and caps they had brought with them from Germany (and

Figure 9.6. Fritz Manasse's ribbon (*Bierzipfel*) from Jewish student fraternities Thuringia Breslau (left) and Sprevia Berlin (right). Jewish Museum Berlin, inventory number 2007/150/235, gift of Susanne Wolff.

sang their old German fraternity songs),[27] and items they had received from fellow members (the exchange of *Zipfel* was part of fraternity ritual, a form of bonding between two students) often adorn the shelves and showcases of their homes.

At the time, only a small number of young people (mainly men) attended universities, and fraternity paraphernalia affirm multiple aspects of the identities of their owners: their German and Jewish heritage and lives as Germans and Jews, their continued bond with their fellow members, and their commitment to the ideals they ascribed to as students in Germany. These insignia do not generate the ambivalence and bitterness often connected to medals from World War I, so migration did not bring about a radical shift in the relation to these objects. Yet they too very rarely served as markers of identity for the following generation, with no small number of second generation donors unaware of the meaning and context of these items.

Quite a few Jewish migrants brought with them paintings of their hometowns, and in their new country these evocations of *place* resonate differently than do the objects connected to groups or to the German nation-state just discussed. A professor of Jewish history, after reading our abstract in which we mentioned that migrants took with them objects that reflected "local pride and identity in cityscapes or drawings of prominent buildings in the cities where the individuals had lived," wrote: "I always wondered why my mother and grandparents took so many paintings, etchings of the famous church in their hometown with them, and now they are on my walls." There are many other instances of people who took just a few paintings, etchings, or drawings, most of which depicted scenes from their hometown. In contrast to Eastern Europe, where many Jews lived in shtetls (small towns with a large and often majority Jewish population), German Jews lived in cities and towns with predominantly non-Jewish populations. The pictures representing these places were never particularly "Jewish" and often featured the local church, which was the most recognizable landmark.

Unlike the example of World War I medals, these objects were much more likely to be proudly and openly displayed in the home. Whereas an attachment to Germany or "Fatherland" was largely eradicated by the rise of Hitler and the war, the connection to a particular region or town and to "Heimat" often remained.[28] These pictures may even have a greater significance for their owners after migration than before, often retaining the power to transmit a sense of place and connection to the past to the next generation. They are perhaps the most straightforward and tangible representation of having been rooted and shaped elsewhere, in a different culture and environment, which apart from the things they brought with them, migrants also convey to their children through food, dialect, or accent as well as many other customs and habits. Such pictures not only point to the formation of identity by place, they also perform this work, emphasizing that identity is constituted in part through the interaction with objects and possessions and that this is an ongoing process that involves a continual reweaving of the various strands of identity.

Trusteeship and Future Encounters

With the transfer of objects from the homes of the refugees and their descendants to the Jewish Museum Berlin, these items make one further migration. They return to the country and in some cases to the city where they were used and often made and pass from a private space into the public domain. For some donors, it is precisely the identification with their *Heimat* that underlines their desire to see the materials preserved and utilized in a museum near their former places of residence. Their transfer to the museum signifies nonetheless a further displacement, although this time voluntary and not forced, as was the case six to seven decades earlier. Passing out of the hands of the family, the object is now resituated in a collection or exhibition that reflects back on its earlier uses and meanings. Yet for a great majority of these objects, their entrustment to the museum constitutes a resuscitation after years of disuse and disregard as well as the loss of meaning, mostly for the descendants but sometimes for the original owners as well. Indeed, very few of these items would have found their way to the museum solely through their owner's initiative but rather came to the fore through conversations and visits. Objects that did not necessarily suggest something representative or significant about one's parents' or grandparents' past are contextualized in the museum to convey various facets of Jewish existence in Germany: personal, familial, religious, economic, and cultural.

In the Jewish Museum Berlin, the potential of the artifacts to capture the curiosity of the visitors lies often in the sheer familiarity of the objects themselves, as very few of them (and none that we have discussed) are intrinsically Jewish. They are not foreign to the visitor, regardless of where she or he is from, and are independent of religious affiliation. All visitors can recognize children's toys, pieces of clothing, musical instruments, even war medals. It is precisely their familiarity that can evoke the question of why such things are on display in a museum devoted to the history and culture of Jews in Germany.

Viewing these objects through the lens of migration sharpens and multiplies these questions by drawing attention to the uses and meanings of these objects at different points in time and in different places. The particular context in which an item is displayed is brought into relief by attending to its migration history, as we then see it both within and outside of this context. One framework for understanding is necessarily brought into contact with others. Attention to migration thereby also heightens a consideration of the materiality of the object, as something that was used, produced, purchased, selected for migration, and interacted with on multiple occasions; as something that has its own history, biography, and life; as something that we gain from by exploring all that exceeds our first encounter with it.

Notes

1. All references to the exhibition of the Jewish Museum Berlin are to its first permanent exhibit that was in place from the opening of the museum in September 2001 through the autumn of 2017. At the time of the completion of this contribution (April 2017), work on a new permanent exhibition at the museum had begun. It is scheduled to open in 2019 and will differ significantly from its predecessor.

2. The various terminology used to describe the migration of Jews from Germany during the period of National Socialism—*emigration, flight, escape*—is fraught with difficulty, with no single term universally applicable to the circumstances and experiences of all individuals. Throughout this paper we will use the term *refugee* to refer to Jews who left Germany between the end of January 1933 and October 1941 in accordance with the definition provided by the League of Nations. See "Convention concerning the Status of Refugees Coming from Germany, February 10, 1938," www.refworld.org/pdfid/3dd8d12a4.pdf, accessed April 1, 2017. Concurrently, we will use the terms *emigration* and *migration* to refer to the process of their departure, which in the overwhelming majority of cases was an organized procedure sanctioned by both the government of Germany and the governments of the countries that the refugees entered.

3. As Leora Auslander insightfully demonstrates in her study of Jewish homes in prewar Berlin, "'Jewish Taste?': Jews and the Aesthetics of Everyday Life in Paris and Berlin, 1920–1942," in *Histories of Leisure*, ed. Rudy Koshar (Oxford: Berg, 2002), 299–318.

4. See among other essays "Migrant Visions: The Scheunenviertel and Boyle Heights, Los Angeles," in *Transit und Transformation*, ed. Verena Dohrn (Göttingen, Germany: Wallstein Verlag, 2010), 320–335; and "Narrative Tensions: The Eyewitness and the Archive," *Partial Answers* 7, no. 2 (2009): 261–278.

5. See Heinz Cohn, "Auswanderung und Mitnahme von Umzugsgut," *C.-V.-Zeitung*, May 19, 1938, 17; Heinz Cohn and Erich Gottfeld, *Auswanderungs-Vorschriften für Juden in Deutschland* (Berlin: J. Jastrow, Jüdischer Buchverlag, 1938), 32–35; "Runderlaß des Reichsministers der Wirtschaft zur Mitnahme vom Umzugsgut durch Auswanderer, April 17, 1939," *Jüdisches Nachrichtenblatt*, April 25, 1939, 1.

6. Their daughter donated two other items that might have been on the *Umzugsliste*, in addition to those mentioned above: another dress and a tablecloth. Documents, letters, and photographs constituted most of what was given to the museum, which is almost always the case.

7. "Aus den Sammlungen des Jüdischen Museums Berlin," website, http://objekte.jmberlin.de/object/jmb-obj-599289, accessed April 24, 2017.

8. Igor Kopytoff, "The Cultural Biography of Things: Commoditization as Process," in *The Social Life of Things: Commodities in Cultural Perspective*, ed. Arjun Appadurai (Cambridge: Cambridge University Press, 1986), 67.

9. Kopytoff, "Cultural Biography," 74.

10. "Aus den Sammlungen des Jüdischen Museums Berlin," website, http://objekte.jmberlin.de/object/jmb-obj-483281, accessed April 1, 2017.

11. See also the first chapter (on the top hat in the Warsaw Ghetto) in Bożena Shallcross, *The Holocaust Object in Polish and Polish-Jewish Culture* (Bloomington: Indiana University Press, 2011).

12. See Sandra Dudley's chapter in this volume.

13. Here is a link to the *Umzugsliste*: http://objekte.jmberlin.de/object/jmb-obj-221459, and to one to the keys: http://objekte.jmberlin.de/object/jmb-obj-224271, accessed April 1, 2017.

14. The cover of the recent *Lexikon der Vertreibungen*, for example, an encyclopedic book about forced migration in Europe during the twentieth century, contains the image of four keys underneath the photo of a group of people who were forced to emigrate. Detlef Brandes, Holm Sunhaussen, and Stefan Troebst, eds., *Lexikon der Vertreibungen: Deportation, Zwangsaussiedlung und ethnische Säuberung im Europa des 20. Jahrhunderts* (Vienna: Böhlau, 2010).

15. Paul Kuttner, *An Endless Struggle: Reminiscences and Reflections* (New York: Vantage, 2009), 119, 129.

16. Mona Körte, "Bracelet, Hand Towel, Pocket Watch: Objects of the Last Moment in Memory and Narration," *Shofar: An Interdisciplinary Journal of Jewish Studies* 23, no. 1 (2004): 111.

17. Körte, "Bracelet," 109, note 1, quoting from Kuttner.

18. Collections of the United States Holocaust Museum, https://collections.ushmm.org/search/catalog/irn510396, accessed April 1, 2017.

19. Notes from Kuttner's conversations with the Jewish Museum Berlin.

20. Ken Gorbey, the original director of the permanent exhibition, stated at one point that in his view, "no other item has yet displaced the hand towel as the most significant item of cultural property in the museum collection"; email from October 2001 from Ken Gorbey to a PhD student, Paul Kuttner file, Jewish Museum Berlin.

21. Wikipedia page for Sergei Rachmaninoff.

22. Marjorie Akin quotes Michael Schiffer: "Michael Schiffer has pointed out that when things no longer serve the purpose for which they were created, they are sometimes transferred into the realm of collected material, a process he has described as 'conserving,' that is, a shifting of material from technofunction to socio- or ideofunction." Akin, "Passionate Possession: The Formation of Private Collections," in *Learning from Things: Method and Theory of Material Culture Studies*, ed. W. David Kingery (Washington, D.C.: Smithsonian Institution Press, 1996), 102–103.

23. On the syringe, see "Aus den Sammlungen des Jüdischen Museums Berlin" website, http://objekte.jmberlin.de/object/jmb-obj-3419932, accessed April 24, 2017.

24. See Marion A. Kaplan, *Dignity and Despair: Jewish Life in Nazi Germany* (New York: Oxford University Press, 1998).

25. "Aus den Sammlungen des Jüdischen Museums Berlin" website, http://objekte.jmberlin.de/object/jmb-obj-371033, accessed April 1, 2017.

26. "Aus den Sammlungen des Jüdischen Museums Berlin" website, http://objekte.jmberlin.de/object/jmb-obj-344457, accessed April 1, 2017. These natural-looking dolls with hand-painted faces and real hair had become the most famous dolls in Germany shortly after the start of their production in the early years of the twentieth century and were the most fervent desire of almost every German girl. To this day they are widely known and treasured.

27. Indeed, the majority of the minutes, reports, and newsletters of the successor organizations were penned in German until well into the 1970s.

28. *Heimat*, most often translated as "home," "homeland," or "native land," is a highly complex term with a broad range of meanings and connotations. On the personal level it can denote the deep sense of (often romanticized) attachment not only to a specific place but also to a certain time, culture, family, and social environment. See Celia Applegate, *A Nation of Provincials: The German Idea of Heimat* (Berkeley: University of California Press, 1990), 3–15, and Friederike Eigler and Jens Kugele, eds., *Heimat: At the Intersection of Memory and Space* (Berlin: De Gruyter, 2012).

10

Paku Karen Skirt-Cloths (Not) at Home

Forcibly Migrated Burmese Textiles in Refugee Camps and Museums

Sandra H. Dudley

Focusing on three skirt-cloths originating among the Paku Karen people from eastern Burma (Myanmar), this chapter looks at forcibly relocated objects as serial migrants and asks what it might mean for them not only to be displaced but also to be "at home."[1] The discussion draws on both ethnographic research with encamped refugees from Burma and work in and on museums. Its premise is that, from the object's perspective, there are notable similarities between a refugee camp and a museum: both entail containment, submission to others' regimes of order and control, and apparent passivity in the face of the viewing outsider (although in neither context are the displaced actually inactive and powerless, as we shall see). Most important, the chapter's approach is not merely object-centered but seeks to take the artifact's point of view; ultimately, this results in an object-*led* focus not only on material continuity and change but also on the actual and potential effects of the object. This approach to displacement is ostensibly rather different to others taken in this volume but, as I shall revisit below, it is complementary to them and provides a way into understanding the effects that objects have and the relationships they have with people, in forced migration contexts and beyond.

"Displacement" conveys both a changed connection to place and an associated sense of movement. An active process, it tends to result in breaks between past and present, there and here; at the same time, the displaced persons or things work both to bridge gaps with the past and to create a new niche. Which of these dynamics appears more dominant may depend on both the position from which we look and the capacity of the displaced to make things happen and to change how people feel. A considerable literature now addresses mobility and translocation in various forms, in contexts of migration (forced or otherwise), transnationalism, diaspora, or global networks (including the digital). Little of this work, however, focuses on objects or seeks fundamentally to widen out to the materiality of the dislocation—as process, experience, or trope—at its heart. Writing on Palestinians in the United States, Zeynep Turan concludes that material culture matters to displaced people because artifacts enable and embody connections to the pre-displacement past, for first-generation migrants through personal memory and for later generations through imagination and collective memory.[2] My own work, however, indicates that these processes are more complex; for example, while objects may indeed act as reassuring, physical links to the past, paradoxically and often simultaneously they may also serve as painful reminders of unpleasant experiences, upheaval, and loss.[3] Parkin sees a shift in which objects become, in forced displacement, deposits "of sentiment and cultural knowledge" that "take the place of interpersonal relations,"[4] so that "social personhood" is objectified in "mementoes of mind and matter" such as artifacts, dance, and ritual.[5] This picture is, however, more reductive than that found in my own field experience, in which refugees work hard and creatively to continue and adapt social relations and personhood. It is not so much that feeling and knowledge are *stored* by (deposited in) material forms such as dress and ritual activity as that they are re-articulated and re-created in an ongoing process—a process that would happen anyway but is (a) intensified by displacement and (b) undertaken by things as well as persons. Material forms, in other words, are dynamic and changing, sociocultural *participants*, not mere repositories.

As participants, objects have capacities to bring about effects, and we misjudge them if we assume that they are nothing but passive lumps, controlled, and ascribed meanings and values, by people in a wholly one-way process. But to understand the capacity of objects fully, I suggest that we have to try to see it from the position from which it operates—in other words, from the perspective of the object—as well as from the standpoint of those affected. We would expect no less if people or institutions were the things in question, so why, if we accept that objects have the capacity to have effects, should we do so here? From an anthropological perspective, objects in this case become, in Geertz's words, "the natives," and the challenge is to produce "an interpretation" that, as he puts it, "is neither imprisoned within their . . . horizons . . . nor systematically deaf to the tonalities of their existence."[6] This is not to anthropomorphize things inappropriately or to negate the real-life entanglement of persons and things, nor is it to imply an ethical equality between the two. Rather, *failure* to seek the object's point of view is anthropocentric and results not only in an oversimplification of our understanding of the relationships between persons and things but also explains nothing about the influence of one inanimate object on another in the absence of people.

Malkki and Clifford urge us to attempt to understand the experience of displacement from the points of view of the displaced.[7] What must that be like from an object's purview? How are rupture and loss, social production and encounter, experienced by displaced artifacts? Extending Malkki's and Clifford's calls into the world of the material, looking beyond a rooted and anthropocentric viewpoint and metaphorically at least taking the object's perspective, may augment our understanding of both the migration process and the relationships between people and things. Taking the object's position is analogous to Holmes's technique in literary biography, seeking "the view *from* the window, rather than the view of the window in the façade."[8] This approach is prosopopoeial rather than fetishistic, as it aims, for methodological purposes, to attribute to objects (imaginatively at least) voice and other qualities that, being human ourselves, we can only conceptualize in human terms.[9] It necessitates both empathy and inventiveness and requires serious attention to the material artifact. It is also, I argue, a rhetorical perspective that enables us to shift not only the direction of gaze but also the level of stress, moving it away from anthropocentric social meanings and toward the objectness of objects.

An object's capacity to bring about effects is such that, once the object exists, if it did not have the inherent characteristics and possibilities that it does, the particular effects that may be produced in any particular encounter with a person or other object would not be what they are. Of course, other factors are at always at play too—how someone responds to an artifact in a museum display case, for example, may be affected by the knowledge and personal background that person brings with them, the mood he or she is in at that moment, the design of the display and the exhibition and museum within which it sits, lighting, adjacent objects, and other people and sounds in the gallery. But the artifact itself has the capacity to affect the viewer; if it were something else, the effects would be different. This capacity is increasingly widely discussed in terms of "object agency," albeit an agency that, unlike that of persons, excludes intentionality.[10] Drawing on Aristotle, however, I prefer to conceptualize it in terms of the potentialities, or inherent possibilities, of things.[11] Potentiality avoids the animistic quality of many formulations of "agency,"[12] in which the agency attributed to objects is still ultimately human agency and no direct potency in particular situations appears to be granted to the particular properties of artifacts. But once objects have been produced, they have an autonomy that goes beyond the intentions and control of their makers—something we do not question in relation to, for example, human beings, but, because they do not have conscious mind, we tend to remove from things, even though *autonomy* and *consciousness* are not synonymous. Potentiality makes room for autonomy. It also embraces the vagaries of temporality or uncertainty. For example, objects change over time, and eventually they may decay and disintegrate. In the process of doing so, their capacities and the effects they may have can change. The surface of a painting may become too dirty or cracked for its original image to be discerned; a landmine may become so corroded that it is no longer capable of detonation. Yet these possibilities—these potentialities, rather than agencies—like so many others were inherent in those objects from the beginning, although they were by no means all deliberately placed there by the objects' creators. Some potentialities may never be actualized;

indeed, we will never know, for any one object, what all of its potentialities are.

For Aristotle, *potentiality* (*dunamis* in ancient Greek) actually had two related meanings, both of which, I suggest, apply to objects more fittingly than *agency* and are relevant to this chapter—indeed, to this book. There is the capacity to bring about an effect, and the potential to become something else. The first is exemplified in this chapter by cloths whose characteristics attract collectors and other kinds of distinctive encounters between themselves and people, as I return to later. Similar effects are observed, in different ways, in other chapters in this book, including those by Noah Benninga, Bonnie Effros, Cathleen Giustino, Alice Goff, Sarah Weicksel, and Jeffrey Wallen and Aubrey Pomerance. Meanwhile the second kind of potentiality, the possibility of transforming into a different thing, is seen in this chapter with cloths that, when seamed into tubes, can become skirts. In so doing, of course, the cloths do not simply take on a different form; they also assume new functions—as well as the new meanings and significances that go along with these. Not all of this is done by them: It is *people* who identify particular colors and patterns as typical of certain Karenni groups, just as it is people operating within specific conditions and limitations who attribute codes and values to specific forms and styles that may arise in those conditions (see Benninga and Iris Rachamimov in this volume). But in all these cases, the potential in the things themselves is an essential part of determining what they might become. Their particular material qualities—fiber type and weave and the textures and fabric behaviors that result; patterns, colors, dullness, or shine—play a central part in the forms and functions that are possible. Unchanneled, they remain potentialities; transmuted, they are, in Aristotle's terminology, actualized.[13]

After introducing the people and material culture from which the skirt-cloth examples in this chapter are drawn, I describe the three distinct objects. Two are now in museum collections (although on different continents and over a century apart in age), and one, while we might think of it as a refugee cloth, has not actually moved anywhere at all. I then consider the sorts of migration trajectories and displacements embodied in each of these cloths and examine their different kinds of connections with their pasts and presents. Finally, the chapter moves on to reflect, through each of the skirt-cloths, on the notion of being "at home" and on how and with what implications this idea can be applied to objects. The direction of the discussion means that many of the social matrices within which the artifacts sit comprise a background rather than a key part of the analysis here, and the chapter includes attention to physical characteristics of the textiles. This should not, however, be read as museum-like description. With the exception of the conservator's recording of changes in condition, the latter is usually thought of as static and untied to the performativity and dynamic change that characterize objects' lives. Here, however, I am concerned with material forms and traces that continue and change, are added to and deteriorate, and with the ways in which their interactions with and effects on people (and vice versa), in a range of mutually influential performances, shape and articulate each other.

Karenni Refugees

The refugees with whom I work use *Karenni* as an umbrella term to encompass around a dozen ethnolinguistically related but self-distinguishing groups, chief among whom are the Kayah, various Kayan groups, the Kayaw, and the Paku Karen. Each of these has its own mother tongue, and each belongs to the overall Karenic language family that also includes the much larger Sgaw and Pwo Karen ethnolinguistic families found in Burma's Kayin (Karen) State and elsewhere in central and southern Burma and western and northern Thailand.[14,15] The Karenni originate in the smallest of Burma's seven ethnic states, Kayah State, a region with a long history of humanitarian and military problems but at peace since a ceasefire was reached between armed opposition groups and the former military regime in 2012.[16] The ethnolinguistic heterogeneity of the state is augmented by diversity in class, education, political engagement, and religion. This diversity is mirrored—and concentrated—in the now long-term Karenni refugee camps in northwestern Thailand. The first significant numbers of Karenni arrived in Thailand in 1989. By July 2016, the population for the two mainly Karenni camps was 13,246, part of a population of over 103,130 refugees from Burma encamped along the Thai side of the border.[17] For over twenty years, there has been in these camps an evolving sense of pan-Karenni-ness, led by the exile-based

Karenni National Progressive Party (KNPP).[18] Meanwhile, long-term displacement has been a very different experience for varied members of the community: all live in self-built, -stilted, and -thatched bamboo huts and have access to food and medical assistance sourced from relief agencies; however, while some refugees work, for example as teachers, drivers, or paramedics, and are paid a modest salary by the KNPP or a relief agency, most eke out what survival they can, a few managing to sell services or home-made or home-grown goods (textiles, baskets, vegetables) to other refugees or outsiders. Many other families and individuals, meanwhile, have been resettled to third countries by the United Nations High Commission for Refugees.[19]

Apart from Lehman's anthropological field research conducted inside Kayah State in the mid-twentieth century,[20] very little ethnographic work was done with the Karenni prior to my own. With the exception of Lehman's work and very few others,[21] almost all research done on any Karenic peoples, whether from Kayah State or beyond, has since the Second World War been done in Thailand rather than in Burma. These groups have to varying degrees straddled and moved around areas that happen to include the national border since well before colonial times. Such historical relocations, and the existence across frontiers of people who consider themselves to be the same or closely connected, provide an important spatiotemporal background for the more recent forced migrations that figure as both reality and metaphor in this chapter.

Textiles and Ethnic Ascriptions

Textiles, most especially women's dress, have long been associated with ethnically ascribed identities in Burma, by insiders and outsiders alike. This close connection between cloth and belonging is a key part of the context for the specific objects discussed here and is approached with an emphasis on what Moerman some time ago described as "emic categories of ascription."[22] This does not only, however, mean the ethnic attributions the Karenni may give to each other, to others, and to items of material culture. As will be seen, it also concerns the labels others may apply too, including outsiders in different places and periods. I take the fluidity and complexity of identity as a given, but at the same time I am concerned with local, quotidian ethnographic realities—and their experiential qualities—in which identities and their connections with, for example, particular forms of dress are credited with considerably more concreteness and authority than is attributed to them by contemporary academic theory. This *matters* (very materially, as will be seen!) to the Karenic groups, now as in the late nineteenth century—however imagined and colonially influenced the ethnic identities may be.[23] It concerns the ways in which people designate, construct, and experience their associations of ethnic identity and cloth.[24] More broadly, this is about shifting perceptions and ascriptions of identity from the subjects' perspective, including their stress on the categories and boundaries of identity, however imagined we might consider them to be. This is, in other words, an emic attempt to understand the subjects' ontological perspectives rather than an etic, epistemological endeavor to explain them.

Trying to make sense of the apparently bewildering collection of peoples among whom they found themselves also *mattered* to early visitors to Burma, and they too are among the subjects of this paper. For them dress offered, in all its colorful visuality, a way to categorize the human array they encountered. Ethnicity and ethnonyms became tied to textiles and styles of dress in fixed and essentialized ways that neither reflected the fluidity of real-life group boundaries and notions of belonging nor were necessarily the same in every area or for every observer. In museums and among collectors, it became—and still is—imperative to know to which group to attribute a textile. Yet making ethnic associations is much more complex and subjective than merely ascribing a label. What local groups call themselves and each other, and thus the attributions they give to particular styles of dress, may be very different to the more "standardized"—though still very varied—versions attributed by outsiders. As Scott observed, referring specifically to the Karenic family, they have "suffered from over-classification. . . . Their clans read like a table of fashion plates or a history of tartans. The only visible distinction between one clan and another was the dress worn."[25] Stylistic features such as small variations in color, style of skirt, and warp striping were all seized upon as apparently ethnically diagnostic in a way that Scott over a century ago was able to read as reductive, over-essentialized, and problematic. Nonetheless, certain textile and clothing traditions were and still are associated with particular groups. Indeed, it may be the groups themselves who consider certain forms or styles so diagnostic or representative of their identity that they deem it worthy of protection or in need of deliberate adaptation to shape its distinctiveness further.[26]

A range of clothing forms can be observed in the Karenni camps, particularly among men, who might pair a T-shirt with trousers, a skirt-cloth, or shorts. For women, however, there are fewer options, and they are almost certain to wear a skirt-cloth. Culturally constituted ideas concerning moral decency render shorts or tight jeans out of the question. Notions of bodily aesthetics also mean that trousers and skirts, as well as the female bodies that wear them, are considered less beautiful than a skirt-cloth wearing woman.[27] The skirt-cloth covers the flesh to lower calf level but at the same time hugs the hips and buttocks and encourages the shorter, slow-stepped walk that is considered graceful. Most women on an everyday basis will wear their skirt-cloth with a T-shirt; sometimes, though, and especially for festivals and church-going, they will coordinate it with a traditionally styled Karenic tunic top. All skirt-cloths, male and female, consist of a long rectangle of fabric with the two ends seamed together so that the whole forms a wide tube (figure 10.3). A man fastens his by centering his body within the tube and pulling the two sides evenly away from his body, before folding the fabric back into the middle and tying in a large knot that hangs down in front of his waist. A woman, in contrast, takes all the fabric out to one side only, before folding it back across her body and tucking it in at the opposite side of the waist, producing a smooth and fitted effect around the lower torso. Most women's cloths are, like most men's cloths, machine-woven. Women's everyday cloths usually consist of cheap cotton produced in Malaysia or Thailand and printed at source with colored patterns that mimic maritime Southeast Asian *batik* designs; this type is ubiquitous in markets throughout the region and in the camps.

Of interest here, however, are the skirt-cloths produced in the camps by refugee women on continuous warp back-strap looms. This technique results in cloth that is only half the necessary width for a skirt cloth, so two pieces are stitched together along the length of one side, in order to make a bigger cloth (figure 10.3).

Some cloths are woven free-style but most deliberately conform to one of two main types, known as "Padaung" and "Paku." Both have a plain black ground; the differences lie in the colors, number, and degree of warp stripes and other effects used for patterning. The three cloths discussed in this chapter are all of the Paku type, so called by the refugees because they are identified by them as typical of cloths traditionally made and worn by women of the Paku Karen sub-group from southwestern Kayah State. Woven using yarn that is purchased ready-spun and ready-dyed (in Kayah State villages, in the recent past at least, thread would have been spun and dyed from home-grown cotton), these cloths may eventually be worn by the weaver, or they may be sold in a camp shop. Near the top and bottom they have a narrow band of colored warp stripes (always including red); in the middle, they display a wider set of warp striping (again, always including red) and subtle warp *ikat* used to create a "python-skin" pattern; most central of all, decorative stitching joins together the two woven strips. When not worn with T-shirts and instead being worn for church or some other special occasion, these cloths are matched with decorated, black tunic-style tops, also described as Paku Karen (figure 10.1).

So garbed, a woman is, the refugees say, "wearing traditional Paku dress." I shall return to performative, habitual, and other aspects of this. Here, however, it is important to note that the cloth so closely identified with a particular ethnicity, wraps the *female* body. There are textile forms and dress styles locally considered typical of particular groups and customarily worn by men, but they are far less commonly seen. It is women's clothing, and knowledge pertaining to it, that is treated by men and women alike as valuable and important to conserve. This is a familiar entwining of gender and culture that I do not have space to discuss here; suffice to say that for the Karenni as for perhaps most other human groups it is women who are at the center of sociocultural as well as biological reproduction. The skirt-cloth and its accompanying garments envelop the female, procreative body; in doing so they are intimately connected to socially and culturally constituted notions of the group and its continuity into both past and future. Woman's bodies and women's dress are together a central aspect of what it means to be Paku (or Karenni and so on). As we shall see, though, these Paku forms of clothing also have a life that extends beyond the camps or Paku communities.

Figure 10.1. Paku Karen women's tunic top from Kawtudur village, southwest Kayah State, traditionally to be worn by a married woman. Such tops are invariably black, and usually—like this one—made of commercially produced cotton. Their neck openings and armholes are often decoratively edged with either red felt or red rickrack braid. The lower portions are usually decorated with colorful, embroidered, floral designs, in notable contrast to the repetitions of circles or blocks found on the tops produced by other Sgaw Karen groups. This one also has an uncommon quilted lower edge. This top was purchased in Kayah State by Naw Rebecca (name changed) and then purchased from her in a Karenni refugee camp in 1997, by the author. Copyright Pitt Rivers Museum, University of Oxford, 1997.28.14.1.

Three Paku Karen Skirt-Cloths

Naw Rebecca's Cloth

The first skirt-cloth is one I can only depict being worn. I not only have no other image of it, I never saw it in any other capacity. Of the three cloths, it is this one that might at first sight seem most clearly to be a migrant cloth. It belongs to a refugee, was made by a refugee, and is worn by a refugee. Yet of the three, this is the only one that has migrated nowhere, having been made and worn and having remained in one place—which happens to be a refugee camp. Naw Rebecca came to Thailand from southwest Kayah State at least fifteen years prior to the photograph in figure 10.2 being taken. Most women in the camp at the time of the photograph would, if they dressed in this style at all, only do so on special occasions, such as church on a Sunday. Naw Rebecca, however, chose this form of clothing as every-day wear. A relatively wealthy and esteemed figure in the camp, and wife of the camp commander, she was respected for doing so, as were other women

Figure 10.2. Naw Rebecca (name changed) weaving at a back-strap loom in a Karenni refugee camp on the Thai-Burma border. She wears a Paku Karen skirt-cloth she wove herself, paired with a Paku Karen–style tunic top. Photograph by the author.

who did the same (they too were generally married, older women and often married to men in positions of political power). These women valued the wearing of traditional-style Paku dress—and the particular ethnic, generational, and political associations it conveyed—more than their younger sisters and daughters appeared to do; through their own weaving skills and their wherewithal to buy materials, they were also able to afford the relative luxury of making and replacing such clothing. In a sense, then, it was a form of dress that both represented and reinforced a relative social position.

Naw Oo May's Cloth

Naw Oo May's skirt-cloth now lies in a museum textile store in Oxford. It was hand-woven in a Karenni refugee camp, having been especially commissioned as part of a larger collection, mostly consisting of textiles,

Figure 10.3. Paku Karen skirt-cloth made by Naw Oo May (name changed) in a Karenni refugee camp on the Thai-Burma border in the late 1990s. Woven on a back-strap loom using pre-dyed yarn from Mae Hong Son market and incorporating faint warp-*ikat* patterning within white warp stripes in central panel. The picture shows one-half of the width of the skirt-cloth tube hanging sideways from a pole. This cloth is, however, as yet unseamed: It consists of two long back-strap loom widths of fabric hand-stitched together down one of each of the long sides (forming the center of this cloth); to be worn as a skirt-cloth, it still needs to have the two raw short sides stitched together. Collected in 1997 by the author. Copyright Pitt Rivers Museum, University of Oxford, 1997.28.15.

which I assembled for the Pitt Rivers Museum during my main period of doctoral field research in the Karenni camps in 1996–97. The composition of the collection, however, was essentially determined not by me but by Karenni refugee women, led by Naw Rebecca.[28]

Mrs. Harris's Cloth

The oldest of the three examples, this skirt-cloth is also the only one to originate inside Burma—though exactly where is unclear. It was collected by Olive Harris, who worked with her husband, the Reverend Norman Harris, as an American Baptist missionary in Burma, based in Moulmein and Shwegyin, between 1846 and 1882.[29] Both areas are somewhat southerly for a significant Paku Karen population. Instead, this cloth is likely to have been given to Mrs. Harris by an already converted Paku Karen individual who may have visited or been working with the Harrises or to have

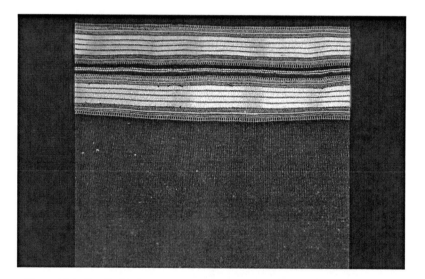

Figure 10.4. Detail of Paku Karen woman's skirt-cloth. Woven principally in black cotton, this cloth is decorated with narrow red, pale yellow, pale green, and white warp stripes and a central band of warp *ikat* python-skin patterning. Made on a back-strap loom, what is not evident here is that one end of the central seam joining together the two back-strap loom strips has, over time, come slightly apart. It dates from the mid- to late nineteenth century. Gift of Mrs. R. Boese from the collection of Mrs. Norman Harris. Copyright Denison Museum, Denison University, P67.114.

been presented to or purchased by her when the Harrises visited the more northerly Toungoo mission post around which many more Paku Karen would have lived.[30] Skirt-cloths were, and still are, common forms of gift to community outsiders and insiders alike.

Displacement and the Object's Point of View

While cloth one has stayed in a refugee camp, made, owned and worn by one woman, cloths two and three have both undergone physical migration—one from the Thai-Burma border to the United Kingdom and one from Burma to the United States. Tracing the routes of these displacements helps to unravel the objects' stories. The trail followed by Naw Oo May's cloth was relatively simple, though staggered. It moved in my hands within the refugee camp from Naw Oo May's house to mine, and thence by road with me, to Chiang Mai. Thereafter, boxed up, it traveled by sea to the United Kingdom, arriving at my house in the English East Midlands several months later, accompanied not only by the other objects I had collected but also a couple of live cockroaches and what were by then, for me, deeply evocative, jungle smells. Several weeks later, I drove the cloth on its final journey, to Oxford. Mrs. Harris's cloth, in contrast, has a far more convoluted travel story, a narrative involving different people and manifold journeys and interludes, within Burma, to the United States (possibly via India, a stop-off point for many traveling to and from Burma), and finally within the United States, at last ending in Granville, Ohio. At some point, probably after the deaths of the Harrises, it left their possession and moved into the ownership of either their son, Dr. Edward Harris and his wife Bessie (who both worked as missionaries in the same stations as Edward's parents, until 1932)[31] or their daughter, Jessie, who also worked in these two stations but only until 1912, when presumably she married. Before the late 1960s, the latest date by which it is likely to have entered the Denison collections, it came into the possession of a Mrs. R. Boese, who may actually have been Jessie. Ultimately, by the late 1960s or before, it entered the Denison collections via Helen Hunt: Herself an American Baptist missionary for many years, she finally retired to Granville, Ohio, in 1951, later moving to California.[32] In her retirement, Hunt busied herself in correspondence with the many former American Baptist missionaries to Burma and their families.[33] She encouraged these individuals to donate objects they had collected in Southeast Asia to the rapidly grow-ing Burmese collections at Denison University, and it is by such means that Mrs. Harris's cloth finally reached its current destination.[34]

So what do these trajectories tell us? The tales of Naw Oo May's and Mrs. Harris's cloths are, like all travel stories, concerned as much with temporal as with spatial distances;[35] that is, the origin points of both objects lie in the past as well as elsewhere. This is most obvious, of course, for Mrs. Harris's cloth, but it matters too for Naw Oo May's; indeed, the situation and demographics of encamped Karenni refugees are now so changed that the historical moment out of which that cloth came is particularly poignant. Moreover, the question of temporal and spatial dis-tance, or more accurately, perhaps, remoteness, is not simply a matter of quantity; that is, occurring longer ago or being physically far-flung does not in itself necessarily make something more out of reach. It is rather that sometimes things can get in the way and make the point of origin *seem* much further away because one cannot reach it. This is an essential difference between travel and displacement. Both are spatial and temporal phenomena, in that the object or person concerned has moved from one set of geographical coordinates to another, from past moment to present instant. For the displaced rather than the merely traveled, however, the traversing, characteristics, and very *existence* of the distances—physical and temporal, actual and metaphorical—between journey's beginning and end, there and then, here and now, become much more significant. For displaced people (I return to displaced things below), it is the ways in which these spatiotemporal distances are constructed that in turn give meaning to being displaced, to the imagination of "home" and to ideas of return.[36] Similar constructions of—and, important, attempts to bridge—distance are also seen in Rachamimov's essay in this volume.

Migration stories show too the extent to which external agencies play important roles in displacement. Mrs. Harris's cloth, for example, has not merely voyaged 8,400 miles and something over a century to get from where it started to where it is now. It has done so as a result of the deci-sions and actions of others: the person who gave or sold it to Mrs. Harris, Mrs. Harris herself, her son or daughter/Mrs. Boese, Mrs. Hunt, and the Denison Museum. We do not know whether or not it has ever been a com-modity during its long life, though it may have been, if Mrs. Harris or a person who gave it to her originally purchased it. We can at least be fairly certain that the cotton from which and the loom with which it was made were not likely ever to have been purchased, as the maker at the time of this cloth's production would have sourced her thread from cotton grown within her own community, spinning and dyeing it herself and turning it into fabric on a loom made for her by her husband (the latter but not the former still common practice today). These kinds of transactions, and the relationships within which objects and their respective productions and movements are associatedly entangled,[37] have been, in one way or another, the focus of most anthropological and other work on material culture. Studying these exchanges and connections reveals a great deal about shifting meanings, values, and power as well as about networks and communities.

But it is illuminating too to look at and for the object per se. For a start, like the human displaced neither Mrs. Harris's nor Naw Oo May's cloth is without power or influence of its own in the processes by which it comes to be where it is. In each case, the particular qualities of the object were central in both its original acquisition by the collector and in its final accessioning by the museum. Mrs. Harris would neither have purchased nor kept her cloth if it did not hold some attraction or significance for her. I would not have bought Naw Oo May's cloth had it not been such an excellent, back-strap loom-woven example of the Paku Karen cloths worn in the late twentieth-century Karenni refugee camps. Both cloths attracted—and held—their collectors at the outset: Had they not been the artifacts they were, they would not have been acquired. Neither would they have been accepted by their respective museums for their collections and documented in the way that they were. Their own material potentialities have thus been significant in their particular trajectories.

Both Mrs. Harris's and Naw Oo May's cloths were removed from their original Paku Karen contexts by others. But from their perspectives, that does not mean that their pasts are necessarily lost. Meanings and values attributed to the cloths by others change—and may be supplanted—over time, but the objects themselves hold manifold elements of the past within them. Some aspects are fairly evident and are a standard part of "reading" material objects. That both Mrs. Harris's and Naw Oo May's cloths remain raw-edged and unseamed into a wearable tube confirms that neither cloth has ever been worn. Moreover, we can assume because of both this feature and the relatively good condition for its age that for most of its life Mrs. Harris's cloth must simply have been stored carefully away. More than this, though, the cloths' very existence manifests both material and temporal continuity with that past: They span the gap between present and past, working as physical connectors or an "object link."[38] In addition to material longevity, individual migrant objects also instantiate the past and the present and their connections in particular ways. In the chapter by Pomerance and Wallen in this volume, for example, we read the powerful story of Paul Kuttner's two hand towels, ironed and folded for him by his mother the night before he left Berlin on a Kindertransport in 1939. Contrary to his mother's intentions, Kuttner never used these towels, wanting instead to keep them as objects bearing her fingerprints and the material form left by her last interaction with them, which she undertook for him; he was never to see his mother again, as she was later killed in Auschwitz. Material traces are essential here—but they are so because of what they mean to Kuttner and how they shape the value he places on the towels. Naw Oo May's cloth too, now resting quietly under acid-free tissue in the textile store of an ethnographic museum, bears into the present not only the form and decorative elements it was given by Oo May when she wove it but also traces of the other hands that folded, carried, exchanged, and ultimately brought it to and have since dealt with it in its current abode. Oils from those different skins, perhaps even microscopic fragments of ink from the sheets of Thai newspaper I used to wrap each collected item before I dispatched them to myself by sea-mail from Chiang Mai . . . even if undetectable by the human eye, these residues are there, and could, if we knew how to read them, tell much of the story of the cloth's path to an English university town. But for most people—indeed, probably for all, most of the time—these traces are meaningless, and in that sense this cloth is very different from Kuttner's towels. For the cloth *itself*, however, they are vestiges of its journey, layered upon its original form, connections not only with the pre-exile past but also with points along the span between origin and now, each an instant of simultaneous pause, action, and change. In that, both the towels and Naw May Oo's cloth share something: looked at from their purview, their *material* continuity and change is highly significant in its own right. Social biography and its material associations, such as the meanings and values attributed to the towels by Kuttner, are of course important too, but when we do not have that (and even when we do), objects themselves still speak, however softly, of the migration both they and people associated with them have undergone.

Important to hearing artifacts, is how change is approached. In this volume, a number of chapters look in different ways at the changing meanings and associations of things in different kinds of incarceral and displaced contexts, but some pay particular attention to the material changes of the objects and—while they might not choose to put it like this—the objects' soft voices. Benninga, Rachamimov, Weicksel, and Brandon Schechter, for instance, among others and in different ways, are all alert to such change. For Naw Oo May's cloth, it was its final transformation, into a museum object, that left the most obvious physical mark of all: a museum textile label, inscribed with an accession number and gently stitched to one of the cloth's corners. But now the cloth is a museum artifact, the label is a *part* of it, not simply a surface append-age. From the textile's perspective, the label is like a wrinkle or a scar, a new but integral element of the object's individuality, not negating what it has been in the past but bringing particular characteristics inherent to its identity henceforth. Naw Rebecca's cloth too undergoes substantive material change as time passes. It becomes increasingly shaped to Naw Rebecca's body, particularly in the seat area, and as it ages it grows not only thinner in parts and worn along some of its edges but also gradu-ally discolored through repeated washings in the muddy river water that runs through the camp. In this case, the alterations are not triggered by the cloth's own physical displacement, and probably it would undergo similar physical modifications over time were it and Naw Rebecca living instead inside Burma's Kayah State. But here, in the camp, Naw Rebec-ca's desire to dress in a style she explicitly constructs as Paku Karen is very keen; one cannot say for sure it would be less strong inside Kayah State, but here, in the concentrated diversity of the refugee camp, the style is essentialized as "Paku Karen and not-Kayah/not-Padaung/not-miscellaneous-*batik*-syle-cloths-and-T-shirts." This, together with the strong likelihood that inside Karenni State Naw Rebecca would have more skirt-cloths or be able to replace them more often, means that in the camp the cloth gets worn more often and thus changes more quickly. Being in a refugee camp, then, even though it started life there, has made life materially different for this cloth than if it had been inside Karenni State. Moreover, imagined from its own perspective, the reality of its strangely non-displaced displacement is materially felt in this greater, faster level of wear and distortion.

Yet just as material form and physical vestiges thread together past and present, they trail into the future too. When Naw Oo May's cloth and the other artifacts I had collected in the refugee camps finally arrived at my house in Leicester, unpacking them rendered me utterly forlorn. Releasing them from their box set free not only textiles and baskets but memories and an overwhelming longing to be back in the camp, the poignancy of which was even greater two weeks later as I watched these things being transformed into museum artifacts in Oxford, numbered, bagged, and frozen. But that sense of loss and yearning was mine, a projection from my settled, human perspective and rooted in my own nostalgia. The displaced themselves, Naw Oo May's cloth and the other objects, having undergone their journey to Europe and now submitting to the museum's processes of documentation, conservation, and storage, were moving forward—taking the past with them in material form but also taking on new ways of being. In these new roles, migrant objects—like migrant people—might not, of course, always behave how others expect (see Goff's chapter in this volume). They may, for example, startle and discompose or at least have the potential to do so, and in this, as the chapter now turns to argue, they could be said to come to be "at home" anew.

Objects "At Home"

For two decades now, there have been strong arguments within studies of refugees and migrants against any suggestion that the displaced lose their culture and against allowing our own views on the poignancy of displacement and the rootedness of culture to blind us to its lived reality.[39] Instead, the reality that migration and displacement are cultural experiences like any other have been emphasized. In relation to material culture, especially in museums, however, it is still commonplace to stress the loss of previous cultural context and even a sense of death in collections. Visitors expect, especially for ethnographic, social-history, or archaeological artifacts, interpretation that provides them with contextual information, and unimaginative labeling and a sense of the object's imprisonment within a vitrine may contribute to a sense of cultural dislocation. In academic studies of museums and their displays, meanwhile, Boon's description of the melancholy of the "fragments wrested from their pasts and else-wheres to be exhibited and categorized, only to yield instead, through their juxtaposition, aphorisms of coincidence" is still frequently cited as an apt portrayal.[40] Yet pessimistic assumptions about an acculturating break with the past and an inevitable loss of context and meaning, anal-ogously to those formerly made about refugees, risk obscuring the con-nections objects may still have and the new meanings they may acquire and overemphasize what *has* been lost and left behind. As we have seen already, the material continuities and changes undergone by an object are part of both its relationship with the past and what makes it what it is at any moment in time.

For refugees and other migrants, there is a close relationship between these dynamic, spatiotemporal processes, on the one hand, and senses of belonging and being at home where one now is, on the other.[41] Thus for Naw Rebecca, wearing Paku Karen clothing makes her feel comfortable, Paku Karen, *and* more "at home" in the camp than she otherwise would. This is both because she wore the same form of dress prior to being dis-placed, and because of its familiarity—in a fundamental, bodily sense, and functionally, as well as visually. Indeed, skirt-cloths like Naw Rebecca's are more than simply an item of clothing. They are modesty-protectors when washing, part-vessels for transporting gathered fruits, baby-carriers (when unworn), signifiers of ethnicity, and so on. The connection between a skirt-cloth and the woman who owns and uses it is at once intimate, performative, and habitual—an association Naw Rebecca's cloth has had throughout its life; indeed, the link between object and person is particu-larly strong in this case as the wearer and owner was also the maker. Naw Rebecca's cloth has been worn many times by her, draping her body and gradually becoming stretched and misshapen by it, and repeatedly washed by her hands. Her hands too have frequently unfolded and refolded the cloth throughout each day it is worn, a common, habitual performance familiar to refugees like Naw Rebecca from their pre-exile past that they were enabled to continue in the camps because of the way cloths like this one, through their form and mode of wearing, are contiguous with that past. At the same time, however, the displacement that Naw Rebecca has undergone and continues to negotiate has not been an issue for her skirt-cloth. Made in the camp, it has never left Kayah State. Yet it is to an extent still displaced: It is constructed by the Karenni as a Paku Karen cloth whose form originates in southeast Kayah State where it does not reside and cannot go; its ability to express or, rather, participate in Karenni-constructed expressions of Paku-Karen-ness is, like Naw Rebecca's, limited by refugee existence and refugee camp existence. Even the few trips out of the camp, for example, cannot be made wearing a Paku Karen—or any other— Burmese-style skirt-cloth, because they will identify the wearer as "Burmese" and thus a potential illegal immigrant liable to arrest by the Thai police.[42] Within the camp, however, there is something comforting about the intimacy of the cloth-wearer relationship and the sense of continuity and normality it provides.

In a prosopopoeial approach, then, what might it mean for an object to be "at home"? In Kayah State, woman and textile participate together in shared cultural practices; in mutually reproducing these in the camp setting, they enable each other, perhaps, to feel more "at home" in that place. In other words, Naw Rebecca's skirt-cloth's "at-home-ness" in the liminal place of the refugee camp might be said to come into being through being worn, as much as Naw Rebecca's does through the wearing.

It is important to note here what I mean by being "at home." It refers to an existential state or quality and is not synonymous with the more substantive "home." The latter has culturally and historically specific connotations that may or may not include elements such as constructions of place, social patterns of settlement or mobility, land ownership, and intragroup socio-political differences including those associated with gender, class, age, and so on. The former, in contrast, is a subjective condition, central to feeling right with the world and one's ability to respond to it—what Gosden describes as cultural aesthetics.[43] Feeling right with the world is less about place and rights than the sense of enough comfort and freedom to exert at least some of one's capacities, to have effects on others as well as being affected by them, to be active as well as passive. Moreover, it is a relative state and does not necessarily imply a lack of restriction or ideal conditions. Thus for Naw Rebecca's skirt-cloth, life in the refugee camp is no more ideal than it is for Naw Rebecca herself; but the cloth's close association with her and her body in everyday life enables it to be itself, to be "at home," as far as is possible.

A close relationship with one woman's body and some notion of cultural or functional continuity from that originally intended by their makers have, however, been opportunities denied to Mrs. Harris's and Naw Oo May's cloths. Neither was ever seamed into a tube and completed as a skirt, and its ultimate destiny as a museum artifact meant that neither was ever able to reach its full potential in being worn—either generally, or specifically to signify Paku-Karen-ness, as is often an explicit intention in the decision to wear them by women like Naw Rebecca. What stops these objects "being themselves" in a museum, however, is not, as Boon and others might have it, that they have been taken away from originating contexts and prevented from performing functions for which they were made. The problem is rather their transformation into representational tools and thus the deactivization of their material possibilities. Subsequent to their removal from their Paku Karen settings, for example, various people along the way may have variously attempted to in some way "recontextualize" them—for instance Mrs. Harris's and ultimately the Denison Museum's documentation, explaining what her cloth was and where it came from—but, like all narratives, these efforts are inevitably incomplete and subjective. The textiles become props in others' attempts to represent the Paku Karen. They turn into synecdoches, used to tell a past story of which they are but fragments; while their role in doing so is important, it is also passive and controlled and viewed by others, negating their very material qualities. In such a delimited and submissive state, these cloths are not fully participating in social life. This is not to say that museums are not social worlds; rather that most of the time the accessioned artifacts appear not able to take a full part in them. Instead, the objects seem at least a little lost, their ties with their "pasts and elsewheres" cut,[44] their museological presence disconnected.

I want to suggest, however, that occasionally museum objects *do* become fully socially participative—though not necessarily as a result of anything planned by the museum's curators and designers. This happens in the moments when an artifact really catches someone's eye, when it takes them by surprise, holds their gaze, makes them stop and stare. These are those instances when an object overwhelmingly intrigues, moves or even appalls, provoking a powerful, affective response even though it cannot be touched and even if (or sometimes especially because) the viewer knows nothing about its origin or intended purpose. Such encounters are capricious: It seems impossible to say which object will bring about what effects for whom. Nonetheless, one can investigate some of their characteristics, such as the impact of artifactual details, the museum visitor's use of imagination and memory to add other sensory modalities to the visual, and the significance to viewers of authenticity.[45] In a prosopopoeial framework, however, these factors in significant object-person encounters need to be considered from the object's perspective. Artifacts that are usually so quiet and obedient to the representational regimes under which they now abide seem, in those unsettling moments, to be staring actively, rebelliously back.[46] Something about the object's form—perhaps a physical trace or surface texture apparent through the glass of the display case, or a combination of material reality and its associations—has reached out and grabbed the observer. The artifact is, however transitorily, no longer a listless representation but has become provocative and recalcitrant. It may not be behaving as it was originally intended to or as it once did; thus any such encounter with Mrs. Harris's or Naw Oo May's cloth would not involve it being worn as a Paku woman's skirt, given as a gift to a missionary, or woven to an anthropologist's commission. Nonetheless, briefly and powerfully the object once again has effects within a social realm, bringing about real changes in the viewer. Whatever its earlier purposes or functions, they too entailed participating and having influence within a social world, and once again, this is happening. In that sense, in an ephemeral but potent person-thing interaction, we might say that the object is, fleetingly at least, able to assert itself, *to be* itself, in its new abode.

Writing on refugees and the concept of home, Malkki argues that home is not necessarily a particular physical location but a place where once can feel "safe and at ease."[47] "Safety," however, is perhaps a more questionable aspect, as it may also pertain, at least in the sense of relative safety from threats, in places of confinement like refugee camps, internment camps, and museums. Good security and basic disciplinary and sustainment practices permitting, refugees, prisoners of war, and artifacts alike may be materially safer in their incarceration than they were before. But perhaps that only demonstrates how much more significant, to any idea of being at home, is the notion of feeling "at ease." In this volume, for example, Rachamimov writes of the efforts made by the occupants of Great War internment camps to enhance the sense of domestic comfort and familiarity in their interiors.[48] In these spaces, "ease" was a deeply elusive quality but was nonetheless something that the interned strove to find. How, then, might an *object* be "at ease"?

Encamped forced migrants and internees and objects in museums can all be hindered by acting according to the culturally "correct styles of action and response" with which they were formerly familiar and at ease.[49] Yet having the capacity to assert and be oneself, even if only occasionally and evanescently and in a different manner than in the past, may still help to enhance the feeling of being "at home" where one now is. Just as refugees and internees, even while the place that has been left behind is a focus of longing and nostalgia, labor to feel as at home as possible in displacement,[50] objects in museums work to make its space and visitors subject to their power. They may succeed only occasionally, in fleeting encounters, but when they do so, they can be said to be at home in the museum.[51] Nonetheless, being themselves or being at home in these terms is, for most museum objects—including Mrs. Harris's and Naw Oo May's cloths—a potentiality that may remain forever latent, capable of being actualized only through particular kinds of interaction. Indeed, for the Denison and Pitt Rivers Museum cloths, potential engagements with anyone except the very occasional curator, conservator, or researcher are precluded by the retention of the artifacts in storage rather than on display. This is in marked contrast to Naw Rebecca's cloth and its quotidian intimacy with its owner and its surroundings. Of the three, it is Naw Rebecca's that is a migrant object coexisting with and being used by an encamped refugee; yet this cloth has migrated nowhere and has the least challenge in working to be "at home." Mrs. Harris's and Naw Oo May's cloths, in contrast, have migrated across continents and into cultural settings very different from those in which they originated; yet they still retain the potential to bring about notable effects.

Concluding Remarks

In exploring some aspects of the displacement of material culture, in particular by attempting to take the object's point of view and by examining what it means for an object to be "at home," this chapter has tried both to challenge and to add nuance to understandings of migration and displacement. In relation to displacement, for instance, the example of Naw Rebecca's cloth suggests that physical migration need not have occurred for displacement to be a valid category. This skirt is both not displaced and always displaced, staying put but still a refugee because of the liminal nature of where it resides and the status of the woman who made and wears it. It is a dislocated thing that does not move; untraveled yet migrated. It is perhaps analogous to a second-generation refugee born in the camp, someone who has not traveled from and cannot visit Kayah State[52] but who nevertheless considers it their real home and point of origin. Although born in the camp, the cloth or the second-generation refugee is not fully "at home" there: The camp is not the place from which its form (for the textile) or group (for the second-generation refugee)—and maker/parents—originate and trace its history. Yet at the same time, each is probably more at home in the camp than anywhere else. Moreover, Naw Rebecca's cloth is certainly more at home in the camp, on an everyday basis, than are the other two cloths in their museum worlds. Naw Rebecca's cloth can co-perform with its wearer and gradually deteriorate, as it was intended to do. The other two cloths, in contrast, were undisplaced at the time of their production but became so almost immediately afterwards. Since then, they have undergone displacement processes that are physically defined by geographical space, but extended too into the temporal, sociocultural, teleological, and beyond. To put it another way, they have moved not only from one place to another, via others; they have done so through time, across social and cultural contexts, and with the result that what they *are* has fundamentally changed, from (potential) skirt-cloths to museum objects. In the process, their material characteristics and accumulated traces carry the past into the present and into the worlds wherein they now reside. That much is true too for Naw Rebecca's cloth in the refugee camp, even though the material changes are different. For the other two, however, feeling "at home" in the sense of being able to be themselves as they were made to be, is not possible. Yet, like other museum objects, they have the potential to assert themselves experientially and transiently in occasional and brief but powerful encounters with museum visitors or professionals. Precisely because of the objects' self-assertion in such encounters, these are the moments in which objects come to be 'at home' in their new (or not so new) abode. Being at home thus emerges as a *condition of possibility* for objects, that can be actualized at any time but in practice is unpredictable and ephemeral.

At the outset of the chapter I indicated that framed in terms of potentiality rather than agency the capacity to bring about effects includes not only the ability to affect others but also the possibility for change within oneself. The material transformations undergone by displaced things, both during their journeys and after they reach their destinations, are important to this. These physical changes—such as the coming undone of the seam end on Mrs. Harris's cloth (figure 10.4)—are as significant a part of the course of displacement as the shifts in meaning and value we are more accustomed to emphasizing in biography and social life approaches to objects. Physical changes will often, of course, be intimately entwined with the accumulated or changed meanings and values accorded to an object by individuals or groups; from the object's *own* perspective, however, its continuing and changing material characteristics participate actively in what it is and what it can do. They also, as Goff's chapter eloquently demonstrates in this volume, can have a central role in how objects dissemble, subvert, and surprise.

Museum objects' recalcitrance and refusal to submit and become recalcitrant, however, and in so doing assert themselves and feel more "at home"—even if only briefly—so too may people. Yet that revealing of capacity by the displaced (human or nonhuman) can be disturbing to the firmly emplaced: What and how we see depends upon our point of view. To paraphrase Mary Douglas, one person's "matter out of place" is another person's dirt, pollution, and provocation.[53] All the chapters in this book have, in different ways, dealt with matter, as well as people, out— and sometimes moving in and out—of place. In some, the objects and the material changes they undergo have been particularly acute. Benninga's chapter, for example, confronts us with a localized material surplus "created by the murder of the Jews." The silks, velvets, leathers, and other items that made up that surplus must have borne traces of their pasts no less than Naw May Oo's cloth and Paul Kuttner's towels. Moreover, in a world of death where clothing was refashioned for a prisoner elite while all "in fact teetered on the brink of a quick death themselves," traces could rapidly accumulate, pajamas, boots, and other items becoming palimpsests of human stories, each one a micro-version of the shocking piles of clothing seen in archive photographs, assemblages of the residues of so many human lives. But Benninga's objects and the others in this book do not simply represent; they do more than stand for the people who have made, owned, worn, used, modified, and exchanged them. They also act: exerting effects, making things happen that would have been different had the objects been different, undergoing change, and turning into something else. They too are displaced, perhaps incarcerated, and subjected to particular regimes. Trying to empathize with objects and to understand at least a little of what it might be like for them to experience displacement just might open up some new ways of thinking about people and things on the move more broadly.

Notes

I am grateful to the two editors of this volume for their kind invitation to contribute. This chapter benefited from comments on earlier versions by the editors, fellow participants at the two workshops that preceded this book, and Distinguished Professor Susan Gal of the University of Chicago. Responsibility for all remaining weaknesses is, however, entirely mine.

1. I use *Burma* in preference to *Myanmar,* as the former is used by the majority of my informants. The Burmese backdrop to this paper is one of various conflicts, including ethnic insurgencies and struggles for democracy, since independence from Britain in 1948. The National League for Democracy won a parliamentary majority in the freely held elections of 2015.

2. Z. Turan, "Material Objects as Facilitating Environments: the Palestinian Diaspora," *Home Cultures* 7, no. 1 (2010): 43–56.

3. S. H. Dudley, *Materialising Exile: Material Culture and Embodied Experience among Karenni Refugees in Thailand* (Oxford and New York: Berghahn Books, 2010).

4. D. Parkin, "Mementoes as Transitional Objects in Human Displacement," *Journal of Material Culture* 4, no. 3 (1999): 317.

5. Parkin, "Mementoes as Transitional Objects," 317.

6. C. Geertz, "'From the Native's Point of View': On the Nature of Anthropological Understanding," *Bulletin of the American Academy of Arts and Sciences* 28, no. 1 (1974): 29.

7. J. Clifford, *Routes: Travel and Translation in the Late Twentieth Century* (Cambridge: Harvard University Press, 1997); L. H. Malkki, *Purity and Exile: Violence, Memory, and National Cosmology among Hutu Refugees in Tanzania* (Chicago: University of Chicago Press, 1995).

8. R. Holmes, *Footsteps: Adventures of a Romantic Biographer* (London: Harper Perennial, 2005), 178, emphasis in original.

9. S. H. Dudley, "What, or Where, Is the (Museum) Object? Colonial Encounters in Displayed Worlds of Things," *International Handbooks of Museum Studies* 1, no. 3 (2013): 41–62.

10. A. Gell, *Art and Agency: An Anthropological Theory* (Oxford: Oxford University Press, 1998); C. Gosden, *Anthropology and Archaeology: A Changing Relationship* (London: Routledge, 1999); B. Latour, *Reassembling the Social: An Introduction to Actor-Network-Theory* (Oxford: Oxford University Press, 2007).

11. S. H. Dudley, *Displaced Things: Loss, Transformation, and Forgetting amongst Objects in Burma and Beyond* (London and New York: Routledge, forthcoming).

12. Gell, *Art and Agency.*

13. My interpretation of actuality (*entelecheia* or *energeia*) diverges slightly from Aristotle, though there is not space to elaborate on this here.

14. In this expansive usage of *Karenic* I follow J. Matisoff, "Linguistic Diversity and Language Contact," in *Highlanders of Thailand*, ed. J. McKinnon and W. Bhruksasri (Singapore: Oxford University Press, 1986).

15. Linguistically, the Paku Karen are actually a sub-group of the Sgaw Karen; geopolitically, however, among the refugee community at least, they identify with the Karenni.

16. For example, see Human Rights Watch, *Burma: Army Attacks Displace Hundreds of Thousands*, 2007, http://hrw.org/english/docs/2007/10/25/burma17168.htm, accessed March 27, 2015.

17. The Border Consortium. *Programme Report July–December 2014*, 2016, www.theborderconsortium.org/media/71671/2016-07-jul-map-tbc-unhcr.pdf, accessed September 20, 2016.

18. Dudley, *Materialising Exile*.

19. By mid-2014, this program had resettled ninety-six thousand refugees from the Thai-Burma border to new countries. The Border Consortium. *Programme Report July–December 2014*.

20. F. K. Lehman, "Burma: Kayah Society as a Function of the Shan-Burma-Karen Context," in *Contemporary Change in Traditional Societies*, vol. 2: *Asian Rural Societies*, ed. J. H. Steward (Urbana: University of Illinois Press, 1967).

21. See, for example, R. B. Jones, *Karen Linguistic Studies* (Berkeley: University of California Press, 1961).

22. M. Moerman, "Who Are the Lue? Ethnic Identification in a Complex Civilization," *American Anthropologist* 67 (1965): 1215–1230.

23. Here as elsewhere, genealogies of ethnicities and nations trace back to the constructions of the colonial state and associated anthropologies. Historians of Burma have argued that ethnicity was not an explicit factor in precolonial political systems and that it was imperial rule and Western conceptions of "nation" that changed this reality. See Victor B. Lieberman, "Ethnic Politics in Eighteenth-Century Burma," *Modern Asian Studies* 12, no. 3 (1978): 455–482; Robert H. Taylor, *The State in Burma* (Honolulu: University of Hawaii Press, 1987; Ronald Renard, *"Kariang": History of Karen-T'ai Relations from the Beginnings to 1923* (PhD diss., University of Hawaii, 1980); Ronald Renard, "The Karen Rebellion in Burma," *Ethnic Studies Report* 6, no. 1 (1988): 24–34; Robert H. Taylor, "Perceptions of Ethnicity in the Politics of Burma," *Southeast Asian Journal of Social Science* 10, no. 1 (1982): 7–22. Less critically explored, particularly in the Burma context but of direct relevance in this discussion, is the topic of missionaries, who were also deeply influential on ideas of ethnicity and nationalism. See Tom Sheahan, "Narrations of Nationalism: An Investigation into the Shifting and Contested Narratives of Karen Nationalism in Burma" (MA thesis, School of Oriental and African Studies, University of London. 1994).

24. On the ethnographic importance of the experience of history rather than history itself, compare N. Tapp, *Sovereignty and Rebellion: The White Hmong of Northern Thailand* (Oxford: Oxford University Press, 1989).

25. J. G. Scott, *Burma: A Handbook of Practical Information* (London: Alexander Moring Ltd., 1911), 120.

26. S. H. Dudley, "Diversity, Identity and Modernity in Exile: 'Traditional' Karenni Clothing," in *Burma: Art and Archaeology*, ed. A. Green and R. Blurton (London: British Museum Press, 2002). Reprinted in S. Knell, ed., *Museums in the Material World* (London: Routledge, 2007).

27. Karenni refugee women who leave the camps to travel into Thailand proper, to visit a hospital for example, will, however, wear a skirt or wide-legged trousers rather than a skirt-cloth, as they are aware that to Thais the latter both appear as if one is not

properly dressed in public (it was described to me by one Thai as "like going out in your nightclothes'").

28. Dudley, *Displaced Things*. I also made a collection for Brighton Museum and Art Gallery, which was similarly shaped by women in the camp.

29. *Burmese Art Newsletter* 1, no. 4 (1969): 3.

30. A Toungoo origin for this cloth is lent credence by the fact that there is another Harris-collected Paku Karen textile in the Denison collection, which is positively described as being from Toungoo.

31. *Burmese Art Newsletter* 1, no. 4 (1969): 3.

32. Denison University, "Helen Hunt," press release, http://cdm15963.contentdm.oclc. org/cdm/singleitem/collection/p15963coll18/id/103/rec/10, accessed April 10, 2015.

33. All of these missionary families who had not previously retired from Burma were, in common with other foreigners, expelled from Burma by Ne Win's military regime, which came to power in the 1962 coup.

34. For more on these collections, see A. Green, ed., *Eclectic Collecting: Art from Burma in the Denison Museum* (Singapore: Singapore University Press, 2008).

35. Compare M. de Certeau, *The Practice of Everyday Life* (Berkeley: University of California Press, 1988).

36. Dudley, *Materialising Exile*.

37. Compare A. Appadurai, ed., *The Social Life of Things: Commodities in Cultural Perspective* (Cambridge: Cambridge University Press, 1988).

38. E. Wood and K. F. Latham, *The Objects of Experience: Transforming Visitor-Object Encounters in Museums* (Walnut Creek, Calif.: Left Coast Press, 2013), 88.

39. For example, J. Clifford, *Routes: Travel and Translation in the Late Twentieth Century* (Cambridge: Harvard University Press, 1997); and L. H. Malkki, *Purity and Exile: Violence, Memory, and National Cosmology among Hutu Refugees in Tanzania* (Chicago: University of Chicago Press, 1995). Compare W. Shawcross, "A Tourist in the Refugee World," in *Forced Out: The Agony of the Refugee in Our Time*, ed. C. Kismaric (New York: Random House, 1989); and B. N. Stein, "The Refugee Experience: Defining the Parameters of a Field of Study," *International Migration Review* 15, no. 1 (1981): 320–330.

40. J. A. Boon, "Why Museums Make Me Sad," in *Exhibiting Cultures: The Poetics and Politics of Museum Display*, ed. I. Karp and S. D. Lavine (Washington, D.C.: Smithsonian Institution Press, 1991), 256.

41. N. Al-Ali and K. Koser, "Transnationalism, Internationalism, and Home," in *New Approaches to Migration? Transnational Communities and the Transformation of Home*, ed. N. Al-Ali and K. Koser (London: Routledge, 2002).

42. Dudley, *Materialising Exile*.

43. C. Gosden, *Anthropology and Archaeology: A Changing Relationship* (London: Routledge, 1999).

44. Boon, "Why Museums Make Me Sad," 256.

45. J. Binnie, "Perception and Well-Being: A Cross-Disciplinary Approach to Experiencing Art in the Museum" (PhD diss., University of Leicester, 2013).

46. J. Elkins, *The Object Stares Back: On the Nature of Seeing* (New York: Simon and Schuster, 1996).

47. Malkki, *Purity and Exile*, 509.

48. Rachamimov also discusses the extent to which internees kept themselves busy in a range of activities. She frames this as a battle to give structure and meaning to what felt, to the prisoners, like a hopelessly unending stretch of time. This response—being *busy*—was something I also found to be a key strategy among Karenni refugees on the Thai-Burma border. See Dudley, *Materialising Exile*.

49. Gosden, *Anthropology and Archaeology,* 203.

50. Dudley, *Materialising Exile,* 9; see also Rachamimov's chapter in this volume.

51. One might argue that in these moments, objects also become *in* and *of* home in the museum, too: They have become museum-ized, and the museum is somewhere now intrinsic to them, and at the same time its museum-ness, and its home-ness for them, is dependent on their presence within it.

52. Currently, the KNPP is in a state of ceasefire with the Burmese military government, which is enabling camp-based refugees to visit friends and relatives in Kayah State (and vice versa). This was not, however, the case during my fieldwork and for most of the period since.

53. M. Douglas, *Purity and Danger: An Analysis of Concepts of Pollution and Taboo* (London: Routledge and Kegan Paul, 1966), 48.

Epilogue

Leora Auslander and Tara Zahra

As the war in Syria rages on, displacing millions of people, the looted and uprooted material possessions of the displaced continue to multiply. If collected into piles, these mountains of Syrian suitcases, toys, shoes, and clothing could fill thousands of rooms in thousands of museums. It will be a long time before a full account can be made of the artifacts violently harvested from Syrian museum cellars (many traded on the black market for cash or arms), of the ancient ruins, mosques, and other cultural heritage sites pulverized into dust, and especially of the family heirlooms and personal possessions hastily packed and dispersed around the world.

What is certain is that this war, like those of the last two centuries, will fundamentally alter not only the material landscape of Syria but also that of the cities, suburbs, and villages around the world where refugees are reconstructing their lives. When the war ends, people and things will not simply have changed places, however. Some objects may have changed their physical form, and many will have even changed meaning. Possession of Syria's remaining cultural treasures will symbolize the defeat of one political order and the consolidation of another. Reconstruction of war-damaged apartment buildings, farms, and businesses will be central to the reconstruction of societies and cultures. Things displaced will become repositories of new memories of former homes and lost family members and will help create new lives and communities in exile.

Every war is different. But this book has demonstrated a striking thread that links modern wars across time and place, from the Napoleonic Wars to the Syrian Civil War: the transformative power of objects in the context of wartime violence and its aftermath. Each section of this book has focused on one of those special powers. In part I, we investigated the ability of looted objects and artifacts to legitimate states and political projects during and after modern wars. Regimes as diverse as the French Empire under Napoleon and Czechoslovakia under Stalin were acutely aware of this power. Modern states and empires have always used material culture to cultivate a sense of belonging to a common polity. But in times of war and revolution, objects and artifacts that are destroyed or stolen from an enemy attained a heightened ability to embody and enact a violent transfer of power.

In part II, we explored the capacity of objects to make and transform individual and collective identities. This power cannot be fully separated from the rise and fall of modern states and mass political movements. In the fervor of war, individual subjectivities and political ideologies often came together or collided in objects. From U.S. Civil War and World War II battlefields to POW camps and Nazi concentration camps, individuals used objects to make sense of their personal experiences of violence, displacement, and internment. Objects or furniture ransacked from a slaveowner's house could serve as material markers of a new identity as a freeman or woman. Clothing stolen from the body of a dead Union soldier might enable his opponent to feel Confederate victory. Medals, guns, and trophies marked a soldier's belonging to and place in a Soviet collectivity, while, alternatively, looting German homes might offer a tiny form of material and psychic compensation for Nazi brutality. A handcrafted armchair could enable a prisoner of war in Siberia to maintain a sense of middle-class domesticity and masculinity, while a tailored suit or a pair of boots extracted from the dead could mark one inmate of a Nazi concentration camp as the social superior of another.

Finally, part III illuminated the critical ability of objects to mediate distances of time and space. Here, objects packed into a trunk in Berlin in 1937; unwrapped in Lahore, India; and then repacked in England twenty years later as a legacy to a son mediate physical distance, cultural and religious difference, and the distance between generations. The objects hastily packed by Jewish refugees, scattered around the world, and then returned to the Jewish Museum Berlin acquired new individual and collective meanings with each leg of their journey. While they might first have been tokens of loved ones left behind, they have since become reminders of Nazi crimes and clues about the texture of German-Jewish daily life before, during, and after the Holocaust. These physical traces of past refugees may have played an important role in Germany's acceptance of around one million refugees from the Syrian conflict three quarters of a century later. Finally, objects forcibly displaced from eastern Burma in the 1990s do not simply mediate distances of time and space, but actually act on people and their environments. Such accounts push us to go beyond thinking about what objects represent to consider how they may transform us and shape historical events. This potential of objects to act on the world may be particularly pronounced in times of war, as the outcome of violent conflict is not only intensely material—in its effects on the human body, the landscape, and state borders—but also often determined by material conditions.

This leads us to one of the most important conclusions of this volume: War is a profound reminder of human materiality and fragility. Conflicts are made and decided through the interaction of human beings and the material world. Objects in this book both move and move us. Their power lies in the political, economic, cultural, and emotional value we ascribe to them but also in the physicality that they impose on us and that escapes our control, in their ability to assault our senses directly.

The ten essays in this volume have only begun to explore this power. We have attempted to outline a research agenda with the potential to illuminate the dynamics and consequences of past and present wars and forced displacements. Many unanswered questions lie within the specificities of time and space, as every conflict is unique. These essays have focused largely on Europe in the nineteenth and twentieth centuries, with brief excursions to North Africa, the United States, and South Asia. Objects and people displaced by violent conflicts in South America, Africa, and

East Asia (as well as other conflicts in Europe or North America) have their own, equally rich stories to tell about particular cultures and traditions that have been uprooted and transformed.

Many other questions remain unanswered here (although some are being addressed by other scholars). We can begin with the role of objects in wartime and postwar state-building projects: The stories told in this volume merely suggest how different kinds or types of occupations and revolutions might shape the power of objects. Is the importance of a stolen object in a democratic revolution different from its role in a fascist seizure of power or an authoritarian coup? Do objects act differently in colonial occupations and anticolonial wars and if so, how do the two reference one another? Those stories remain to be told.

At the level of the individual, the range of potential subjects for future research is equally vast. The essays chosen here have focused largely on the objects used or stolen in battle or taken in and out of camps. Important questions remain about the kinds and types of objects that are transported by refugees and the meanings they acquire through their displacement—for the construction of both diasporic communities and individual subjectivities. These questions require further refinement. How do gender, social class, religion, and race shape the objects chosen for flight, their journeys, and their meanings? How do forced migrations transform the material culture of communities left behind?

Finally, there remains significant research to be done on the memory work of objects—not simply monuments and memorials but everyday objects that bridge miles and generations. We have limited our focus here to portable objects and artifacts (along with a single chateau), but new insights could be gleaned from analyzing other types of material artifacts and structures and embodied practices—from food, commodities, and plants, to technologies and skills, to music and dance, apartments, businesses, and farms. We could also further consider practices of curation, display and circulation, and reception.

Scholars of material culture have long called on historians and other scholars to look "beyond words" in their research.[1] At the same time, historians in particular have, over the past several decades, become more attentive to many forms of materiality—from the history of the physical body, the emotions, and the senses to the environment and visual as well as material culture. Scholars of war and migration, meanwhile, are more interested than they once were in the everyday, cultural, and social history of war and forced displacement. Bringing the study of material culture together with the history of war and forced migration has the potential to offer new insights on questions that have long preoccupied scholars in both fields as well as raise new questions altogether. We have not answered all of these questions here, of course, but hope that the essays in this volume have been suggestive of the work yet to be done.

These essays have begun to demonstrate, for example, how states have used material culture to secure and maintain popular participation in warfare even to the extent of sacrificing one's life. We have gained suggestive insights into the relationship between the battlefront and the "home front" by studying objects transported between the two and made or used in captivity. The histories of looting and expropriation explored here have shed light on how modern wars have transformed understandings of property and social class, gender, race, and sexuality. Finally, incorporating material culture has illuminated relationships between states and social groups that were marked by material culture either as privileged or as excluded through the deprivation of personal possessions.

Scholars of material culture will also have found new routes into familiar debates even as they foster new discussions, by focusing their attention on violence and forced displacement. These essays have suggested collectively that the process of cultural transfer and transformation in the modern era has been inseparable from the history of war, forced migration, and occupation. The prism of war has offered a concentrated site to explore the ways in which human beings and things interact. And of course, examining material culture in times of war has highlighted the many ways in which things shape individual subjectivities and collective loyalties.

While nontextual sources are valuable to scholars in many disciplines and fields, we hope that this volume has made a persuasive argument for the particular importance of material culture in the study of war as well as of war in the study of material culture. The essays in this book collectively suggest that things take on heightened meaning in extreme situations. This amplification of meaning has historical origins in the modern era—in the process by which modern nation-states and empires have consolidated legitimacy through cultural symbols; in the rise of consumer culture and its importance for constituting the self; in the ambitions of mass political movements and regimes to remake subjectivities; and finally, in the terrifying ability of modern warfare and technology to devastate the material world. But this special relationship linking war, forced migration, and material culture may also have deeply psychological origins, as traumatic experiences and memories that are painful or difficult to retain or express in words are transposed onto objects.

The inquiries started here offer the foundation for a historically informed investigation of this interaction in the new forms of warfare in an age in which the virtual often seems to have more presence than the material. New technologies have radically changed the materiality of war. In the wake of the massive destruction of the built and natural environment of Europe and Japan during the Second World War, state-supported scientists developed the neutron bomb, a nuclear weapon designed to kill people but leave their material world intact. The vision was one of a "clean" battlefield, one that could be quickly occupied and settled. This was, of course, completely illusory, since radiation would leave the areas bombed uninhabitable for decades, if not centuries. More intensive study of how soldiers and civilians lived the consequences of the "dirty" wars of the nineteenth and twentieth centuries would elucidate the reasoning that led to the investment in these "enhanced radiation weapons" as well as the decision not to deploy them. Although it is thought that these bombs lie at the ready in many arsenals around the world, they have been left dormant in favor of other de-materialized forms of warfare that have become widespread.

Rather than physically encountering the enemy on the battlefield or entering homes as they invade enemy territory, for example, many soldiers are now sitting thousands of miles away launching missiles or operating drones that do first the reconnaissance and then the killing for them. Unlike the soldiers in this volume, who were completely and physically immersed in war (whether on the battlefield, in trenches, or in POW camps), these drone operators commute to their workplace from suburban homes. They do their eight-hour shift, punctuated by coffee and lunch breaks, then return home in the evening to supper with their families and Little League games. Keeping soldiers safely out harm's way engaging in remote warfare provokes far less public opposition than does massive deployment of bodies to the battlefield. This shift has radical consequences for the material experience of war.

These soldiers have no opportunity for intimate, affectionate relations with their weapons and no opportunity for looting. No trophies will be taken and no teapots or dresses sent home. These soldiers are also never at risk of spending time in an all-male POW camp constructing a fantasy of heteronormative domesticity to keep their sanity while waiting for the war to end. These are, furthermore, gender-integrated armies. Although women have always been present on the field of battle, until the new millennium the battlefront was an overwhelmingly masculine site with a feminized homefront as its counterpart. Now, both women and men wield the weapons, and both husbands and wives wait for them in the homes that have become the new "home front," paralleling the civilian lives around them. The lives of some of these soldiers remain secure at the same time as they are ending lives and destroying the homes, schools, hospitals, workplaces, and sites of worship and governance of others. We do not yet know, cannot yet imagine, what the long-term consequences of this remote warfare will be. More research into how the relations between soldiers and things worked in earlier forms of war will surely lend insight into this new age.

At the same time as wealthy and powerful states have more often had recourse to *dematerialized* means of waging war, insurgent groups have turned to *more material* forms of engagement. Material destruction along with bodily harm is in fact a primary goal of terrorist action. Al-Qaeda, ISIS, and other terrorist organizations have been as resolute iconoclasts as seventeenth-century radical Protestants or French, Russian, or Chinese revolutionaries. Each of their territorial incursions has been accompanied by the systematic destruction of religious and political monuments and the looting of libraries and museums. The targets of the 9/11 attack, for example, were chosen as much for their symbolic as their pragmatic function; the World Trade Center towers were icons of Western capitalism, the Pentagon of American militarism, while the third hijacked airplane was presumably aimed at another government building in Washington, D.C. The method used was equally iconic; commercial airliners are not only a means of transportation but a symbol of the free movement of people, goods, and ideas. Weaponizing civilian aircraft and killing the passengers and the occupants of the buildings going about their everyday lives was a means of taking war into the everyday in a new way. The impact extended, as it was intended to do, far beyond the direct targets of the attack.

This means of waging war, like aerial bombing in the last century and the use of drones and remotely launched missiles, is characterized by their suddenness and arbitrariness; death and destruction appear with no warning from the sky. They also produce many victims among the aggressed and few among the aggressors. Those who survive the attacks, and the relatives and friends of those killed, are faced with the task of returning to life forced to reckon with both loss of life and the destruction of the material environment and possessions that gave that life form. The research presented in part II of this volume is suggestive of how to think better about that process.

The commemorative responses to the death and destruction of the attack on the World Trade Center have been threefold. Above ground, a new gleaming tower, even taller than the one destroyed, rises from the site. The message that a certain vision of modernism, capitalism, and prosperity will not be defeated could hardly be more vividly concretized. The memorial, composed of ponds marking the footprint of the destroyed towers, sits at ground level. Thus, the memorial, like the new tower, insists on life and continuity while marking the violence of the day by reminding visitors and passersby of the void left by the two towers and by the loss of life. Deaths are individualized through the inscription of the names of those who were killed that day. Deep below ground, the museum leaves the present and the future behind, taking the visitor to a place of death and destruction. The underground galleries are claustrophobic and noisy, assaulting the visitor with moving and still images, with the voices of those about to die, and, above all, with the banal things of everyday life at the office. Handbags, a single shoe, a telephone, a framed photograph from someone's desk, a lunchbox. Case after case displays bloody everyday things, mangled by their fall, scorched by fire, stained with smoke.

At a moment when curators wonder more and more about the status of the object and the purpose of "bricks and mortar" museums in the age of the virtual, the intense materiality of the memorial museum is particularly striking. The designers clearly believed that the truth of the moment could only be conveyed through the things that had been present that day, or their traces: the real shoe, the real recorded voice, the real film footage. Both the perpetrators of this act of extreme violence marking the beginning of the new millennium and those who seek to commemorate it and assure that those killed will not be forgotten are still convinced of the power of linking war with things.

Terrorists have not only weaponized technologies of movement, they have weaponized the human body itself. In sharp distinction to infantrymen's or pilots' fetishization of, or drone operators' distance from, their weapons, suicide bombers and their weapons are one. Soldiers who lavished care on their guns or pilots and who painted faces on their airplanes did so because they depended on those tools of destruction for their own survival. They hoped that the attention and affection would be reciprocated by their machines and that they would live to return home. Although one could argue that they were behaving like animists, their actions are evidence that they knew that there was a boundary between a thing used to kill and the person who used it. They knew that they used their guns and their planes to kill people and destroy things and that they themselves risked death and the destruction of their own homes. Drone warfare has been designed to obscure the former and avoid the latter. Unlike guns or fighter aircraft, drones are also used for perfectly benign uses. They are sold as toys, and Amazon and Walmart may soon be using them to deliver packages to customers' doors. And, also in contrast with a rifle or a plane, a drone is not individualized, nor would a malfunction put its operator at risk. Drones, in other words, create maximum distance among the soldier, the weapon, death and material destruction; the loss is necessarily all one-sided. Suicide bombers, by contrast, collapse all of these distinctions. Suicide bombers see what and whom they will destroy, and they know that they will not leave the site they have defined as a battlefield.

And yet, governments have weaponized human beings in another way: by transforming them into refugees, explicitly or implicitly threatening to unleash "weapons of mass migration" on neighboring states if their own demands are not met.[2] Governments feeling under siege by suicide bombers, insurgent violence, and undesired migrants (and things) have turned to building walls to keep them out—a contrast to the Cold War era, when walls were often intended to keep people in. This very material response to mass migration and violence stands in stark contrast to those same states' increased emphasis on adopting dematerialized practices of waging war. It is also striking in its willful conflation of the movement of bodies and the movement of violence. Walls may be effective in keeping out unwanted people, but the moment has long since passed when they could keep out agents of destruction. From medieval besiegers who forced surrender by catapulting carcasses of dead animals into walled cities, decimating the inhabitants by disease, to the present moment, when boundaries are much more permeable, wall-building merely serves to create the illusion of safety and sovereignty.[3]

This example, taken along with that of the 9/11 memorial and new commemorative museums still being founded across the world, demonstrate that the project undertaken here, to understand the relationships linking war, material culture, and movement, matters. It is not only that intersection that matters but also the interdisciplinary and inter-institutional approach. More conversation among historians, anthropologists, and curators is essential if we are to grasp how violence and its commemoration work.

Wars continue to uproot people and things in ways that we can only begin to comprehend. But as we seek to understand the history and the modern experience of warfare or material culture, we cannot neglect their relationship to one another. The objects of war—carried, hidden, looted, remade, returned, forgotten, and rediscovered—offer powerful clues to how people and things interact to shape our societies and ourselves.

Notes

1. Leora Auslander, "Beyond Words," *American Historical Review* 110, no. 4 (2005): 1015–1045.

2. The phrase comes from Kelly Greenhill, *Weapons of Mass Migration: Forced Displacement, Coercion, and Foreign Policy* (Ithaca: Cornell University Press, 2011).

3. See especially Wendy Brown, *Walled States, Waning Sovereignty* (Cambridge: MIT Press, 2010).

Notes on Contributors

Leora Auslander is Arthur and Joann Rasmussen Professor of Western Civilization at the University of Chicago. Her work lies at the intersection of politics and material culture in Europe and the Atlantic world. Her publications include *Cultural Revolutions: Everyday Life and Politics in Britain, North America, and France* (Berg, 2008; University of California, 2009) and *Taste and Power: Furnishing Modern France* (University of California, 1996). She coedited three issues of the French gender history journal, *Clio: Femmes, Histoire, Genre.* She is currently finishing a book, "Paradoxes of Citizenship: Jewish Parisians and Berliners in the Twentieth Century," and is at work on two more, "Race and Racism in the Twentieth Century Atlantic World" (with Thomas C. Holt) and "Commemorating Death, Obscuring Life? The Conundrums of Memorialization."

Noah Benninga is a postdoctoral fellow at the Richard Koebner Minerva Center at the Hebrew University. His PhD dissertation, "The Material Culture of Prisoners in Auschwitz" (Hebrew University), uses witness testimony to study the material culture and everyday life of prisoners in the "Metropolis of Death." He is the author of a number of scholarly publications, including "The First Person Inversion: Conscious Engagement and the Practical Past," in *Holocaust Studies: A Journal of History and Culture*, 2015; "Jean Amery and the Negative Materiality of Language in Auschwitz," in *Jean Améry: Als Gelegenheitsgast, ohne jedes Engagement*, ed. Ulrich Bielefeld and Yifaat Weiss (Wilhelm Fink, 2013); and the entry on *Auschwitz* in Dan Diner's prestigious *Enzyklopädie jüdischer Geschichte und Kultur* (2011). His coedited volume *Personal Engagement and the Study of the Holocaust* (Vallentine Mitchell, 2015) includes contributions from Hayden White, Otto Dov Kulka, and Aleida Assmann, among others. His prizes and honors include the President's Fellowship, the Wolf Prize for graduate students, and the Franz Rozenzweig Minerva Fellowship.

Sandra H. Dudley is head of the School of Museum Studies at the University of Leicester. She gained her DPhil in social anthropology from the University of Oxford and has held postdoctoral research posts in Oxford's Institute for Development Studies and the Pitt Rivers Museum. Her books include *Materialising Exile* (Berghahn, 2010) and *Museum Objects* (Routledge, 2012), and she is currently completing a monograph on displaced things. She is joint chief editor of the annual journal *Museum Worlds: Advances in Research*, and has recently been co-running a project researching object encounters in museums and heritage sites in India and the United Kingdom.

Bonnie Effros is professor of European history and holder of the Chaddock Chair of Economic and Social History at the University of Liverpool; she previously served as the Rothman Chair and director at the Center for the Humanities and the Public Sphere at the University of Florida. She is the author of *Caring for Body and Soul: Burial and the Afterlife in the Merovingian World* (Pennsylvania State University Press, 2002), *Merovingian Mortuary Archaeology and the Making of the Early Middle Ages* (University of California Press, 2003), *Creating Community with Food and Drink in Merovingian Gaul* (Palgrave, 2002), and *Uncovering the Germanic Past: Merovingian Archaeology in France, 1830–1914* (Oxford University Press, 2012). Her book, *Incidental Archaeologists: French Officers and the Rediscovery of Roman North Africa*, will be published by Cornell University Press in 2018.

Cathleen M. Giustino is the Mills Carter Professor of History at Auburn University and a 2017 Carnegie Fellow. She earned her PhD in Modern Central European History from the University of Chicago. She is author of *Tearing Down Prague's Jewish Town: Ghetto Clearance and the Legacy of Middle-Class Ethnic Politics around 1900* (East European Monographs, 2003) and coeditor, with Catherine Plum and Alexander Vari, of *Socialist Escapes: Breaks from Ideology and the Everyday in Eastern Europe, 1945–1989* (Berghahn Books, 2013). Her articles include "Rodin in Prague: Modern Art, Cultural Diplomacy and National Display," which appeared in *Slavic Review,* and "Socialist Industrial Design and the Czechoslovak Pavilion at EXPO '58," which was published in the *Journal of Contemporary History.* She is currently writing a book on racism, ethnic hatred, and museums made out of persecuted people's things in former Eastern Europe.

Alice Goff is assistant professor of German history and the College at the University of Chicago. From 2015 to 2017 she was a postdoctoral fellow with the Michigan Society of Fellows at the University of Michigan in the departments of Germanic Languages and Literatures and History. She received her PhD in history from the University of California at Berkeley in 2015. She is currently working on a book, titled "The God Behind the Marble: Transcendence and the Object in the German Aesthetic State," which is about the French looting of German art collections in the Napoleonic period and its aftermath in Prussian cultural politics during the first half of the nineteenth century.

Gerdien Jonker is a historian of religion. She is the author of *The Ahmadiyya Quest for Religious Progress: Missionizing Europa 1900–1965* (Leiden, 2016), in which she addresses Muslim missionaries in interwar Europe. Within this framework she encountered the private archives of Jewish Germans who had converted to Islam, the subject of her book *Zwischen Juden und Muslimen: Eine europäische Familiengeschichte 1836—2016* (Göttingen, 2017). She is affiliated with Erlangen University in Germany.

Aubrey Pomerance is the head of archives at the Jewish Museum Berlin and the director of the branch of the archives of the Leo Baeck Institute New York and the branch of the Wiener Library at the Jewish Museum Berlin. He has written on Jewish memorial culture, Jewish lives and fates during the period of National Socialism, Jewish photographers in Berlin in Weimar and Nazi Germany, and archive studies and archival pedagogy.

Iris Rachamimov is an associate professor of modern history at the Department of History, Tel Aviv University. She received her PhD in 2000 from Columbia University. Her book *POWs and the Great War: Captivity on the Eastern Front* (2002) was awarded the Fraenkel Prize for Contemporary History for a first major work. Her article "The Disruptive Comforts of Drag" was published in the April 2006 issue of the *American Historical Review,* and she wrote the chapter on military captivity in the latest edition of *The Cambridge History of War: War and the Modern World* (2012). She was the director of the Cummings Center for Russian and East European Studies at Tel Aviv University (2009–15), a senior visiting fellow at the Stanford Humanities Center (2008–9), and a senior visiting fellow at the University of Oxford-St. Antony's College (2015–16). Since 2014 she has been the editor of the Hebrew-language journal *Zmanim: A Historical Quarterly.* She is currently working on a book on gender and warfare, titled "Islands of Men: Shifting Gender Boundaries in World War I Internment Camps."

Brandon Schechter is the Elihu Rose Scholar in Modern Military History at New York University. He received his PhD in history at the University of California at Berkeley in 2015. Recently he was a postdoctoral fellow at the Davis Center for Russian and Eurasian Studies at Harvard University. Prior to finishing his PhD he studied at Smolny College, European University in St. Petersburg, Kazan Federal University, the Higher School of Economics in Moscow and St. Petersburg (with support from Fulbright IIE) and received a BA in Russian Studies from Vassar College (2005). He is currently finishing a book titled "Government Issue: The Material Culture of the Red Army 1941–1945," which tells the story of the Great Patriotic War through objects from spoons to tanks.

Jeffrey Wallen is a professor of comparative literature at Hampshire College in Amherst, Massachusetts (dean of humanities, arts, and cultural studies from 2012 to 2015). He has also taught as a visiting professor at the Free University Berlin and at the University of Toulouse and is the director of Hampshire's semester-long study abroad program in Berlin. He has published widely on nineteenth- and twentieth-century European literature; on biography and literary portraiture; on testimony, Holocaust literature, and Berlin Jewish history; and on debates about education. His book *Closed Encounters: Literary Politics and Public Culture* was published by the University of Minnesota Press in 1998. Some of his most recent publications are "The Witness against the Archive: Towards a Microhistory of Christianstadt," "Testimony and Taboo: The Perverse Writings of Ka-Tzetnik 135633," "The Lure of the Archive: The Atlas Projects of Walid Raad," "Migrant Visions: The Scheunenviertel and Boyle Heights, Los Angeles," "Twemlow's Abyss," and "Narrative Tensions: The Eyewitness and the Archive." He is currently working on a study of the archive in contemporary thought and art.

Sarah Jones Weicksel received her PhD in history from the University of Chicago in 2017. In 2015 and 2016 she was a Committee on Institutional Cooperation-Smithsonian Institution Fellow at the National Museum of American History and the National Museum of African American History and Culture. She holds an MA in American Material Culture from the Winterthur Program at the University of Delaware and a BA in History from Yale University. She is the author of several articles and is currently working on a book titled "The Fabric of War: Clothing, Culture, and Violence in the American Civil War Era."

Tara Zahra is professor of East European history at the University of Chicago. Her most recent book is *The Great Departure: Mass Migration from Eastern Europe and the Making of the Free World* (Norton, 2016). She is also the author of *The Lost Children: Reconstructing Europe's Families after World War II* (Harvard University Press, 2011), and *Kidnapped Souls: National Indifference and the Battle for Children in the Bohemian Lands, 1900–1948* (Cornell University Press, 2008). She is currently working on a history of the First World War in the Habsburg Empire with Pieter M. Judson as well as on a book on deglobalization in interwar Europe, tentatively titled *Against the World: Deglobalization and the Decline of Democracy in Interwar Europe* (Norton, forthcoming).

INDEX

CPSIA information can be obtained
at www.ICGtesting.com
Printed in the USA
LVOW12s0359050418
572308LV00004B/174/P